17-8 The Cross

Participating
in Christ

Participating in Christ

Explorations in Paul's Theology and Spirituality

MICHAEL J. GORMAN

B
Baker Academic
a division of Baker Publishing Group
Grand Rapids, Michigan

© 2019 by Michael J. Gorman

Published by Baker Academic
a division of Baker Publishing Group
PO Box 6287, Grand Rapids, MI 49516-6287
www.bakeracademic.com

Printed in the United States of America

Library of Congress Cataloging-in-Publication Data
Names: Gorman, Michael J., 1955– author.
Title: Participating in Christ : explorations in Paul's theology and spirituality / Michael J. Gorman.
Description: Grand Rapids, MI : Baker Academic, a division of Baker Publishing Group, [2019] |
    Includes bibliographical references and index.
Identifiers: LCCN 2018047595 | ISBN 9781540960368 (pbk.)
Subjects: LCSH: Bible. Epistles of Paul—Theology. | Bible. Epistles of Paul—Criticism,
    interpretation, etc. | Jesus Christ—Person and offices.
Classification: LCC BS2651 .G646 2019 | DDC 227/.06—dc23
LC record available at https://lccn.loc.gov/2018047595

ISBN 978-1-5409-6159-4 (casebound)

For Brent Laytham,
colleague, dean, friend,
and fellow participant in Christ;

and for my students,
far and near, formal and informal

Contents

Part 2: Paul and Participation Today   237

Acknowledgments

This volume has taken shape over several years, which means that I am indebted to many people for their input and feedback. It also means that I will probably forget more than one person, so I ask their forgiveness in advance. I begin with colleagues, who have also sometimes been formal or informal editors, especially Todd Billings, Ben Blackwell, Douglas Campbell, Stephen Chester, Athanasios Despotis, Susan Eastman, Steve Fowl, John Goodrich, Joel Green, Kathy Grieb, Richard Hays, Andy Johnson, Brent Laytham, Jason Maston, Frank Matera, Walter Moberly, Markus Nikkanen, Ian Paul, Klyne Snodgrass, Mike Thompson, and Tom Wright.

I am also thankful to the various institutions that asked me to give lectures that eventually became chapters of this book, and to my gracious hosts and my respondents (formal and informal) at each institution. These include the British New Testament Society; Northeastern Seminary, and especially J. Richard Middleton and Doug Cullum; North Park Theological Seminary, and especially Klyne Snodgrass and Stephen Chester; Washington Adventist University, and especially Zack Plantak (now at Loma Linda University); and various units of the Society of Biblical Literature.

I am grateful as well to my research assistants in recent years: Daniel Jackson (now Dr. Jackson), Michelle Newman Rader, and Gary Staszak. They have not only completed various research and editorial tasks; they have also been valuable conversation partners. Michelle, in particular, has been a major aide in the preparation of the book for publication.

Once again, I express my deep gratitude to my colleagues at St. Mary's Seminary & University for their support, especially Deans Brent Laytham and Tom Burke and President-Rector Phil Brown.

My gratitude to the entire staff at Baker Academic is enormous. I am especially grateful to editors Bryan Dyer and Tim West, once again, for their support and guidance, and to Ryan Davis.

I am also grateful to the following publishers and publications for permission to use and revise previously published material:

- Grove Books for permission to adapt the booklet *Participation: Paul's Vision of Life in Christ* for chapter 1;
- The *Journal of Moral Theology* and T&T Clark for permission to adapt, respectively, "Paul and the Cruciform Way of God in Christ" and "The Cross in Paul: Christophany, Theophany, Ecclesiophany" (from *Ecclesia and Ethics: Moral Formation and the Church*, ed. E. Allen Jones III, John Frederick, John Anthony Dunne, Eric Lewellen, and Janghoon Park [2016]) for chapter 2;
- Wipf and Stock and the journal *Ex Auditu* (vol. 33 [2017]) for permission to adapt "Cruciform or Resurrectiform? Paul's Paradoxical Practice of Participation" for chapter 3;
- Wipf and Stock (Cascade imprint) for permission to adapt "A New Translation of Philippians 2:5 and Its Significance for Paul's Theology and Spirituality" (from *Conception, Reception, and the Spirit: Essays in Honor of Andrew T. Lincoln*, ed. J. Gordon McConville and Lloyd K. Pietersen [2015]) for chapter 4;
- Fortress Press for permission to adapt "The Apocalyptic New Covenant and the Shape of Life in the Spirit according to Galatians" (from *Paul and the Apocalyptic Imagination*, ed. Ben C. Blackwell, John K. Goodrich, and Jason Maston [2016]) for chapter 5;
- Mohr Siebeck for permission to adapt "Reading Gal 2:15–21 Theologically: Beyond Old and New, beyond West and East" (from *Participation, Justification, and Conversion: Eastern Orthodox Interpretation of Paul and the Debate between Old and New Perspectives on Paul*, WUNT 2/442, ed. Athanasios Despotis; copyright © Mohr Siebeck Tübingen [2017]) for chapter 6;
- Mohr Siebeck and William B. Eerdmans for permission to adapt "Paul's Corporate, Cruciform, Missional Theosis in Second Corinthians" (from *"In Christ" in Paul: Explorations in Paul's Theology of Union and Participation*, ed. Michael J. Thate, Kevin J. Vanhoozer, and Constantine R. Campbell; copyright © Mohr Siebeck Tübingen [2014]; copyright © William B. Eerdmans Publishing Co. [2018]) for chapter 9;

- The *Canadian-American Theological Review* (vol. 4, no. 2 [2015]) for permission to adapt "Being 'In Christ' Today: Paul's Letter to the Contemporary Church in North America" for chapter 10; and
- *Priest* magazine / *Our Sunday Visitor Weekly* and *The Living Pulpit* for permission to adapt "St. Paul and the Resurrection" and "Preaching and Living the Resurrection Today," respectively, for chapter 11.

I dedicate this volume to Brent Laytham, my good friend and fellow interpreter of Scripture (as well as my dean). I have known few theologians or readers of Scripture as perceptive as he. I dedicate it also to my students, both near and far, formal and informal; it is an honor to be your teacher, and to learn from you too.

Abbreviations

JTC	*Journal for Theology and the Church*
JTI	*Journal of Theological Interpretation*
LNTS	Library of New Testament Studies
LXX	Septuagint
mg.	marginal note
MJG	denotes the author's translation
NCB	New Clarendon Bible
NETS	Pietersma, Albert, and Benjamin G. Wright, eds. *A New English Transla-tion of the Septuagint*. New York: Oxford University Press, 2007.
NIGTC	New International Greek Testament Commentary
NovT	*Novum Testamentum*
NovTSup	Supplements to Novum Testamentum
NTL	New Testament Library
NTS	*New Testament Studies*
PCNT	Paideia Commentaries on the New Testament
SHBC	Smyth & Helwys Bible Commentary
SJT	*Scottish Journal of Theology*
SNTSMS	Society for New Testament Studies Monograph Series
SP	Sacra Pagina
SVTQ	*St. Vladimir's Theological Quarterly*
THNTC	Two Horizons New Testament Commentary
TS	*Theological Studies*
WBC	Word Biblical Commentary
WUNT	Wissenschaftliche Untersuchungen zum Neuen Testament
ZECNT	Zondervan Exegetical Commentary on the New Testament
ZTK	*Zeitschrift für Theologie und Kirche*

Introduction

Paul did not coin them [terms for communion with Christ] for the Universities of the nineteenth or twentieth centuries. If he had written his letters for future generations he would not have coined these wonderful expressions for Anselm or Johann Gerhard, but for Johann Sebastian Bach.

—Adolf Deissmann (1923)[1]

Human existence is full of participation: in families, workplaces, groups of friends, society as a whole, and more. It is also replete, when at its best, with union: husband and wife, soul mates, partners in business or service or travel. The search for God—or, rather, God's search for us—is also ultimately about participation (the heart of the incarnation); indeed, it is about union. How has God connected intimately with us, and how do we, in response, connect intimately with God?

The theme of participation, which includes or implies union, has captured my attention for a very long time. I remember, as a new Christian believer, being amazed at the words of Colossians: "Christ in you, the hope of glory" (Col. 1:27). At that time, of course, I had no idea where meditation on, and investigation of, such words would take me.[2] But in many ways those words have guided and shaped both my spiritual and my scholarly journey ever since I first encountered them.

---

1. Deissmann, *The Religion of Jesus and the Faith of Paul*, 202. The eminent theologian Anselm lived in the eleventh century; Gerhard, a Lutheran scholastic theologian, in the seventeenth.
2. For instance, wondering whether we should translate this verse as "Christ among you [plural], the hope of glory."

Adolf Deissmann (quoted above), a New Testament scholar himself, believed that Paul's language of participation—"Christ in me . . . I in Christ"—was "not dogmatical but poetical" language.[3] It is a mystical idiom, worthy of a setting by Bach, for when we sing, or perhaps listen to a Bach fugue, we pray twice. Despite Deissmann's comment, and in part because of it, the theme of participation is back in vogue within most theological schools and many universities across the theological and ecclesial spectrums. Moreover, this renewal exists within the various theological subdisciplines: biblical studies, systematic theology, historical theology, theological ethics or moral theology, spirituality, and practical theology. Participation has been proposed as an essential aspect of Christian theology and spirituality, of New Testament theology and spirituality more specifically, and of Pauline theology and spirituality in particular.[4] Assorted terms are used to refer to this theme, including (in addition to "participation" itself), "union with Christ," "mysticism," and the "theosis" family of words: theosis, deification, divinization, Christosis, and Christification. Thus contributors to the conversation do not always agree about terminology or, more importantly, substance.[5] But participation is on the table in a major way, and this development is one of the most exciting and fruitful directions in theology in recent decades. Moreover, inseparable from the theme of participation is its corollary, transformation.

My own participation in this participationist approach to the New Testament, especially to Paul (but also to John and the New Testament more broadly),[6] has resulted in various publications. In this book I attempt first, in

3. Deissmann, *The Religion of Jesus and the Faith of Paul*, 202; cf. 201, 219.

4. For example, the annual Symposium on the Theological Interpretation of Scripture at North Park Theological Seminary near Chicago had "participation" as its subject in 2017. This interdisciplinary, international event was the culmination of years of planning by its organizers, especially Klyne Snodgrass and Stephen Chester. Biblical scholars, systematic theologians, ethicists, pastoral theologians, pastors, and others came together to discuss and debate the meaning of participation—specifically, participation in God, Christ, and/or the Spirit—in Christian theology and for Christian practice. Presentations focused on participation in Old Testament theology, Paul, Acts, Augustine, Calvin, and so on. The conference papers were published in *Ex Auditu* 33 (2017). The conference and journal volume are just the tip of the iceberg of interest in participation, as the journal's lengthy annotated bibliography indicates. Also in 2017, the Society of Biblical Literature included at least a dozen presentations on participation in the writings and theology of Paul in its annual meeting program. In addition to purely academic works, a number of scholarly books also have significant pastoral and practical implications. See, e.g., Billings, *Union with Christ*; Owens, *Shape of Participation*.

5. Richard Hays has proposed that we adopt the word for participation used by Gregory of Nyssa, *metousia*, but so far it has not caught on (Hays, "Apocalyptic *Poiēsis* in Galatians," 214–15).

6. For participation in John, see my *Abide and Go*; for the New Testament more broadly, see my *Death of the Messiah*.

chapter 1, to briefly summarize some of my earlier work and offer my general perspective on Paul and participation. I then proceed, in subsequent chapters, both to explore some of the claims made in chapter 1 in more depth and to develop new areas of investigation.

Interest in participation in Paul has a long pedigree. An account of this development would take a full chapter, if not an entire book, but a few introductory remarks are in order.

The Study of Paul and Participation

Discussion of Paul, participation, and transformation (whatever theological label is given to it), as we will see below, has its roots in certain early church fathers, including Irenaeus and Athanasius. The discussion continues in many subsequent Christian theologians, whether Roman Catholic, Orthodox, Protestant, Anglican, or Pentecostal/charismatic. Protestants are frequently surprised to see the theme of union with Christ (and even, according to some, deification), often connected to justification, in theologians such as Luther, Calvin, and Wesley.[7] The seventeenth-century Scottish theologian Henry Scougal speaks for many from all the Christian traditions: "True religion is a union of the soul with God, a real participation of the divine nature, the very image of God drawn upon the soul, or, in the apostle's phrase, 'It is Christ formed within us.'"[8]

In modern scholarship, interest in Paul and participation can be traced back especially to Adolf Deissmann, Albert Schweitzer, and James Stewart in the late nineteenth and early twentieth centuries.[9] These three were hardly in complete agreement, however. For example, Deissmann saw justification and union/participation as complementary realities.[10] Schweitzer, however, famously claimed that "the doctrine of righteousness by faith,"

7. For Luther and Calvin, see Chester, *Reading Paul with the Reformers*. On Luther and theosis, an older, brief survey (with bibliographical references) is still valuable: Kärkkäinen, "Salvation as Justification and *Theosis*." For John Wesley, a good place to start is Christensen, "John Wesley: Christian Perfection," in Christensen and Wittung, *Partakers of the Divine Nature*. (That volume also has excellent articles on Paul, Luther, Calvin, and others.) For an in-depth study of Charles Wesley, see Kimbrough, *Partakers of the Divine Life*.

8. Scougal (1650–78), *The Life of God in the Soul of Man*, 3.

9. See, e.g., Deissmann, *The Religion of Jesus and the Faith of Paul*; Deissmann, *Paul*; Deissmann, *Die neutestamentliche Formel "in Christo Jesu"*; Schweitzer, *Mysticism of Paul the Apostle*; Stewart, *A Man in Christ*. The German original of Schweitzer's work was titled *Die Mystik des Apostels Paulus*, published in 1930 (but first drafted in 1906, according to the preface to *Mysticism* [written on a ship returning him to Africa], xxiii), with a second edition in 1954.

10. See, e.g., Deissmann, *The Religion of Jesus and the Faith of Paul*, 175, 207–19.

or justification, is "a subsidiary crater, which has formed within the rim of
the main crater—the mystical doctrine of redemption through the being-
in-Christ."[11] Like Deissmann, he called this "Christ-mysticism," which for
him was both sacramental—that is, effected by baptism (here disagreeing
with Deissmann)—and eschatological/apocalyptic, meaning an experience
of future redemption now.[12] Schweitzer rightly pointed out that Paul's emphasis on being in Christ was no late development, for it had been worked
out no later than his writing of 1 Thessalonians (probably the earliest extant
letter), as evidenced by several occurrences of the "in Christ" formula in
that letter.[13]

The interest in participation waned, though it never died,[14] before it was
dramatically jump-started in recent times by E. P. Sanders, one of the archi-
tects of the "New Perspective on Paul."[15] Sanders eschewed Schweitzer's term
"mystical" but still argued that participation in Christ—specifically Paul's
"participationist eschatology"—is at the center of Paul's theology. Paul "is
not primarily concerned with the juristic categories [of "righteousness by
faith"]," for "the real bite of his theology lies in the participatory categories."[16]
However, unlike Schweitzer but like Deissmann, Sanders did not see justification by faith and participation as ultimately disconnected or antithetical, but
as connected and complementary.[17]

Since Sanders's initial work on participation, this theme has been explored
by a wide variety of Pauline scholars who might fervently disagree about,
say, Sanders's view of "works of the law" in Second Temple Judaism and in
Paul. It is nearly impossible to engage Paul seriously today without recognizing the centrality of participation to his lived experience ("spirituality") and
his theology. Participation is not merely one aspect of Pauline theology and
spirituality, or a supplement to something more fundamental; rather, it is at
the very heart of Paul's thinking and living. Pauline soteriology (theology of
salvation) is inherently participatory and transformative.

---

11. Schweitzer, *Mysticism*, 225.
12. See the helpful discussion in Claussen, "Albert Schweitzer's Understanding of Righteousness by Faith."
13. Schweitzer, *Mysticism*, 224.
14. See, e.g., Tannehill, *Dying and Rising with Christ*.
15. Sanders, *Paul and Palestinian Judaism*, esp. 447–74.
16. Sanders, *Paul and Palestinian Judaism*, 502; see 549 for "participationist eschatology."
17. E.g., Sanders, *Paul and Palestinian Judaism*, 440–41. See also Sanders, *Paul: The Apostle's
Life, Letters, and Thought*, 264–66, 611–14, 665–66, where Sanders says that "having righteousness by faith is the same as sharing the death and resurrection of Christ" (612) but that
the "heart and soul" of Paul's theology is not justification by faith but participation in Christ
(666). Jeanette Hagen Pifer (*Faith as Participation*, 1–38) surveys recent scholarship on faith in
Paul and concludes that the "bifurcation of justification and participation" is unnecessary (36).

It is sometimes said that Sanders was not quite sure what this participation actually entails, though this is to partially misread Sanders.[18] Still, it has been left to others to further unpack the meaning of participation in Paul's theology, and also in terms of its significance for the church. For instance, James D. G. Dunn, another advocate of the New Perspective, pays significant attention to the theme of participation, especially in his Pauline theology.[19] Dunn echoed Deissmann's and Sanders's claims that justification and participation are complementary.[20] Another theology of Paul that stresses participation is that of the German scholar Udo Schnelle.[21]

It is Richard Hays, however, who has responded directly to Sanders's incompletely developed discussion of the substance of participation. Hays wrote an essay dedicated to Sanders in which he outlined four aspects of participation in Christ according to Paul: (1) belonging to a family; (2) having political or military solidarity with Christ (as in Rom. 6, with its language of being baptized into Christ and presenting our bodily members as "weapons" of righteousness); (3) participating in the *ekklēsia* (Greek for "assembly," "church"), the body of Christ; and (4) living within the Christ-story ("narrative participation").[22] It is the last of these four that Hays, as a major advocate of the participationist perspective, has emphasized in his own work,[23] and it has been central to my interpretation of Paul too.[24]

Several contemporary interpreters of Paul who have stressed participation, including Morna Hooker, David Litwa, Ben Blackwell, and the present author, connect it implicitly or explicitly with the theme of theosis or deification. Blackwell has especially stressed the similarity between Paul's soteriology and that of some of the early church fathers. Blackwell sees the patristic claim that "God/Christ became what we are so that we could become what God/Christ is" as foreshadowed in Paul's soteriology of being conformed to Christ—what he calls "Christosis."[25] Morna Hooker focuses on similar "interchange" texts, such as 2 Corinthians 5:21 and Galatians 3:13.[26] Litwa is especially interested in versions of deification in Paul's own religious world.[27] My own approach,

---

18. See Sanders, *Paul and Palestinian Judaism*, 447–73.
19. Dunn, *Theology of Paul the Apostle*, 390–441.
20. Dunn, *Theology of Paul the Apostle*, 396.
21. Schnelle, *Apostle Paul*.
22. Hays, "What Is 'Real Participation in Christ'?"
23. See, e.g., Hays, *Faith of Jesus Christ*; Hays, *Moral Vision of the New Testament*, 16–59.
24. See esp. my *Cruciformity*; Gorman, *Apostle of the Crucified Lord*.
25. Blackwell, *Christosis*. Relevant texts from the fathers include, e.g., Irenaeus, *Against Heresies* 5.preface.1, and Athanasius, *Incarnation of the Word* 54.
26. Hooker, *From Adam to Christ*, 13–69.
27. Litwa, *We Are Being Transformed*.

as this book will further display, is grounded primarily in textual analysis and connections within the Pauline corpus itself.[28]

Furthermore, both Douglas Campbell (from the "apocalyptic" approach to Paul) and N. T. Wright (from the New Perspective—and beyond) occasionally use the word "theosis" to characterize Paul's understanding of transformation.[29] Furthermore, and even more significantly, each of them agrees on the importance of participation in Paul. Wright views participation within the framework of covenant, while Campbell sees it within the framework of apocalyptic incursion and liberation.[30]

Additionally with respect to theosis, in an important book edited by Orthodox scholar Athanasios Despotis, Orthodox interpreters of Paul—whose tradition sees theosis as the main substance of salvation—are brought into conversation with the New Perspective and with other Pauline interpreters. Among the contributors to *Participation, Justification, and Conversion: Eastern Orthodox Interpretation of Paul and the Debate between Old and New Perspectives on Paul* are Edith Humphrey, who is Orthodox, and the present writer. At the same time, there are of course interpreters who stress participation in Paul but who do not find terms like "theosis" and "deification" to be accurate descriptors. Grant Macaskill, for instance, prefers the term "union."[31]

Another significant volume on participation is *"In Christ" in Paul: Explorations in Paul's Theology of Union and Participation*, edited by Michael J. Thate, Kevin J. Vanhoozer, and Constantine R. Campbell. In addition to the editors, contributors include Douglas Campbell, Susan Eastman, Joshua Jipp, Grant Macaskill, Isaac Augustine Morales, and more. Vanhoozer's survey of Pauline scholarship on participation is a helpful supplement to this brief overview.[32] Coeditor Constantine Campbell has himself published an important book, *Paul and Union with Christ: An Exegetical and Theological*

---

28. See, e.g., my *Inhabiting the Cruciform God*; Gorman, "Romans: The First Christian Treatise on Theosis"; Gorman, *Becoming the Gospel*.

29. See D. Campbell, *Deliverance of God*, 211, 265; Wright, *Paul and the Faithfulness of God*, 546, 583, 955, 1021–23, 1031. On various approaches to Paul, see my *Apostle of the Crucified Lord*, 1–9.

30. Commenting on Gal. 3, for instance, Wright says, "What has been meant by 'participationist' theology joins up at once with the 'salvation-historical' perspective, both finding their meaning within a 'covenantal' frame of thought" (*Paul and the Faithfulness of God*, 875). D. Campbell finds in Phil. 3, for instance, a "vibrant, participatory, and apocalyptic understanding of the Christ event" (*Deliverance of God*, 897)—which is a good, succinct description of his overall reading of Paul.

31. Macaskill, *Union with Christ*. See also Powers, *Salvation through Participation*.

32. Vanhoozer, "From 'Blessed in Christ' to 'Being in Christ.'" For longer surveys, see Macaskill, *Union with Christ*, 17–41; C. Campbell, *Paul and Union with Christ*, 31–58.

Study. Campbell calls union with Christ the "webbing" that holds Paul's thought together.[33]

The focus on participation has led in other interesting directions. A few recent examples will have to suffice:[34]

- Douglas Campbell, a leading interpreter of Paul from within the "apocalyptic" school of Pauline studies for whom participation has always figured prominently, has written a major Pauline theology in which "Trinitarian communion"—participation in the eternal life of the Father, Son, and Spirit—is seen as the goal of God's work in Christ and through the Spirit.[35]
- Susan Eastman has produced an eloquent and insightful interdisciplinary study of Paul's anthropology, arguing that participation is at the heart of being human and at the core of Pauline anthropology; moreover, human participation in Christ depends on, and is subsequent to, God's participation with humanity in the person of Christ.[36]
- Another interdisciplinary study, this time by Pathipati Victor Paul from a very different context (India), explores the sociocultural aspects of corporate participation in Christ in view of caste, racial, and other disunifying forces.[37]
- Laura Hogan has written a careful study of Paul's spirituality, a "living Christ pattern" grounded in Philippians 2:5–11, that has three dimensions: kenosis, enosis (presence, union, solidarity), and theosis.[38]
- Jeanette Hagen Pifer demonstrates that, for Paul, faith means denial of any form of self-salvation, dependence on God, and self-involving participation in Christ's death and resurrection.[39]
- Haley Goranson Jacob's study of glory in Romans interprets glorification as participation in Christ's benevolent messianic rule.[40]

---

33. C. Campbell, *Paul and Union with Christ*, 441.

34. Because many of these volumes appeared after this book's manuscript was largely complete, I have been unable to interact in substantive ways with most of them.

35. D. Campbell, *Pauline Dogmatics*. For Campbell, this communion/participation has concrete relational consequences (e.g., sharing meals and money).

36. Eastman, *Paul and the Person*. For a similar emphasis on divine participation (both within the Trinity and, especially, in the incarnation) preceding and enabling participation in Christ—with the incarnation being the "epicenter" of Paul's theology—see Ware, *Paul's Theology in Context*.

37. Paul, *Exploring Socio-cultural Aspects of Pauline Ecclesiology*.

38. Hogan, *I Live, No Longer I*.

39. Pifer, *Faith as Participation*.

40. Jacob, *Conformed to the Image of His Son*.

- Wesley Thomas Davey has produced a study of the theme of suffering as participation in Christ, including its missional impact, in both the undisputed and the disputed Pauline letters.[41]
- Finally, Siu Fung Wu has edited a collection of essays on suffering in Paul, written by scholars from across the globe, that focus on the importance of various social locations for suffering but are united by the Pauline motif of participation in Christ.[42]

The Conversation Continues

Although participation is now widely recognized by Pauline scholars as a significant dimension of Paul's theology and spirituality (or "mysticism"), some interpreters have made it the focus, or a major aspect of the focus, of their own interpretation of Paul over time.[43] This book, and the rest of my work on Paul, is representative of this sort of "participationist perspective."[44] This perspective is intended not to exclude other approaches to Paul but to give pride of place—with Deissmann, Schweitzer, and Sanders—to "being in Christ" when interpreting Paul. My own contributions, like those of Hays, have a specifically narrative approach to participation that understands dying and rising with Christ as taking on a particular shape, or embodiment, in the world that resembles the trajectory of the Christ-story. My work has also attempted to end the divide between theology and spirituality, as well as the one between justification and participation. My challenge to Adolf Deissmann would be that participation in Christ is worthy of both the most serious academic theological investigations and the most profound expressions of Christian spirituality—precisely what we find in Paul himself.

It is clear that the study of participation in Paul shows no signs of abating. There are many texts to examine more carefully and important questions to explore more fully. The primary focus of this book is an array of specific texts, yet certain big questions will inevitably arise. One of these is the relationship between participation and justification. Despite recent developments in the study of Pauline soteriology, many students of Paul remain unconvinced that

41. Davey, *Suffering as Participation with Christ.*

42. Wu, *Suffering in Paul.*

43. Some interpreters who identify primarily as part of the apocalyptic school of Pauline interpretation see participation as a major aspect of that approach. I think especially of Douglas Campbell and Susan Eastman. Richard Hays could be identified primarily as part of the participationist approach to Paul, but with a strong apocalyptic emphasis as well.

44. For an excellent overview of this perspective that mentions much of the recent literature and has a focus on narrative (and with which I am largely in agreement), see Aernie, "Participation in Christ."

justification is anything other than a declaration of acquittal. This book again challenges that understanding, proposing (as I have before) an interpretation of justification as both participatory and transformative. Another big issue that emerges in Pauline studies is that of imitation, or mimesis. We will look carefully at the issue of whether Paul advocates the imitation of Christ, and what that has to do with participation. Yet another important question that will surface repeatedly is the relationship between a cross-centered and a resurrection-centered spirituality and theology. I will refer to this relationship as *resurrectional cruciformity*, developing it in various chapters. Still another significant issue is whether and how the term "theosis" is a good characterization of Paul's theology and spirituality.[45]

The present book, then, continues the participationist and narrative perspective on Paul's theology and spirituality I have developed especially in three major monographs, two editions of a comprehensive textbook on Paul, and numerous articles. This volume is neither a summation of those publications nor a complete, systematic treatment of participation in Paul. Rather, it is a set of interconnected explorations in Paul's participatory theology and spirituality that look in depth, and in new ways, at certain critical components of that theology and spirituality. Some of these components are examined in print here for the first time; others expand, deepen, or reiterate arguments (or suggestions) that have been made elsewhere. The chapters build logically on one another, yet many can also be read as stand-alone contributions. My intent is to offer a coherent reading of Paul that helps all interpreters of the apostle, in both academy and church, see him and his efforts through a fully participatory lens.

In much of my previous work, pride of place has gone to certain texts, among which are especially Philippians 2:6–11 (which I call Paul's master story), Galatians 2:15–21, and Romans 6. These texts continue to function significantly in the interpretation of Paul offered in this book. But if there is a highlighted letter in this volume, it is 2 Corinthians, and if there is a "theme text," it is 2 Corinthians 5:14–21, with special emphasis on verse 21: "For us [or "For our sake"] God made the one who did not know sin [the

---

45. One issue not addressed in this book, however, is the question of origins: What is the source, or what are the sources, of Paul's theology and spirituality of participation? Elsewhere (Gorman, "Romans and the Participationist Perspective") I have suggested that its source is likely the participationist implications of (1) the prophetic promise of the indwelling of God's Spirit that (2) the Jesus tradition connects to Jesus' baptizing with the Spirit and his death as a baptism. For other recent proposals, see, e.g., Jipp, *Christ Is King* (ancient and messianic royalty); Macaskill, *Union with Christ* (representative scriptural/messianic figures and corporate solidarity); and Nikkanen, "Participation in Christ" (covenant/Torah, Passover, pre-Pauline eucharistic practices).

Messiah Jesus] to be sin so that we ourselves would become the justice [or "righteousness"] of God in him" (my translation).[46] We will return frequently to this letter, this passage, and this verse.

I conclude this introduction with a brief overview of what is to come. Part 1, "Paul and Participation," consists of nine chapters. Chapter 1 is an overview of various aspects of being in Christ, presented as thirteen propositions. Many of these are developed more fully throughout the book. Chapter 2 examines the revelatory function of the cross and thus of life in the crucified Messiah. Chapter 3 considers the paradox that life in Christ—who is the *resurrected* crucified Messiah—is not only cruciform but also resurrectional. Chapter 4 proposes a new translation of a disputed text (Phil. 2:5) and the importance of that translation for Paul's in-Christ theology and spirituality. Chapter 5 explores aspects of life in the Spirit according to Galatians.

Chapters 6–8 follow a "justification" trajectory, looking at connections among Galatians 2:15–21 (chap. 6), 2 Corinthians 5:14–21 (chap. 7), and Romans (chap. 8) that show the participatory and transformative character of justification. Chapter 9 returns to 2 Corinthians and argues for the appropriateness of the term "theosis" for Paul's theology and spirituality.

Part 2, "Paul and Participation Today," consists of two chapters, one more general (though focused on the North American context) and one focused on the resurrection. These chapters reflect on the significance of Paul's participationist theology and spirituality for contemporary Christian praxis.[47]

---

46. From now on, my own translations will be indicated by "MJG."

47. It is encouraging to see other interpreters of participation in Paul engaging in similar sorts of reflections. See, e.g., Billings, *Union with Christ*, and now Macaskill, *Living in Union with Christ*.

Part 1

Paul and Participation

The nine essays in this first part of the book are primarily careful exegetical studies of various key passages in Paul's letters that demonstrate the significance of participation for the apostle's theology and spirituality. These exegetical studies are connected to one another and thus also make claims about Paul's theology and spirituality as a whole. Furthermore, this part of the book also makes claims—often more implicit than explicit—about the significance of that theology and spirituality for today. Some of these claims are addressed more explicitly in the two essays in part 2.

one

Participating in Christ

An Overview

Participation is back in the (theological) news. The energy and, indeed, excitement about participation is palpable at conferences, in publications, and even occasionally from the pulpit. This renewed interest in participation is due in no small measure to the apostle Paul. This chapter briefly considers Paul's language of participation before sketching some of the major aspects of Paul's theology and spirituality of transformative participation in Christ. This sketch will take the form of thirteen propositions divided into four sections: the cross, cruciformity, dying and rising with Christ, and mission. These propositions do two things: they summarize much of my previous work on Paul and participation, and they anticipate some of the areas that will be explored in more depth in later chapters of this book.[1]

Paul's "In Christ" and "With Christ" Language

Paul expresses participationist ideas in several ways.[2] One common way is by using prepositions and prefixes. He often uses the language of being "in Christ," as well as related phrases like being "with Christ." This assumes that there has been an initial movement, through faith and baptism, from "outside

---

1. For another brief overview of the participationist approach to Paul, see Gorman, "Romans and the Participationist Perspective."
2. See, e.g., his various metaphors, discussed in C. Campbell, "Metaphor, Reality, and Union with Christ."

of" and "away from" Christ to being "in" and "with" Christ: "Do you not know that all of us who have been baptized **into Christ Jesus** were baptized **into his death?**" (Rom. 6:3).[3]

For Paul it is as natural to speak about a person or persons being "in Christ," "in Christ Jesus," "in the Lord Jesus," or "in the Lord" as it is for Christians today to refer to themselves as "Christians." Take, for instance, the evidence from his letter to the Romans; all the boldfaced phrases begin with the Greek preposition *en* ("in"):[4]

> So you also must consider yourselves dead to sin and alive to God **in Christ Jesus.** (6:11)

> [1]There is therefore now no condemnation for those who are **in Christ Jesus.** [2]For the law of the Spirit of life **in Christ Jesus** has set you free from the law of sin and of death. (8:1–2)

> I am speaking the truth **in Christ**—I am not lying; my conscience confirms it by the Holy Spirit. (9:1)

> So we, who are many, are one body **in Christ,** and individually we are members one of another. (12:5)

> I know and am persuaded **in the Lord Jesus** that nothing is unclean in itself; but it is unclean for anyone who thinks it unclean. (14:14)

> **In Christ Jesus,** then, I have reason to boast of my work for God. (15:17)

> [1]I commend to you our sister Phoebe, a deacon of the church at Cenchreae, [2]so that you may welcome her **in the Lord** as is fitting for the saints, and help her in whatever she may require from you, for she has been a benefactor of many and of myself as well. [3]Greet Prisca and Aquila, who work with me **in Christ Jesus.** (16:1–3)

> [7]Greet Andronicus and Junia, my relatives who were in prison with me; they are prominent among the apostles, and they were **in Christ** before I was. [8]Greet Ampliatus, my beloved **in the Lord.** [9]Greet Urbanus, our co-worker **in Christ,** and my beloved Stachys. [10]Greet Apelles, who is approved **in Christ.** Greet those who belong to the family of Aristobulus. [11]Greet my relative Herodion. Greet those **in the Lord** who belong to the family of Narcissus. [12]Greet those

---

3. As we will see throughout this chapter, the connection between being in Christ and being "in" his death is absolutely central to Paul's theology and spirituality.

4. For a helpful analysis of "in Christ" language in Paul generally, including the history of interpretation and a brief note on Romans, see R. Longenecker, *Epistle to the Romans*, 686–94.

workers **in the Lord**, Tryphaena and Tryphosa. Greet the beloved Persis, who has worked hard **in the Lord**. [13]Greet Rufus, chosen **in the Lord**; and greet his mother—a mother to me also. (16:7–13)

I Tertius, the writer of this letter, greet you **in the Lord**. (16:22)

The natural way in which Paul uses this "in" language does not mean he is unreflective about it or that it is void of content. Rather, such expressions are rich in meaning; they constitute Paul's main idiom for "the intimate and personal relationship that exists between the exalted Christ and those who have committed themselves to him."[5] Some of the phrases in Romans, especially in chapter 16, use "in Christ" almost as a title. But in earlier chapters there is clearly significant theological content associated with the various phrases. To be in Christ is to have life and to be alive to God (6:11; 8:1–2); it is to live according to certain ethical norms (9:1); it is to be part of a community, a body (12:5); and it is to possess certain convictions and attitudes (14:14; 15:17).

We should assume that most, if not all, of these theological dimensions of being in Christ—and more, if we look outside Romans—are also to be associated with the various people described as being in Christ/in the Lord in chapter 16. At the same time, aspects of chapter 16 can also be generalized with respect to all who are in Christ: being in Christ is the result of a transfer from being outside Christ (16:7); there is missional work to be done in Christ (16:9, 12–13); and there is accountability in Christ (16:10). Moreover, it is clear that being in Christ both includes and transcends the local community; those who are in Christ in Corinth (like Paul) and in Rome are in Christ *together*. "In" language is a spatial idiom that signifies a relational reality that is both personal and corporate, both "vertical" and "horizontal," both local and universal.

Not to be forgotten in considering this language is that "Christ" (Gk. *Christos*) means "Messiah." Paul is saying that he and all believers are located in the crucified and resurrected Messiah and Lord whose name is Jesus. And this reality reminds us, furthermore, that our participation in the Messiah is possible only because God the Father has first participated with us by being present in the Messiah Jesus, a presence revealed both in the Messiah's incarnation and death and in his ongoing resurrected life:[6]

5. R. Longenecker, *Epistle to the Romans*, 692. Longenecker (691–92) rightly ⸱ "in Christ" is more than an adjective (i.e., "Christian") for Paul.

6. Both here and in the next group, the Greek preposition *en* is used phrases.

In Christ God was reconciling the world to himself, not counting their trespasses against them, and entrusting the message of reconciliation to us. (2 Cor. 5:19)

[38]For I am convinced that neither death, nor life, nor angels, nor rulers, nor things present, nor things to come, nor powers, [39]nor height, nor depth, nor anything else in all creation, will be able to separate us from **the love of God in Christ Jesus our Lord.** (Rom. 8:38–39)

Sometimes the "God in Christ" and "us in Christ" realities seem to merge, for Christ is the place where human beings meet God and receive salvation:

For the wages of sin is death, but the free gift of God is **eternal life in Christ Jesus our Lord.** (Rom. 6:23)

They are now justified by his grace as a gift, through **the redemption that is in Christ Jesus.** (Rom. 3:24)

As noted above, the close association between believers and Christ is also expressed in the language of "with Christ," a reality that is both present and future (and is expressed, grammatically, in several ways).[7] For example:

For through the law I died to the law, so that I might live to God. **I have been crucified with Christ** [*Christō synestaurōmai*]. (Gal. 2:19)

And if [we are God's] children, then [we are also] heirs, heirs of God and **joint heirs with Christ** [*synklēronomoi de Christou*]—if, in fact, we **suffer with him** [*sympaschomen*] so that we may also **be glorified with him** [*syndoxasthōmen*]. (Rom. 8:17)

But if we have **died with Christ** [*apethanomen syn Christō*], we believe that we **will also live with him** [*kai syzēsomen autō*]. (Rom. 6:8; cf. 1 Thess. 4:17)

I am hard pressed between the two: my desire is to depart and **be with Christ** [*syn Christō einai*], for that is far better. (Phil. 1:23)

Because we know that the one who raised the Lord Jesus **will raise us also with Jesus** [*kai hēmas syn Iēsou egerei*], and will bring us with you into his presence. (2 Cor. 4:14)

7. The "with Christ" idea can be expressed by means of a preposition (*syn*, "with"; sometimes *pros* [2 Cor. 5:8]), a prefix (*syn*, meaning "with" or "co-," and its various forms), or case usage; see C. Campbell, *Paul and Union with Christ.*

Of course, participating in Christ in Paul is about more than a handful of expressions, no matter how often they are used or how important they are. We turn now, therefore, to a more careful, if basic, analysis of participation in Paul by considering the thirteen propositions, divided into four sections, mentioned at the beginning of this chapter. (The thirteen propositions are also collected together at the end of the chapter.)

The Cross

We begin with the cross, because Paul proclaimed to the Corinthians, "I resolved to know nothing among you except Jesus the Messiah—that is, Jesus the *crucified* Messiah" (1 Cor. 2:2 MJG). To be sure, for Paul, Jesus would not have been the Messiah had he not been raised from the dead, and on many occasions the apostle speaks specifically, in the same breath, of Jesus having both died and been raised (e.g., Rom. 4:25; 6:10; 8:34; 14:9; 1 Cor. 15:3–4; 2 Cor. 5:15; 1 Thess. 4:14). And yet Paul grants a certain priority and emphasis to the death of Jesus, to his being the Crucified One. Why is that so? Three main points may be offered in response to this query.

1. The cross is "the signature of the one who is risen."

These words come from the pen of the great twentieth-century German New Testament scholar Ernst Käsemann.[8] Käsemann was insisting, against perverted forms of theological and political notions of power and glory, that the resurrected Lord of the church is continuous with the crucified Jesus. The cross remains forever a part of the identity of the Messiah.

Paul is not alone among New Testament writers in making this point. For instance, the Gospel of John depicts this reality in the most literal way possible by noting that Jesus appeared to the disciples and to Thomas with his scars (John 20:19–29). The book of Revelation portrays the same reality in the image of the Lamb who was slaughtered and yet stands (Rev. 5:6–14). Though once dead and now alive forever (Rev. 1:18), this Jesus can only be encountered and worshiped as the slaughtered Lamb (see also Rev. 13:8), the one forever marked with his own blood (Rev. 7:14; 12:11; 19:13).[9] And the Gospel of Luke represents the same reality, though more subtly, when the resurrected Jesus is identifiable only when he is associated with the breaking

8. Käsemann, "Saving Significance of the Death of Jesus," 56.
9. There is debate about whose blood covers the robe of "the Word of God" (Christ) in Rev. 19:13, but given the significance of associating blood and death with Jesus throughout Revelation, it is almost certainly his own blood.

of bread, the remembrance of the meal that is both the predecessor and the symbol of his death (Luke 24:13–35, esp. vv. 30–31, 35).

For both Paul and these other New Testament theologians, the cross is a Christophany—a manifestation of Christ's identity, not merely a moment in his life that is succeeded and superseded by the resurrection. He is forever the crucified Messiah, the crucified Lord. Yet Paul wants to say something more about the cross of Christ.

2. The cross is not only a Christophany but also a theophany—the definitive self-revelation of God, which means that God is kenotic (self-emptying) love; the cross is the signature of the Eternal One.

One of Paul's most radical claims about the cross and about the character of God is that the cross reveals not only the identity of Christ but also the identity of God. That is, the cross is the signature not only of the Crucified One but also of the Eternal One.

The text of 1 Corinthians 2:2 quoted above ("I resolved to know nothing among you except Jesus the Messiah—that is, Jesus the *crucified* Messiah") is found within the context of Paul's asserting that the crucified Messiah is the definitive revelation of divine power and wisdom. Over against both Jewish and gentile notions of these essential divine attributes, says Paul, "we proclaim a crucified Messiah . . . the Messiah who is God's power and God's wisdom" (1 Cor. 1:23–24 MJG). If, philosophically and theologically speaking, we cannot separate God's attributes from God's actual identity, then we can only conclude that Christ crucified reveals the divine identity; the cross is a theophany. In the same context, Paul also implies that the Messiah who "became" wisdom from God—that is, who revealed divine wisdom on the cross—"became" and thus revealed divine justice/righteousness as well (1 Cor. 1:30). Paul restates this claim with emphasis in Romans 3:21–26.

In two other key texts, Paul also likely refers to Christ's cross and to the incarnation that both preceded it and, in important ways, resembled it as divine revelation.[10] First, we have 2 Corinthians 8:9. The critical word in this text, a Greek participle (*ōn*, from the verb "to be"), is normally translated as a concessive participle, with the word "though": "For you know the generous act [*charin*, "grace"] of our Lord Jesus Christ, that though he was [*ōn*] rich, yet for your sakes he became poor, so that by his poverty you might become rich." But as John Barclay has persuasively argued, the context here makes it

---

10. On the appropriateness of the language of incarnation in reference to Paul, see Macaskill, "Incarnational Ontology."

likely that the participle should be translated causally, not concessively.[11] Thus we might render the verse as follows: "For you know the grace of our Lord Jesus Christ, that *because* he was rich, yet for your sakes he became poor, so that by his poverty you might become rich" (emphasis added).

This translation means that Christ acted in self-giving graciousness *because* of the richness he possessed—not *in spite* of it. That is, the Messiah's self-impoverishment, probably meaning both his incarnation and his crucifixion, was a Christophany: a true revelation of his identity. The text does not explicitly say that the incarnation and cross also constitute a theophany. Nevertheless, we should still draw that conclusion because, in the same context, Paul tells us that the grace of Christ was also the "indescribable gift" of God (2 Cor. 9:15). This is the case because "God was in the Messiah, reconciling the world to himself" (2 Cor. 5:19 MJG).

Our second key text on this subject is more explicit. In Philippians 2:6, which is part of the famous "Christ-hymn" or "Christ-poem" of Philippians 2:6–11—a text that likely stands behind the briefer theological statement of 2 Corinthians 8:9—we find a situation similar to that of 2 Corinthians 8:9. Once again there is a participle that is normally translated concessively ("though") when it could, even should, be translated causally ("because"). The NRSV, for instance, has "though he was in the form of God, [he] did not regard equality with God as something to be exploited." But a good case has been made by numerous scholars that another rendering is both possible and correct: "*because* he was in the form of God . . ." (emphasis added).[12] In other words, Christ did what he did—what the poem narrates as his self-emptying (kenosis) and self-humbling in both incarnation and death (Phil. 2:6–8)—not *in spite of* his equality with God but *because* of it.

If this translation is correct—and it seems to be completely in line with the implications of the texts from 1 and 2 Corinthians cited above—then, once again, we have Paul asserting that what Christ did in his self-giving incarnation and death was a revelation of divinity, a theophany. Since the context of both Philippians 2:6–8 and 2 Corinthians 8:9 tells us that Christ's incarnation and death constituted an act of gracious love (not to mention other texts about both his love and the Father's love),[13] we can only conclude

11. Barclay, "'Because He Was Rich He Became Poor.'"
12. See my *Inhabiting the Cruciform God*, 9–39, which is a revision of "'Although/Because He Was in the Form of God.'" More precisely, the view developed there is that we should read the text with both causal and concessive senses, but the argument for that view cannot be delineated here.
13. E.g., Rom. 5:8; 8:35–39; 2 Cor. 5:14; Gal. 2:20. Cf. Eph. 5:2, 25.

that the cross, as the culminating revelation of Christ's kenotic, cruciform love, is simultaneously the revelation of God's self-giving love.

This fundamental divine trait of self-giving, kenotic love, which has manifested itself concretely and supremely in the cross of Christ, is also for Paul the essential trait of the person and the people who have received this divine love in Christ.

3. The cross is not only the definitive revelation of Christ and of God (i.e., it is both Christophany and theophany) but also the definitive revelation of what humans and the church are to be.

What does it mean to say that the cross reveals what *we* are to be, both as individuals and as the corporate body of the church (Gk. *ekklēsia*)? This query is one of the driving questions in all my work on Paul, but for the purposes of this chapter I can respond briefly in three ways.[14]

First, the word "incarnation" means not only that God became human but also that God became *true* humanity; that is, God became the kind of human that humans were intended to be.[15] For Paul, then, the story of Christ, the Incarnate One, is both the story of God and the story of what humans were meant to be. Paul refers to this interconnection between Christ and God the Father, on the one hand, and human beings, on the other, as a process of being transformed into the image of Christ, which means the image of God (2 Cor. 3:18; 4:4).

Second, as is well known and has already been noted, a critical element of Paul's theology and spirituality is expressed in the language of being "in Christ," or "in the Messiah." The Messiah is where "the action" was and is. He is both the "place" where God has acted ("God was in the Messiah," 2 Cor. 5:19) and the "place" where believers now are, individually and corporately. And if the exalted Messiah in whom believers live remains forever the crucified Messiah, then his cross defines both him and those who indwell him. Furthermore, it is "in him" (Christ), as Colossians puts it, that "all the fullness of God dwells bodily" (Col. 2:9 MJG; cf. 1:19), and thus it is "in him" that "you are completely fulfilled" (Col. 2:10 MJG). As in 2 Corinthians 5:14–21, according to Colossians the incarnation was for the purpose of reconciliation

---

14. See also chap. 2 below, where I will introduce the terms "anthrophany" and "ecclesiophany" to indicate that the cross reveals what humanity and what the church are supposed to be in Christ.

15. Although Paul does not use the exact language we find in John 1:14 ("the Word became flesh"), we have a similar theological claim in Phil. 2:6–8, especially if the interpretation of that text just offered is taken into account. Moreover, Paul also uses the language of the Father sending the Son (e.g., Gal. 4:4), which is similar to the frequent "sending" language in John and which implies both Christ's preexistence and his incarnation.

through the cross (Col. 1:20). In other words, the incarnation of God and the cross of Christ are inseparable; to be Godlike and thus "full" as a human being, then, will mean to be cross-like. (We will have much more to say about "cross-shaped Godlikeness" below.)

Third, one of Paul's favorite images of the church is that of the Messiah's body (Rom. 12:3–8; 1 Cor. 12; cf. Eph. 4). More than a metaphor, this reality implies that Jesus continues to live in and as his church. As the body of Christ, the church continues, in a sense, the incarnation and therefore continues its inseparable connection to the cross. The body of Christ is inherently a cross-shaped body, a people that incarnates the self-emptying, self-giving Messiah who is the incarnation of the kenotic God. It is this cross-shaped existence of the church that is summarized in the term "cruciformity."

Cruciformity

The term "cruciform," meaning cross-shaped, was originally applied to churches that were built in the form of a cross. Over time, it came to be used in biblical and theological circles as an adjective to describe the form of life inspired and shaped by Jesus' crucifixion—that is, by the values and practices that both led up to the cross and were displayed on the cross. The adjective was, and is, frequently used to characterize certain aspects of New Testament theology, such as Mark's vision of cruciform discipleship, or Paul's understanding of cruciform ministry. When transformed into a noun, "cruciform" becomes "cruciformity."[16] What can be said about it briefly?

4. The cross is not only the source but also the shape of our salvation, and cross-shaped living (cruciformity) means that all Christian virtues and practices are cruciform: faith/faithfulness, love, power, hope, justice, and so forth.

Most Christians believe that the cross of Christ is the source of their salvation and that Paul himself affirms that conviction. To be sure, neither Paul nor good theology limits the source of salvation to the cross, for it involves also Christ's incarnation (as we have already noted), earthly ministry, resurrection, ascension, and parousia (coming). Moreover, some Christians, especially Orthodox Christians, put at least as much weight on the incarnation as on the cross. But no one should deny the role of Jesus' death in salvation.

16. In addition to my *Cruciformity*, see esp. my *Apostle of the Crucified Lord* for the importance of cruciformity throughout Paul's writings.

Debates about the "mechanics," or specific means and meaning, of the atonement have swirled around the church for centuries. Moreover, several new theories, or "models," of the atonement, in addition to the three or four principal ones, have been proposed in recent times.[17] Whatever one's preferred model of the atonement, what is often lacking in the models is any application of the model to actual life. For Paul, however, the cross is more than the *source* of salvation; it is also its *shape*. Paul cannot talk for long, if at all, about the cross without connecting it to life in Christ, and he cannot speak of life in Christ for long, if at all, without linking it to Christ crucified.

Of particular importance is the way Paul interprets the theological virtues of faith(fulness), love, and hope (a triad that he was likely the first to formulate), plus the practice of power, in light of the cross.[18] Love, for instance, is cross-shaped in many ways, not least because it seeks the good and edification of others, rather than of the self.[19] Love "does not seek its own advantage" (1 Cor. 13:5 MJG) but rather, in humility, seeks the good of others, because that is what Christ did on the cross (Phil. 2:3–4, 6–8). The strong or powerful in the church must look out for the weak, because that is what Christ did on the cross, welcoming the weak (Rom. 15:1–4; cf. 5:6).

So too, faith is connected to the cross; Paul seems to have claimed that Christ displayed his faith, or faithfulness (Rom. 3:22, 26; Gal. 2:16, 20; 3:22; Phil. 3:9), toward God,[20] which means his obedience (Rom. 5:19; Phil. 2:8). For this reason, Paul describes the goal of his ministry as eliciting "the obedience of faith" ("faithful obedience," or even "believing allegiance"), especially from the gentiles (Rom. 1:5; 15:18; 16:26; cf. 10:16; 11:30–32).[21] The positive reputation of a particular church can be described in terms of its faithfulness (1 Thess. 1:8) or its obedience (Rom. 16:19; Phil. 2:12[22]). Even hope for Paul is cruciform, because it is experienced, paradoxically, most fully when suffering with Christ (Rom. 8:17–25).[23]

---

17. For a survey, see Baker and Green, *Recovering the Scandal of the Cross*. For my own proposed model, see *Death of the Messiah*.

18. Gorman, *Cruciformity*, 95–348.

19. See esp. Gorman, *Cruciformity*, 155–267.

20. This is not the place for a full discussion of this issue, to which we return briefly below. For the discussion, see Bird and Sprinkle, *Faith of Jesus Christ*. For my own defense of the subjective-genitive reading ("the faith of Christ"), see *Cruciformity*, 95–121.

21. See, e.g., Bates, *Salvation by Allegiance Alone*, 85–87. Bates uses terms like "enacted allegiance" and "embodied allegiance."

22. The NRSV's rendering of Phil. 2:12 erroneously introduces the pronoun "me" after "obeyed."

23. See Gorman, *Cruciformity*, 304–48.

Furthermore, other virtues and practices are likewise defined in terms of the cross. For instance, Paul exhorts the Corinthians not to practice the injustice of taking their "siblings" to the pagan courts, and even to accept rather than inflict injustice (1 Cor. 6:1–11).[24] Why? Explicitly, it is because believers have identified completely with the identity of Christ at their baptism into his name. This was the public expression of their justification, their being incorporated into the community of the just (1 Cor. 6:11). Implicitly, it is because accepting rather than inflicting injustice is precisely what Christ himself did on the cross.[25]

There is a fairly consistent pattern that Paul either uses explicitly or implies throughout his exhortations to cruciformity. He grounds these exhortations in the narrative of Christ's incarnation and crucifixion found in Philippians 2:6–8. The basic pattern is that those who have a certain status, right, or prerogative are called, shaped, and empowered by Christ to relinquish the right for the good, edification, or salvation of others. The grammar of the pattern is "although [x] not [y] but [z]," meaning "although [status], not [selfishness] but [self-giving]."[26] This is the pattern of Christ's own kenosis and crucifixion.

By the power of the indwelling Christ/the Spirit (Phil. 2:1, 5), the story of Christ is "re-incarnated" in the church and in each individual believer.[27] Paul calls the members of the church to embody this narrative in the way they deal with divisions over the eating of meat offered to idols (1 Cor. 8:1–11:1), the practice of the Lord's Supper (1 Cor. 11:17–34), the use of spiritual gifts (1 Cor. 12–14), and more. Moreover, Paul himself serves as a kind of "middle term" between Christ and the churches. He calls on them to become imitators of him, but only inasmuch as he is an imitator of Christ (1 Cor. 11:1), for he embodies the story of Christ in the way he lovingly cares for his churches, especially in renouncing his right to compensation, working with his hands so as not to burden them (1 Thess. 2; 1 Cor. 9).

As we have just seen and will see again below, all of this means being narrated into the story of the crucified Messiah. Paul's spirituality of the cross is a *narrative* spirituality. It incarnates the story of Christ—which means the story of God.

24. See my "Justification and Justice in Paul"; also my *Becoming the Gospel*, 212–96.
25. Note the reference to Christ the sacrificed paschal lamb in the immediately preceding passage (1 Cor. 5:7).
26. Which can also be construed, in light of proposition 2 above, as "because [x] not [y] but [z]." We will return to this pattern in more detail in the next chapter. For the basic pattern, see esp. Gorman, *Cruciformity*, 90–91, 164–77, 186–88, 192, 197, 230–38, 243, 252, 261, 330; Gorman, *Apostle of the Crucified Lord*, 80–81, 125–26, 310, 507–9.
27. On the role of the Spirit, see my "Holy Spirit and Cruciformity."

5. Cruciformity is also theoformity, or theosis; that is, cross-shaped existence is God-shaped existence, and this existence is for both individuals and communities in the Messiah.

If Paul's spirituality is a *narrative* spirituality of conformity to the crucified Messiah, and if the story of the crucified Messiah is also the story of God, then the logical conclusion to draw is that *cruci*formity is also *theo*formity. To become Christlike is to become Godlike, for Christ is the image of God, the one in whom God's fullness lives, the one in whom God has acted. If "in Christ" is the heart of Paul's theology as well as his spirituality, then when human beings are incorporated into Christ to take on his identity and be transformed into his image, they are also being incorporated into God the Father (1 Thess. 1:1; 2 Thess. 1:1) to be transformed into the image of God—to have their original Godlikeness restored. If the cross is a theophany as well as a Christophany, then cruciform existence is theoform, or God-shaped, existence. In the Christian tradition, the language for this theology and spirituality is theosis, or deification.

It is this logic—along with other factors—that has led several interpreters of Paul, including the present author, to connect Paul's soteriology to the theology of theosis, or deification.[28] (When I first proposed using this language with reference to Paul, in the early years of this millennium, I was nearly run out of town at a scholarly conference. That is no longer the case.) This is an aspect of Christian theology that is prominent in Orthodoxy, is present but far less prominent in Roman Catholicism, and has been barely known in much of Protestantism, until recently.

Like participation, theosis (or deification/divinization) is back in the theological news. Of course, these are all terms that need to be defined carefully. None of them implies that human beings ever become God or gods; humans become Godlike, never crossing the line—the chasm—between creature and Creator. But because of this possible misunderstanding, some people prefer the term "Christosis" or "Christification"—becoming like Christ.[29] The point to be made is that, whichever of these terms is used (or not used), Paul is proclaiming that when the church is inhabiting Christ, it is inhabiting God—the cruciform God.[30]

---

28. For a full exposition of this thesis, see my *Inhabiting the Cruciform God*. For a concise exposition of the theme, see Gorman, "Romans: The First Christian Treatise on Theosis," revised in *Becoming the Gospel*, 261–96; and chap. 9 below. See also, e.g., Blackwell, *Christosis*; Litwa, *We Are Being Transformed*; Litwa, "2 Corinthians 3:18."

29. E.g., Blackwell, *Christosis*.

30. See esp. my *Inhabiting the Cruciform God*: "For Paul, to be one with Christ is to be one with God; to be like Christ is to be like God," which is to say that "for Paul cruciformity . . . is

The patristic claim noted earlier is helpful here: God/Christ became what we are so that we could become what God/Christ is. There are similar texts in Paul's letters, which Morna Hooker refers to as "interchange" texts.[31] The one that is perhaps closest to the patristic formula is 2 Corinthians 5:21: "For us [or "For our sake"] God made the one who did not know sin [the Messiah Jesus] to be sin so that we ourselves would become the justice [or "righteousness"; Gk. *dikaiosynē*] of God in him" (MJG). Although this text is often interpreted as a witness to Paul's (alleged) theology of imputation (the notion that Christ's righteousness is reckoned to sinners), many recent scholars have rightly recognized that this is a text of transformation, and particularly of taking on one of the most fundamental divine attributes: justice/righteousness. This text reveals that for Paul justification involves transformation, and it is inseparable from justice.[32] It is a text to which we will return several times in this book.[33]

We must keep in mind that, for Paul, all spirituality is not only individual but also communal. In 2 Corinthians 5:21 he says that God's goal is that "we"— not merely "I"—become the justice of God in the Messiah.[34] This is why the Pauline images of being *together* in Christ are so critical to his theology: the church as the temple of the Holy Spirit (1 Cor. 3:16) and the body of Christ. Being "in Christ" signifies many things for Paul, but one of its most fundamental meanings is being in the community, the body, of the Messiah.

The key to individual and corporate transformation, then, is being "in Christ," where the powerful ongoing work of the risen Lord takes place by the Spirit, who is the Spirit of both the Father and the Son (Gal. 4:6; Phil. 1:19).

6. Cruciformity/theoformity is a matter not of imitation but of transformative participation: being in the Messiah/the Spirit and having the Messiah/the Spirit within (mutual indwelling).

One of the great Christian spiritual practices is the "imitation of Christ." Despite its popularity, this notion is somewhat at odds with Paul's own spirituality. This claim may sound surprising, since Paul himself says, "Imitate me," does he not? The answer is "Yes, but . . ." The critical verse is

---

really theoformity, or theosis" (4). That is, it is appropriate to use "theosis" to describe Paul's understanding of transformative participation in the "kenotic, cruciform character of God through Spirit-enabled conformity to the incarnate, crucified, and resurrected/glorified Christ" (162).

31. Hooker, *From Adam to Christ*, 13–69.

32. See further Grieb, "'So That in Him.'"

33. See esp. chaps. 7 and 9.

34. There are debates about the specific referent of the "we"—all Christians or just Paul's apostolic team—but, in either case, the transformation is of a group, not merely of the individual.

1 Corinthians 11:1, where Paul says, "Be imitators of me, as I am of Christ."[35] Actually, the verb "be" is "become" (Gk. *ginesthe*), which implies a transformative process. More importantly, as we have just seen, transformation takes place in Christ by the working of the Spirit. Because this divine "force" is at work on us and within us, says Paul, we are being transformed into the glory and image of Christ (2 Cor. 3:18; 4:4). It is this presupposition of divine transformative activity that allows Paul to issue the exhortation to be transformed: "Be transformed by the renewal of your mind" (Rom. 12:2 MJG). This call is in the passive voice because it is not merely our own effort that makes it happen.

At the center of Paul's spirituality of participation and transformation is his notion of mutual indwelling, or reciprocal residence—that is, Christ in believers and believers in Christ, which means also the Spirit in believers and believers in the Spirit. This language signifies a relationship of deep intimacy and allegiance. Romans 8 expresses this spirituality most succinctly:

> [1]There is therefore now no condemnation for those who are **in Christ Jesus.** . . . [9]But you are not in the flesh; you are **in the Spirit,** since **the Spirit of God dwells in you.** Anyone who does not have the Spirit of Christ does not belong to him. [10]But if **Christ is in you,** though the body is dead because of sin, the Spirit is life because of righteousness. [11]If **the Spirit of him who raised Jesus from the dead dwells in you,** he who raised Christ from the dead will give life to your mortal bodies also through **his Spirit that dwells in you.** (Rom. 8:1, 9–11)

It is this life-giving, life-changing Spirit that makes the imitation of Paul, and—more importantly—of Christ, possible. It is *in* Christ that we become *like* Christ, thanks to the Spirit:

> [1]If then there is any encouragement in Christ . . . any participation [*koinōnia*] in the Spirit . . . [4]Let each of you look not to your own interests, but rather to the interests of others. [5]Cultivate this mindset [and its corollary behavior] in your community, which is in fact a community in the Messiah Jesus. (Phil. 2:1, 4–5 MJG)[36]

These lines are the preface to the famous Christ-poem in Philippians 2:6–8, in which the "mindset" of the Messiah is described as consisting of self-emptying and self-humbling activity for the good of others, as we noted earlier: cruciformity/theoformity. The point here is that the "imitation" of Christ's mindset,

---

35. We find "imitation of Paul" language also in 1 Cor. 4:16, Gal. 4:12, Phil. 3:17 (cf. 4:9), and 1 Thess. 1:6–7, generally containing the verb "become" and the noun "imitators."

36. Phil. 2:5 is often rendered, "Let the same mind be in you that was in Christ Jesus" (so NRSV), but the translation offered here is to be preferred. Chapter 4 discusses this text in detail.

his way of life, is the result of participation in the life of the living Lord, not merely the imitation of a historical figure or an external example.

It may seem to some that we have thus far been putting the proverbial cart before the horse. To speak of being in Christ and in God, and of a corresponding life of cruciformity/theoformity, implies that people are actually located in Christ. That is not the case for all human beings, however, from Paul's perspective. He does not agree with the ancient Stoics, who found a spark of the divine reason, the universal Logos, resident in everyone. Rather, there must be a "transfer"—to use the language of E. P. Sanders[37]—into Christ, at which time Christ also takes up residence in that person. In Paul's theology and spirituality, this transfer occurs in the act of faith and baptism.

Dying and Rising with Christ

Most Christians associate the language of dying and rising with Christ with baptism, and rightly so (Rom. 6). But it is also, for Paul, the idiom of justification, and that is no less important.

7. We enter the Messiah by means of faith/baptism; justification by faith is a participatory event of dying and rising with the Messiah, meaning that justification is resurrection to new life by means of co-crucifixion with the Messiah.

The "doctrine" of justification is often claimed to be at the center of Paul's theology. Whether or not that is precisely the case, it is certainly true that justification has been both central to and controversial in discussions of Paul and of his significance for Christian theology.[38] The interpretation of justification has been a major focus of my work on Paul, and it will be a major focus of several chapters in this book.[39]

Justification remains a contested subject in Pauline theology and in theology more generally. This is the case despite the *Joint Declaration on the Doctrine of Justification*, issued by Roman Catholics and Lutherans in 1999, and then later endorsed, in one way or another, by certain significant Methodist (2006), Reformed (2017), and Anglican (2017) bodies.

In my view, some interpreters of justification in Paul commit one or more methodological errors:

37. See Sanders, *Paul and Palestinian Judaism*, 463–72.
38. For an overview of recent perspectives, see A. Johnson, "Navigating Justification."
39. See esp. chaps. 6–8.

1. Some interpreters wrongly assume that Paul's understanding of justification is defined and confined by the meaning of the term provided by the lexicon or Second Temple Jewish sources. This position does not allow sufficiently for Paul's theological creativity: his reconfiguration of justification in light of the Messiah and the Spirit and in light of his own personal experience. A conversion in Paul's life yields a conversion in his understanding of justification.[40]

2. Some interpreters fail to note, or fail to synthesize, the intimate connections among the various members of the *dikai-* family of words in Greek. This is partly a function of the two English word-families that are used to render the single *dikai-* family: "righteous," "righteousness," and "rectification" versus "just," "justice," and "justification." But even some scholars who know the words are related do not, or will not, make all the connections. Which leads to the third error.

3. Some interpreters fail to make other sorts of connections and stop short of certain kinds of exegetical and theological conclusions because of fear of sounding, or even becoming, Roman Catholic or Orthodox (or Jewish?). For instance, a predisposition toward a "juridical" (forensic, legal) view of justification can obscure the connection between justification and justice, or rule out the possibility of seeing justification as that which actually makes people just. Theological concerns about "works-righteousness" or "synergism" may prevent an interpreter from seeing what Paul actually says.

The threefold antidote to this set of errors is simply to expect creativity from Paul, explore connections in Paul, and hold theological presuppositions about Paul more loosely.

A strong case can be made that Paul's understanding of justification is much more participatory and transformative than is often thought, especially by many Protestant interpreters. (Recent work on the sources of Protestant thought on justification, including Luther, Calvin, and Paul himself, suggests that we cannot understand justification appropriately apart from union with Christ—that is, apart from participation and transformation.)[41] This claim will also be developed in detail in several chapters later in this book. For now, a brief summary of some of my earlier work will suffice.

40. A similar point is made by Jonathan Linebaugh regarding the phrase "the righteousness of God": "Paul does not look in the lexicon of apocalyptic Judaism to define" the righteousness of God, for the "Pauline definition . . . is a christological *redefinition*" ("Righteousness Revealed," 236, 237; emphasis added).
41. See esp. Chester, *Reading Paul with the Reformers*; Canlis, *Calvin's Ladder*.

A careful study of two critical passages in Paul's theology and spirituality—Galatians 2:15–21 and Romans 6—reveals that Paul has a basic soteriology of dying and rising with Christ that he associates with both justification by faith/faithfulness (Gal. 2:15–21) and baptism (Rom. 6). In each passage, Paul speaks of co-crucifixion with the Messiah Jesus:

> For I myself, through the law, died in relation to the law so that I could live in relation to God. **I have been crucified with the Messiah.** (Gal. 2:19 MJG)

> We know that **our old self was crucified with him** so that the body defined by Sin would be destroyed, and we would no longer be enslaved to Sin. (Rom. 6:6 MJG)

In fact, there are multiple parallels between Galatians 2 and Romans 6, suggesting that justification and baptism are two sides of the same coin—the coin of initial participation, or conversion.[42] Of these additional similarities, two are most important. First, co-*crucifixion* with Christ is immediately followed (implicitly or explicitly) by co-*resurrection* with Christ: resurrection to new life in covenant relation to God.[43] Second, these realities of justification and baptism entail being transferred into Christ. Paul says both that we "came to faith [that incorporates us] into [Gk. *eis*] the Messiah" (Gal. 2:16 MJG) and that we have been baptized "into" (*eis*) the Messiah (Rom. 6:3; Gal. 3:27), into his "body" (1 Cor. 12:13).

Whether Paul is speaking of the internal confession of faith or the external confirmation of that faith in baptism, the reality is the same: co-crucifixion and co-resurrection *with* Christ that means transfer *into* Christ and thus new life *in* him, which means also in his body, the *ekklēsia*. One would be hard-pressed to think of ways to indicate participation more strongly, yet succinctly, than with the trio of prepositions "with," "into," and "in."

This initial experience of dying and rising that entails transfer and entry continues for believers once they are in Christ. The life of cruciformity is the natural outflowing of the initial co-crucifixion. That is why Paul can say, "I have been crucified with the Messiah" (Gal. 2:19 MJG), using the perfect tense; it is a reality with an initial starting point that continues into the present. Those who are in Christ have "crucified" the deeds that characterized their former way of life, and yet they must constantly "put them to death" (Rom. 6:6–14; 8:10–13; Gal. 5:24; Col. 3:5). The paradox, as we will see later in this

---

42. For a detailed argument for this thesis, see my *Inhabiting the Cruciform God*, 40–104, esp. 63–85.

43. Some scholars have insisted that both the language and the theology of resurrection in Paul are reserved for eschatological, bodily resurrection. For discussion of this issue, see chap. 3.

chapter (and especially in the next), is that this life of constant co-crucifixion (cruciformity) is also suffused with the resurrection.

8. To enter the Messiah is to be incorporated into his body and caught up into his story; Pauline spirituality and ethics have a narrative character.

It should be evident from the discussion thus far that Paul's understanding of life in Christ, from beginning to end, has a certain shape to it: it is an experience of death and resurrection. These two defining moments in the story of the Messiah, as Paul understands it,[44] become for him also the defining moments in the story of those in Christ, both individually and corporately.

Christ's story, then, is also the church's story; the church is the community of those who are baptized—immersed—into the story of Jesus. Or, to be more precise, the church is the community of those who are immersed into Jesus, who is definitively narrated in that story of death and resurrection.

This immersion, though it begins in faith/baptism, does not end there. It is enacted daily, and it is remembered regularly in the celebration of the Lord's Supper. The Supper is an event of *koinōnia* with the Lord Jesus (1 Cor. 10:16–17), concretely present in the bread and cup, and of *koinōnia* among those gathered (1 Cor. 11:17–34), in and among whom Christ is also present.[45] It is therefore at the Supper that the community's foundational story of Jesus' death is told, guided by the assurance of his presence as the resurrected and coming Lord (1 Cor. 11:26).[46]

Accordingly, it is appropriate to speak of Paul's spirituality and ethics—his understanding of life in Christ—as having a *narrative* character. There will be certain discernible patterns, such as the narrative movement that can be discerned in the Christ-poem of Philippians 2 discussed above (although [x] not [y] but [z]).[47] These will be patterns of renouncing rights, looking out for the needs of the neighbor, welcoming the other (such as those of lower social

---

44. See references, above, under "The Cross" (p. 7).

45. Paul uses "body of Christ" language to designate both the bread of the Supper and the gathered community (1 Cor. 10:16–17; 11:23–29). The word *koinōnia* does not appear in 1 Cor. 11:17–34, though it is implied. See further M. P. Baker, "Participating in the Body and Blood of Christ"; Nikkanen, "Participation in Christ."

46. Unless, of course, the community's behavior essentially expels the Lord from the gathering (1 Cor. 11:20). For further perspective on the Lord's Supper and participation/transformation, see Gorman, *Apostle of the Crucified Lord*, 312–14, 318–22; R. Morales, "Liturgical Conversion of the Imagination"; Barber and Kincaid, "Cultic Theosis"; Nikkanen, "Participation in Christ"; Pitre, Barber, and Kincaid, *Paul, a New Covenant Jew*, chap. 6.

47. A similar pattern is found in Hogan, *I Live, No Longer I*. She uses the language of "kenosis" (self-emptying), "enosis" (union), and "theosis."

status, as should have been the practice at the Corinthian Lord's Supper), and even loving the enemy.

The crucifixion-resurrection pattern is sometimes described as one of suffering-glory (e.g., Rom. 8:17; 2 Cor. 4:17–18). In each case there is a sequence, with the emphasis in the present on co-crucifixion. While this co-crucifixion will normally entail actual suffering at some point, as it often did in Paul's case, it is not only, or even primarily, about suffering. This is the case because the death of Jesus is not simply about suffering, as we will now see.

9. Sharing in the Messiah's story is first of all sharing in his death, which means sharing in his covenant faithfulness to God and his covenant love toward others.

For Paul, the first and primary thing to say about the Messiah's death is not that it was an event of suffering (though it was that) but that it was an event of obedience and faithfulness to the Father, and of love for humanity, for us. As we saw earlier, Paul clearly describes Jesus' death in terms of obedience (Rom. 5:19; Phil. 2:8), and he probably also describes it in terms of faithfulness (Gk. *pistis*). The latter part of this claim depends on interpreting certain Greek phrases, generally known as *pistis Christou* texts, to mean "the faith of Christ" or "the Messiah's faithfulness" rather than the more traditional "faith in Christ."[48]

Although I cannot offer a defense of the "faith of Christ" (subjective genitive) interpretation here, it does make sense of many things in Paul without in any way taking away the role of the human response of faith.[49] Of particular interest to us, if the "faith of Christ" reading is correct, is the presence of references to both Christ's faithfulness and his love in one text: "I myself no longer live," says Paul, "but the Messiah lives in me; and the life I do now live in the flesh, I live by means of the **faithfulness** of the Son of God, who **loved** me by giving himself for me" (Gal. 2:20 MJG). Here we see that the combination of faithfulness to God and self-giving love for others is what defines the Son of God—and what defines those whom that same Son of God inhabits (cf. 2 Cor. 5:14 for love as the governing power of, and in, Christ).

---

48. As listed above, these include, in the undisputed letters, Rom. 3:22, 26; Gal. 2:16 (twice), 20; 3:22; and Phil. 3:9. There may be other references to Christ's faithfulness when just the word *pistis* occurs. In the disputed letters, see the possible references to Christ's faithfulness in Eph. 3:12; 4:13, and to Christ's "steadfastness" in 2 Thess. 3:5. Bates (*Salvation by Allegiance Alone*, 80–87) speaks of Jesus' allegiance.

49. On "the faith of Christ," see esp. Hays, *Faith of Jesus Christ*. For the theological implications of reading the *pistis Christou* texts as examples of the subjective genitive, see Stubbs, "Shape of Soteriology." See also Bates, *Salvation by Allegiance Alone*, 80–87, who argues that Paul expects a response of allegiance to the allegiance (faithfulness) of Jesus.

The conjunction of faithfulness and love is no accident; it is a succinct summary of the requirements of the covenant between God and Israel that is reinforced by Jesus (Mark 12:28–34; Matt. 22:34–40; Luke 10:25–28). The biblical call to love God is a call to faithful obedience, while the call to love neighbor includes practicing justice. This pair of basic covenantal responsibilities is central also to Paul. Although he speaks occasionally of our love for God or the Lord (1 Cor. 8:3; 16:22), his emphasis is on God's love for us, and his preferred terms for our love for God are the same ones he uses of Christ: faith and obedience, or "the obedience of faith" (see esp. Rom. 1:5; 16:26; cf. 15:18; Phil. 2:12; 1 Thess. 1:3; 3:6). In Galatians 2:20, after describing Christ's cross as the embodiment of faithfulness and love, and clearly implying their relevance for those who are in Christ, he explicitly makes faithfulness and love the essential hallmark of believers in Galatians 5:6: "In Christ Jesus neither circumcision nor uncircumcision carry any weight, but rather faithfulness being worked out through love" (MJG).[50]

10. Paradoxically, cruciform (cross-shaped) existence is also resurrectional (resurrection-suffused); cruciform ministry is life-giving because the death of the Messiah means life for all who share in that death.

Paul's theology and spirituality, like that of Jesus, is full of paradox. "Amen, amen, I tell you," said Jesus, "unless a grain of wheat falls into the earth and dies, it remains just a single grain; but if it dies, it bears much fruit" (John 12:24 MJG). And, "Whoever wants to be first must be last of all and slave of all" (Mark 9:35 MJG). Paul likewise saw Jesus the Lord as the "slave of all" (e.g., Phil. 2:6–8; Rom. 15:8), and he saw his own apostleship as being the slave of Christ and of all whom he served in the gospel (e.g., Rom. 1:1; 1 Cor. 3:5, 9; 4:1; 2 Cor. 4:5; 6:4; Gal. 1:10; Phil. 1:1; Col. 1:7, 23, 25). Life in Christ is, paradoxically, a life of freedom that entails being the slave of others (Gal. 5:13).

But perhaps the most distinctive paradox of Paul's theology and spirituality is his claim that power comes in and through weakness. This symbiosis of power and weakness comes to its most memorable expression in Paul's famous lines in 2 Corinthians:

> [9][The Lord] said to me, "My grace is sufficient for you, for [my] power is perfected in [your] weakness." So I will boast even more gladly of my weaknesses, so that the power of Christ may indwell me [as his tabernacle; Gk. *episkēnōsē*]. . . . [10]For whenever I am weak, then I am strong. (2 Cor. 12:9–10 MJG)

50. See also Hays, "Christology and Ethics in Galatians."

Paul's paradoxical fusion of power and weakness is rooted in the gospel of the crucified Messiah, who is the revelation of God's power (1 Cor. 1:18–2:5). The paradox of the cross, however, is not only that it displays God's counterintuitive power but that, because of the resurrection, it is also the source of life. Christ's one act of obedience and righteousness delivered us from the powers of Sin and Death, resulting in life (Rom. 5:17–18).

Accordingly, those who live in Christ, including especially all who exercise ministry in Christ, experience the paradoxical reality of strength during suffering, of life in the midst of death. Once again, in 2 Corinthians Paul expresses this reality both succinctly and forcefully:

> [11]For while we are alive, we are always being handed over to death because of Jesus so that the life of Jesus may also be made visible in our mortal flesh. [12]Thus death is at work in [or "among"] us, but life is at work in [or "among"] you. (2 Cor. 4:11–12 MJG)

Not only does this text encapsulate Paul's spirituality of power-in-weakness; it also implicitly reveals the union of faithfulness and love in Paul's ministry.

To speak of cruciform existence, then, is to speak also of an existence suffused, paradoxically, with the resurrection. It is life-giving both for the "practitioner" and for the recipient. Although Paul certainly understands life in Christ to have a fundamental sequential pattern of death followed by resurrection, of suffering followed by glory, he also realizes that there is life *in the midst of* death, glory *during* suffering. The death-resurrection dynamic is not only *sequential* but also, paradoxically, *simultaneous*; cruciformity is what we might call "resurrectional"—suffused with the life-giving power of the resurrection.[51] That is why Paul can say that "we all, with unveiled faces, gazing at the glory of the Lord, are being transformed into the same image from glory to glory" (2 Cor. 3:18 MJG). The cruciform life is the life of transformational participation in the paradoxical glory of God revealed in Christ; it is corporate Christosis, or theosis.

Mission

Our consideration of resurrectional cruciformity, of transformational participation in the life of Christ, has already touched on several aspects of Paul's theology and spirituality that we could call "missional"—embodiments of

---

51. This topic is explored at length in chap. 3. Laura Hogan (*I Live, No Longer I*) maintains that kenosis, enosis, and theosis are often not sequential but simultaneous and integrated.

resurrectional cruciformity. We may now make a few additional observations about the missional character of life in Christ.

11. The church is called not merely to *believe* the gospel but also to *become* the gospel and thereby to *advance* the gospel; the church is a living exegesis of the gospel.

We have already seen that the church for Paul has a fundamental narrative quality: it participates in, and thereby "tells," the story of Christ's death and resurrection, the story of his self-giving, life-giving love. Paul summons people not merely to "believe in" Christ or even just to "believe *into*" him (Gal. 2:16) but to become part of a community, the body of Christ, that "re-incarnates" the Messiah in the world. His story becomes the community's story, and when that happens, the in-Christ community bears witness—in word and deed—to the gospel of the crucified and resurrected Messiah.

Paul makes it clear that the churches with which he is most pleased have been, and are called to continue being, such embodiments of the gospel. For instance, he praises the young Thessalonian church for its faithful witness despite persecution (1 Thess. 1:2–10; 2:13–16; 3:1–10). That community is exemplary in its love as well as its faithfulness, so Paul calls them to "keep on keeping on" in holiness—faithfulness to God, and love for one another and for "all" (1 Thess. 3:11–13; 4:1–12; 5:6–24).[52]

Similarly, Paul writes with great fondness to the church at Philippi, commending those believers' participation (Gk. *koinōnia*) with him in the gospel (Phil. 1:5), which includes the "grace" of "not only believing in Christ, but suffering for him as well" (Phil. 1:29 MJG).[53] Throughout the letter, Paul urges the Philippians, as a community, to continue to embody the kenotic, life-giving death of Jesus, which will make them more holy, more joyful, more unified, and more faithful in their public witness. Of special importance is the exhortation following the Christ-poem:

> [12]Therefore, my loved ones, just as you have always obeyed [like Christ],[54] not only in my presence, but much more now in my absence, work out [put into practice] your salvation together, with fear and trembling; [13]for it is God who is at work in you, enabling you both to will and to work for his good pleasure. [14]Do all things without murmuring and arguing, [15]so that you may become blameless and morally undiluted, children of God without blemish in the midst of a crooked and perverted generation, in which you shine like stars in the

52. The exhortation to do good to all, meaning outsiders, is found in 1 Thess. 5:15. See further Gorman, *Becoming the Gospel*, 63–105.

53. See esp. the discussion in Davey, *Suffering as Participation with Christ*, chap. 2.

54. As noted above, the reference is not to obeying Paul; it is to Christlike obedience to the Father (cf. Phil. 2:8).

world, [16]steadfastly holding forth the word of life, so that I can boast on the day of Christ that I did not run in vain or labor in vain. (Phil. 2:12–16 MJG)[55]

Paul is suggesting that the Christlike church is an obedient church, even to the point of suffering with and like Christ, faithfully displaying "the word of life"—the life-giving gospel—in both word and deed. If "exegesis" is the careful interpretation of a biblical text, a commentary on Scripture, then Paul is calling on the church to be a *living* exegesis of the gospel of the crucified and resurrected Lord.

We may refer to this embodiment of the gospel as "becoming" the gospel. Of course, this does not mean in any sense that the church replaces the gospel of Christ and becomes the object of attention and devotion. *May it never be!* (to quote Paul). What it does mean, however, is that the church's vocation is to represent the gospel faithfully in its public witness, such that the watching world can see, even if it does not always understand, something of the counterintuitive power of God displayed in the faithful and loving death of his Son. And this will mean that the church has certain practices, not merely beliefs, that are essential to its identity. Corporately, the *ekklēsia* becomes good news to the world.

12. Becoming the gospel means embodying the missional practices of love, peace-making, reconciliation, restorative justice, forgiveness, nonviolence, and so on that correspond to what God has done in the Messiah.

As the writer of Hebrews would say (Heb. 11:32), time would fail us if we attempted to explore all the necessary missional practices of the church that correspond to the counterintuitive, self-giving, life-giving, cruciform revelation of God in Christ. The fundamental reality of participation in Christ, and thereby in the mission of God, is—as we have seen—resurrectional cruciformity. This is not one of many aspects of life in Christ, but rather it is the umbrella term for that life.

When Paul implicitly or explicitly calls the church to practice, say, reconciliation, he is simply saying something like, "God was in Christ engaging in reconciliation, we are in Christ, and thus we have the privilege and responsibility of practicing Godlike, Christlike reconciliation." (See, e.g., 2 Cor. 5:12–6:2.) When he calls the church to practice justice (Gk. *dikaiosynē*) rather than injustice (*adikia*), he essentially means, "God was in Christ manifesting God's own (counterintuitive) justice, we are in Christ, and thus we have the

55. There is debate about the sense of v. 16—does it mean to "hold forth" or "hold fast to" the word of life? I think both senses are in play, and have indicated such with the translation "steadfastly holding forth."

privilege and responsibility of practicing Godlike, Christlike justice." (See, e.g., 1 Cor. 6:1–11; 2 Cor. 8–9.) Or, when he calls the church to welcome the weak, he is fundamentally saying, "God was in Christ welcoming the weak, we are in Christ, and thus we have the privilege and responsibility of welcoming the weak." (See, e.g., Rom. 14:1–15:13.)

In other words, for Paul every summons to virtue, every commandment, every exhortation is a call to practice "the law of Christ" (Gal. 6:2; cf. 1 Cor. 9:21), the narrative pattern of the crucified Messiah. His self-giving love is what gives life to the *ekklēsia* and, through the *ekklēsia*, to the world.

13. To be in the Messiah is to be in community, to be in mission, and to be in trouble—simultaneously.

Throughout this brief introduction to Paul's theology and spirituality of transformative participation, we have repeatedly seen that this life in Christ is lived not in isolation but only in community. (We must keep in mind that most of the words for "you" in Paul's letters are *plural* pronouns, and most of the imperatives are given in the second- [or third-] person *plural* form.) We have also seen that this life in Christ, in his body, is a life of mission. It is not a "holy huddle," an isolationist sect. And finally, we have seen that if this missional life in Christ/in community is practiced faithfully, it may very well lead to opposition, to persecution. It is difficult to look at the life of the apostle Paul, or of his Lord, and conclude anything less. Suffering per se may not be the only manifestation of cruciformity, but it is often the inevitable consequence of life in Christ. As 2 Timothy puts it, "All who wish to live devoted lives in Christ Jesus will be persecuted" (2 Tim. 3:12 MJG).

The Christian church in many parts of the world today knows this reality of persecution firsthand. If participation in Christ's body means anything at all, it clearly entails weeping with those who weep as well as rejoicing with those who rejoice (Rom. 12:15). Sometimes, paradoxically, those who weep are also precisely those who rejoice; their joyful witness in the presence of persecution is Paul-like—or, better said, Christlike.

Conclusion

To be "in Christ," to be in the exalted crucified Messiah, is the fundamental reality of Paul's spirituality, what some have called his "mysticism." But this is not an empty mysticism; nor is it a self-centered spiritual journey. Rather, Paul's spirituality is both individual and corporate; his mysticism is missional. To be in Christ is to participate fully in the fullness of God,

Father, Son, and Spirit. Paul's letter to the Colossians expresses this sense of fullness in remarkably simple but profound language: "For in him [Christ] the whole fullness of deity dwells bodily, and you have come to fullness in him" (Col. 2:9–10a).[56]

This chapter's overview of Paul's theology and spirituality of participation in Christ has focused on thirteen aspects of four closely related topics: the cross, cruciformity, dying and rising with Christ, and mission. The cross-centered nature of participation in Christ depends, of course, on the reality of his resurrection. The cross of Christ has saving significance only because God raised the crucified Jesus from the dead, and—likewise—participation in Christ is possible only because God has raised him from the dead.

The paradox of cruciformity is that it is resurrectional: we die *and* we rise; we receive, and we give, life through death. In some traditions (especially Roman Catholicism), therefore, Christians rightly speak of participating in the Paschal Mystery, the mystery of Christ's death and resurrection. Life in Christ, we might say (with Paul's consent), is the spiritual fusion of Good Friday and Easter.[57] When people inhabit that space, they inhabit Christ, and they bear public witness to the fullness of God.

In the next chapter, we return to Paul's starting place: the cross.

Appendix: The Thirteen Propositions

The thirteen propositions presented in this chapter are listed here, section by section:

The Cross

1. The cross is "the signature of the one who is risen."

2. The cross is not only a Christophany but also a theophany—the definitive self-revelation of God, which means that God is kenotic (self-emptying) love; the cross is the signature of the Eternal One.

3. The cross is not only the definitive revelation of Christ and of God (i.e., it is both Christophany and theophany) but also the definitive revelation of what humans and the church are to be.

---

56. I am part of the growing number of scholars who consider Paul to be the author of Colossians.

57. See, e.g., Matera, *Spirituality of Saint Paul.*

Cruciformity

4. The cross is not only the source but also the shape of our salvation, and cross-shaped living (cruciformity) means that all Christian virtues and practices are cruciform: faith/faithfulness, love, power, hope, justice, and so forth.

5. Cruciformity is also theoformity, or theosis; that is, cross-shaped existence is God-shaped existence, and this existence is for both individuals and communities in the Messiah.

6. Cruciformity/theoformity is a matter not of imitation but of transformative participation: being in the Messiah/the Spirit and having the Messiah/the Spirit within (mutual indwelling).

Dying and Rising with Christ

7. We enter the Messiah by means of faith/baptism; justification by faith is a participatory event of dying and rising with the Messiah, meaning that justification is resurrection to new life by means of co-crucifixion with the Messiah.

8. To enter the Messiah is to be incorporated into his body and caught up into his story; Pauline spirituality and ethics have a narrative character.

9. Sharing in the Messiah's story is first of all sharing in his death, which means sharing in his covenant faithfulness to God and his covenant love toward others.

10. Paradoxically, cruciform (cross-shaped) existence is also resurrectional (resurrection-suffused); cruciform ministry is life-giving because the death of the Messiah means life for all who share in that death.

Mission

11. The church is called not merely to *believe* the gospel but also to *become* the gospel and thereby to *advance* the gospel; the church is a living exegesis of the gospel.

12. Becoming the gospel means embodying the missional practices of love, peacemaking, reconciliation, restorative justice, forgiveness, nonviolence, and so on that correspond to what God has done in the Messiah.

13. To be in the Messiah is to be in community, to be in mission, and to be in trouble—simultaneously.

two

The Cross

Revelation of Christ and God, of Humanity and the Church

I resolved to know and make known among you nothing other than Jesus the Messiah—meaning Jesus the *crucified* Messiah.

1 Corinthians 2:2 MJG

These remarkable words summarize Paul's bold claims about the interrelated identities of Jesus, himself as an apostle, and, at least implicitly, all communities and individuals in the Messiah. In their immediate context (1 Cor. 1:18–2:5), moreover, they imply something profound about the nature of God and of divine activity, and about how we know what we know about God. In other words, in this one sentence from 1 Corinthians we have an indication not only of Pauline Christology but also of Pauline theology proper (i.e., the doctrine of God), pneumatology, ministry, ecclesiology, spirituality (in-Christ-ness), anthropology, epistemology, and morality (or ethics)—at least. In effect, Paul could not, and we cannot, speak about Christ without also speaking about a wide range of related topics.

This chapter was previously published as "Paul and the Cruciform Way of God in Christ," *Journal of Moral Theology* 2 (January 2013): 64–83; and "The Cross in Paul: Christophany, Theophany, Ecclesiophany," in *Ecclesia and Ethics: Moral Formation and the Church*, ed. E. Allen Jones III, John Frederick, John Anthony Dunne, Eric Lewellen, and Janghoon Park (London: Bloomsbury T&T Clark, 2016), 21–40.

The church and Christian theology are facing three major questions across cultures: (1) Who, or what, is God, and who, or what, is the church? For example, is God the omnipotent Western deity of military, political, economic, and colonial power? (2) Is the church an arm of the state, or of a particular culture, or an embodiment of that kind of power? (3) What does it mean to be fully human in a world full of unchecked political and personal power?

The claim of this chapter is that the cross of Jesus Christ supplies the substance of an answer to all three questions, and that it is also the bridge that connects them. This chapter will contend, in other words, that the cross is not only a *Christophany* (a revelation of Christ's identity) but also a *theophany* (a revelation of God's identity). Furthermore, the cross is also an *ecclesiophany* (a revelation of the church's identity in Christ and God—what it means to be the church) and an *anthrophany* (a revelation of human identity—what it means to be human).[1] This thesis will be developed by examining some of the work of Paul the theologian, for Paul was not merely a letter writer or a counselor.

But first we must ask what kind of theologian Paul was. Five dimensions of him as a theologian, all arising from chapter 1, may be considered for our purposes. Paul is

- a *messianic theologian* whose entire theological program is grounded in the conviction that God's resurrection of the crucified Jesus means that Jesus is both the Messiah of Israel and the Lord and Savior of all peoples; in Jesus God has inaugurated the messianic, or eschatological, age;[2]
- a *theologian of the cross and resurrection* who sees in the cross the representative, reconciling, and revelatory activity of God in his Son, which is the central scene of the central act in a grand narrative of salvation; this salvific death is confirmed and completed by the resurrection of Jesus;
- a *narrative theologian* whose christological narrative carries within it a corresponding narrative spirituality—that is, an account of how participants in the reality of Christ crucified and resurrected ought to live, including concrete practices that derive from the narrative itself;[3]

1. "Anthrophany" is a neologism that I have shortened from what is probably its appropriate form, "anthropophany" (Gk. *anthrōpos* = human being).

2. For a Messiah-centered theology of Paul, see Wright, *Paul and the Faithfulness of God*.

3. On Paul as narrative theologian, see Hays, *Faith of Jesus Christ*; B. Longenecker, *Narrative Dynamics in Paul*. On the narrative character of Paul's spirituality, see my *Cruciformity*. On Paul, narrative, and ethics, see also Fowl, *The Story of Christ in the Ethics of Paul*. As we will see, the narrative character of Paul's Christology will also have something to say about theology proper (the doctrine of God).

- an *ecclesial theologian* who is confident that God has called the church to be the sign of the new age,[4] and as such it is shaped by the story of Jesus the Messiah, in whom the church lives and who lives in the church; and
- a *spiritual or even mystical theologian* whose fundamental conviction about individuals and communities being "in Christ" means that Christology inherently has spiritual and ethical consequences (both personal and corporate), as well as theological consequences with respect to our overall understanding of the God encountered in Christ.

Some Christians, including some theologians, are wary of the term "mystical." Certain earlier accounts of Paul's "in-Christ mysticism" fell short of a full account of their subject, describing an individualistic communion with Christ that failed to recognize either the corporate or the narrative— and thus the inherently moral—dimensions of Paul's participationist language.[5] With others, I define mystical experience as occasional or ongoing encounters with God (for Christians this may mean specifically Jesus) in which God's presence, holiness, power, and/or love are known in an intimate and transformative way. These encounters lead to renewed commitment to activity in the world.[6] We might, therefore, call Paul a mystical-narrative, or a spiritual-narrative, theologian. Encountering the resurrected "Christ crucified" always and everywhere implies "cruciformity," because those who confess Jesus as the crucified Messiah are now, through faith and baptism, "in" him, and he, by the Spirit (received through faith and baptism), is in them, enabling a sort of nonidentical repetition of his salvific and paradigmatic story.[7]

In this chapter we will explore the implications of these claims about Paul the theologian in more detail, with special emphasis on Paul the mystical-narrative (or spiritual-narrative) theologian. In doing so, we will see the close interconnections in Paul among the cross, the church, the individual, and God—God (Gk. *theos*) being the first and most fundamental subject of *theo*logy, but one that is often neglected.

---

4. See also Wright (*Paul and the Faithfulness of God*, 1492), who refers to the church as a "microcosmos" and "prototype" of what is to come.

5. The term "in-Christ mysticism" summarizes the important, if incomplete, contribution of Adolf Deissmann to our understanding of the center of Paul's experience. See Deissmann, *The Religion of Jesus and the Faith of Paul*; Deissmann, *Paul*. We should note that such accounts of Paul's mysticism have generally failed to recognize the distinctively Jewish character of Paul's participationist spirituality. For a major corrective to this mistake, see Wright, *Paul and the Faithfulness of God*, esp. chap. 9.

6. See further Gorman, "This-Worldliness," and the references there.

7. On nonidentical repetition, see Fowl, "Christology and Ethics," esp. 148.

First, however, we will further explore the term "cruciformity" introduced in the previous chapter and make some preliminary observations about its significance in Paul, highlighting its spiritual (or mystical) and narrative dimensions. We will then explore three moral themes (one at length, two briefly) in Paul in which the story of Christ is interpreted *morally* as paradigmatic for the Christian life (individually and corporately) and also *theologically* as divine action—and the significance of that two-step dance. Finally, along the way we will briefly note some possible implications of Paul's perspectives for contemporary Christian praxis.

Cruciformity: Its Meaning and Its Mystical and Narrative Character

The term "cruciformity," from "cruciform" (cross-shaped) and "conformity," may be defined simply as conformity to Jesus the crucified Messiah. Cruciformity is the spiritual-moral dimension of the theology of the death of Jesus by crucifixion found in Paul, in the rest of the New Testament, and throughout much of the Christian tradition. With respect to Paul, at least, this conformity to the crucified Messiah is not an abstract moral principle but a spiritual or mystical reality. This mystical reality is rooted, paradoxically, in a profoundly this-worldly reality (Jesus' crucifixion) and produces, no less paradoxically, a variety of very this-worldly results.

It will be helpful to summarize the basic roots and structure of this this-worldly Pauline mysticism. For Paul, Jesus is the crucified Messiah whom God raised from the dead, vindicating him as Messiah, validating his path of lifelong, self-giving, faithful obedience that led to the cross, and establishing him as the Lord of all who shares in the divine name, glory, and worship.[8] As the resurrected, glorified, and living Lord, Jesus remains the crucified Messiah. Those who respond in faith to the gospel of his death, resurrection, and lordship are baptized "into" him and henceforth live "in" him, as we saw in chapter 1. At the same time, this crucified but resurrected Jesus takes up residence in and among those who live in him, such that we can refer to the resulting relationship as the mutual indwelling, or reciprocal residence, of the crucified but resurrected Messiah and his people, individually and corporately. To further complicate matters, however, Paul can use the same language of reciprocal residence in reference to believers and the Spirit, who dwells in believers and they in him (e.g., Rom. 8:9, 11).[9] To add

8. See, e.g., Rom. 10:8–13; Phil. 2:6–11.
9. Furthermore, at least once (twice if, as I think, Paul wrote 2 Thessalonians), Paul speaks of the church being in both God the Father and Jesus the Messiah and Lord (1 Thess. 1:1; cf. 2 Thess. 1:1).

even more complexity to this situation, Paul can speak of the Spirit both as the Spirit of Christ/the Son and as the Spirit of God.[10] And if that were not enough, he can do all of this in the same breath, specifically in the first half of Romans 8. Those who participate in this relationship of mutual indwelling thereby manifest the "fruit" of the Spirit, especially the qualities of faith (or faithfulness) and love that Jesus the Messiah exemplified in his death on the cross (Gal. 5, esp. vv. 6, 22).[11]

Cruciformity, then, is cross-shaped existence in Jesus the Messiah, what N. T. Wright calls "cruciform authenticity" or "cross and resurrection authenticity."[12] It is *participating in* and *embodying* the cross. Paul himself might put it this way (a paraphrase of Gal. 2:19–20): "It is no longer I or we who live our own lives, but it is God's crucified and resurrected Messiah who lives in me and in us by his Spirit, empowering us to embody his kind of faithfulness and love." Because of the relational quality of this reality, we must be careful to focus not on the cross per se but on the *crucified*—that is, on the living, present Jesus. Furthermore, although Paul can use the language of imitation (e.g., 1 Cor. 11:1), we must distinguish this Pauline spirituality from a simple ethic of *imitatio Christi*, since Paul's focus is on the activity of the living, indwelling Messiah, which is at the same time the work of God's indwelling Spirit. The living Lord Jesus, identical with the crucified Messiah, enables the individuals and communities he indwells to engage in acts of non-identical repetition that constitute their individual and communal narratives.

Philippians 2:6–11

As we saw in the last chapter, fundamental to Paul's Christology is the narrative poem (often called a hymn) included in his letter to the Philippians. It is widely recognized that Philippians 2:6–11 contains some of the most significant christological affirmations in the New Testament. It has even been designated the place "where Christology began."[13] Whether or not Paul wrote it (and the older consensus that he did not do so has been disintegrating), he clearly owned it, both internalizing it and proclaiming it as his story, meaning his gospel, or at least one articulation of it. In fact, the importance of this narrative in Paul's theology and his widespread use of it throughout his

10. Spirit of Christ/the Son: Rom. 8:9; Gal. 4:6; Phil. 1:19. Spirit of God: Rom. 8:9, 11, 14; 15:19; 1 Cor. 2:11–14; 3:16; 6:11; 7:40; 12:3; 2 Cor. 1:22; 3:3; Phil. 3:3; 1 Thess. 4:8.

11. On the intimate link between Christology and ethics in Galatians, which is indicative of Paul's thought more generally, see the classic article by Hays, "Christology and Ethics in Galatians."

12. Wright, "Paul, Ethics, and the Church," 92.

13. Martin and Dodd, *Where Christology Began.*

letters suggest that we ought to call it his master story.[14] Although the precise significance of nearly every phrase in this narrative poem has been debated, there is no argument about its overall importance. We would need an entire chapter to offer an extended analysis of this epic in miniature, so I will limit my remarks to four basic points.[15]

Christophany

First, the christological story as a whole has a clear structure and movement, similar to a parabola: movement from height to depth and back to height. The first part of the poem (Phil. 2:6–8, before the exaltation), in which the Messiah Jesus alone is the actor, has a syntactical and narrative structure that can be described, as we saw in chapter 1, as "although [x] not [y] but [z]." It may be represented graphically in table 2.1 on page 35.[16]

As this figure shows, it is possible to divide the [z] portion of the narrative into two parts, [z_1] and [z_2]. Thus three key verbs in verses 6–8 characterize Christ's actions: (1) he *did not regard* (or *consider*) equality with God as something to be exploited;[17] (2) he *emptied* himself; and (3) he *humbled* himself. The second and third verbs ([z_1] and [z_2]) correspond to Jesus' two acts of self-emptying (incarnation) and self-humbling (crucifixion), but the point in each case is the same: the rejection of selfish exploitation of status in favor of self-giving action. The climax of this downward mobility, this course of ignominies, is crucifixion, a perfectly Roman conclusion to a perfectly un-Roman trajectory from the highest heights to the lowest depths.[18] For Paul the Messiah's incarnation (kenosis; self-emptying) and crucifixion are two stages in a unified act of self-donation, and therefore his death on the cross is not a unique, independent, or unexpected act but rather a continuation of the "mind" expressed in the incarnation.[19]

Paul reuses, adapts, abridges, and alludes to this narrative structure throughout his letters, both to express his Christology and to describe the nature of apostolic ministry and of general "Christian" existence that is appropriate

---

14. See esp. Gorman, *Cruciformity*, 23, 88–94, 164–75, 214–15, 366–67.

15. For further discussion, see chap. 4 below, as well as my *Inhabiting the Cruciform God*, 9–39; Wright, *Climax of the Covenant*, 56–98; and Wright, *Paul and the Faithfulness of God*, 680–89.

16. For fuller discussion, see Gorman, *Cruciformity*, 90–91, 164–77, 186–88, 192, 197, 230–38, 243, 252, 261, 330; Gorman, *Apostle of the Crucified Lord*, 80–81, 125–26, 310, 507–9.

17. "Something to be exploited" translates the Greek *harpagmos*, a term that occurs only here in the NT and the meaning of which is much debated. Some render the phrase "something to be grasped."

18. See esp. Hellerman, *Reconstructing Honor in Roman Philippi*.

19. See Gorman, *Inhabiting the Cruciform God*, 9–39.

Table 2.1. Syntax and Sense in Phil. 2:6–8

Syntax	Narrative	Sense
although [x]	though he was in the form of God	possession of status
not [y]	[he] did not regard equality with God as something to be exploited	rejection of selfish exploitation of status
but [z]	but	decision to act in self-giving, seeking the good of others
[z_1]	emptied himself, taking the form of a slave, being born in human likeness.	stage 1: incarnation (kenosis)
[z_2]	And being found in human form, he humbled himself and became obedient to the point of death—even death on a cross.	stage 2: death on the cross

for those who live in this Messiah.[20] Although Paul will most often highlight Jesus' death when he uses this narrative, he can also point to the incarnation as the warrant for specific Christian practices (e.g., generous giving, as in 2 Cor. 8:9, discussed below and in chap. 9).

Ecclesiophany and Anthrophany

Second, already here in Philippians, Paul offers the poem to his readers as the christological basis for their life together, and this in two ways: Jesus the incarnate, crucified, and exalted/living Messiah is both the *paradigm* and the *provider* of the rights-renouncing, others-regarding, cruciform humility and love needed for existence in the Christian community.

That Jesus is the paradigm of such cruciform love is clear from the parallels between the actions ascribed to him in Philippians 2:6–8 and the communal practices expected of the Philippians that are enunciated in Philippians 2:3–4: "Do nothing from selfish ambition or conceit, but in humility regard others as better than yourselves. Let each of you look not to your own interests, but to the interests of others." One could hardly ask for a more succinct application of the Christ-narrative to life in Christian community.

No less important, however, is the mystical, or spiritual, aspect of this life together. It is an expression of life "in Christ" and of "sharing [participation, *koinōnia*] in the Spirit" (Phil. 2:1). It is an instantiation of the "mind" of the Messiah Jesus (Phil. 2:5). The transition in Philippians 2:5 between the exhortations in 2:1–4 and the narrative poem in 2:6–11 makes this clear: "Cultivate this mindset—this way of thinking, feeling, and acting—in your

---

20. For the use of this pattern in Philippians, see the next chapter. For an example of this pattern in a description of apostolic ministry, see 1 Thess. 2:5–12. Various uses are discussed in detail throughout my *Cruciformity*; see, e.g., 91–92, 167–73, 186–88, 192–95, 230–43, 252, 261.

community, which is in fact a community in the Messiah Jesus" (MJG).[21] In other words, it is by virtue of their being *in* the Messiah, which means also their participation in the Spirit, that the Philippians will be able to embody in their corporate life the narrative *of* the Messiah. The indwelling Messiah creates and shapes a community that manifests his presence in concrete practices of Messiah-like love.

Third, it is self-evident that one cannot have Christian community without Christian individuals. The community-indwelling Messiah is simultaneously the individual-indwelling Messiah. The messianic pattern, or master story, reveals not only what the in-Christ community is called to be but also what each in-Christ person is called and enabled to be. This is because, as the fully human (incarnate) one, the Jesus of this Christ-poem defines and reveals what true humanity looks like: self-giving love.

Scholars debate whether Philippians 2:6–8 alludes to the story of Adam in Genesis.[22] If it does (as I think), it reinforces the claim of the previous paragraph; the human Messiah Jesus fulfilled what it means to be human, the image of God, by not misusing that God-given status—in contrast to Adam. If there is no allusion to Adam, that does not negate the claim of the previous paragraph, for the incarnation, in and of itself, means that humanity is on display.

Theophany

Fourth (and perhaps most controversially), the poem suggests that what Christ did is not only rewarded by God but is also, because of Christ's equality with God (Phil. 2:6), a manifestation of God's character.[23] That is, this Christophany is also a theophany. Theologically, this is because incarnation means that divinity is manifested precisely in the humanity on display. Moreover, as suggested in the previous chapter, an additional valid way of interpreting and translating the opening of the poem (2:6a) in Philippians is by replacing, or supplementing, concessive ("although") language with causal ("because") language (see table 2.2 on p. 37).

The critical words in support of this claim are the first few of verse 6: *hos en morphē theou hyparchōn* (lit., "who, being in the form of God"). The participle *hyparchōn* ("being") needs to be interpreted: Does it imply a rather

21. For the justification of this translation, see chap. 4 below.

22. An allusion to Adam is likely, but this does not mean (as some suggest) that Christ was neither divine nor preexistent. See the discussion in Gorman, *Inhabiting the Cruciform God*, 9–39.

23. For further exploration and defense of this claim, see Gorman, *Inhabiting the Cruciform God*, 9–39. Most exegetes now agree that the poem's grammar affirms that Jesus possessed equality with God, but the full implications of that affirmation are still being debated.

Table 2.2. Alternative Syntax and Sense in Phil. 2:6a

Syntax	Narrative	Sense
because [x]	because he was [lit., "being"] in the form of God	possession of status

neutral sense of simultaneity—"while being [i.e., while he was] in the form of God"? Or does it have a concessive sense—"although being [i.e., although he was] in the form of God"? This latter option has been the interpretation of nearly every modern English translation;[24] it is not incorrect, but it may be incomplete. The causal sense I am proposing—namely, "because of being in the form of God" (= "because he was in the form of God")—does not need to supplant but can supplement the concessive sense.[25] This causal ("because") interpretation had also been suggested by notable recent interpreters (e.g., C. F. D. Moule, N. T. Wright, and Stephen Fowl) and is now catching on more widely.[26]

The upshot of all this is that Christ did what he did not merely *in spite of* being in the form of God and equal with God but also precisely *because* he was in the form of God and equal with God.[27] The poem tells us something profound not only about Jesus and what it means to be the Messiah but also about God and what it means to be divine. God, it says, is by nature self-emptying (kenotic), self-humbling, self-giving—vulnerable and "downwardly mobile."[28]

The Messiah's refusal to exploit his existing equality with God for selfish advantage does not imply that the essence of deity is the possession of some sort of status (glory, power, etc.) that is, or can be, exploited for the deity's own self-serving benefit. Rather, although "normal" deities in the

24. NASB has "although"; CEB, ESV, NAB, NET, NLT, NRSV, and RSV all have "though." NIV has the neutral "being in very nature God"; translations into other languages (e.g., several major French translations) sometimes prefer this neutral interpretation too.

25. Maintaining both "although" and "because" is not a case of wrongly trying to have one's cake and eat it too; it is rather a matter of the text's surface structure ("although") and its deep structure ("because"). See Gorman, *Inhabiting the Cruciform God*, 9–39.

26. See, e.g., Barclay, "'Because He Was Rich He Became Poor,'" 340n19, 343–44; Blackwell, *Christosis*, 11–12, 205–6; Cooper, *Christification*, 56; Tan, "Conformity to Christ," 79.

27. For a similar conclusion, see Larry Hurtado's analysis of Phil. 2:6–11 in light of Philo's *Embassy to Gaius* 110–14: "'The Form of God.'"

28. Some readers may sense a degree of theological and exegetical concern about this claim because they (rightly) affirm that God is the Exalted One. The main point to be made, theologically, is that the Triune God is a communion of persons whose nature is self-donating love. I use "self-emptying" here in a metaphorical sense as one way to describe this love (as does Philippians, I suggest) and thus (since God is love) God's nature. For a similar view in connection with the church's missional participation in God/Christ, see Holmes, "Trinitarian Missiology." Holmes writes, "Just as purposeful, cruciform, self-sacrificial sending is intrinsic to God's own life, being sent in a cruciform, purposeful and self-sacrificial way must be intrinsic to the church being the church" (89).

pagan world might be expected to act in such a way, Jesus the Messiah's equality with the one true God, the God known in Israel's Scripture and history, was displayed in radical self-giving. Implicitly, then, Paul is associating the activity of Jesus the Messiah with the activity of God (the Father). In other texts, as we will see below, this association is more explicit, with Christ's death interpreted as an act of divine love (e.g., Rom. 5:6–8; 8:32), and the entire Christ-event as an act of divine reconciliation (e.g., 2 Cor. 5:19). The spiritual and ethical payoff of this association is that those who become like Christ by the power of the Spirit are instantiating not only the narrative of Christ but also the story of God.

To summarize: Paul's spiritual/mystical and narrative Christology provides both the framework and the content for his vision of cruciform existence: what it means to be human, what it means to be the church. At the same time, this Christology is inseparably connected to Paul's theology proper (his "doctrine" of God), expressed in the spiritual reality that existence in Christ is existence in the Spirit of God, and in the narrative reality that what Christ did on the cross was also the activity of God. It is nearly impossible to avoid the conclusion that Paul has experienced God in Christ by the Spirit in a way that can only be described as trinitarian in nature.[29] At the very least, we could speak, as others have, of Paul's christological monotheism or Christology of divine identity.[30] Here, however, I would suggest that a more appropriate term might be Paul's *theological Christology*.

The remainder of this chapter focuses on Paul's theological Christology: the relationship between God the Father and Christ the Son in Paul's understanding of the cross and of cruciformity.[31] We will look specifically at the following aspects of this God-in-Christ activity:

- the cruciform, reconciling enemy-love of God in Christ;
- the cruciform generosity of God in Christ; and
- the cruciform hospitality of God in Christ.

Reconciliation will receive rather sustained attention, followed by much briefer comments about generosity (explored in more detail in chap. 9) and hospitality. We will consider what Paul says about God in Christ and about cruciform existence in him (remembering, from the previous chapter, the importance of "location") and, briefly, how theologians and Christians gen-

---

29. See further my *Cruciformity*, 63–74; Hill, *Paul and the Trinity*.

30. See, e.g., Bauckham, *Jesus and the God of Israel*, esp. 182–232.

31. For more on what I am calling Paul's theological Christology, in addition to Bauckham, *Jesus and the God of Israel*, see, e.g., Tilling, *Paul's Divine Christology*; Capes, *Divine Christ*.

erally might incorporate the practices Paul describes more fully into the life of the church.

In doing this, we will essentially move from a theologically shaped Christology to a christologically shaped (cruciform) ecclesiology and then, therefore, to a theologically shaped ecclesiology. The church, in this approach to Christ, becomes a witness not only to Christ and to life in Christ, but also to God and to life in God (as Paul puts it in 1 Thess. 1:1). That is,

Theological Christology → Christological (Cruciform) Ecclesiology →
Theological Ecclesiology

Christ crucified, in other words, is the bridge between God and the church (and thus also between God and individuals within the church), revealing the identity of each, and giving the church (and the individual) the privilege and responsibility of representing God, but only inasmuch as it (and each individual) maintains its (and his/her) cruciform shape through cruciform practices.

The Cruciform, Reconciling Enemy-Love of God in Christ

Few passages in the Pauline correspondence are as rich or as dense as 2 Corinthians 5 and Romans 5, each of which describes the reconciling enemy-love of God in Christ and also provides, either explicitly or implicitly, guidelines for cruciform existence.

2 Corinthians 5

As noted in the introduction to this book, we will return frequently to 2 Corinthians 5, for various reasons, throughout this book. At the heart of 2 Corinthians 5 is the affirmation that "in Christ God was reconciling the world to himself" (5:19). There are several significant translational and interpretive problems in this verse that we cannot examine here. One critical issue is simply the translation and meaning of the opening phrase. Is it "in Christ God was reconciling the world to himself" (NRSV; a sort of instrumental Christology); or, similarly, "God was reconciling the world to himself in Christ" (NAB, NIV); or "God was in Christ reconciling the world to himself" (more of an incarnational Christology; cf. NRSV mg., NASB, KJV)? My own preference is "God was in the Messiah reconciling the world to himself."[32] In any case,

---

32. The translation of 2 Cor. 5:14–21 used here comes from chap. 7.

it is probably best to understand the text as a reference to the entirety of the Christ-event (or at least those aspects of it that Paul stresses in his letters), inclusive of Christ's death (as 5:21 makes clear in the immediate context) but also of his incarnation (especially in light of 2 Cor. 8:9, in the wider context).

What is fascinating about this passage is that it is a clear example of how the Messiah's death is, for Paul, both an act of Christ's love and an act of God's reconciliation and forgiveness—that is, of divine love:

> [14]For the Messiah's love compels us, since we have concluded this: that one died for all [*hyper pantōn*], and therefore all died. [15]And he died for all [*hyper pantōn*] so that those who live would live no longer for themselves, but for the one who died for them [*hyper autōn*] and was raised. (2 Cor. 5:14–15 MJG)

> [18]And all these things are from the God who reconciled us to himself through the Messiah and who gave us the ministry of reconciliation; [19]that is, God was in the Messiah reconciling the world to himself, not counting their trespasses against them, and entrusting to us the message of reconciliation. . . . [21]For us [or "For our sake," *hyper hēmōn*] God made the one who did not know sin [the Messiah] to be sin so that we ourselves would become the justice [or "righteousness"] of God in him. (2 Cor. 5:18–19, 21 MJG)

In 5:14–15, Christ is the actor, the one who displayed his love in his death "for all," a complement to the expression "for their sins" (cf. Rom. 5:6; 1 Cor. 15:3; Gal. 1:4; 3:13; 1 Thess. 5:10). In 5:18–19, 21, God is the actor and apparently even the originator of Christ's atoning death, as the source of "all these things," as the one acting "in the Messiah," and as the one who made the Messiah to be sin (however that is to be interpreted) "for us/our sake" (cf. Rom. 3:25; 5:8).

What both texts have in common, however, is that the goal of this messianic and divine action is human transformation: "so that those who live would live no longer for themselves, but for the one who died for them and was raised" (2 Cor. 5:15); "so that we ourselves would become the justice [or "righteousness"] of God in him" (5:21b). More precisely, we can say that the goal is transformation into Christlikeness and thus Godlikeness. Those transformed by Christ's death will stop living for themselves and live for Christ, meaning implicitly to live *like* Christ—that is, with others-centered love.[33] Similarly, those reconciled to God by the Messiah's death will "become the justice [NRSV, "righteousness"; Gk. *dikaiosynē*] of God," which, at the very least,

---

33. The connections between love for neighbor and devotion to Christ are developed more fully and explicitly in 1 Cor. 8 and Rom. 14.

means to embody the kind of justice or righteousness that is characteristic of God as displayed in Christ's death.[34] In context, this justice is clearly associated with reconciliation, suggesting that the justice/righteousness expected of the community includes the practice of what we would call restorative justice— that is, bringing people together with God and one another.[35]

Each of these texts also contains an echo of the narrative structure we found in Philippians 2:6–11. The deep structure, so to speak, of 2 Corinthians 5:14–15 can be summarized as follows:

> Although the Messiah Jesus could have selfishly ignored the plight of humanity in its self-centered existence, he did not do so but freely and willingly expressed his love for all by dying for them, and now, by virtue of his resurrection, he is able to empower those who believe this good news to live for him by living in love for others too.

Similarly, 2 Corinthians 5:18–19, 21 could be summarized in these words:

> Although God was fully aware of humanity's sins, unrighteousness, and alienation from himself, God did not in righteous displeasure leave humanity in this condition but entered fully into it in the Messiah, whose death was God's act of forgiveness, reconciliation, and transformation for all.

In 2 Corinthians 5, then, Paul presents us with brief narrative summaries of the reconciling love of God in Christ and with (even briefer) summaries of the transformative power and the existential consequences of this divine action. Reconciliation, therefore, is a central aspect of Paul's understanding of God's crucified Messiah and therefore of loving, righteous/just, cruciform existence "in him" (2 Cor. 5:21). Cruciform reconciliation grounded in this text will have two critical dimensions: forgiveness and restoration.

One thinks immediately of the truth and reconciliation commissions in South Africa and elsewhere, and of certain Christian (and other) groups that seek reconciliation between victims of crimes, and/or their families, and those who have perpetrated crimes against them. Such forms of reconciliation require a spiritual depth and power that is also reflected in our text, the source of a love that empowers a person or community to forgive even though

---

34. On this text, see Grieb, "'So That in Him.'" See also my "Justification and Justice in Paul" and chap. 7 below.

35. I agree with Grieb ("'So That in Him'") that the "we" of 2 Cor. 5:21 refers to the entire believing community, as does the "us" that is the object of reconciliation (5:18), even if the "we" and the "us" of 5:18–20 that are linked to "ambassadors" refer only to Paul and his colleagues in apostolic ministry.

it has every right to seek retribution. In this regard, we remember the Amish community of Nickel Mines, Pennsylvania, after the schoolhouse shooting in October 2006.

Why is it that truth and reconciliation commissions and Amish communities appear to be the exception rather than the norm in Christian practice? No doubt there is no single or simple answer to this question. But one wonders whether cruciform reconciliation receives the attention in Christian theological ethics, and in Christian spirituality and theology more generally, that it deserves.[36] In this regard, two positive examples of appropriate attention are the Center for Reconciliation at Duke Divinity School, with its programs and publications that foster reconciliation rooted in Christian faith, and the more politically oriented Kroc Institute for International Peace Studies at the University of Notre Dame.[37] These and other such centers of scholarship and activism are important for the church's ongoing witness, and more are needed.

Romans 5

In Romans 5 the subject is once more reconciliation, and its source is again stated as both the Messiah's death and God's activity in that death. These two aspects of the chapter emerge in the following verses:

> [1]Therefore, since we are justified by faith, we have peace with God through our Lord Jesus Christ. . . . [6]For while we were still weak, at the right time Christ died for the ungodly [*hyper asebōn*]. [7]Indeed, rarely will anyone die for a righteous person—though perhaps for a good person someone might actually dare to die. [8]But God proves his love for us in that while we still were sinners Christ died for us [*hyper hēmōn*]. [9]Much more surely then, now that we have been justified by his blood, will we be saved through him from the wrath of God. [10]For if while we were enemies, we were reconciled to God through the death of his Son, much more surely, having been reconciled, will we be saved by his life. [11]But more than that, we even boast in God through our Lord Jesus Christ, through whom we have now received reconciliation. (Rom. 5:1, 6–11)

Divine Participation

This text possesses several striking features. For one thing, one of Paul's most distinctive theological themes, justification, is here inseparably linked

---

36. The general inattention to peacemaking in New Testament theology and ethics/spirituality has been rightly documented—and to a degree corrected—by Willard M. Swartley in his *Covenant of Peace*. See also my *Death of the Messiah*, 132–202, and *Becoming the Gospel*, 142–211.

37. See the Center for Reconciliation (http://divinity.duke.edu/initiatives/cfr) and the Kroc Institute (http://kroc.nd.edu).

to reconciliation.[38] Reconciliation, in turn, is described in the vivid image of dying for people who are unjust, sinners, and enemies of God. The Messiah's death is here depicted as his own death for (*hyper*) the ungodly, which should be understood primarily as an act of love (cf. 2 Cor. 5:14–15), as the demonstration of God's love for sinners, and as the means of God's reconciliation and justification of enemies. The syntactical and narrative parallels are quite striking:

> For while we were still weak, at the right time Christ died for the ungodly. (Rom. 5:6)

> But God proves his love for us in that while we still were sinners Christ died for us. (5:8)

> For if while we were enemies, we were reconciled to God through the death of his Son . . . (5:10)

Thus this death "for us" occurred, on the one hand, at the initiative of the Messiah and out of his love for others and, on the other hand, at the initiative of God and out of God's *own* love (*tēn heautou agapēn*) for us.

Most importantly here, the Messiah's death is the demonstration of God's way of dealing with rebellious humanity—spiritual insurgents, we might say. It is the definitive sign of God's love for enemies and God's nonviolent reconciliation of them.[39] There is once again, at least at the semantic level, an echo here of Christ's love depicted in Philippians 2. Although God had every right to allow sinful humans to receive the just consequences of their actions—the divine wrath (Rom. 5:9)[40]—God chose not to allow humanity to stew in its own juices forever but rather, in an act of unexpected and unheard-of love, sought his enemies' reconciliation and ultimate salvation in and through the Messiah's death.[41]

What is absent from Romans 5, however, is any explicit call to cruciform existence in the form of loving enemies or practicing reconciliation. This lacuna is more a function of context than conviction, however. At this point

38. The parallels between Rom. 5:1 and 5:11 make this especially clear. Second Corinthians 5:18–21, with its language of reconciliation and transformation into the justice/righteousness of God, makes the same connection (see above), though perhaps not as clearly (the verb "to justify" not being present, though the noun "justice/righteousness" is). See further chaps. 7 and 8 below.

39. See further my *Inhabiting the Cruciform God*, 129–60.

40. Cf. Rom. 1:18; 2:5, 8; 3:5.

41. For a brilliant exposition of this extravagant, incongruous grace, see Barclay, *Paul and the Gift*.

in Romans Paul has been establishing the need for, and the reality of, God's rescue of Sin-enslaved humanity in and through the Messiah's death and resurrection. Romans 5:1–11 serves as a sort of bridge passage to the apostle's discussion of the existential significance of that reality. Later in the letter Paul will, in fact, draw parallels between the love of God and Christ for enemies and the praxis of those in Christ. But even here there is a hint in that direction, as Paul indicates that "God's love has been poured into our hearts through the Holy Spirit that has been given to us" (5:5). In other words, those who have received the Spirit of God have also received the dynamic love of God and will, implicitly, love others—even enemies—as God in Christ has loved them.[42] That is, the love of God that was in Christ has now become, by virtue of the Spirit, the love of God in the Christian and the Christian community. This is what we might call *double participation* or, perhaps, *redundant participation*: what God has done in Christ God now does in an analogous way in us.

The Fruit of Double Participation

The implicit call to enemy-love becomes explicit in Romans 12. After a general overview of the new life as the corporate spiritual sacrifice of daily, bodily existence (Rom. 12:1–2) and remarks about the use of gifts in the corporate body (12:3–7), Paul introduces the subject of love as a community practice:

> [9]Let love be genuine; hate what is evil, hold fast to what is good; [10]love one another with mutual affection; outdo one another in showing honor. . . . [13]Contribute to the needs of the saints; extend hospitality to strangers. [14]Bless those who persecute you; bless and do not curse them. [15]Rejoice with those who rejoice, weep with those who weep. [16]Live in harmony with one another; do not be haughty, but associate with the lowly; do not claim to be wiser than you are. [17]Do not repay anyone evil for evil, but take thought for what is noble in the sight of all. [18]If it is possible, so far as it depends on you, live peaceably with all. [19]Beloved, never avenge yourselves, but leave room for the wrath of God; for it is written, "Vengeance is mine, I will repay, says the Lord." [20]No, "if your enemies are hungry, feed them; if they are thirsty, give them something to drink; for by doing this you will heap burning coals on their heads." [21]Do not be overcome by evil, but overcome evil with good. (Rom. 12:9–10, 13–21)

We focus first on the exhortations in verse 14 and verses 17–21, and then on the creative tension regarding believers and evil that emerges in this passage, especially in verses 9, 17, and 21.

---

42. The best current work on the Spirit and ethics is that of Volker Rabens. See, e.g., his *Holy Spirit and Ethics in Paul*.

The call to bless rather than curse persecutors (12:14) is likely an echo of the Jesus tradition preserved in Gospel texts such as Matthew 5:43–48 and Luke 6:27–33.[43] If that is true, then we have in Romans a remarkable confluence of the *teaching* of Jesus and the *death* of Jesus on the subject of loving enemies/persecutors, for although Romans 5 is not explicitly recalled here, the astute hearer/reader of the letter will not have forgotten the triple emphasis in that chapter on Jesus' death as God's reconciling of enemies. Moreover, Paul is calling his Roman audience to do precisely what he claims to have done himself throughout his cruciform ministry "for the sake of Christ":[44] "When reviled, we bless; when persecuted, we endure; when slandered, we speak kindly" (1 Cor. 4:12b–13a).

Verses 17–21 of Romans 12, using the ancient image of heaping coals of fire on people's heads, offer a prohibition of practices that would contradict the call to bless persecutors. Christians are to hate evil but not return evil to the evildoer. Paradoxically, Paul suggests that the ability to love enemies depends, not on ignoring evil, but on recognizing and naming it. Just as God in Christ named humans as sinners and enemies, Paul's audience must "hate what is evil" (Rom. 12:9) and must be able to name it as such in order not to "repay" it (12:17) or "be overcome" by it (12:21). *This is precisely what God has done in the Messiah: to name evil and to overcome it with good.*

Following the infamous text in Romans 13:1–7 (which might be, in part, a practical example of how to love enemies),[45] Paul returns to the topic of love as the sine qua non of life in Christ, claiming that those who love (by the powerful presence of God's Spirit—Rom. 5:5) fulfill the divine law (Rom. 13:7–10). Then vividly, in his apocalyptic dialect, Paul calls his audience to disrobe themselves of inappropriate practices characteristic of "the night" and to clothe themselves instead with "the Lord Jesus Christ" (Rom. 13:11–14). The wider context, then, suggests that Paul considers nonretaliation and enemy-love as constitutive of being in Christ; they are two of the cruciform practices that are characteristic of the new day, the new creation, ushered in by the Messiah's death and shaped by it. In addition to being Christlike practices, however, they are also Godlike practices. *To be like Christ is to be like God,* for God was in Christ, loving enemies, reconciling the hostile world. *Cruciformity is, therefore, theoformity.*[46]

---

43. There is some scholarly debate about this, since Jewish traditions also preserve texts about enemy-love, and Paul may have been influenced by such sources. But since we know he had some access to the Jesus tradition, it is at least as likely that he (also?) knew Jesus' views on the subject.

44. 1 Cor. 4:10. Cf. Paul's self-description in 1 Cor. 4:17: "my ways in Christ Jesus."

45. For a brief exposition of this text in light of certain political misuses of it, see my "Romans 13 and Nonconformity."

46. This is the fundamental premise of my book *Inhabiting the Cruciform God.*

Accordingly, one suspects that Richard Hays is right in his claim that "there is not a syllable in the Pauline letters that can be cited in support of Christians employing violence."[47] Hays implies that Paul would not allow us to distinguish between personal and state violence, or between justified and unjustified violence, as in the case, for example, of war.

A Thought Experiment: Radical Reconciliation

Although I agree with Hays about (non)violence in Paul, I would nonetheless like to engage in a thought experiment. How would Paul structure an argument with someone who claims, let us say, the right to the use of violence in self-defense? Paul might be willing, for the sake of argument, to grant the existence, and the Christian appropriation, of the just-war tradition and thus of the so-called right of self-defense.[48] But then he would almost certainly turn the logical consequence of accepting that tradition, with its implicit right, on its head:

[x] Although you have been wronged, and
although you do have an authoritative tradition that gives you the right of self-defense as a last resort,

[y] do not make use of that right and thereby return evil with evil, but rather

[z] continue in practices that overcome evil with good.

To the pragmatic, Paul (or at least this argument put on his lips) will sound naïve. After all, human beings are not God; they cannot overcome evil at will. Of course not, Paul would say. But then he would add that this is not the point. Christian existence requires conformity to the pattern of God's action in the Messiah, meaning good in the face of evil, even when logic and moral authority seem to say otherwise.

That Paul would actually construct such an argument seems quite clear from a careful reading of 1 Corinthians 9, where he offers just this type of christological moral reasoning for his self-support by tent making and against

---

47. Hays, *Moral Vision of the New Testament*, 331.

48. In 1 Cor. 9 Paul appeals to several possible sources that Christians might use (Scripture, church tradition, common sense) to build the case for the existence of certain rights, just as Christians today might appeal to various sources, and not necessarily only Christian ones, to build the case for something like self-defense, and the right to use violence in self-defense, or the right to go to war (or participate in a just war) more generally. In what follows, and in all the examples in this chapter, I am speaking about Christians making arguments about appropriate Christian ethics and praxis.

his being supported financially by Corinthian patrons. In making that case, he argues evangelically and christologically against the moral norms of apostolic example (9:5–6), common sense and cultural practice (9:7), Scripture (9:8–10), spiritual wisdom and ecclesial practice (9:11–12), priestly practice (9:13–14), and even the teaching of Jesus (9:14). All of these norms are overturned by the call of the gospel and the cross:

> [12]Nevertheless, we have not made use of this right, but we endure anything rather than put an obstacle in the way of the gospel of Christ. . . . [15]But I have made no use of any of these rights, nor am I writing this so that they may be applied in my case. . . . [19]For though I am free with respect to all, I have made myself a slave to all, so that I might win more of them. (1 Cor. 9:12b, 15a, 19)

I am not so naïve or foolish as to think that this one example from Paul, or his hypothetical argument in response to the use of the right of self-defense in war, will become the norm in Christian moral reasoning about complex matters. But I would contend that in a moral universe like ours (especially in the West) that is so dependent on the establishment and exercise of rights, with respect to warfare and much more, Paul offers a uniquely Christocentric and theocentric way of moral reasoning that we neglect to our own detriment.[49]

One last example, very briefly:

> [1]When any of you has a grievance against another, do you dare to take it to court before the unrighteous [adikōn; NAB, "unjust"; NIV, "ungodly"], instead of taking it before the saints? . . .
>
> [7]In fact, to have lawsuits at all with one another is already a defeat for you. Why not rather be wronged [adikeisthe; NAB, "put up with injustice"; MJG, "be treated unjustly"]? Why not rather be defrauded? [8]But you yourselves wrong [adikeite; NIV, "do wrong";[50] NAB, "inflict injustice"] and defraud—and believers [adelphous; NAB, NIV, "brothers"] at that.
>
> [9]Do you not know that wrongdoers [adikoi; NAB, "the unjust"; NIV, "the wicked"] will not inherit the kingdom of God? Do not be deceived! Fornicators, idolaters, adulterers, male prostitutes, sodomites, [10]thieves, the greedy, drunkards, revilers, robbers—none of these will inherit the kingdom of God. [11]And this is what some of you used to be. But you were washed, you were sanctified, you were justified [edikaiōthēte; MJG, "incorporated into the community of the just"] in the name of the Lord Jesus Christ and in the Spirit of our God. (1 Cor. 6:1, 7–11)

49. If 1 Cor. 8:1–11:1 as a whole is any indication (see esp. 1 Cor. 10), Paul would also instruct the church in the harm that violence does to the perpetrator, not just to those on whom the violence is inflicted.

50. NIV has "cheat and do wrong," apparently reversing the order of the Greek verbs.

Note here the call to radical cruciform existence, which is rooted in God's action (implied in the passive voice used in 6:11b) of washing, sanctifying, and justifying sinners, moving them from outside the community of the just into that community—into the Messiah. To be in the church, to be in Christ, is to become empowered by God's very own Spirit to become like Christ by accepting rather than inflicting injustice.[51] This is a radical form of reconciliation, or at least the start of reconciliation, because it nips the cycle of violence or other forms of retaliation in the bud. In a litigious culture (Roman or other), such alter-cultural ecclesial practices bear profound witness to the gospel.

The Generosity and Hospitality of God in Christ

The overall spiritual-theological point being argued in this chapter has two foci: (1) the specific narrative shape of Paul's cruciform gospel, existence in Christ, and moral reasoning about individual and ecclesial life; and (2) the theological (i.e., referring to God) character of that christological, narrative ethic and spirituality. There are, of course, other texts and themes that demonstrate the overlap of christological and theological action, and thus moral reasoning, in Paul. We will attend to some of those texts and themes in later chapters. For now we may briefly examine two significant examples.

2 Corinthians 8–9

In chapters 8 and 9 of Paul's Second Letter to the Corinthians (to which we will return in more detail in chap. 9), the apostle appeals to his problem children in Corinth to fulfill their commitment to the collection for the church in Jerusalem. He grounds his appeal first of all in the self-giving of Messiah Jesus, using language that echoes his master story from Philippians 2:6–11: "For you know the generous act of our Lord Jesus Christ, that though he was rich, yet for your sakes he became poor, so that by his poverty you might become rich" (2 Cor. 8:9). As we saw in the previous chapter, in both Philippians 2 and here, the Greek could also be translated with an introductory "because": "For you know the generous act of our Lord Jesus Christ, that because he was rich, for your sakes he became poor."[52] Paul also grounds his appeal in the generosity of God, who is himself a generous giver and the one who supplies the needs of those who are generous in return (2 Cor. 9:6–15).

---

51. Note the many "justice/injustice" interconnections within the passage, boldfaced in the bracketed text because they are often missed in translations, including the NRSV cited here. For further discussion, see my *Becoming the Gospel*, 234–40.

52. For the 2 Corinthians passage, see Barclay, "'Because He Was Rich He Became Poor.'"

Paul concludes his brief discussion of God's generosity and provision with an exclamation: "Thanks be to God for his indescribable gift!" (2 Cor. 9:15)—a clear reference to the gift of Jesus, the Son and Messiah. Taking these two chapters together, we see once again what "in Christ God was reconciling the world" (2 Cor. 5:19) means for Paul on the ground. The Corinthians are to embody the Christ-narrative of generous self-giving (even to the point of renouncing their implied "right" to hold on to their money), which is in turn a narrative of divine giving. The goal of their generosity is, in some unspecified but tantalizing way, economic "equality" (2 Cor. 8:14).[53] They will become the justice of God (2 Cor. 5:21; 9:9–10).

We should not be so naïve as to think that international economic crises or long-term issues such as global poverty will be solved simply by appeal to Paul's theological argument for economic justice and "equality" among early Christian communities. Nevertheless, Paul's argument means that Christians exercise their vocational and, yes, *spiritual* obligations properly when they care about economic injustice—but only when they do so within the framework of christologically construed divine generosity and justice; that is, when they operate with a theological end (justice, shalom) and a theological/christological means (generosity, self-giving) as their framework. Such a framework will generate economic practices within the Christian community that embody the gospel, challenge the status quo, and serve others in need—whether or not they are Christians.[54] This is one critical dimension of a Christlike, Godlike, fully human Christian community.

Romans 14–15

As in 2 Corinthians 8–9, we find in Romans 14–15 both christological and theological grounds for Paul's call to practices of hospitality within the multicultural (gentile and Jewish) Christian communities in Rome. At that moment, mutual judgment was the order of the day in Rome, but the Christ-story and the divine actor within it will not countenance such inhospitality: "Those who eat must not despise those who abstain, and those who abstain must not pass judgment on those who eat; for God has welcomed them" (Rom. 14:3). Echoing his own words offered to the Corinthians, Paul speaks

53. So NAB, NIV. NRSV's "fair balance" may approximate Paul's point, but it aborts the interpretive summons issued by the noun *isotēs*. For a helpful analysis of the Jerusalem collection as the expression of an unprecedented challenge and alternative to Greco-Roman social and economic structures, see Ogereau, "Jerusalem Collection as Κοινωνία."

54. The text of 2 Cor. 9:13, "sharing with them and with all" (NRSV, "all others") refers to generosity toward both believers and others. Otherwise it would not reflect the divine generosity of the cross. On economic justice and spiritual formation, see Barram, *Missional Economics*.

of living for the Lord Christ now and appearing before God's judgment later as the existential framework within which judgmentalism about indifferent matters of diet makes no sense (Rom. 14:7–10). Moreover,

> [17]the kingdom of God is not food and drink but righteousness [or justice] and peace and joy in the Holy Spirit. [18]The one who thus serves Christ is acceptable to God and has human approval. [19]Let us then pursue what makes for peace and for mutual upbuilding. (Rom. 14:17–19)

Already in Romans 14 the blending of Christology and theology is evident. It becomes much more poignant in chapter 15:

> [1]We who are strong ought to put up with the failings of the weak, and not to please ourselves. [2]Each of us must please our neighbor for the good purpose of building up the neighbor. [3]For Christ did not please himself; but, as it is written, "The insults of those who insult you [God, being addressed by Christ] have fallen on me." . . . [7]Welcome one another, therefore, just as Christ has welcomed you, for the glory of God. (Rom. 15:1–3, 7)

Thus, in this section of Romans, Paul calls the story of Jesus both the paradigm of Christian hospitality and the fulfillment of the divine hospitality initiative itself. Christ's hospitality (15:7b) is God's (14:3), and it must now become the church's and each individual's in it (15:7a), especially those who perceive themselves to be "strong" (15:1). *As in the case of reconciliation/ peacemaking and in the case of generosity, the story of Christ is at once Christophany, theophany, ecclesiophany, and anthrophany.*

Paul's theological Christology and its spiritual-ethical corollaries may again inform contemporary Christian moral reasoning and praxis. To return to the fundamental narrative logic of Paul's spirituality, we remember that "although [x] not [y] but [z]" underlies all of Paul's accounts of God's action in Christ and thus of cruciform existence. The christological logic of Paul might result today in a sentence such as this:

> Although we have the "right" to neglect or even reject certain people because of their status in the eyes of the law, we will not do so because we have been saved by, and now will live by, a different law—namely, the law of divine hospitality, the law of Christ. (cf. 1 Cor. 9:21; Gal. 6:2)

Conclusion

This chapter has explored Paul's notion of cruciformity as the central spiritual and moral dimension of his story of the crucified Messiah. We have considered the distinctive narrative pattern Paul puts forward in a variety of ways, and we have looked at three spiritual-moral themes—reconciliation, generosity, and hospitality—in Paul's letters as aspects of his message of cruciformity. Furthermore, and perhaps most importantly, we have seen that this christological narrative is inherently and simultaneously also a story about God, and that therefore Paul's call to *cruci*formity, or *Christo*formity, is also a call to *theo*formity—perhaps even theosis.[55] Paul does not speak about Christ's salvific and paradigmatic death without also speaking of it, both theologically and spiritually, as the action of God. His is a theological Christology. At the same time, the story of Christ and of God is also the story of the church (what it is and what it is called to be) and of humanity (what it is and what it is called to be). The cross is Christophany, theophany, ecclesiophany, and anthrophany.[56] If we wish to speak of Paul's mysticism, it is a mysticism with legs, a this-worldly other-worldliness.

The church—the in-Christ community—needs to take all the dimensions of this Pauline contribution seriously. It will not be sufficient, if we follow Paul's lead, to speak about God and morality without also speaking about Christ and morality, or vice versa. Nor will it be sufficient to speak about Christ and morality without speaking of Christ and ecclesiology. And it will not be sufficient to speak about Christ and morality or ecclesiology without speaking of the mystical-narrative reality to which Paul attests in his letters, and which must be embodied in the church and in each Christian, on the ground.

In terms of concrete moral consequences, Paul offers a vision of divine enemy-love/reconciliation, generosity, and hospitality. Christian ethicists, biblical scholars, spiritual writers, and all Christians need to work together to discern the concrete ways in which we can instantiate the story of God in Christ in our own communal and individual practices by the power of the Spirit of the Father and the Son.

We may summarize all of this in three phrases:

- *theological Christology*—the God-shaped Messiah and the Messiah-shaped (cruciform) God;
- *cruciformity as theoformity*—the Messiah-shaped church as the God-shaped church; and

55. See further my *Inhabiting the Cruciform God* and chap. 9 below.
56. Some might object that the cross is actually revelatory only of God and of Christ (i.e., it is descriptive), and that it does not reveal what the church or the person is, but only what it or he/she should be (i.e., it is prescriptive). This objection misses the inseparable links in Paul's mind between divinity and humanity in Christ, and between Christ and the church. Because Christ is fully and truly human, that which reveals Christ also reveals humanity—true humanity. And because the church is Christ's body, that which reveals Christ also reveals what the church truly is.

- *mystical-missional cruciformity*—the church in the Spirit, and each of its members, becoming a living exegesis of the gospel by its ecclesial practices: becoming like Christ, becoming like God, representing God more faithfully to the world.[57]

The cross, in other words, is the revelation of the identity not only of Christ but also of God and of the church and of humanity. Accordingly, Christification is divinization is humanization.

The question that arises in the midst of Paul's (and my) emphasis on the cross—recall 1 Corinthians 2:2, cited at the head of this chapter—is, Where is the resurrection? Although this chapter has made it clear that the power that enables cruciform existence is the power of the indwelling Christ, we will need to explore the relationship between crucifixion and resurrection more fully in the next chapter.

57. See further my *Becoming the Gospel.*

three

Cruciform or Resurrectiform?

Paul's Paradoxical Practice of Resurrectional Cruciformity

In the previous chapter we took seriously Paul's claim in 1 Corinthians 2:2 that he had decided to know nothing except the crucified Messiah, and we saw that for Paul (and for those who consider Paul's letters Christian Scripture) the cross is both Christophany and theophany, both ecclesiophany and anthrophany. That is, the cross reveals the identity of Christ, of God, of the church, and of true humanity. But what about the resurrection? Did Paul not also stress the resurrection of Christ in, for example, 1 Corinthians 15? And did he not speak of not only dying but also *rising* with Christ in Romans 6? So is life in Christ cross-shaped or resurrection-shaped? That is the question before us regarding Paul's understanding of participation in Christ.

As noted in the introduction to this book, despite wide-ranging interest in participation among Pauline scholars, they disagree on a variety of topics, including what participation in Christ means concretely. Some initial remarks about my own place in this discussion will be useful in considering the question at hand.

Perhaps not surprisingly (at least not for those who have read chaps. 1 and 2, or are familiar with my work more generally), my computer lists some two thousand files containing some form of the word "cruciform." Still more significant, however, is the fact that my computer reveals nearly four thousand files with some form of the word "participate" and nearly four thousand containing some form of the word "mission." These three words—"cruciform," "participation," and "mission"—constitute a fair summary of what I have been doing in my exegetical and theological work, especially in Paul, but also in the rest of the New Testament.

My previous three monographs on Paul (an accidental trilogy), as well as the two introductory texts I have written, have all developed these three themes, though each of the three monographs highlights one theme in particular. *Cruciformity: Paul's Narrative Spirituality of the Cross* (2001) obviously focuses on cruciformity; *Inhabiting the Cruciform God: Kenosis, Justification, and Theosis in Paul's Narrative Soteriology* (2009) stresses participation; and *Becoming the Gospel: Paul, Participation, and Mission* (2015) highlights mission.

The first and third volumes have been nearly universally well received, but the second volume (*Inhabiting the Cruciform God*)—in which the word "theosis" appears not only in the subtitle but also as the content of the book's primary thesis—has been subject to more criticism. Additionally, in the longest chapter of that book, I contend that for Paul justification is *participatory* and *transformative*, the beginning of "an experience of participating in Christ's resurrection life that is effected by co-crucifixion with him."[1] The phrase "resurrection life" should be carefully noted.

Two of the main questions about *Inhabiting the Cruciform God* that have repeatedly emerged are the following: (1) Is justification really an act of participatory transformation, an event of co-crucifixion and co-resurrection with Christ? (2) Is "theosis" an appropriate designation for what happens to those who participate in the life of the Triune God by being so crucified and raised with Christ?

It is tempting to pursue one or both of those questions in this chapter. However, I have already addressed them in various places and ways elsewhere.[2] For example, although I believe strongly that theosis language is *appropriate* in discussing Paul and should not be abandoned, I do not think the term itself is *necessary* if other language can suffice. I do insist, however, that everything Paul is about, including justification, must be understood as transformative participation in Christ the image of God, and hence as transformative participation in the very life of God.[3]

This chapter will therefore focus on a question that has arisen from my work as a whole: Is it adequate to focus on the "cruciform" character of participation in Christ? Or, in other words, what happened to the resurrection

---

1. Gorman, *Inhabiting the Cruciform God*, 40.

2. Nonetheless, I am unable to resist the temptation and will return to these questions in later chapters.

3. For "theosis" as an appropriate term, see, e.g., chap. 9 below. In *Becoming the Gospel* (e.g., 7–8), I stress that the term is not necessary. With respect to justification, see Gorman, *Inhabiting the Cruciform God*, 40–104, as well as chaps. 6–8 below.

and its implications for Christian practice? Is participating in Christ not also resurrection-shaped—that is, "resurrectiform" or "anastiform" (a term based on the Greek word for resurrection, *anastasis*)? This question has been raised by such scholars as Stephen Finlan (proposing "anastiform"), Andrew Boakye (proposing "resurrectiform" or "reviviform"), and Rachael Tan.[4]

At first, this might seem a bit like asking Martin Luther if he would want to balance his *theologia crucis* (theology of the cross) with a hearty theology of glory. "*Mē genoito!*"—"May it never be!"—he would perhaps answer.[5] But I wish to take this question with utmost seriousness and probe it carefully. (For the record, I also have some 3,300 computer files containing a form of "resurrection.")

The thesis of this chapter is, on the one hand, a qualified affirmative response: cruciform participation in Christ is also, paradoxically, participation in Christ's resurrection, as already stated. On the other hand, I will insist that we must maintain Paul's emphasis on the cross and therefore grant the word "cruciform" a certain priority. Therefore, rather than using a term like "resurrectiform" in conjunction with "cruciform," I will argue that we need a different term that better captures the crucifixion-resurrection dynamic, or dialectic, of participation in Christ according to Paul. As we will see, this contention is not merely a minor episode of "wrangling over words" (2 Tim. 2:14), but a significant exegetical and theological claim about the substance of Paul's theology and spirituality—and their contemporary significance.

The Proposal That Participation Is Anastiform/Resurrectiform

Of the three scholars mentioned above who explicitly or implicitly propose language such as "anastiform" or "resurrectiform," we will focus briefly on Andrew Boakye's article "Inhabiting the 'Resurrectiform' God: Death and Life as Theological Headline in Paul." Boakye says the title is a deliberate adaptation of the title of my book *Inhabiting the Cruciform God*.[6]

In his essay Boakye first states his basic agreement with what he rightly understands to be three of the primary cross-centered claims of *Inhabiting*:

1. "Justification is by crucifixion, specifically co-crucifixion, understood as participation in Christ's act of covenant fulfillment."

---

4. Finlan, "Can We Speak of *Theosis* in Paul?"; Boakye, "Inhabiting the 'Resurrectiform' God"; Boakye, *Death and Life*; Tan, "Conformity to Christ."

5. This phrase appears fourteen times in Paul's letters (all in Romans, 1 Corinthians, and Galatians), generally to answer rhetorical questions. See, e.g., Rom. 6:1–2.

6. Boakye, "Inhabiting the 'Resurrectiform' God," 53. Some of this article is restated in Boakye's *Death and Life*, 13–14.

2. "Co-crucifixion leads to co-resurrection which draws those of faith into a cruciform lifestyle (i.e. informed by the cross), for which Jesus was template and Paul was example."

3. "God's cruciform nature gave shape to Jesus' self-giving act."[7]

While these claims, according to Boakye, are "hermeneutically sound" and, "pastorally, [offer] a sharp upward call," the more fundamental claim of my book, which "equates being 'in Christ' with 'inhabiting the *cruciform* God'"[8] (emphasis his), troubles Boakye. He therefore offers two lines of critique. The first critique, somewhat ironically (given the article's title and thesis), challenges my own use of resurrection language for Paul's understanding of present existence in Christ; Boakye finds the notion of present resurrection with Christ only in post-Pauline (to his mind) letters—namely, Colossians and Ephesians—so he prefers the language of "revivification" with respect to Paul's theology.[9] The second critique mistakenly attributes the phrase "resurrection shaped" to me as a description of Paul's view of life in Christ, while correctly noting that I do speak of "co-resurrection." Boakye then affirms my thesis that "'inhabiting the God of life-in-death and power-in-weakness'" is "the heart of 'Paul's cruciform spirituality.'"[10] Accordingly, Boakye argues, we "better comprehend both the church's ethical program and Paul's ministry career as 'resurrectiform'" since "a resurrection requires a death, [while] the reverse is not true."[11] He expands this thesis as follows:

> It seems to me precisely because power comes from weakness (Gal. 2:19; 2 Cor. 12:9), life from death (Gal. 5:24–25; 2 Cor. 4:11) and victory from suffering (Gal. 3:4; Rom. 8:17), emphasizing crucifixion over resurrection . . . *creates a hierarchy that Paul never intended.* This brief paper will explore whether the ministry of Paul and the lives of the rectified are actually resurrection shaped.
>
> I propose that a simple survey of Paul's death-life lexicon will elucidate just how resurrection shaped the life and ministry of Paul was, and how pro-

---

7. Boakye, "Inhabiting the 'Resurrectiform' God," 53. In points 1 and 2 in the numbered list, Boakye indicates he is quoting me, but only point 1 is a direct quotation, while point 2 is a paraphrase; in point 3 he is also paraphrasing me, as he rightly indicates.

8. Boakye, "Inhabiting the 'Resurrectiform' God," 53.

9. Boakye, "Inhabiting the 'Resurrectiform' God," 54.

10. Boakye, "Inhabiting the 'Resurrectiform' God," 54, referring to *Inhabiting the Cruciform God*, 150–52.

11. Boakye, "Inhabiting the 'Resurrectiform' God," 54. In *Death and Life*, 14, Boakye states that the term "reviviform" would be more accurate, but since he does not employ that term in the article, or elsewhere in the book, I will generally stay with "resurrectiform" in this essay.

foundly ideas of resurrection inform the lives of those rectified through faith in Christ.[12]

Boakye then offers a spirited defense of this thesis, with a particular focus on 2 Corinthians. His major claim, building on a brief examination of the language of life and death in Paul, is that "the twinned concepts of life *and* death is [*sic*] critical to Paul's depiction of God's work to rectify the world, Paul's evaluation of his own role within that work and how he remedies aberrant theology and behaviour in the Jesus assemblies."[13] He then appeals to 2 Corinthians to defend this three-part claim.

In other words, with respect to salvation, ministry, and spirituality, cruciformity needs to be balanced with "resurrectiformity."[14] Although I basically agree with much of the substance of what Boakye says, I want to maintain that Paul actually does create a hierarchy of sorts, privileging the cross in several ways, and not least in 2 Corinthians. In making this argument, I am not "marginalizing" the resurrection, as Boakye implies at the end of his essay;[15] nor am I attending only to "half" of Paul's message, as Finlan claims (Boakye concurring),[16] or attending only "partially" to Paul's theology of conformity to Christ, as Rachael Tan argues.[17]

12. Boakye, "Inhabiting the 'Resurrectiform' God," 55 (emphasis added). In a note in the middle of this passage, Boakye mentions Finlan's neologism "anastiform" and affirms Finlan's critique of my work: that we leave out half of Paul's message if we only call life in Christ cruciform (Finlan, "Can We Speak of *Theosis* in Paul?," 74–75).

13. Boakye, "Inhabiting the 'Resurrectiform' God," 56.

14. Boakye uses this noun twice ("Inhabiting the 'Resurrectiform' God," 59).

15. Boakye, "Inhabiting the 'Resurrectiform' God," 62.

16. Writes Finlan: "In chapter 3 [of Philippians], the believer's re-formation or conformation begins with sharing in Christ's sufferings and death, and then with participation in resurrection. Conformity with Christ, then, is first 'cruciform,' and then 'anastiform.'. . . Theosis has to do with 'anastiform' experience, both in this life and the next. If we want to call Paul's gospel 'cruciform,' as Michael Gorman does, we must also call it 'anastiform,' or we leave out half his message" ("Can We Speak of *Theosis* in Paul?," 74–75). At first Finlan appears to find a sequential pattern of cruciform conformity followed by ("then . . .") anastiform conformity, but then he says that theosis is an anastiform experience both now and later. He understands this anastiform existence primarily as transformation into a Spirit-led, instead of a fleshly, life (72–74), describing it also as "living as though already in the kingdom of God and receiving eternal light and truth" (77). He further describes theosis as being "transformed into Christlikeness," which "always involves both cruciform and anastiform living, but points to a thoroughly anastiform destiny" (78). For Boakye's agreement, see his "Inhabiting the 'Resurrectiform' God," 55n12.

17. Tan ("Conformity to Christ," 179) agrees with me that Paul advocates conformity to Christ (rather than mere imitation of him) but then remarks,

> Although cruciformity captures the meaning of conformity partially, it could mislead one to focus only on the cross (*crux*) without the resurrection, dying without the rising, and sufferings without the power. It is clear from our exegesis that Paul's conformity includes both the power of Christ's resurrection and the participation in his sufferings. He wants

Rather than turning this chapter into a direct response to Boakye (or Finlan or Tan), I will instead think theologically with Paul about the resurrection and the resurrectional character of participation in Christ, doing so partly in dialogue with these scholars. Unlike them, however, I think it best, as stated above, not to use terms like "resurrectiform" or "anastiform" in parallel with "cruciform" to refer to the *form*, or narrative structure, of participation in Christ according to Paul. Rather, it is better to speak of participation in Christ as having a resurrection *quality*—or perhaps even a resurrection *ethos* and *effect*. There may not be a suitable term with the ring of "resurrectiform," but—as we will see—the neat parallelism between "cruciform" and "resurrectiform" is actually (if unintentionally) misleading. Terms like "anastiform" could imply the present completion, or fullness, of a process that does not conclude until the eschaton, and they could minimize the ongoing cruciform character of present existence in Christ. Thus I will propose that terms like "resurrectional" or "resurrection-suffused," in conjunction with "cruciform," are better, more accurate descriptors of Paul's paradoxical understanding of participation in Christ.[18]

First Response: Cautious Affirmation

Even with that thesis, my first response to the concerns of Boakye, Finlan, and Tan is generally affirmative. Participation in Christ is of course participation in the resurrected Christ and is therefore in a profound sense "informed" by the resurrection.[19] Several important commonsense and specifically Pauline perspectives justify both these scholars' concerns and my affirmation of what I think they are trying to convey with terms like "resurrectiform."

---

to know Christ, his mindset, his attitudes, and everything related to Christ. No doubt the cross is central to Paul's theology and forms the basis of conformity, but conformity is more than that. It is this comprehensive aspect which pervades the whole of life that is highlighted in this passage [Phil. 3:7–11].

18. In the second edition of my *Apostle of the Crucified Lord*, I was more appreciative of terms like "anastiform," though with the same basic understanding offered here: "To die with Christ is also to be raised to new life—resurrection life (Rom. 6). Some scholars have suggested that we speak not only of cruciform existence in Paul but also of resurrectiform, reviviform, or anastiform existence. . . . This is true, but it is true only paradoxically: cruciform existence is anastiform, and vice versa. It is also true only partially and provisionally, for full resurrection life will be known only in the future, in the eschaton" (151–52, with references to Boakye and Finlan in a note).

19. See Boakye's phrase cited above that for Paul "the resurrection inform[s] the lives of those rectified" ("Inhabiting the 'Resurrectiform' God," 55). I have, in fact, recognized my own need to give greater emphasis to the resurrection. The second edition of *Apostle of the Crucified Lord* attempts to do precisely that.

First is the commonsense assumption that one cannot truly participate in any meaningful way in the life of a dead person. If Christ has not been raised from the dead, Paul might say, our (so-called) participation is in vain.

Second, the God Paul knows and worships in Christ is the living God, the God of resurrection, the God of new creation who "gives life to the dead and calls into existence the things that do not exist" (Rom. 4:17).[20] Thus the God of Paul's gospel and Paul's ministry on behalf of God is life-giving; this is in part what Boakye means by "resurrectiform" and what I mean by "resurrectional"—resisting the "form" language in connection with resurrection because (paradoxically, as I will emphasize later) the character or "shape" of this resurrecting God revealed in Christ is cruciform.[21]

Third, Paul himself grounds our salvation not only in the cross but also in the resurrection. For instance, in Romans 4:24–25 Christ's death and resurrection are so inseparable that they essentially constitute one saving event, and elsewhere Paul both assumes this inseparability and sometimes articulates it (e.g., Rom. 8:34—Jesus is the one "who died, yes, who was raised, who is at the right hand of God, who indeed intercedes for us").[22] Moreover, 1 Corinthians 15 makes it clear that there is no salvation, no hope, and no purpose without both Christ's resurrection and ours, but that with resurrection comes purposeful life now and permanent eschatological life in the future.

Fourth, Paul can characterize the gift of salvation effected by Christ's death and resurrection as "life" and even, in some sense, as resurrection. In Romans 5:18 Paul declares that "one man's act of righteousness leads to justification and life for all." Although this life is predicated on Jesus' singular act of righteousness (his death), the result is clearly the opposite of death (see Rom. 5:15), and thus the "life" effected by Christ's death is a form of resurrection. This is also the strong implication of the Abraham story: that despite the deadness of Abraham's body and his wife's womb (Rom. 4:19), the God of Abraham (and of Paul) is the one "who gives life to the dead" (Rom. 4:17)—the God of resurrection, new creation, and new life.[23]

Fifth, therefore, the ongoing experiential side of salvation (ethics, spirituality) involves participating not only in Christ's death but also in his resurrection. This is not limited to Colossians and Ephesians, whether Paul authored

20. See also 2 Cor. 1:9, which Boakye rightly explores while also briefly noting Rom. 4:17 ("Inhabiting the 'Resurrectiform' God," 56).

21. Boakye is right to stress that "2 Corinthians houses a deeply embedded nucleus of revivification language exemplary of Paul's self-perception of the political, social, and theological dynamics of ministry" ("Inhabiting the 'Resurrectiform' God," 62).

22. See also, e.g., 1 Thess. 4:14; Rom. 5:10.

23. For more on Rom. 4, see chap. 8 below.

those letters or not.[24] It is especially clear in Paul's treatment of the implications of baptism in Romans: "Therefore we have been buried with him by baptism into death, so that, just as Christ was raised from the dead by the glory of the Father, so we too might walk in newness of life" (Rom. 6:4).[25] Thus Paul can say that we are "those who have been brought from death to life" (Rom. 6:13) in anticipation of eternal life (Rom. 6:23); that is, present resurrection life ("newness of life") is a foretaste of future resurrection life ("eternal life").[26]

The Priority of Cruciformity in Paul's Understanding of Participation

Nevertheless, although I agree with my critics that we need to keep the cross and resurrection together, and I affirm that we need to speak of participation in Christ's resurrection, I suggest that it is imperative that we maintain the priority of cruciformity and of the term "cruciform" to describe the shape, or structure, of life in union with Christ. Moreover, because throughout Paul's writings there is a discernible cruciform substance, even a pattern (i.e.,

24. See, e.g., Col. 2:12; 3:1–3; Eph. 2:5–6.

25. Despite the claims of certain interpreters, including Boakye, that Paul does not promote a present resurrection but restricts resurrection language completely to the future, Daniel Kirk, Ann Jervis, and others have demonstrated that Paul sees believers as participating in Christ's resurrection now, this present participation taking the form of new life. See, e.g., Kirk, *Unlocking Romans*; Jervis, "Time in Romans 5–8," esp. 145; Tappenden, *Resurrection in Paul*.

26. This seems to be Finlan's point in speaking of both present and future anastiform existence. Although Boakye prefers the term "revivification" to "resurrection" in describing my fourth and fifth points, we are in essential agreement about the importance of life in Christ having a resurrection-like quality. For a methodologically unique approach to this issue that arrives at conclusions similar to mine, see Tappenden, *Resurrection in Paul*. Tappenden writes, "For Paul, resurrection is an ongoing event whereby both Christ's death and Christ's life are continually manifested in the Christ-believing body" (226). Present resurrection is the result of the presence of the divine spirit, who effects "a trajectory of transformative embodiment" in a "single resurrection event" (155) from baptism to eschatological completion: "The already risen interior thus awaits the achievement of the not yet risen exterior" (157). For Tappenden, this ongoing, participatory, transformational resurrection is expressed in "certain patterns of embodiment" (177) that involve dying with Christ: (1) "life in death" (190–207), which is complementary to life through death (199, 234), and (2) "ecstasy, ethnicity, and resurrection" (207–25). Although the latter pattern may seem closer to Finlan, Boakye, and Tan than to me, Tappenden stresses that in all aspects of this experience, "the nature of the enspirited earthly body's present experience of resurrection . . . is characterized by a process of ongoing outer death and inner life" (226). (Although Tappenden does not use the word "theosis," his insistence on participation in Christ as a single resurrection—an ongoing process and trajectory—is actually quite theotic in nature. I do not agree with him, however, that Christ's *pneuma*, or Spirit, received at baptism, in which we participate, is a material spirit [103–33, 175–227].) In my words, I would say that the shape of resurrection life in the present is cruciform, and that theosis involves cruciformity.

although [x] not [y] but [z]), that describes participation in Christ, but not a discernible "resurrectiform" substance or pattern, there really is no parallel between cruciform and "resurrectiform" life.[27] Rather, the profound Pauline paradox of participation is that the cruciformly structured life in Christ is, simultaneously, participation in Christ's resurrection. This is the case in two closely connected senses that we might cautiously call "spiritual" and "missional": experiencing newness of life (spiritual) and being a channel of life for others (missional). That is, the cruciform life is suffused with the power of the resurrection; it is *resurrectional*, but not *resurrectiform*.[28]

I will substantiate this claim by looking at a few key texts from Paul's letters, specifically the Corinthian correspondence and Philippians. Many other texts could be considered to corroborate the argument.

1 Corinthians 2:2 in the Context of 1:18–2:5: The Theophanic Cross

In 1 Corinthians 2:2, as we briefly noted in both chapter 1 and chapter 2, Paul claims that he had "decided to know nothing among you [the Corinthians] except Jesus Christ, and him crucified," which should probably be translated as "nothing among you except Jesus the Messiah—that is, Jesus the *crucified* Messiah" (MJG; cf. 1 Cor. 1:23). How could Paul possibly make this claim about his allegedly myopic focus on Christ crucified in the letter that contains his most sustained exposition of the resurrection of both Jesus and believers (1 Cor. 15)?

On the one hand, the most immediate context suggests that 1 Corinthians 2:2 is a rhetorically charged claim, bordering on hyperbole, in which Paul contrasts his own message with the showy rhetorical practices of certain unnamed preachers who may have "come proclaiming the mystery of God to you in lofty words or wisdom" (1 Cor. 2:1). In other words, we should perhaps not take Paul literally. On the other hand, if we expand the context just a bit to include the entire rhetorical unit of 1:18–2:5, it becomes clear that we *should* take Paul very literally. In this passage Paul makes astonishing claims about Christ crucified both as divine self-revelation and, hence, as epistemological criterion for discerning the activity of God.

27. The closest we get to a resurrection "pattern" in Paul is the dynamic of life in death (so Tappenden), but that is more of a principle in search of a concrete pattern than it is an actual pattern. The concrete pattern itself, as we will see below, is specific and cruciform.

28. By denying the appropriateness of the term "resurrectiform" to describe Paul's theology and spirituality, I have in mind a theology and spirituality of present glory, triumph, or power that minimizes or even dismisses the centrality of ongoing participation in Jesus' crucifixion. Indeed, as noted, the central Pauline paradox is that the resurrection life is cross-shaped (cruciform) from start to finish, meaning until the parousia or the bodily resurrection.

By claiming that Christ crucified constitutes the power and wisdom of God (1 Cor. 1:24), Paul is saying that the cross is not only a Christophany but also, and in a sense more fundamentally, a theophany, as we explored in chapter 2. As such, the cross is the criterion for knowing how and where God works—that is, both *among* the weak (the Corinthians: 1:26–31) and *through* the weak (Paul: 2:1–5). The implicit corollary of this epistemological criterion for discerning the *means* by which God works, and the *space* in which God works, is that we participate in God's sort of activity—which is of course the work of God's Spirit (2:4, 6–16)—by means of, and in spaces of, human weakness. (This corollary will become both more fully developed and turned into a memorable slogan in 2 Corinthians: "Whenever I am weak, then I am strong" [2 Cor. 12:10]).

In other words, the word (*logos*; 1 Cor. 1:18) of Christ crucified is not a minor part of Paul's gospel or an optional supplement, nor is it even merely a prelude to the more important reality of the resurrection. Rather, the cross tells us something about Christ, about God, about God's Spirit's work in the world, about us, and about our benefiting from and participating in God's work that even the resurrection does not tell us. That is, Christ crucified is the sine qua non of the substance of the gospel because of its theophanic, christophanic, anthrophanic, ecclesiophanic, and pneumatophanic character.[29] Even the Spirit is not, and should not be, separated from Christ crucified.

To be sure, the word of the cross is no gospel, and it has no soteriological consequence, apart from the resurrection. The mini-creed that Paul inherited, passed on to the Corinthians, and quotes back to them (1 Cor. 15:3–5) names both the crucifixion and the resurrection as the fulfillment of Scripture and the basis of salvation. Without the resurrection, says Paul in 1 Corinthians 15, everything else Christians say and do is meaningless. Paradoxically, however, the cross maintains a priority in emphasis throughout the rest of 1 Corinthians. This is because for Paul one function of the resurrection is to validate his fundamental claim that the cross is both how and where God acts savingly for the world. The salvific, theophanic, and paradigmatic character of the cross obtains only because the resurrection validates it as such. We participate in Christ, in the Spirit, in the life of the Triune God by participating in the reality that the resurrected Christ in whom we live and move and have our being is the crucified Christ, and none other.

29. Which means that Christ crucified reveals the character of God, Christ himself, the human person, the church, and the Spirit. See the previous chapter, which referred to all of these revelatory dimensions except that of the Spirit (pneumatophanic).

In the words of Andy Johnson, Jesus is "stamped forever with the legacy of being crucified."[30]

The resurrected Christ does not displace the crucified Christ as the place of divine life and of our participation in that life. On the contrary, we participate in Christ truly only when we know this Christ as the crucified Messiah, the one whose obedient faithfulness to God and self-giving love on the cross determine the shape of our own lives, individually and corporately, in the power of the Spirit. (This is essentially the message of 1 Corinthians 13, which is applied to various concrete situations throughout the letter.)[31] For Paul, as we shall see further below, the cruciform life is—paradoxically—the resurrection-suffused life, and vice versa.

Philippians 2 in Context: The Cross as Divine Self-Revelation and Paradigm

We turn next to Philippians, and specifically once again to its famous christological poem, but this time with a focus on its use within the letter. It will be important to recall the main claims I have made, especially in the previous chapter, about the contents of this narrative poem: (1) the christophanic and theophanic character of the cross, and (2) the corollary participatory, paradigmatic character of Christ crucified for the Philippians and for all Christians—that is, the ecclesiophanic and anthrophanic character of the cross. In other words, the self-emptying (kenotic), self-humbling, self-giving, vulnerable, and "downwardly mobile" God revealed in Christ crucified generates a self-emptying (kenotic), self-humbling, self-giving, vulnerable, and "downwardly mobile" community of people in Christ.

The specific narrative structure of this downward mobility is a critical dimension of Paul's understanding of Christ and, as we will see below, of participation in Christ. This narrative structure, or form, of Christ and thus of those in him is the "although [x] not [y] but [z]" pattern that we explored in the last chapter. That pattern depicts the fundamental character—the life story, so to speak—of God and of God's Messiah. It also characterizes Paul, and it is supposed to characterize all who are in Christ. Ultimately, the pattern is also to be understood as "*because* [x] not [y] but [z]." That is, God, Christ, Paul, and all in Christ do what they do not merely *in spite of* possessing some status but precisely *because* they possess that status.

---

30. Personal correspondence, September 1, 2017, based on his own published work. Similarly, in the last century Ernst Käsemann wrote that the cross is "the signature of the one who is risen" ("Saving Significance of the Death of Jesus," 56).

31. Particularly important is the phrase "does not insist on its own way" (*ou zētei ta heautēs*) in 1 Cor. 13:5, which is echoed in 1 Cor. 10:24, 33, and Phil. 2:4.

This counterintuitive pattern about the nature of being truly divine and messianic both reinforces and unpacks what we observed in 1 Corinthians 1:18–2:5. Of course, the story of Christ ends not with crucifixion but with exaltation; the two-step, sequential structure of the poem in Philippians as a whole is from crucifixion to exaltation. But it is the cruciform x-y-z pattern of the first part that becomes normative for present life in Christ.

Throughout Philippians, this "although/because [x] not [y] but [z]" Christ-paradigm of humility, self-emptying, concern for others, and even suffering to the point of death is consistently described and prescribed, as many interpreters have recognized. (It occurs throughout the rest of Paul's letters too.)

First of all, in the poem's most immediate context, Paul prescribes genuine participation in Christ/in the Spirit (which means in Christ/Christ's body, the *ekklēsia*) in terms that echo the poem and its narrative structure of not seeking self-interest but seeking the interests of others:

> ¹If then there is any encouragement in Christ, any consolation from love, any sharing in the Spirit, any compassion and sympathy, ²make my joy complete: be of the same mind [*to auto phronēte*], having the same love, being in full accord and of one mind [*to hen phronountes*]. ³Do nothing from selfish ambition or conceit [or "empty glory"; see 2:7, 11], but in humility [see 2:8] regard [see 2:6] others as better than yourselves [*heautōn*]. ⁴Let each of you look not to your own interests [*ta heautōn*], but to the interests of others. (Phil. 2:1–4)[32]

The theme of "one mind" is directly related to the exhortation to have the mind (*phroneite*) of Christ (2:5) that connects this passage to the poem itself in 2:6–11. Moreover, near the end of the letter (4:2), Paul prescribes cruciform harmony ("to be of the same mind," *to auto phronein*) for Euodia and Syntyche, who are in some sort of dispute, by using the language of unity from 2:2 ("be of the same mind . . . of one mind," *to auto phronēte . . . to hen phronountes*) and from the introduction to the poem describing the mind of Christ (*phroneite*).

Furthermore, Paul describes living examples of such cruciform participation by briefly narrating stories of himself and others that borrow the ideas and even the language of the poem. Paul's own desire to die and be with Christ is held in check by his Christlike commitment to put the needs of others first (1:21–26). His own suffering (1:7, 12–24) is clearly for him participation in

---

32. Some aspects of the echoes from the poem are discernible only in Greek, such as the twofold use of the reflexive pronoun in 2:3–4 (*heautōn*) and in 2:7–8 (*heauton*). The Greek of 2:4 also echoes that of 1 Cor. 13:5, noted above.

Christ's sufferings (3:10).[33] And his "conversion"[34] autobiography echoes the Christ-poem in multiple ways, not least in the threefold repetition of the verb that characterizes Christ's fundamental act of "considering" or "regarding":

[Christ Jesus] did not regard [*hēgēsato*] . . . (Phil. 2:6)

[7]Yet whatever gains I [Paul] had, these I have come to regard [*hēgēmai*] as loss because of Christ. [8]More than that, I regard [*hēgoumai*] everything as loss because of the surpassing value of knowing Christ Jesus my Lord. For his sake I have suffered the loss of all things, and I regard [*hēgoumai*] them as rubbish [or "filth," "excrement"], in order that I may gain Christ. (Phil. 3:7–8)

In addition, Paul says of Timothy, "I have no one like [lit., "equal in soul to" (*isopsychon*)] him" (2:20), and that "he has served [*edouleusen*] with me in the work of the gospel" (2:22), statements that together echo the description of Christ as the one equal (*isa*) to God (2:6) who took on the form of a servant, or slave (*doulou*, 2:7). And of Epaphroditus Paul writes that he "came close to death [*mechri thanatou*] for the work of Christ" (2:30), using the exact phrase from the poem that announces Christ's obedience unto death: "He . . . became obedient to the point of death [*mechri thanatou*]—even death on a cross" (2:8).[35]

Where is the resurrection in the midst of all this death and deathlike living? If we look for the term itself in the poem, we will look in vain, for it speaks of Christ's exaltation (Phil. 2:9), not resurrection. Even this event in the Christ-narrative is something in which believers will share, however, as Christ "will transform the body of our humiliation that it may be conformed to the body of his glory" (Phil. 3:21). Thus the two-step structure of the poem, from humiliation to exaltation, becomes the present-future pattern of believers, a pattern that is fundamentally synonymous with the pattern of death-resurrection that we also find in Philippians 3 (and elsewhere) for both Christ and those in Christ:

[10]I want to know Christ—that is, (a) the power of his resurrection [*anastaseōs*] and (b) the participation [*koinōnian*] in his sufferings by (b′) being conformed [*symmorphizomenos*] to his death, [11]if somehow I may attain (a′) the resurrection [*exanastasin*] from the dead. (Phil. 3:10–11 MJG)

The chiastic (a-b-b′-a′) structure of this text suggests that knowing the power of Christ's resurrection refers, at least in part, to the future resurrection

---

33. See esp. the discussion in Davey, *Suffering as Participation with Christ*, chap. 2.

34. I use the term "conversion" in the sense of dramatic transformation, not to mean a change of "religion."

35. For a fuller discussion, see Gorman, *Apostle of the Crucified Lord*, 489–91.

from the dead. As in Romans 8:17 (God's adopted children are "joint heirs with Christ—if, in fact, we suffer with him so that we may also be glorified with him"), the sequential pattern of suffering and death followed by future resurrection is evident here. But the close grammatical connection between knowing that resurrection power and participating in Christ's sufferings also strongly suggests that those who are in Christ paradoxically experience the power of Christ's resurrection, as well as his sufferings, *as they are conformed to Christ's death.* For Paul, participating in Christ ("be[ing] found in him," Phil. 3:9) consists of knowing him in two inseparable senses: (1) experiencing the power of his resurrection now, even while (2) sharing in his sufferings and thus being conformed to his death.

In other words, participating in Christ's resurrection *now* and participating in his sufferings and death *now* are simultaneous—indeed, in many ways, overlapping—realities. That is, *present participation in Christ is resurrection-empowered and resurrection-suffused but cross-shaped.* This simultaneity of cruciformity and resurrectionality is the point also of 2 Corinthians 12:10: "Whenever I am weak, then I am strong." Indeed, it is the present cruciform life, which is paradoxically but profoundly an experience of knowing Christ's resurrection power, that leads to future bodily transformation and resurrection—that is, to resurrectiform life. The *simultaneous* reality of *cruciform* existence being *resurrectional* existence is paired with the *sequential* reality of *cruciform* existence leading to *resurrectiform* existence.

The key to present participation in Christ, then, is participatory *simultaneity*—sharing in Christ's death and resurrection at the same time—and the shape of that sharing is *cruciform*.[36] This cruciformity can take the form of actual suffering (as it did for both the Philippians and Paul) as well as the more general form of kenotic, self-giving love. In fact, the two forms of cruciformity can coexist in the same person or community, as they did in Christ. That is why Paul consistently commends and advocates cruciform existence throughout the letter (and throughout all his correspondence), even calling participation in Christ's suffering a "grace" (*charis*): God "has graciously granted [*echaristhē*] you the privilege not only of believing in Christ, but of suffering for him as well" (Phil. 1:29).

Yet one more thing needs to be said about this cruciform participation: it is—once again, paradoxically—far from morbid. Indeed, as everyone recognizes, Philippians is a letter of joy (see 1:4, 18, 25; 2:2, 17–18, 28–29; 3:1; 4:1, 4, 10).[37] This too is undoubtedly part of what Paul means by knowing the power

36. Similarly, Hogan, *I Live, No Longer I*, esp. 86–139.
37. See the eloquent discussion in Hogan, *I Live, No Longer I*, 108–39.

of the resurrection: joy in the midst of suffering. Paul might even paraphrase the Letter to the Hebrews (on the assumption he did not write it!) by saying this:

> We should look to Jesus the pioneer and perfecter of faithfulness, who for the sake of the joy that was both given to him in the midst of suffering and set before him as the end result of suffering, endured the cross, disregarding its shame, and has taken his seat at the right hand of the throne of God. (cf. Heb. 12:2 NRSV alt.)

For Paul, then, participating in Christ is constituted by *a pattern of death and resurrection that is both sequential and simultaneous.* In this present life, corresponding to Christ's earthly life, the fundamental shape of participation is cruciform, but this cruciform participation is empowered by the resurrection—or, more accurately, by the (Spirit of the) resurrected crucified Messiah (see Gal. 2:19–20; Rom. 8:9–11). The Christian experience of *sequential* death and resurrection is grounded in the narrative sequence of the Christ-story, while the Christian experience of *simultaneous* death and resurrection is grounded in the reality that the Resurrected One remains the Crucified One. Accordingly, whether it is Paul, Timothy, Epaphroditus, Euodia and Syntyche, the Philippian community in ancient Macedonia, or Christians today, *the power of the resurrection is manifested in similar ways: through cruciform participation in Christ.*

2 Corinthians 3–5, Focusing on 4:7–12: The Power of Resurrectional Cruciformity

Paul's claims in Philippians about the simultaneity of cross and resurrection, with the stress on cruciform life in Christ, could hardly be more robustly affirmed than they are in 2 Corinthians. This symbiosis of cross and resurrection is revealed as Paul describes his and his colleagues' ministry (2 Cor. 1–7), as he redescribes that ministry in contrast to the activity of the "super-apostles" (2 Cor. 10–13), and as he encourages the Corinthians themselves to practice joyful, Macedonian-like cruciform generosity (2 Cor. 8–9).

At the same time, Andrew Boakye's argument for the importance of the "resurrectiform" dimension of Paul's theology is made primarily from this letter. Our goal will be to discern what Paul says on these matters and how best to articulate them theologically, proposing once again that Paul advocates resurrectional cruciformity rather than a resurrectiform existence. We will focus on one critical text, 2 Corinthians 4:7–12.[38]

---

38. According to Boakye, in 2 Cor. 4:11–12, "the resurrectiform shape of the Pauline gospel exhibits the cruciformity of which Gorman speaks" ("Inhabiting the 'Resurrectiform'

Analysis of 2 Corinthians 4:7–12

Paul has just told the Corinthians that he and his colleagues are ministers of a gospel about the glory of God, the glory of Christ (4:1–6; cf. 3:1–18). He has also told them that the role he and his coworkers play in proclaiming this gospel is to preach Jesus' lordship and to practice Jesus' servanthood (4:5). The paradox inherent in the comingling of a story of glory and a story of shame (servanthood/slavery) needs now to be spelled out in terms of its existential implications for apostolic ministry. How Paul and his coworkers *live* (and therefore also how all ambassadors of Christ should live, he implies) is as much a part of their ministry as what they *say*, for ministers embody in themselves the slave-like existence of their Lord (see Phil. 2:6–8; 1 Cor. 9:19). Paul's life of affliction in the service of others is proof of his status as slave rather than lord, as well as a demonstration of a fundamental theological claim of the letter, already made in 1 Corinthians (esp. 1:18–2:5): that God's power operates in and through human vulnerability and weakness (see esp. 2 Cor. 1:3–6; 12:9–10).

The paradoxically coupled images of slavery and glory propel the rest of this section of 2 Corinthians (through 5:10). Paul senses the tension between a gospel of glory and a life of slavery and affliction. He resolves it by finding the conjunction of death and resurrection in Jesus to be the pattern of his own life. Moreover, if the claims of 4:7–12 are not at odds with the bold claim of 3:18—that contemplating the glory of the Lord changes people into the likeness of the Messiah—then all believers, apostles or otherwise, are being called to participate in a transformation into glory that comes about only by becoming vessels of death-through-life.

Paul begins 4:7–12 with an image of having treasure in clay jars that functions as the thesis of the paragraph (4:7).[39] He proceeds to give a brief but eloquent catalog of apostolic sufferings (4:8–9).[40] He then interprets this ministerial experience of affliction as a paradoxical dynamic of life being made manifest in death (4:10–12). Weakness has a purpose, as Paul will say in three ways with three parallel purpose clauses ("so that," Gk. *hina*) in verses 7, 10, and 11.

God," 58). For a recent analysis of this passage that comes to conclusions similar to my own, see Pifer, *Faith as Participation*, 96–115.

39. Some translators and other interpreters consider 4:7 to be the conclusion to the previous paragraph, but the parallel language of 4:1 ("since . . . we are engaged in [lit., "since we have"] this ministry") and 4:7 ("But we have this treasure"), together with the stark shift from the images of glory and light in 4:6 to the image of clay jars in 4:7, suggests that 4:7 begins a new discourse unit.

40. Lisa M. Bowens ("Investigating the Apocalyptic Texture of Paul's Martial Imagery") argues convincingly that the language used in 4:8–9 occurs elsewhere in military contexts and thus implies apocalyptic conflict.

The "treasure" named in 4:7 is clearly first of all the gospel of the glory of God in the face of the Messiah Jesus (4:4, 6), while the "clay jars" are the lives of those in and through whom the gospel is proclaimed.[41] The treasure is also, in a profound sense, Jesus himself, whose dying and life Paul and his colleagues "carry" and make visible. With this clay-jar image, and then throughout the paragraph, Paul points out the necessary (and, in his case, actual) correspondence between the narrative shape of the gospel about Jesus and the narrative shape of ministerial life: power in weakness, life through death (not merely power *and* weakness or life *and* death). Paul also makes it clear that this is the *only* way that truly divine power—the power of cross and resurrection, of new covenant and new creation—can be manifested in and through human beings. As Paul had previously told the Corinthians (1 Cor. 1:18–2:5, discussed above), the gospel reveals that this is simply the way God works, whether in the crucifixion of Jesus (1:18–25), the calling and composition of the Corinthian community (1:26–31), or the ministry of Paul (2:1–5).

Cruciform existence, then, is paradoxically the manifestation of divine power—indeed, of resurrection power. The mission of God is accomplished in and through suffering and weakness, or else the power of the cross is no power at all, and the gospel that Paul preached is utter nonsense. Theosis, or participating in the life of God through dwelling in Christ and being empowered by the indwelling Spirit of the Father and the Son, is a foretaste of future resurrection that is presently—paradoxically—cross-shaped. This (present) theosis is necessarily both cruciform and missional, for God in Christ was letting loose the divine power of creation to re-create people into a new people of the new covenant ready and able to continue the manifestation of God's work in Jesus in the world. That is, they were to be a people who would practice resurrection (to use the words of Eugene Peterson and Wendell Berry) by embodying the cross.[42]

"Power" (*dynamis*), then, is the critical word in Paul's thesis statement in 2 Corinthians 4:7. Paul does not merely aver that the treasure *is* contained in clay jars so that its divine source will be evident (so NIV, NRSV, RSV), but rather implies that the treasure *must* be in clay jars because clay jars are fragile and thus "weak," and when the gospel of God is contained in other kinds of

41. Paul may also be alluding to the prophetic image (e.g., Isa. 29:16; 45:9; 64:8; Jer. 18–19) of God's people as God's pottery, as he does in Rom. 9:21–23.

42. Boakye reads this passage somewhat similarly, finding in it both cruciformity and resurrectiformity, in his words ("Inhabiting the 'Resurrectiform' God," 58–59). But what he fails to articulate sufficiently clearly is that it is precisely Paul's cruciform ministry that is the vehicle and mode of God's resurrecting activity, such that calling Paul's ministry "resurrectiform" rather than "resurrectional" risks underemphasizing this paradox.

Table 3.1. Power/Life in Weakness/Death (2 Cor. 4:7–12)

Verse	Weakness/Death	Power/Life
4:7	But we have this treasure in clay jars, so that [*hina*]	it may be made clear that this extraordinary power belongs to God and does not come from us:
4:10	always carrying in the body the death [or "dying"] of Jesus, so that [*hina*]	the life of Jesus may also be made visible in our bodies.
4:11	For while we live, we are always being given up to death for Jesus' sake, so that [*hina*]	the life of Jesus may be made visible in our mortal flesh.
4:12 (summary)	So death is at work in us,	but life in you.

vessels—vessels of power, such as those of the "super-apostles" described in chapters 10–13—the gospel is distorted and the power of the gospel becomes the power of someone or something else. Yes, the gospel is the power of God for salvation (Rom. 1:16), but only when it is contained within, and channeled through, jars of clay.

Paul expresses the necessity and purpose of such oddly construed divine resurrection power, and its modus operandi, in the three parallel "so that" (*hina*), or purpose, clauses noted above, followed by a summary statement (table 3.1 above).

The three parallel purpose clauses and the summary statement all proclaim that cruciform existence has a paradoxical purpose: the manifestation of the transformative power of God and the "life" of Jesus—the transformative, resurrection power of Jesus to bring life out of death, as 4:12 says in conclusion. That is, through the cruciform ministry of weakness and suffering, the transformative, life-giving power of God manifested in Jesus' resurrection is unleashed in the life of Corinth and beyond. To be sure (once again, paradoxically), this resurrectional life brought forth in Jesus will be cruciform, for cruciformity is not just for apostles, as Paul has said clearly elsewhere (e.g., in Philippians) and will make plain in 2 Corinthians 8–9 when he discusses the collection for Jerusalem.[43]

Conformity and Participation

All of this is because the exalted, living, life-giving, resurrected Lord is identical to the crucified Messiah. The life he produces corresponds to the life

43. In *Christosis* (e.g., 203), Ben Blackwell likewise stresses both that the life of Jesus—and of God—is manifested in the apostolic dialectic of life through death and that this form of revealing the divine life is not restricted to apostles.

he led and the death he died. There are not two things operating, crucifixion *and* resurrection, or death *and* life, but rather life *in* death, power *in* weakness, resurrection *in* crucifixion (cf. 2 Cor. 12:9–10). God's uncanny, paradoxical power works this way both *in* us and *through* us, Paul says.[44] This cruciform life is not only one of participating in Christ's sufferings, as cataloged in 2 Corinthians 4:8–9 and elsewhere, but also one of participating in Christ's love, as the catalog in 1 Corinthians 4:9–13 makes clear: "When reviled, we bless; when persecuted, we endure; when slandered, we speak kindly" (1 Cor. 4:12b–13a)—words that echo Jesus' own teaching and praxis. The Messiah's suffering on the cross was the ultimate manifestation of a life of cruciform love; so too, participation in his life will be manifested as love that will likely culminate in suffering.[45]

The similarity of the apostle's sufferings to those of Jesus is reinforced by the Greek verb Paul uses in the phrase "we are always being given up [or "handed over"] to death" (2 Cor. 4:11): *paradidometha*, a passive form of the verb *paradidōmi*. This verb is frequently used in all four Gospels, in both passive and active forms, to signify Jesus' betrayal and his being handed over to the authorities.[46] Paul knew at least an oral tradition about Jesus' deliverance to death that used this verb: "For I received from the Lord what I also handed on [*paredōka*] to you, that the Lord Jesus on the night when he was betrayed [or "handed over," *paredideto*] took a loaf of bread" (1 Cor. 11:23). The apostle also uses the verb to signify Jesus' own active self-giving in death (Gal. 2:20),[47] as well as his being delivered to death by his Father (Rom. 4:25; 8:32). The verb occurs additionally in texts about Jesus' followers being handed over to authorities.[48] In fact, in Acts, Paul is both one who hands disciples over to others (Acts 8:3; 22:4) and, later, one who is handed over (Acts 15:26; 21:11; 28:17).

Although *paradidōmi* does not always signify "hand over to death," that is clearly the sense of most of these texts, especially those concerning Jesus, but also those focused on the disciples.[49] What is significant for reading

44. Similarly, see Paul's use in 2 Cor. 2:14 of the Roman triumph as an image of apostolic ministry. Paul depicts himself as the conquered captive (death) who is "in Christ" (resurrection/life). In Christ, he is both defeated and victorious, dying and living.

45. I agree with Billings (*Union with Christ*, 142n52) that "cruciform" with respect to Christ characterizes his entire life, not only its culmination.

46. See, e.g., Matt. 10:4; 17:22; 20:18–19; 26:2, 15, 16, 21, 23–25, 46, 48; Mark 3:19; 9:31; 10:33; 14:10, 11, 18, 21, 42, 44; 15:1, 15; Luke 9:44; 18:32; 21:12; 22:4, 21, 22, 48; 24:7; John 6:64, 71; 12:4; 13:2, 11, 21; 18:2, 5, 30, 36; 19:11, 16a; 21:20; see also Acts 3:13.

47. See Eph. 5:2, 25. See also Gal. 1:4, where the related verb *didōmi* is used.

48. E.g., Matt. 10:19; Mark 13:11–12; Luke 21:12; see also Acts 12:4.

49. Occasionally there is a contextual reference to prison or punishment rather than death per se, but the word "death" or "kill" often appears in the context, and the context usually implies that death is the goal of the handing over.

2 Corinthians 4:11 is that *Paul tells his story of apostolic suffering in the language that both he and the evangelists use to narrate Jesus' own deliverance to death and in the language that those same writers employ to describe the similar fate of Jesus' followers, including Paul himself.* To be handed over to death constantly ("always" in 4:10–11), then, is to share repeatedly in the fate of Jesus, which has now become the fate of his disciples—as Jesus himself predicted, according to the Gospel writers: "Take up [your] cross daily" (Luke 9:23).[50] But since death cannot literally happen repeatedly, Paul is obviously talking about the deathlike practices and brushes with death that he describes and prescribes, both here and elsewhere.

The best word to characterize this is not "imitation," as if Paul were deliberately seeking these situations and inviting others to do the same. Rather, the passive voice of *paradidometha* suggests that he and his colleagues are being acted on, and thereby being conformed to the story of Christ. Thus "participation" and "conformity" characterize Paul's experience better than "imitation."[51] This does not, however, mean that Paul is an unwilling participant in these sufferings, nor does it mean that the only forces at work in his life of conformity to the sufferings of the Messiah are those of his enemies. Rather, as we see here (and in the subsequent sentences: 4:14–15), Paul views the sufferings as beneficial—even life-giving—for others, and he believes he is empowered to endure them by God. Indeed, God is mysteriously at work in and through these sufferings.

In 2 Corinthians, of course, Paul also speaks about transformation "from glory to glory" (3:18 MJG), implying some type of present, as well as future, glory. But the context of that verse, especially the following sentences in chapter 4 that we have just examined, suggest that Paul has in mind a present, *cruciform* glory and Christlikeness that will eventually become an eschatological, fully resurrectiform glory.[52] As in 2 Corinthians, so also in Philippians, Romans, and elsewhere: present glory is power in weakness, life in death, glory in suffering. But it is nonetheless glory—cruciform glory. And it is nonetheless participation in the life and power of God in Christ by the Spirit—cross-shaped participation. In other words, there is real participation in divine power, in the resurrection, even in glory, but this participation is

50. Consider also Jesus' many predictions of literal suffering and persecution (e.g., Matt. 5:10–12; 10:16–36; Mark 10:28–31; Luke 21:12–19; John 15:18–21; 16:1–4, 33), and cf. 1 Cor. 15:31, "I die every day!"

51. Similarly, D. Campbell, *Deliverance of God*, 914–24. See also the next chapter's analysis of Phil. 2:5.

52. In Rom. 8:30, similarly, Paul can speak of glorification in the past tense because in Christ the process of restoring humanity into the image and glory of God—into Christlikeness—has begun (see Isa. 55:3, 5–7).

paradoxically marked by what appears to be the *opposite* of power, resurrection, life, and glory. The apostolic practices of being afflicted and persecuted, of nonretaliation and blessing when cursed, and so on are fundamentally experiences of glory—*the glory of the cross*. They are spiritual practices, cruciform practices, theotic practices.[53]

To repeat: that such paradoxical resurrection-suffused participation in the cross is not limited to apostles is clear in numerous ways. Not only do we have the testimony of other letters with similar paradoxical dynamics, such as Philippians, but we also have the explicit witness of 2 Corinthians itself (esp. chaps. 8–9).[54] Moreover, elsewhere Paul speaks autobiographically of being in Christ in ways that are appropriate for all believers (e.g., Gal. 2:19–20), and he invites others—specifically the Corinthians—to become imitators of him in his cruciform mode of participation in Christ (1 Cor. 4:16; 11:1; cf. Phil. 4:9; 2 Thess. 3:7–9).[55]

Conclusion: The Pauline Participation Paradox— Resurrectional Cruciformity

Many other texts in Paul could be considered to see how the themes we have explored in parts of Philippians, 1 Corinthians, and 2 Corinthians are so thoroughly enmeshed in Paul's articulation of his theology and spirituality.

For instance, Romans 6 speaks of both dying and rising with Christ as liberation from sin (or Sin, understood as a cosmic power), but the freedom of "newness of life" (6:4; cf. 6:13)—of being alive to God (6:10–11)—is paradoxically one of dying to sin (6:11) and of self-giving to God (6:13–23). Or consider Romans 8, a robust text on participation in Christ; it contains numerous "in" passages indicating a spirituality of mutual indwelling ("in" Christ and vice versa; "in" the Spirit and vice versa; 8:2, 9–11); numerous words that begin with a form of the Greek prefix *syn* (meaning "with," "co-"; 8:16–17, 22, 26, 28–29); and the metaphor of adoption as God's children (8:14–25), which has frequently been associated with theosis, or deification, in the Christian tradition. Indeed, no passage on participation in Paul is more filled with exuberant life in the Spirit than Romans 8—it radiates resurrection power (8:11). At the same time, however, Paul makes it clear that life in Christ, life in the Spirit, is cruciform in several ways, especially ongoing dying to the flesh (8:1–6) and suffering, both with all creation and for the gospel (8:17–39).

53. Paul's association of the cross with glory is reminiscent of the Gospel of John (e.g., John 12:23; 13:31–32; 17:1).
54. On which, see chap. 9 below.
55. See also 1 Thess. 1:6; 2:14. See as well Aernie, "Faith, Judgment, and the Believer."

These texts, among others, reinforce the central claim of this chapter: for Paul, resurrectional life in Christ is the cruciform life, and vice versa. This is the paradox of participation for Paul. Furthermore, this chapter has emphasized that it is best to use "cruciform" for the shape, structure, or form of this present life in Christ, avoiding the additional use of the parallel term "resurrectiform" or "anastiform" for present participation in Christ. Rather, it is more appropriate to use terms like "resurrectional" or "resurrection-suffused" (meaning "resurrection-enabled" and "life-giving") for present participation, reserving any other "-form" language for the fully transformed eschatological future (e.g., "resurrectiform," "reviviform," "anastiform"). Hence "resurrectional" or "resurrection-suffused" characterizes that which enables and sustains cruciform participation in Christ and that which results from such participation: abundant life (cf. John 10:10). Yes, we have been crucified *and* raised with Christ—raised to newness of life; revivified, if you prefer. But the fundamental shape of present resurrection life is cruciform.[56] We participate in the resurrected Christ by continually carrying his death in our mortal but resurrection-empowered bodies, both personally and missionally. Such is the Pauline paradox of participation in Christ. *To be in Christ is to embody continuously and simultaneously Good Friday and Easter.* This is participating in the Paschal Mystery. This is resurrectional cruciformity.

We might say that the former dimension of the story and reality (Good Friday) supplies the *pattern*, while the latter dimension (Easter) supplies the *power*, for participation in the resurrected crucified Messiah. But both are constantly present, inseparable from each other. This spiritual simultaneity is rooted in the christological simultaneity of Jesus the resurrected crucified Lord. Resurrectional cruciformity is not only experienced in daily living and ministry; it is also reaffirmed, celebrated, and experienced in the Lord's Supper, when the resurrected Lord—the Supper's host—is vividly recalled, even reenacted, as the crucified Messiah and is embodied (or should be embodied) in practices of cruciform love and hospitality (1 Cor. 11:17–34).[57]

Paul's paradoxical spirituality of resurrectional cruciform participation in Christ is a matter of critical importance. The gospel is not the gospel of Paul, or of God, if it loses its focus on the cross—rightly understood as the

---

56. Even Ephesians, which speaks of life in Christ as being "raised . . . up with him and seated . . . with him in the heavenly places" (Eph. 2:6), connects the resurrected life to Christ's cross: "Therefore be imitators of God, as beloved children, and live in love, as Christ loved us and gave himself up for us" (Eph. 5:1–2). This text both demonstrates the cruciform, earthly character of life in/with Christ "in the heavenly places" and implicitly claims that cruciformity ("as Christ loved us and gave himself") is theoformity ("imitators of God").

57. Markus Nikkanen speaks of "embodied remembering" that participates in Christ's death and resurrection by means of cruciform behaviors ("Participation in Christ," 236–47).

theophany of God's self-giving, life-giving love. "To be truly human is to be Christlike, which is to be Godlike, which is to be kenotic and cruciform."[58] Life in Christ is not truly life in Christ when it loses its cruciform shape of participation precisely in that divine love and life. This assertion may be illustrated with one extreme but important example.

Shortly after the Charlottesville, Virginia, white-supremacist rally in August 2017, I watched a documentary about a Ku Klux Klan (KKK) group in which the filmmakers were permitted to witness a ceremonial cross "lighting." As the ceremony began, the hooded KKK members encircled a tall wooden cross. The "grand knight" (if that is the correct title) began the ceremony by announcing that this was to be a cross lighting, not a cross burning. He then approached each member with a burning torch, lighting each one's own torch in turn as he asked, "Do you accept the light of Jesus Christ?"—to which each member replied, "I do." The grand knight then set the cross aflame, announcing to all that they together were proclaiming the cross of Jesus Christ.

My gut reaction was to call aloud words like "heresy," "abomination," and "blasphemy." To be sure, these folks believed they were proclaiming the cross. I suspect they also believed they were proclaiming a risen, living savior; perhaps some of them even sing about such a savior on a regular basis. But their ceremony and their lives are neither resurrection-suffused nor cross-shaped. And their sort of distortion of Christian faith plagues the world, not only in Charlottesville, but also elsewhere; it is death-dealing rather than life-giving.

I am not in any way accusing any of the scholars proposing "resurrectiform" language of deliberately pushing the church in the wrong direction. I am, however, saying that Paul advocates a specific form of spirituality and discipleship that is as critical for our time as it was for Paul's—and for Dietrich Bonhoeffer's. *In fact, the very integrity of the church and of the gospel are at stake.* "Cheap grace," Bonhoeffer famously wrote, "is grace without discipleship, grace without the cross, grace without the living, incarnate Jesus Christ."[59] The corollary of this bold assertion is that the only way we know the living, incarnate Christ is through cruciform discipleship. For Bonhoeffer, as for Paul (and for the present author), "form" language is critical. Speaking of the "form of the incarnate one" that "transforms the church-community into the body of Christ," Bonhoeffer wrote, "The form of Christ on earth is

---

58. Gorman, *Inhabiting the Cruciform God*, 39.
59. Bonhoeffer, *Discipleship*, 44. Unfortunately, numerous preachers advocate some (alleged) form of resurrection life without any ongoing cruciform existence.

the form of death [*Todesgestalt*] of the crucified one. The image of God is the image of Jesus Christ on the cross. It is into this image that the disciple's life must be transformed. . . . It is a crucified life (Gal. 2:19)."[60] It is, said Jesus, taking up one's cross, not enjoying one's eschatological glory.[61]

This is a summons for the church to be faithful in its calling to be *resurrectional* by being *cruciform*.

60. Bonhoeffer, *Discipleship*, 285.
61. I owe this reminder to Michelle Rader, my research assistant. See also Gorman, *Death of the Messiah*, esp. 32–50, 78–98, 106–8, 114–18.

four

A New Translation of Philippians 2:5 and Its Significance for Paul's Theology and Spirituality

Touto phroneite en hymin ho kai en Christō Iēsou . . .

Philippians 2:5

In each of the previous chapters I have devoted attention to the Christ-poem of Philippians 2:6–11, which I refer to as Paul's "master story." But I have said nothing substantial about the verse that introduces this poetic narrative, Philippians 2:5. The interpretation of this verse relates directly to a claim made briefly in the previous chapter: "participation" and "conformity" characterize Paul's spirituality, theology, and ethics better than "imitation" does.

Philippians 2:5 remains an exegetical and translational conundrum, yet it is a *crux interpretum*—a critical interpretive juncture.[1] Word by word, it says something like the following:

> This think [*Touto phroneite*]
>> in [or among] you [plural] [*en hymin*]
>> which also [*ho kai*] in Christ Jesus [*en Christō Iēsou*].

1. O'Brien, *Epistle to the Philippians*, 203. His treatment of 2:5 is one of the most thorough in print (203–5, 253–62). I cite it here for that reason, despite the fact that this commentary is now known to have been produced in part by plagiarism on the part of the author. For that reason, it should be used with caution.

The NRSV renders the verse as "Let the same mind be in you that was in Christ Jesus." The bridge between a key exhortation in the letter (Phil. 1:27–2:4) and its poetic, theological foundation (Phil. 2:6–11), Philippians 2:5 needs to be interpreted well in order to understand the nature of the connection between the exhortation and the foundation. Furthermore, since the great significance of Philippians 2:6–11—in multiple respects—is universally acknowledged, we will gain the highest degree of clarity about it only if we properly explicate 2:5.

This chapter is an extended case for a translation and interpretation of 2:5 that I have previously presented briefly:[2]

> Cultivate this mindset—this way of thinking, feeling, and acting—in your community, which is in fact a community in the Messiah Jesus . . .

The key element of my proposal is not the language of cultivation or the three-part definition of "mindset."[3] Rather, it is the last half of the verse, "which is in fact . . ." This relative clause is the link between the imperatival clause *Touto phroneite en hymin* ("Think this in/among you") and the following poem, and it is what has most thoroughly beguiled translators. In this chapter I argue that this translation best captures the point Paul is making in Philippians and also has highly significant implications for understanding Paul's theology and spirituality as a whole. (Readers should note that this chapter is rather linguistically technical, but the theological repercussions are significant.)

A Sample of Two Basic Interpretations

The exegesis of Philippians 2:5 affects the interpretation of the connection between poem and exhortation, between Christology and spirituality. The basic question that has divided interpreters is this: Does Paul exhort the Philippians to adopt a mindset that Christ had, or does he tell them to maintain a mindset that they already have "in Christ" and under his lordship? Does he promote imitation of the suffering, dying Jesus, or does he promote obedience

---

2. In chap. 1 the translation that is argued for here is briefly presented. See also, e.g., my *Cruciformity*, 39–44; Gorman, "The Self, the Lord, and the Other," 694–98. This specific formulation, with minor changes (from "Christ" to "the Messiah"; reordering the verbal participles), derives from my *Becoming the Gospel*, 117–18.

3. For this three-part understanding of "mindset," see Fowl, *Philippians*, 88–90; cf. 28–29. We might also render the main verbal idea as "Let this same mindset be operative in your community." For this sort of rendering, see my "Participation and Ministerial Integrity."

to Christ the Lord? Or, somehow, does he do both? Or, again—as I will argue here—does he do something different?

Two basic interpretive options have been proposed in modern scholarship:

1. something like "Have the attitude that was in Christ" or "Have the mindset that Christ had"
2. something like "Have the attitude that is yours in Christ"

The first interpretation is purely imperatival, urging imitation of Christ. The second includes an indicative statement about already possessing the attitude, or condition, that is the basis for the imperative. These two basic interpretations are sometimes referred to as (1) the "ethical" and (2) the "kerygmatic," "doctrinal," or "soteriological," respectively. I prefer the terms (1) "imitative" and (2) "locative" to characterize these two basic perspectives. The former stresses imitation *of* Christ, the latter being *in* Christ.

Bible translations largely represent one or the other of these two interpretations, with the imitative option being the more popular:

Imitative Translations

Adopt the attitude that was in Christ Jesus. (CEB; cf. NASB)

Think the same way that Christ Jesus thought. (CEV)

You should have the same attitude toward one another that Christ Jesus had. (NET; cf. NLT)

In your relationships with one another, have the same mindset as Christ Jesus. (NIV)

Make your own the mind of Christ Jesus. (NJB)

Let the same mind be in you that was in Christ Jesus. (NRSV)

Locative Translations

Have this mind among yourselves, which is yours in Christ Jesus. (ESV)

Have among yourselves the same attitude that is also yours in Christ Jesus. (NAB)

Have this mind among yourselves, which is yours in Christ Jesus. (RSV)

This is how you should think among yourselves—with the mind that you have because you belong to the Messiah, Jesus. (*Kingdom New Testament* [N. T. Wright])[4]

Recent commentators who provide their own translations fall generally into one of these two interpretations too. An example of each will suffice:

Let this be your pattern of thinking, acting, and feeling, which was also displayed in Christ Jesus. (Stephen Fowl; imitative)[5]

Think in this way among yourselves; it is the way you also think "in Christ Jesus." (John Reumann; locative)[6]

Although, as we will see, the exegetical issues are quite complex, there is one fundamental difference between the imitative and the locative interpretations. It is whether one understands the missing Greek verb in the relative clause—"which also [verb] in Christ Jesus" (*ho kai* [ὃ καί] [verb] *en Christō Iēsou*)—as referring to Christ or to the Philippians.[7]

Most often, the verb supplied for the imitative reading is something like "was" (*ēn*), or occasionally "you see/saw" (perhaps *blepete* or *eidete*),[8] with Jesus as the one who possessed the disposition: "Have this attitude that was in Christ"; "Think how Christ thought."[9] "In Christ Jesus" refers to the location of the *disposition* in *Jesus*.

The verb supplied for the locative reading, on the other hand, is normally an indicative form of the explicit imperative "think" (*phroneite*), with the Philippians as the ones who possess the disposition: "Have the mindset you have"; "Think what you think." "In Christ Jesus" refers to the location of the *Philippians* in *Christ*.[10]

The kerygmatic or soteriological approach—what I am calling the locative interpretation—was championed especially by Ernst Käsemann (in 1950) and

4. Though technically similar to other locative translations, Wright's rendering is quite close in spirit to the interpretation offered in this chapter.

5. Fowl, *Philippians*, 88.

6. Reumann, *Philippians*, 333.

7. In this chapter I have occasionally included Greek text, in addition to transliteration, when it is necessary or helpful for the argument.

8. This would be similar to Paul's descriptions of what could be seen in him (Phil. 1:30; 4:9).

9. As noted, and as we will see further below, the verb *phronein* means more than simply "think."

10. In the locative reading, the location of the disposition is ultimately also in Christ, such that believers have the disposition only by virtue of their being in Christ. But the emphasis in this interpretation is on the location of believers in Christ, not the location of the disposition in Christ.

then Ralph Martin (in 1967), each expressing concern about the pervasive ethical (imitative) interpretation.[11] They rightly emphasized that Paul was focused on the lordship of Christ and on the church's being in Christ and under his lordship. For them, Christ and the hymn do not constitute the *model* of Christian ethics but the *foundation* of it. Nevertheless, their reaction was an overreaction, a textbook example of throwing the baby out with the bathwater. What looked to Käsemann and Martin like a necessary exegetical and theological choice between two opposite readings of the text, one ethical and the other kerygmatic, is a false dichotomy, as Larry Hurtado ably showed in a 1983 essay.[12]

A Third Option

In a similar spirit, Markus Bockmuehl has proposed a third option for the translation of Philippians 2:5 that attempts to blend the two basic approaches, as follows:

> This is the attitude you should have among yourselves, which [attitude] is also in Christ Jesus.[13]

Bockmuehl is onto something important. He contends that Paul is clearly making an ethical point, as the "close parallels" between 2:1–4 and 2:6–11 reveal.[14] Furthermore, he agrees with many exegetes that an appeal to Jesus' example probably requires a form of the verb "to be." But rather than using the commonly supplied "was," Bockmuehl offers "is." He claims that

> the simplest reading is to supply the *present* tense of "to be" [i.e., *estin*]: "have this attitude amongst yourselves, which *is* also in Christ Jesus." While it leaves intact the moral analogy with the narrative that follows, this reading has the advantage that the indicated attitudes of the mind of Christ are seen to be not just a past fact of history but a *present reality*.[15]

Bockmuehl continues: "In some sense, therefore, the 'mind-set' of unselfish compassion which Paul encourages in the Philippians 'is present' in Christ Jesus both historically and eternally." Furthermore, "this translation may

---

11. Käsemann, "Critical Analysis of Philippians 2:5–11," esp. 83–84; Martin, *Hymn of Christ*, esp. xii–xix, 68–88.

12. Hurtado, "Jesus as Lordly Example in Philippians 2:5–11."

13. Bockmuehl, *Epistle to the Philippians*, 114. Cf. REB, "what you find in Christ Jesus," as Bockmuehl himself suggests (124). See also Meeks, "Man from Heaven in Paul's Letter to the Philippians," 332, and the (French) Bible de Jérusalem: "Ayez entre vous les mêmes sentiments qui sont dans le Christ Jésus."

14. Bockmuehl, *Epistle to the Philippians*, 122–23.

15. Bockmuehl, *Epistle to the Philippians*, 123–24.

narrow the gap between the usual two options."[16] What is more, Bockmuehl briefly suggests that the continuity between the Jesus Christ of faith and of history implies *participation* more than mere remembrance.[17]

Bockmuehl advances the conversation by focusing on the likelihood of the implied verb being in the present tense, as well as the theological implications of that with respect to the presentness of Jesus and his ongoing disposition of self-giving love. He does not, however, develop the insight about participation (though that theme figures in his commentary as a whole). His translation of 2:5 itself remains a variation on the imitative reading because it does not recognize "in Christ Jesus" as the location of the church; Christ is still the location of a disposition, even if the disposition "is" rather than "was" located in him.

Two observations might be helpful at this point. First, like Bockmuehl, most interpreters of Philippians today—even if chastened a bit by Käsemann and Martin—recognize that Paul is presenting Jesus as a model for Christian behavior in some sense. Precisely how Paul envisions the relationship between Jesus and the Philippian believers, or Christians more generally, is still debated and sometimes articulated in less precise and less accurate language than should be the case.[18]

Second, since the phrases *en hymin* ("in you") and *en Christō Iēsou* ("in the Messiah Jesus") are *syntactically* parallel, they are almost certainly in some sense *semantically* parallel. Indeed, I would submit that the most critical exegetical question for the translation and interpretation of Philippians 2:5 is the semantic significance of the parallelism between these two phrases. I would further submit that the key to understanding this parallelism lies in (1) assuming that the phrase *en Christō Iēsou* here means what similar phrases most often mean in Paul—namely, "within the community of Christ the Lord"; and (2) rethinking the sense of the phrase that connects the two parallel phrases—that is, *ho kai* (normally understood to be ὃ καί, a relative pronoun followed by the word for "and" or "also").

In other words, it is time for a fresh exegesis of the text that might yield a true third option. To do this, we need to step back a bit in order to name and discuss the various exegetical issues. The solutions I will propose to a series of questions will lead to the translation noted at the beginning of the chapter.

---

16. Bockmuehl, *Epistle to the Philippians*, 124.

17. Bockmuehl, *Epistle to the Philippians*, 124.

18. A number of commentators in the imitative tradition have rightly suggested that "conformity" is a better description of Paul's ethics than "imitation" (e.g., Hooker, *From Adam to Christ*, 90–92; O'Brien, *Philippians*, 205). This suggestion approaches the language of participation. For Christ's participation in humanity enabling our participation in him, see Eastman, "Philippians 2:6–11," though she does not deal directly with 2:5.

I will refer to this option as the *participatory* interpretation, an alternative to the traditional imitative and locative interpretations.

Some Key Exegetical Questions

The standard critical editions of the Greek New Testament provide the interpreter with this text of Philippians 2:5:[19]

Τοῦτο φρονεῖτε ἐν ὑμῖν ὃ καὶ ἐν Χριστῷ Ἰησοῦ

Touto phroneite en hymin ho kai en Christō Iēsou

This think in [or "among"] you [plural] which also [or "that is"] in Christ [or "the Messiah"] Jesus.

This short text raises a host of exegetical issues, which can be summarized as five main questions.

1. Does the neuter demonstrative pronoun Τοῦτο/*Touto* look backward, forward, or both? That is, is it retrospective, prospective, or both?
2. What is the sense of φρονεῖτε/*phroneite*?
3. Does ἐν ὑμῖν/*en hymin* mean "in [each of] you" or "among you"? That is, does the phrase refer (or refer primarily) to individuals or to the community?
4. What is the meaning of the phrase ὃ καί/*ho kai*?

   a. Is the first word a neuter relative pronoun (ὅ/*ho*), as generally assumed and therefore universally printed, or is it possibly a masculine, singular, nominative article (ὁ/*ho*)?
   b. If it is the neuter relative pronoun ὅ/*ho*, does it refer back to Τοῦτο/*Touto*, or is there another option?
   c. If it is the article ὁ/*ho*, what is its significance?
   d. What is the force of καί/*kai*?
   e. What verb (if any) should be supplied, or is inferred, after the phrase ὃ καί/*ho kai* or ὁ καί/*ho kai*?
   f. In what sense (if any) are the phrases ἐν ὑμῖν/*en hymin* and ἐν Χριστῷ Ἰησοῦ/*en Christō Iēsou*, which are linked by ὃ καί/*ho kai*, parallel, both syntactically and semantically?

19. I will not discuss the variants, none of which has found significant acceptance among textual critics or exegetes. I will, however, propose a possible variant rendering of the omicron that is assumed to be the relative pronoun ὅ/*ho*.

5. To what does ἐν Χριστῷ ᾿Ιησοῦ/*en Christō Iēsou* refer—to something "in" Christ or to the community of believers as those who are "in" Christ? Is there any significance to the presence of ᾿Ιησοῦ/*Iēsou* in a phrase that is normally in Pauline usage simply ἐν Χριστῷ/*en Christō*?

It would take a book, rather than a chapter, to offer a full response to each of these issues, so relatively brief replies will be necessary. We will consider them in sequence, though some overlap with and anticipation of subsequent questions is unavoidable. In general (apart from subheads and references to the Greek lexicon), from now on I will include only the transliteration of Greek words, except in the case of the critical word ὅ (*ho*) and the phrase ὅ καί (*ho kai*) because, as we will see, this relative pronoun might actually be the article ὁ (also transliterated *ho*).

1. Retrospective Τοῦτο (Touto)

There are two main reasons to think that *touto* is primarily retrospective. First, forms of the verb *phronein*, of which *touto* is the direct object, appear twice in the immediate context of 1:27–2:4, specifically in 2:2:[20]

> *plērōsate mou tēn charan hina to auto **phronēte**, tēn autēn agapēn echontes, sympsychoi, to hen **phronountes***

> Make my joy complete: be of the same **mind**, having the same love, being in full accord and of one **mind**. (NRSV)

Paul uses the neuter pronoun *touto* in 2:5 to sum up the *phronēsis* ("mind/mindset") that he has described in 2:1–4—a *phronēsis* that is characterized by unity, love, humility, and concern for others rather than self. This is clearly a community *phronēsis*, one that originates in the shared reality identified in 2:1 as being in Christ (*en Christō*) together and being co-participants in the Spirit (sharing the *koinōnia pneumatos*). The retrospective neuter pronoun *touto* does not refer to a grammatically neuter linguistic entity (such as a noun) in 2:1–4, but rather to the "idea," or the existential reality, described in those verses.[21] It is therefore unnecessary to posit an allegedly suppressed word (as may be necessary later in the verse), such as [*to*] *phronēma* ("mind, thought").[22]

20. The verb appears also in 1:7, to which we will return.
21. See BDAG, s.v. οὗτος/*houtos* 1 b α; the neuter demonstrative pronoun can be used for what precedes it in a text.
22. As suggested by, e.g., O'Brien, *Philippians*, 205, following Moule, "Further Reflexions on Philippians 2:5–11," 265.

Second, in both the previous and the following chapters of Philippians (1:7; 3:15), Paul also combines the neuter singular pronoun with a form of *phronein*, and in each case the pronoun functions retrospectively. In 1:7 Paul tells the Philippians that it is appropriate for him to feel or think a certain way about them:

*Kathōs estin dikaion emoi touto **phronein** hyper pantōn hymōn.*

It is right for me to **think** this way about all of you. (NRSV; NIV, NJB, RSV: "feel")

Paul has described this fitting mindset of thanksgiving, joy, and confidence in the previous verses (1:3–6). Philippians 3:15 is also a sentence in which *touto* is clearly retrospective, as indicated both by the preceding content to which it refers and by the presence of the conjunction *oun* ("therefore, so"):

*Hosoi oun teleioi, **touto phronōmen**.*

So all of us who are spiritually mature should **think this way**. (CEB)

The *phronēsis*, or way of thinking, to which Paul refers in 3:15 is contained in the paradigmatic autobiographical account found in the previous two verses, 3:3–14.

Of course we cannot restrict Paul's use of *touto* ("this") to retrospective senses, as Philippians itself makes clear,[23] but it does seem to be the case that the combination of *touto* and *phronein* is routinely retrospective. Furthermore, it appears to be the norm in Paul that the sense of a demonstrative pronoun before an imperative, as in 2:5, is retrospective.

This *syntactical* conclusion does not, however, mean that there is no prospective *semantic* significance to 2:5 as a whole. The verse functions clearly as a bridge between what precedes and what follows, and there is an obvious material, or semantic, parallel between at least 2:2–4 and 2:6–8. However, if *touto* is syntactically retrospective, then the relative pronoun ὅ/*ho* (if that is what it is) does not have to refer back to the demonstrative pronoun, because the content of *touto* has already been identified. We will return to the implications of this conclusion below.

2. φρονεῖτε *(phroneite): "Cultivate this way of thinking, feeling, and acting"*

It is quite obvious that *phronēsis* ("mindset") is on Paul's mind in Philippians (pun intended!). Forms of the verb *phronein* appear ten times in the

---

23. *Touto* is retrospective in 1:7, 19, 22, 25, 28; 3:15, but prospective in 1:6, 9. In addition, the plural *tauta* ("these things") is retrospective in 3:7; 4:8, 9.

letter, in 1:7; 2:2 (twice); 2:5; 3:15 (twice); 3:19; 4:2; and 4:10 (twice). The only other Pauline letter that remotely resembles Philippians in this regard is Romans, especially where concerns and exhortations similar to those of Paul in Philippians are expressed in Romans 12–15.[24]

The noun *phronēsis*, a common word in ancient moral philosophy, may be defined as "practical reasoning."[25] It is more than just thinking; we might refer to it as an attitude with consequences. As noted above, Stephen Fowl has translated it as a "pattern of thinking, acting, and feeling" or, more simply, "a common pattern of thinking and acting."[26] It is a combination of a perspective and a set of corollary practices. "There is clearly an intellectual component to this activity. Equally important . . . is the assumption that such a common perspective will generate, direct, and sustain a particular course of action."[27]

This practical *phronēsis* also has an emotional dimension. New Testament scholars have often neglected this aspect of early Christian spirituality.[28] But in the immediate context of 2:5 we have references to the emotional as well as the practical dimensions of Christian *phronēsis*: *paraklēsis . . . paramythion agapēs . . . splanchna kai oiktirmoi* ("encouragement . . . consolation deriving from love . . . deep affection and compassion," 2:1 MJG). Moreover, Paul expresses his profound, emotional (as well as practical) love for the Philippians by saying that he shares in the deep affection of Christ Jesus: *en splanchnois Christou Iēsou* (1:8). That is, Paul's practical-emotional affection for them has its source in the practical-emotional affection of Christ Jesus.

Paul's claim implies three things: (1) the story of Christ Jesus can be described as one of deep affection; (2) this deep affection persists into the present because Jesus is not dead but alive; and (3) others can participate in this deep affection by loving others in similar practical-emotional ways. This is in essence what it means to be "in Christ" (2:1) for both Paul and his communities. Already in Philippians 1:7, then, Paul anticipates the main point of 2:1–4 and suggests that both his and the Philippians' practical-emotional affection have a common source in the story and the living reality of Jesus, narrated in 2:6–11.

24. See the nine occurrences of forms of *phronein* in Rom. 8:5; 11:20; 12:3 (twice); 12:16 (twice); 14:6 (twice); and 15:5. Cf. the occurrences of *phronēma* in Rom. 8:6 (twice), 7, 27, and of the related adjective *phronimoi* ("understanding, sensible, wise") in Rom. 11:25 and 12:16.

25. Meeks, "Man from Heaven in Paul's Letter to the Philippians," 333.

26. See Fowl, *Philippians*, 77, 82–83 (without "feeling" in his discussion of 2:2) and 88–90 (with "feeling" in his exegesis of 2:5). Fowl does not explain why he adds "feeling," but its inclusion is appropriate, as we will see.

27. Fowl, *Philippians*, 82.

28. For exceptions, see Barton, "Spirituality and the Emotions in Early Christianity"; Hogan, *I Live, No Longer I*, 108–39.

So the *phronēsis* of which Paul speaks involves thinking, feeling, and acting. I have translated the imperative *Touto phroneite* as "Cultivate this mindset" as a way of summarizing Paul's call to this three-dimensional *phronēsis*, and followed that general imperative with an explanatory phrase that names these three elements. I have chosen the word "cultivate" to suggest that this is a process that has begun but also needs attention and, thereby, growth.[29]

3. ἐν ὑμῖν *(en hymin): "in your community"*

The translation of the phrase *en hymin* is probably the least difficult and controversial of the various parts of this verse. Both from the strong emphasis on community in Philippians and from Paul's overall understanding of ethics and spirituality as a communal experience and responsibility, we can be quite certain that the imperative is directed primarily to the community and refers to communal relations. As in 1:6 and 2:13, *en hymin* means "among yourselves," "in your community," rather than "in you as individuals in your individual lives." In fact, the attitudes and corollary practices described in 2:1–4 only make sense as community attitudes and practices, elements that should characterize life together "in Christ" and inspired by the Spirit. Moreover, as Moisés Silva suggests, Paul would probably have used the plural reflexive pronoun (*en heautois*) if he had meant to say "within yourselves."[30] The phrase *en hymin* is similar, instead, to *en allēlois* ("in/among one another") in Romans 15:5, where Paul again issues a call to unity using the verb *phronein: ho de theos . . . dōē hymin to auto phronein en allēlois* ("May the God [of steadfastness and encouragement] grant you to live in harmony with one another").

At the same time, however, there can be no community without individuals, and no community mindset without individuals displaying that mindset. This becomes especially clear and explicit in Philippians 2:4 with its emphasis on the individual (*hekastos*, "each") in relation to others. Thus Paul is really making his plea to each and to all, to the individual and to the body, to cultivate certain appropriate ways of thinking, acting, and feeling toward one another.

4. ὃ/ὁ καί *(ho/ho kai): "which is in fact" ("that is")*

If the phrase *en hymin* is the least difficult and controversial, we come now to the most challenging aspect of the verse. Its complexity has already been signaled by the six subquestions listed above. Although the phrase is clearly

---

29. That the Philippians already experience some measure of unity and love in Christ (Paul's desire expressed in 2:1–4) is clear from their joint support of Paul (1:5, 7) and his wish that their love would increase (1:9).

30. Silva, *Philippians*, 95–96.

functioning to link two parts of the verse, there is no verb after it to indicate what precisely is being linked to what, and what the significance of that link is. Hence we have the various translations, each nuancing one of the two basic options, the imitative or the locative.

I want to propose two alternatives to the standard interpretations of this phrase, either of which would provide a fresh reading of the text, a true third option beyond the imitative and locative options. Each of these alternatives yields a similar final result: that ὅ/ὁ καί (ho/ho kai) means something like "that is," a kind of id est phrase.[31]

Interpreters universally assume that the first word in this two-word phrase is the neuter singular relative pronoun ὅ/ho, "which." I will suggest shortly that since the unmarked Greek letter omicron could be either the neuter relative pronoun ὅ/ho or the masculine article ὁ/ho, this assumption needs to be challenged. But for now, let us assume that ὅ καί/ho kai (the phrase with the relative pronoun) is the right transcription of the Greek text.[32]

Alternative One: ὅ καί/ho kai (Relative Pronoun)

I argued earlier that touto is retrospective. If that is the case, then another unexamined assumption about the phrase ὅ καί/ho kai needs to be challenged immediately: the supposition that ὅ refers back to touto. But ὅ/ho only *needs* to refer to touto if touto is prospective, for then it must have something to define its content, to fill the semantic space called "this." Such content would be provided either by a vague, implicit reference to that which the Philippians already "think" (so the locative interpretation) or by the poetic narrative in 2:6–11, or at least in 2:6–8 (so the imitative interpretation). If, however, the content of "this" (touto) has already been defined as the "mindset" depicted in 2:1–4, it is not necessary for the demonstrative pronoun to be linked, via the relative pronoun, to something later in the text. Although ὅ/ho *might* still refer back to touto, it has been essentially liberated from its assumed *obligatory* syntactical and semantic role, resulting in the interpreter's freedom to explore other possible roles.

Like neuter demonstrative pronouns, neuter relative pronouns can also refer "generally to the idea or sense of the context"[33] and therefore to grammatical constructions or other generic, nongendered linguistic or semantic entities. It is quite common for a neuter relative pronoun to refer back to a phrase, clause, or word that is then explained in the clause introduced by the

---

31. Latin for "that is," often abbreviated "i.e."

32. The earliest manuscripts of the NT lacked nearly all diacritical marks, accents, etc.

33. Boyer, "Relative Clauses in the Greek New Testament," 244. According to Boyer (243, 244), more than 20 percent of the antecedents of relative pronouns in the New Testament need to be determined from the context.

relative pronoun.[34] The antecedent may be a prepositional phrase.[35] In such cases, there is *ad sensum* agreement between the neuter pronoun and the antecedent. For instance, the rather common phrase ὅ ἐστιν/*ho estin* is often used as a formula of translation (e.g., Mark 7:11; Heb. 7:2) or explanation (e.g., Mark 15:42) and is roughly equivalent to the Latin *id est*.[36]

Something like this, I suggest, is happening in Philippians 2:5 if the omicron is in fact the relative pronoun ὅ/*ho*. It is referring not to *touto* but to the nearest neuter, or neutral, linguistic item—namely, the phrase ἐν ὑμῖν/*en hymin*. In conjunction with ὅ καί/*ho kai*, the result is something approximating *id est*, an explanation formula, making the phrase *en Christō Iēsou* an apposition to *en hymin*:

> *en hymin* = in you (pl.), or in you all
> *ho kai* = "that is" (literally, "which also")
> *en Christō Iēsou* = in Christ Jesus

The missing verb, then, is the present tense of "to be"—namely, *estin*.[37] What we have here, it appears, is the suppression of the verb *estin* from the explanatory phrase *ho estin*—a common phenomenon, especially in impersonal constructions[38]—and the addition of the particle *kai*, to which we will return momentarily. We might also translate the phrase as "which is also" or "which is to say"; it functions to link the two syntactically parallel prepositional phrases and thus to show their semantic parallelism too. The point is not, however, that what is supposed to be "in you" (a certain mindset) is already in Christ, as Bockmuehl has suggested. It is rather that *en Christō Iēsou* ("in Christ Jesus") is another way of saying *en hymin* ("in you all"). G. B. Caird interpreted 2:5 similarly, calling ὅ καί/*ho kai* the equivalent of *id est* and translating the text as "This is the disposition which must govern your common life, i.e., your life in Christ Jesus, because he . . ."[39]

The expression *en Christō Iēsou* ("in Christ Jesus") is not, however, just an *additional* way of describing *en hymin* ("in you all"). It is a more

---

34. BDAG, s.v. ὅς/*hos* 1 g α, β.

35. Boyer, "Relative Clauses," citing Acts 2:39; 2 Tim. 1:5; and Heb. 12:25–26 as examples.

36. See Boyer, "Relative Clauses," 246, 248. He does not distinguish between "translation" and "explanation" formulae, lumping all NT examples into the former category, but Mark 7:11, at least, is more explanatory than translational. On *ad sensum* agreement, see also BDAG, s.v. ὅς/*hos* 1 c β. On ὅ ἐστιν/*ho estin*, see BDAG, s.v. ὅς/*hos* 1 g β; BDF 132 (2); Robertson, *Grammar of the Greek New Testament*, 713–14. The phrase is essentially genderless.

37. The imperfect *ēn* was almost never omitted (BDF 128 [3]).

38. BDF 127.

39. Caird, *Paul's Letters from Prison*, 118–19.

theologically thick way of saying *en hymin*. The reality that can be described as *en hymin* is better and ultimately understood as *en Christō Iēsou*. The particle *kai* functions adverbially, then, not merely to mean "also" but to mean "indeed" or "in fact." It is a strengthening, not merely an additive, particle in this instance.[40] The life of the corporate entity ("in [= among] you") is further defined as life in Christ. The result in our translation is "Cultivate this mindset . . . in your community, which is in fact a community in the Messiah Jesus." This interpretation, substituting "in fact" for "also" as the translation of *kai*, means that Paul is exhorting the Philippians to cultivate a mindset not because *it* was also in Christ, but because *they* are in Christ.

Alternative Two: ὁ καί/ho kai (Article)

We return now to the other potentially erroneous assumption about the phrase ὃ καί/*ho kai*. It is possible that the phrase ὃ καί/*ho kai* is really ὁ καί/*ho kai*.[41] That is, the first word may be the masculine singular nominative article. The phrase ὁ καί/*ho kai* was used in inscriptions and elsewhere to equate two names as references to one person, to say that so-and-so was also called such-and-such. There is one definite example of this linguistic phenomenon in the New Testament, in Acts 13:9:

> *Saulos de, ho kai* [ὁ καὶ] *Paulos, plēstheis pneumatos hagiou atenisas eis auton*
>
> But Saul, also known as Paul, filled with the Holy Spirit, looked intently at him . . . (NRSV)

This kind of formulation was often used to identify a Roman citizen with respect to his various names (the *praenomen, nomen,* and *cognomen*), as well as to indicate someone's alternative name used among close friends—his nickname (Latin *signum* or *supernomen*). The Latin equivalent was normally *qui et.* The phrase ὁ καί/*ho kai* was a kind of technical term for expressing the common phenomenon of "double names."[42]

---

40. See BDF 442 (10) and (11) for epexegetical ("i.e.") and ascensive ("even") uses of καί/*kai*, in addition to adjunctive ("also"). The particle can give emphasis to what follows, and after a relative pronoun it often gives a sense of independence to the following clause (BDAG, s.v. καί/*kai* 2 b, f). In some instances the particle καί/*kai* may be "colorless" (i.e., without semantic significance) when it follows the relative (so Cadbury, "Relative Pronouns in Acts and Elsewhere," 157), but in this case it seems to point emphatically to what (who) follows.

41. It is worth noting that there appears to have been some confusion among Greek speakers about the uses of ὃ/*ho* and ὁ/*ho*, resulting in some overlap in usage. See BDF 249.

42. For an older but still significant discussion, see Harrer, "Saul Who Also Is Called Paul." See also BDF 268 (1) and BDAG, s.v. καί/*kai* 2 h, for the phenomenon and secondary literature.

It is highly likely that Paul would have been familiar with the use of ὁ καί/*ho kai* to indicate double names from inscriptions, literature, or daily conversation. It is therefore quite possible that in Philippians 2:5 Paul has instinctively introduced a common expression for indicating someone's other name as he writes to the community of believers at Philippi about their double identity. He characterizes them not merely as a community but as an in-Christ community. "Have this mindset in you, since your true identity is being in Christ Jesus."

Conclusion: Renaming the Community

We now have before us two ways of construing the phrase in question, whether read as ὃ καί/*ho kai* or as ὁ καί/*ho kai*, that point in the same direction: away from seeing it as having an antecedent in *touto* and toward seeing it as equating *en hymin* and *en Christō Iēsou*. In either case, the phrase does not indicate the existence of a disposition in both "you" (the Philippians) and Christ, but rather refines the description of the Philippian community as an in-Christ community. That is who they are in the most fundamental and significant sense.

The parallelism in the text is only between *en hymin* and *en Christō Iēsou*, not between the initial clause "*Touto phroneite . . .*" and a hypothetical related clause consisting of "[verb +] *en Christō Iēsou*." The particle *kai* functions to indicate that the Philippian fellowship has another name, another—and more significant—identity. Its perspectives and practices exist not merely in a human community, but in a community constituted at the core of its being as participating in the sphere of Christ's lordship and in his identity-shaping narrative.

5. ἐν Χριστῷ Ἰησοῦ *(en Christō Iēsou): "a community in the Messiah Jesus"*

Nearly every interpreter acknowledges some sort of parallelism between *en hymin* and *en Christō Iēsou*. As already noted at various points, the phrase *en Christō Iēsou* is best read as an appositional prepositional phrase to *en hymin* and thus a description of the church's true identity: participating "in" Christ. The phrase is not, then, a reference to something (e.g., an attitude) that existed and/or continues to exist in Christ. (On this point, the locative [kerygmatic] interpreters are correct.) There are two main reasons for this position.

The first reason is the larger context of Paul's writings. Although the phrase *en Christō* and variants in Paul have various senses, they most often refer to life in the community, life together in personal relation to Christ the

Lord.[43] If 2:5 is referring to "something" in Christ, it would be a unique use of *en Christō* in Paul.

The second reason is the context of Philippians itself. A similar phrase in the immediate context (2:1) is clearly a reference to the community: *Ei tis oun paraklēsis en Christō* ("Therefore, if [there is] encouragement in Christ"). Paul is beginning a series of four conditional ("if") phrases that are actually assumptions, or "since" phrases. Together they form the basis of the imperative *plērōsate* ("make [my joy] complete") in 2:2. The phrase *en Christō* should be understood as associated with all four of these "since" phrases: since encouragement, consolation from love, participation in the Spirit, and deep affection and compassion do indeed exist in Christ (i.e., in the church), the Philippians should follow the exhortations in 2:3–4 and thereby make Paul's joy complete by the way in which they live in community, as those in Christ.

The occurrences of *en Christō* [*Iēsou*] at the beginning (2:1) and the end (2:5) of the preface to the Christ-poem function together as bookends, forming an inclusio that sets off the description of concrete practices. Another similar phrase occurs in Philippians 4:2: *Euodian parakalō kai Syntychēn parakalō to auto phronein en kyriō* ("I urge Euodia and I urge Syntyche to be of the same mind in the Lord"), which clearly echoes both 2:5 and the general exhortation at the beginning of 2:2: *hina to auto phronēte* ("be of the same mind"). Paul wants these two women to be unified in their relationship within the community constituted by the Lord Jesus.

Thus *en Christō Iēsou* in 2:5 is referring to the church, not to Christ. At the same time, however, the practices Paul calls for can and do exist in Christ (i.e., in the church) because they are analogous to what Christ himself did; those who participate in his life are shaped by him. Paul has already spoken of his participation in Christ's compassion (1:8), and he is about to narrate Christ's self-emptying and self-humbling (2:6–8) in ways that echo the exhortations in 2:3–4. Thus, although it is wrong to interpret "in Christ" as an indication of Christ's inner attitude, it is nonetheless true that there is a correlation between Christ and those in Christ, as 2:6–8 will make especially clear.[44]

43. C. Campbell, *Paul and Union with Christ*, 73, though he interprets Phil. 2:5 as a reference to Christ's interior disposition (105–6).

44. Some interpreters come to similar conclusions about the overall thrust of the passage by supplying a phrase like "as is fitting in Christ" or "as is necessary in Christ," suggesting that [*ho*] *dei phronein* (cf. Rom. 12:3), [*ho*] *prepei phronein*, or a similar phrase is implied. See, e.g., Silva, *Philippians*, 97: "Be so disposed toward one another as is proper for those who are united in Christ Jesus." This is closer to a participatory than to a purely imitative reading. Rom. 15:5 makes it clear, in either case, that Christ is the norm for the church's unified disposition: *to auto phronein en allēlois kata Christon Iēsoun* ("to live in harmony with one another, in accordance with Christ Jesus").

It is probably the vivid parallelism between the story of Jesus in 2:6–8, which stresses his death, and the community life Paul prescribes for the Philippians that explains why Paul has added "Jesus" to his typical expression "in Christ." As in 2 Corinthians 4 (discussed in the previous chapter), where the name "Jesus" appears nine times and his dying is the chapter's christological focal point, in Philippians 2 Paul is saying that the normal shape of Christian ministry and life is one that resembles the dying of Jesus. This is the kind of very human life, one of obedience to the point of death, that Jesus the Messiah and Lord lived. Paul's vision of cross-shaped participation in Christ is coherent with the Gospels' portrayal of Jesus' understanding of messiahship and his call to radical, deathlike discipleship as participation in his death. This tradition of Jesus as suffering Messiah likely stands behind Paul's own spirituality of cruciformity, and for this reason it is better to refer to the community "in Christ Jesus" as the community "in the Messiah Jesus."[45] Paul is describing not an ethic of imitation but a spirituality of participation.

The Significance of Philippians 2:5 for Paul's Theology and Spirituality

I have argued that Philippians 2:5 is best translated as "Cultivate this mindset— this way of thinking, acting, and feeling—in your community, which is in fact a community in the Messiah Jesus." This interpretation means that what is "in" Christ is not a disposition that is to be adopted or imitated, but a community that is to be shaped by the person the community inhabits, the person whose story is narrated in 2:6–11. Thus, while 2:5 is not imitative, it is also not merely locative. The location is inseparable from the story; the Messiah is inhabited only as his story is continued in analogous ways in the community. This is a theology and spirituality of participation, as Paul had already hinted in 1:8. Paul presumes a continuity between the self-emptying and self-humbling Messiah Jesus and the reigning Lord Jesus in whom the church exists.[46]

Thus Philippians 2:5 is indeed a bridge between 2:1–4 and 2:6–11, but it does not connect potential imitators to the model. Rather, Philippians 2:5 grounds Paul's exhortation in 2:1–4 in the narrative of Christ in 2:6–11, on

45. On the correspondence between Jesus and Paul in this regard, see my *Death of the Messiah*, 78–94, 106–11, 114–27. The participatory language of Jesus is about sharing in his cup and baptism (e.g., Mark 10:38).

46. This is what Bockmuehl emphasizes in arguing that the present-tense *estin* rather than the imperfect *ēn* is the missing verb in 2:5 and briefly raising the subject of participation. I agree with Bockmuehl about the suppressed verb but contend that what is in Christ is not a disposition but a community.

the assumption that this narrative defines the suffering Messiah not merely as a historical figure but as the present, living Lord. The Messiah Jesus who emptied and humbled himself is the Lord in whom the Philippians, and all Christians, live, and he in them (e.g., Gal. 2:19–20; Rom. 8:10; Col. 1:27). Because the Philippians' life together is life together in the Messiah Jesus, that common life must have the same basic pattern as did Christ's; *their* story must be shaped by *his* story, because his story identifies him and therefore them.

Paul's mode of exhortation, then, is not simply to present Christ as an example of the correct inner attitude, nor even of correct actions. Rather, Paul emphasizes the "in the Messiah Jesus" dimension of the church's existence, grounding his exhortation in that dimension: those who live in the Messiah are to be conformed to the pattern of his self-humbling and self-emptying, not merely as imitators of a model, but as persons whose fundamental identity is to participate in him and thus in his story. Paul may speak of "obedience" (Phil. 2:12), but it is an obedience to the Obedient One (2:7) and enabled by participation in him.[47]

If Philippians 2:6–11 can in some sense be called Paul's "master story,"[48] then the significance of Philippians 2:5 and of how it is a bridge between Christ and the community is weighty indeed. Again and again in Paul's letters, what looks like imitation is really participation. Even calls to "be[come] imitators of me" (e.g., 1 Cor. 4:16; 11:1) are really invitations to more thoroughgoing participation in Christ.

Furthermore, participation for Paul is a two-way street; it is not merely believers being in the Messiah but also the Messiah being in believers, as Galatians 2:19–20 and Romans 8:1, 9–10 make especially clear. Indeed, these two texts from outside Philippians remind us that the reciprocal residence of Christ and the community also exists between Christ and the individual believer. Paul may be speaking representatively in Galatians 2, but he is also speaking personally. So too, he may be speaking about the community in Philippians 2, but he also envisions a parallel personal relationship with the Messiah for all believers, as Philippians 3 makes clear.

Finally, if Philippians 2:5 is about participation in the person and story of the Messiah Jesus, it is also about the inseparability of that participation from participation in the Spirit and indeed in God the Father. We have already noted the important language about participation (*koinōnia*; "sharing" in CEB, NIV, NRSV) in the Spirit in 2:1. Paul's theological ethic (if that is even the right name for it), or spirituality (or mysticism), is one in which the reality

---

47. The obedience to which Paul calls the Philippians is not to himself (contra CEB, NRSV).
48. See esp. Gorman, *Cruciformity*, 23, 88–94, 164–74, 366–67, 383–85, 400–401.

of a living Messiah and an active Spirit make the Christlike life possible. We must also note that Paul credits God (the Father) as well, in 2:13, as he says that "God . . . is at work in your community [*en hymin*], enabling all of you together both to will and to work for his good pleasure" (MJG). Furthermore, if the case for translating *en morphē theou hyparchōn* in 2:6 as "because he was in the form of God," rather than (or in addition to) "although he was in the form of God," is found convincing (see chaps. 1–2 above), it will be necessary to conclude that Paul's participatory spirituality is about self-giving love as sharing in the very character and life of God.[49]

All of this is to say that Paul's theology and his notion of participation, his spirituality, is not merely cruciform or Christocentric; it is not merely charismatic, focusing on the Spirit; it is inclusive of Father, Son, and Spirit. Here in Philippians 2 we see yet more evidence that Paul's theology and spirituality of participation were inherently trinitarian, even if his language did not fully express what came to fruition later. And this implicit trinitarian theology and spirituality is why it is appropriate to speak of Philippians 2:5 not only as a *textual* bridge but also as a *theological* one: a bridge from Paul to the doctrine of the Trinity and to the spirituality of theosis, or deification: transformative participation in the life of the Triune God.[50]

But Philippians 2:5, in context, makes it quite clear that such theosis—or, more simply, transformation and life, or resurrectional cruciformity—comes primarily not through contemplation or private holiness but through service to others and faithful, even sacrificial witness to the world (Phil. 1:27–2:4; 2:12–16).[51] It is by such participation in the exalted crucified Jesus that fullness of life and of God is found.

---

49. Cf. my *Inhabiting the Cruciform God*, 9–39, and the literature cited there.
50. On Paul and the Trinity, see Hill, *Paul and the Trinity*, and the literature cited there.
51. On missional theosis in Paul, see my *Becoming the Gospel*.

five

The Apocalyptic New Covenant and the Shape of Life in the Spirit according to Galatians

I n the last chapter we saw that the life of resurrectional cruciformity is a communal life in Jesus the Messiah. At the end of the chapter, we noted that this life is actually life in the Father, Son, and Spirit. Thus far we have spoken at length about life in Christ and even in the Father, and thus about Christosis and theosis. In this chapter we explore more fully the meaning of life in Christ as life in the Spirit. We do so by looking at the Letter to the Galatians and at two aspects of Paul's theology and spirituality that are sometimes thought to be in tension with each other: covenant theology (specifically new-covenant theology) and apocalyptic theology.

Paul the Apocalyptic Figure

There is more than one sense to the term "apocalyptic," and more than one way in which Paul was an apocalyptic figure. There is little doubt that Paul viewed the coming, death, and resurrection of Jesus as a disruptive, divine, liberating "invasion" or "incursion," and that the term "apocalyptic" can be appropriately used to characterize that saving event. But Christopher Rowland has rightly drawn our attention to Paul's apocalyptic autobiographical statements in Galatians 1:

96

For I did not receive it [the gospel] from a human source, nor was I taught it, but I received it through a revelation of Jesus Christ [*alla di' apokalypseōs Iēsou Christou*]. (Gal. 1:12)

[15]God . . . was pleased [16]to reveal his Son to me [*apokalypsai ton huion autou en emoi*; or "in me," NET, NIV, NJB], so that I might proclaim him among the Gentiles. (Gal. 1:15–16)

Rowland argues that Paul was an apocalyptic figure because he received a revelation, an *apokalypsis*, and not because of a particular theological perspective or agenda that could be called "apocalyptic."[1]

I want to develop, but also nuance, Rowland's view, the nuance being the rejection of the possible implications in his statement that (1) experience and theology should be pitted against each other and (2) Paul is only, or at least primarily, apocalyptic experientially. We should resist this kind of unnecessary and ultimately unhelpful dichotomy.[2] Paul's apocalyptic experience shaped his apocalyptic theology (including his "politics"), and his apocalyptic theology helped him to interpret, and likely also shaped, his apocalyptic experience.

Focusing on Galatians, I wish to make four main points about Paul as an apocalyptic figure under the general rubric of the apocalyptic new covenant and the shape of life in the Spirit—an attempt to hold together Paul's apocalyptic experience and his apocalyptic theology as well as his apocalyptic and his new-covenant perspectives:[3]

1. With N. T. Wright and others, I contend that Paul is both an *apocalyptic* theologian and a *covenant* theologian—and specifically a *new*-covenant theologian. What is revealed, or "apocalypsed," is the radically unexpected and new way in which the new covenant has come to fruition.[4]

---

1. See, e.g., Rowland, "Paul and the Apocalypse of Jesus Christ."

2. I do not mean that Rowland himself is necessarily guilty of such a dichotomy.

3. For another effort at holding two perspectives (similar to the ones described here) together with respect to Galatians, see Bird, *Anomalous Jew*, 108–69.

4. See esp. Wright, *Paul and the Faithfulness of God*, e.g., 1013, 1025, 1038, 1071–72, 1262–63, 1513. Wright appears to concur (e.g., 725, 984) that Paul is speaking of what I am calling the "apocalyptic new covenant." See also Shaw, "Apocalyptic and Covenant." Shaw argues that recent "apocalyptic" interpreters actually unknowingly espouse new-covenant themes. Shaw erroneously maintains, however, that apocalyptic interpreters need to admit "a greater place for forensic categories in Paul's thought" in order to acknowledge his new-covenant framework (168). Rather, in this chapter I argue that full recognition of a claim made by J. Louis Martyn, which Shaw cites approvingly (160n9), is closer to what is needed: recognizing an analogy between divine invasion and the prophetic promise of a new heart and spirit (Martyn, "Afterword: The Human Moral Drama," 164n13). See also Davies, *Paul among the Apocalypses?*; Davies, "Two Ages and Salvation History"; and Hays, "Apocalyptic *Poiēsis* in Galatians."

2. Borrowing Wright's language, we need to recognize how Paul has re-worked his theology of the new covenant in light of God's apocalyptic incursion into human history and life in the Messiah and the Spirit—and specifically Paul's *experience* of the Messiah and the Spirit.

3. A critical aspect of the content of Paul's revelation is that the gracious "invasion" of God's Spirit (Ezekiel) and Law (Jeremiah) into the hearts of God's people that was associated with the promised new covenant has, in fact, occurred, but in a shocking, cruciform mode. This fulfill-ment is expressed in the language of the faithful and loving Messiah who now indwells Paul (and, implicitly, all believers; Gal. 2:19–20), the presence of the Spirit of the Son in believers' hearts (Gal. 4:6), and believers' fulfilling the "Law of the Messiah" (Gal. 6:2).[5]

4. Thus, to return to the conjunction of Galatians 1:12 and 1:16, the reve-lation *to* Paul and the revelation *in* Paul are inseparable—a claim that is developed most fully in 2 Corinthians but also in Galatians itself. By means of the invading and indwelling Messiah / Spirit / Law of the Mes-siah, Paul becomes his gospel (i.e., embodies his gospel), and he expects others to do so similarly—to live out the new covenant of faithfulness and love, the beginning of the new creation.

That is to say, the in-breaking of God into human history in Jesus' new-covenant-inaugurating death and in the gift of the Spirit necessarily includes a divine in-breaking into the lives of individual human beings to create a community of the new covenant that embodies the character of that divine invasion. The result is both shockingly new and surprisingly continuous with the prophetic promises in Scripture.[6]

The Promise of the New Covenant

Promises of a renewed or new covenant are associated with the prophets Jer-emiah and Ezekiel as well as Deuteronomy. Jeremiah and Ezekiel addressed similar situations with similar, though not identical, promises. Both employ the idiom of the covenant: YHWH being the people's God, and the people

5. Throughout this chapter I have deliberately used an uppercase initial letter for most occur-rences of the words "Law" and "Spirit" (altering English translations where necessary) in order to indicate that they are proper nouns, having specific referents and functioning essentially as technical terms. This is true even for translations of *nomos* in Paul, even if there is debate about whether a specific occurrence should be rendered "Torah," "Jewish Law," or something else.

6. See also my *Death of the Messiah*, esp. (for Paul) 51–68, 89–94, 109–11, 118–27, 135–36, 141–61, 186–95.

being YHWH's people. Yet Jeremiah actually uses the term "new covenant" and speaks of the *Law* being put within God's people, specifically in their hearts, while Ezekiel does not use the term "new covenant" (though he does speak of a "covenant of peace" and "an everlasting covenant"[7]) and talks about God's own *Spirit* being put within the people.[8] This is certainly the language of divine-human interaction, and thus explicitly of presence and participation, and implicitly of transformation.

Moreover, both prophets speak metaphorically but realistically of something happening to the people's heart(s), though precisely what that is varies: the inscription of God's Law (Jer. 31:33);[9] a transplant (Jer. 24:7; Ezek. 18:31; 36:26), involving a softening or "fleshification" (Ezek. 11:19; 36:26); circumcision (Jer. 4:4; cf. Ezek. 44:7, 9);[10] and unification (Jer. 32:39; Ezek. 11:19). *For both Jeremiah and Ezekiel, then, the heart is the heart of the problem.*[11] The purpose of the divine activity on and in the people's hearts is clearly indicated by Ezekiel: "so that they may follow my statutes and keep my ordinances and obey them," and thus "they shall be my people, and I will be their God" (Ezek. 11:20; cf. 36:27). This is the language of both covenant fulfillment and the covenant "formula"—the idiom of a unified people in proper relation to God.[12] At the same time, it is obviously the language of transformation. Similarly, Deuteronomy 30:6–10 promises a covenant renewal that will consist of heart-circumcision followed by love of God and observation of the commandments (cf. 10:16–22).

Jeremiah's "I will write it [my Law] on their hearts; and I will be their God, and they shall be my people" (Jer. 31:33; 38:33 LXX, with "laws" plural) is more or less equivalent to Ezekiel's "I will remove the heart of stone from

7. E.g., Ezek. 16:60 (everlasting covenant); 34:25 (covenant of peace); 37:26 (both).

8. See Ezek. 36:26–27 (NETS): "And I will give you a new heart, and a new spirit I will give in you [*en hymin*], and I will remove the stone heart from your flesh and give you a heart of flesh. And I will give my spirit in you [*en hymin*] and will act so that you walk in my statutes and keep my judgments and perform them." Cf. Ezek. 11:19 (NETS): "And I will give them another heart, and I will impart a new spirit in them [*en autois*]." Although NETS renders *pneuma* as "spirit" (lowercase *s*), I will discuss these texts from Ezekiel using "Spirit" (uppercase *S*) on the assumption that what is being given is the actual presence of God.

9. Jer. 38:33 LXX (NETS): "I will give my laws in their mind [*eis tēn dianoian autōn*], and I will write them on their hearts [*kardias*]."

10. Ezekiel describes the foreigner as "uncircumcised in heart and uncircumcised in flesh" (Ezek. 44:7, 9 NETS), implying the need for circumcision of the heart to be part of the covenant people. Thus, as we will see below, internalization and obedience to the law are not antithetical; the latter results from the former, as Paul also says in, e.g., Rom. 8:3–4.

11. E.g., Ezek. 3:7; 14:3–7; 16:30; 28:5, 17; Jer. 5:23; 9:14; 12:2; 17:1; 32:40 (39:40 LXX).

12. The prophetic promises of land restoration (e.g., Ezek. 36:24, 28) also stress the recreation of such a covenant community and carry through into Paul in terms of community, if not in terms of land itself.

their flesh and give them a heart of flesh, so that they may follow my statutes and keep my ordinances and obey them" (Ezek. 11:19–20). Furthermore, Ezekiel's parallel phrases "a new heart I will give you" and "a new spirit I will put within you" (Ezek. 36:26; cf. 11:19; 18:31), which is in fact "my [God's] Spirit" (Ezek. 36:27), suggest that his understanding of what God will do to the heart with the Spirit is fundamentally synonymous with Jeremiah's vision of the inscription of the Law on the people's hearts. The new covenant will be a powerful act of divine grace entailing

- the people's receipt of the Law or the Spirit within;
- their inner transformation; and
- their consequent faithfulness to the covenant.

Clearly, for both Jeremiah and Ezekiel, as well as Deuteronomy, there is no disjunction between internalization of the covenant and external adherence to its stipulations, between the heart and obedience. Taking the two prophets together, we must also deny any disjunction between the Spirit and the Law—a subject to which we will return in considering Paul.

Indeed, it is likely that Paul, like certain other scriptural interpreters of his era, read these key texts from Jeremiah, Ezekiel, and Deuteronomy together, as a collective witness to God's anticipated activity among and within the people of God.[13] Moreover, this coming divine action was envisioned not only as a new (or renewed) covenant but also as the restoration of Israel and as a new creation—and more.[14] This merger of metaphors is especially potent in Ezekiel 36–37, where images of forgiveness and cleansing, a new heart, a new spirit (the indwelling of God's Spirit), restoration to the land, and abundant living (Ezek. 36:25–38) are then graphically displayed as resurrection (or re-vivification), as new creation, in the famous vision of dry bones in Ezekiel 37.

It is difficult, then, not to think about this promised new-covenant activity of divine heart surgery as a sort of divine incursion—in other words, as an apocalyptic event. Paul appears to have been thinking similarly. As J. Louis Martyn said, Paul's "divine *invasion* . . . has a highly illuminating theological analogue in Ezekiel 11:19."[15] If Ezekiel is any indication, Paul himself could

13. See Wells, *Grace and Agency*, esp. the summaries on 221 (including n. 52) and 275; cf. 12–13, 24, 134–39, 255–69.

14. On eschatological restoration (including new exodus), see Wells, *Grace and Agency*; R. Morales, *The Spirit and the Restoration of Israel*. On new creation specifically, see Yates, *The Spirit and Creation in Paul*, with special attention to Ezek. 36–37 in Paul's theology.

15. Martyn, "Afterword: The Human Moral Drama," 164n13, in a discussion of agency in Paul (emphasis his).

also blend images of covenant renewal and new creation, resulting in what we are calling an "apocalyptic new covenant." We find the phrases "new covenant" and "new creation" (the latter generally understood in an apocalyptic sense), of course, in 2 Corinthians (3:6; 5:17), but only "new creation" in Galatians (6:15). Yet Martyn's insightful observation, together with the merger of metaphors in both Ezekiel and 2 Corinthians, suggests that we should anticipate both apocalyptic language and new-covenant language in Galatians. As Richard Hays notes, "God's 'apocalyptic' act in Christ does not simply shatter and sweep away creation and covenant; rather, it hermeneutically reconfigures creation and covenant, under the guidance of the Spirit, in light of cross and resurrection."[16]

The Apocalypse "in" Paul

As noted at the beginning of this chapter, in Galatians 1:15–16a Paul claims that God was pleased "to reveal his Son to me [*apokalypsai ton huion autou en emoi*]," as many translations render it. But some also translate this phrase as "to reveal his Son *in* me" (emphasis added).[17] So what does Paul mean when he states that God was pleased to reveal the Son *en emoi*? To consider this question, we turn to the recent work of one of the self-identified apocalyptic interpreters of Paul, Martinus de Boer. De Boer summarizes the scholarly debate about *en emoi* in 1:16 as offering three main interpretations, to which he adds his own (no. 4):[18]

1. "to me" (equivalent to a simple dative)
2. "through me" (through Paul's preaching)
3. "within me" (an inner, subjective experience)
4. "in my former manner of life"

While each of the first two interpretations is possible, the strength of the last two is that each recognizes the "locative" semantic value of *en*, implying that Paul would have used a simple dative or a preposition such as *dia* ("through") had he intended to signify either mere receipt of the revelation (no. 1) or kerygmatic instrumentality (no. 2). The translation "within me" (no. 3), referring primarily to an inner, subjective experience, does not,

16. Hays, "Apocalyptic *Poiēsis* in Galatians," 205.
17. The translation "to" is found in, e.g., CEB, NAB, NRSV, RSV; "in" is used in, e.g., NASB, NET, NIV, NJB.
18. De Boer, *Galatians*, 93.

however, correspond to the way Paul elsewhere narrates his encounter with the risen Christ as the Lord's appearing to him (cf. 1 Cor. 9:1; 15:8).

De Boer's proposal (no. 4) is therefore helpful because it retains the locative sense of the subjective interpretation (no. 3) while foregrounding the apocalyptic and public character of the experience. That is, "God entered into the life of Paul, the persecutor of God's church . . . in order to bring that manner of life to a complete and irrevocable end." In other words, "Paul personifies the radical discontinuity between the two ages (this one and the one to come) of all apocalyptic eschatology."[19] What God has done apocalyptically in Christ to and for the world, God has also done apocalyptically to and for Paul.

What Paul is referring to in Galatians 1:16, therefore, according to de Boer, is Paul's "conversion" (de Boer's term).[20] Moreover, argues de Boer, Paul continues this apocalyptic interpretation of his conversion and its aftereffects in Galatians 2:15–21, especially in 2:19–20, where (de Boer contends) Paul re-narrates the "Damascus road" experience in which he was crucified with Christ and died to the Law, as his nomistically determined self was ended and a new life was begun.[21] The crucifixion of the old self, says de Boer, is another way of interpreting the death of Paul's old, Pharisaical self. Not only Paul, however, but everyone who believes in Christ (2:16) "participates in, is joined to or taken up into, this all-embracing, cosmic, apocalyptic event that spells the end of the old age."[22]

De Boer rightly notes Paul's reuse of the phrase *en emoi* from 1:16 in 2:20—Christ lives *en emoi*. The difference between the two uses, he avers, is that the earlier one refers to Paul's *former* life and the later one to Paul's *apostolic* life.[23] Although de Boer does not "exclude the notion of Christ's dwelling inside Paul (or the believer) in some sense"—he points to Galatians 4:6 ("God has sent the Spirit of his Son into our hearts")—Paul's emphasis, according to de Boer, is on the public domain of human affairs and interpersonal relationships.[24]

Although de Boer moves in the right direction by interpreting the revelation "in" Paul as a reference to a public reality and connecting it (strongly) to Galatians 2:15–21 and (less strongly) to Galatians 4:6, he also unnecessarily limits the referent of *en emoi* to Paul's conversion and misses Paul's allusions to the new covenant. What I propose, then, is that Paul's self-portrayal as the

---

19. De Boer, *Galatians*, 93.
20. De Boer, *Galatians*, 89. By "conversion" de Boer means God's conversion of Paul "from his manner of life in Judaism to Christ" (89n143; cf. 77n120).
21. De Boer, *Galatians*, 159–63. "Damascus road" is again his term (160).
22. De Boer, *Galatians*, 161.
23. De Boer, *Galatians*, 161–62. I will offer a different interpretation below.
24. De Boer, *Galatians*, 162n242.

apocalyptically "invaded" persecutor, who has been crucified (and raised) with the Messiah, is simultaneously a self-portrayal as the recipient of the surprising Spirit of the new covenant that enables him, and all believers, to embody the cruciform pattern of the Messiah's self-giving love: the "Law of the Messiah" (Gal. 6:2 MJG). This is the case, I suggest, even though the term "new covenant" does not appear in Galatians and the Spirit is explicitly associated with the fulfillment of the "old" (that is, the original) covenant with Abraham.[25]

Rereading Galatians as Witness to the Apocalyptic New Covenant

De Boer rightly sees three key passages in Galatians as interconnected texts: 1:15–16; 2:20; and 4:4–6. We will consider them in reverse order.

Galatians 4:4–6

The first thing to note about Galatians 4:4–6 is its apocalyptic flavor. The phrase about "the fullness of time" is, among other things, "an apocalyptic assertion."[26] But this apocalyptic event of benign invasion, of liberation and redemption, occurs in two steps: (1) the sending forth of the Son followed by (2) the sending forth of the Spirit. The cosmic divine event in Christ becomes existentially real for human beings through the work of the Spirit (cf. Rom. 5:1–11). What takes place "out there" must, and does, also take place "in here," in the intimate space of knowledge and imagination (the heart) that issues in corresponding activity in the world. Paul will later speak about this activity as walking "by," or better "in," the Spirit (*pneumati*, Gal. 5:16) and being led by the Spirit (5:18) in order to bear the fruit of the Spirit (5:22–23).[27]

The next thing to note about Galatians 4:4–6, then, is the phrase "God has sent the Spirit of his Son into our hearts [*exapesteilen ho theos to pneuma tou huiou autou eis tas kardias hēmōn*]" (4:6). The divine action is described, by its use of "Spirit" and "hearts" (cf. Rom. 5:5), in language echoing the

25. Even Richard Hays, in arguing for a similar understanding of "the law of Christ," does not mention the phrase "new covenant." See Hays, "Christology and Ethics in Galatians." His thesis is that a "careful reading of the evidence will suggest that 'the law of Christ' is a formulation coined (or employed) by Paul" as a reference to "the paradigmatic self-giving of Jesus Christ" as the "definitive expression" of *agapē* (274–75).

26. De Boer, *Galatians*, 262.

27. "In" the Spirit is to be preferred for *pneumati* in 5:16 because it indicates the sphere in which the community of believers exists and moves forward. The location of the Spirit in believers, and vice versa, may be called "mutual indwelling" or "reciprocal residence" (discussed below).

prophetic promises of a new covenant in Jeremiah and Ezekiel, though it is not a direct quote from either prophet.[28] The focus on the heart as the object of divine action appears also in Romans 2:25–29, where the image of heart-circumcision is reminiscent of both prophets as well as Deuteronomy. Paul sees the prophetic promise of a new covenant fulfilled in the gift of the Spirit's being sent into people's hearts. Curiously, although de Boer correctly notes the echo of Ezekiel 36:26 and Jeremiah 31:33–34 in Galatians 4:4–6, he does not mention the phrase "new covenant."[29] Similarly, in his commentary, Martyn notes the allusion to Jeremiah and Ezekiel, and he speaks vividly and apocalyptically of the divine "invasion" of the heart/the human being, but he does not call this the inauguration of the new covenant.[30]

It seems clear, however, if we put our first two observations about this passage together, that what Paul is talking about is an apocalyptic new covenant. There are elements of both continuity and discontinuity with the specific prophetic promises. We should not be surprised if there is something unexpected about the fulfillment of these promises, especially since the promised Spirit arrives with a significant qualifier—as the *messianic* Spirit.

The third thing to note about Galatians 4:4–6, then, is that this Spirit is specifically the Spirit of the Son (cf. Rom. 8:9; Phil. 1:19). The identity of the *promised* Spirit, now the *present* Spirit, has been reconfigured in terms of God's Son, the Messiah Jesus. In other words, this is the apocalyptic Spirit, and that in two senses: the Spirit of the Jesus who has been apocalypsed, and the Spirit who participates in the divine apocalyptic activity of liberating people from this age and giving them a share in the life of the age to come that was inaugurated by God's action in Christ. Thus, Paul is continuing here (cf. 3:1–5) to forge an inseparable bond between the Spirit and the Messiah Jesus, which of course means the *crucified* Messiah, now raised by the Father.

Although Paul's main point in using the language of sonship and adoption is the connection between Jesus' sonship and ours, the language of knowing God as "Abba, Father" also continues the new-covenant theme. In Jeremiah's promise of a new covenant and similar texts, we see the covenant formula about the intimate bond between God and the people: "I will be their God, and they shall be my people" (Jer. 31:33 [38:33 LXX]).[31] The "Abba, Father" relationship described in Galatians 4:4–6 (cf. Rom. 8:15–16) is, in part, the restatement of

---

28. See esp. Boakye, *Death and Life*, 65–71.

29. De Boer, *Galatians*, 265.

30. Martyn, *Galatians*, 391–92. In fairness to de Boer and Martyn, I note that most commentators do not mention the new covenant in commenting on this text. In personal conversation, however, de Boer (my teacher) told me that Martyn (his teacher) effectively forbade mention of the word "covenant."

31. Cf. Jer. 24:7; 30:22; 32:38 (39:38 LXX); Ezek. 11:20; 14:11; 36:28; 37:23, 27.

that covenant formula in light of the apocalypse of Jesus as God's Son, and the corollary reconfiguration of the Spirit as the one who relates people covenantally to both God the Father and Jesus the Son. This covenantal, Father-Son relationship now extends, surprisingly, beyond Israel to include the gentiles. In the giving of the Messiah and the Spirit of the Messiah, God is speaking the language of (new) covenant, saying, "I am your Father, and you are my children" (cf. Rev. 21:7). God's people/children, both Jew and gentile, respond, "Abba!"

So what we have, finally, is an apocalyptic new covenant in which, at the initiative of God the Father, Christ effects humanity's liberation and redemption, and the Spirit establishes and maintains a residential, new-covenant relationship between God the Father and God's adopted children. It is nearly impossible (once again)[32] to resist a trinitarian conclusion regarding Paul's theology and spirituality. His explicit language elsewhere, in one breath, of the Spirit being the Spirit of both the Son and the Father (Rom. 8:9) makes this conclusion even more inevitable. In any case, the identification of the indwelling Spirit as the Spirit of the Son drives us back to Galatians 2:15–21.

Galatians 2:15–21

I will argue in the next chapter, as I have done more briefly elsewhere, that the one and only subject of Galatians 2:15–21 is justification.[33] Co-crucifixion with Christ and being inhabited by Christ are not separate or additional topics but key elements in Paul's reconfiguration of justification around a crucified and resurrected Messiah. Justification is both participatory and transformative. It is transformative as an experience of death and resurrection, of co-crucifixion and new life. It is participatory as an event that occurs "in the Messiah" (*en Christō*, 2:17) and results in having the Messiah living within (*zē de en emoi Christos* ["but the Messiah lives in me"], 2:20). The phrase *en emoi* in 2:20 is of particular interest to us in this chapter.

The Indwelling of the Son/Spirit as Identity Marker

Galatians 2:20 can be translated "Thus I myself no longer live, but the Messiah lives in me; and the life I do now live in the flesh, I live by means of the faithfulness of the Son of God, who loved me by giving himself for me" (MJG).[34] I contend that Paul is also here speaking about the apocalyptic new

32. See the final section of the previous chapter, "The Significance of Philippians 2:5 for Paul's Theology and Spirituality."

33. See also my *Inhabiting the Cruciform God*, 63–72.

34. It is beyond the scope of this chapter to defend in any detail the translation and interpretation offered of the critical texts in this passage. See, briefly, my *Inhabiting the Cruciform God*, 63–72, 76–85, and chap. 6 of the present book.

covenant and, specifically, the existential impact of God's incursion into his life and indeed the life of all believers. Paul's first-person language is meant to be representative.

Although explicit covenant or new-covenant language does not appear in this passage, it has been widely and rightly advocated by the "New Perspective" on Paul that justification is about membership in the covenant, even if the New Perspective occasionally overemphasized ecclesiology (or, more precisely, the corporate dimension of justification) at the expense of the individual. What has completely reshaped the terms of justification for Paul, and thus also of covenant membership, is the apocalyptic event of Jesus' death and resurrection. Covenant membership, or the right relations with God that effect or demonstrate covenant membership, is by death and resurrection with the Messiah. The crucified person, whether Jew or gentile, rises to new life, a new life characterized most fundamentally by the presence of the indwelling Messiah/Son of God. This means, according to most interpreters, that the Spirit inhabits believers. As suggested above, this interpretation is implicitly confirmed by the following passage, Galatians 3:1–5, in which Paul associates the coming of the Spirit with the preaching of the crucified Messiah, and it is explicitly confirmed in 4:6 when Paul writes about God's sending "the Spirit of his Son into our hearts."[35] That is, the crucified Messiah is the resurrected Messiah, and his Spirit brings new life, effecting revivification—as God's Spirit, according to Ezekiel 37, was poised to do.[36]

It is thus absolutely critical for Paul that Christ (or, better, the Messiah) is the indwelling one, that this Spirit is specifically the Spirit *of the Son* (4:6). The apocalyptic event that has made justification, liberation, and redemption a reality is the concrete faithful and loving activity of the Son in his death. Galatians 2:20 picks up from Galatians 1:4 that the death of Jesus was his self-sacrificial activity, telling us now that it was not only apocalyptically liberating ("who gave himself for our sins to set us free from the present evil age," 1:4) but also covenantally faithful to God and loving toward us: "I live by means of the faithfulness of the Son of God, who loved me by giving himself for me" (2:20 MJG). Paul is describing the Son's apocalyptic death as the fulfillment of the covenantal requirements of love for God (meaning faithfulness to God) and love for others. It is the crucified and now resurrected Son who embodies, indeed who *is*, this apocalyptic-covenantal reality that "invades" human beings. The implication is that to be inhabited by *this* Messiah, to

35. Richard Longenecker (*Galatians*, 174) calls the phrase "into our hearts" from 4:6 a "collective synonym" for the phrase "in me" in 2:20. It may be better to say that 2:20 individualizes the more corporate, prophetic perspective of 4:6.

36. On Gal. 2:19–20 and Ezek. 37, see Boakye, *Death and Life*, 112–19.

receive the Spirit of *this* Son in fulfillment of the prophetic promises about the new-covenant gift of the Spirit within, is to die and rise to a new self, to a new, apocalyptically shaped form of covenant existence characterized by cruciform faithfulness and love. The identity marker of covenant membership is now the presence of the (lovingly) invading, indwelling Messiah/Son of God—that is, the Spirit of the Son—who enables covenant fulfillment (cf. Rom. 8:3–4).

The Law of the Messiah

An immediate objection to this line of thinking would be simply to quote Galatians 2:19a: "For I myself, through the Law, died in relation to the Law so that I might live in relation to God [*egō gar dia nomou nomō apethanon, hina theō zēsō*]" (MJG). The antithesis of the Law and God would seem to rule out any implicit reference to the new covenant, which is said to reinscribe the Law on people's hearts. But if, as Paul later says, the fundamental issue about the Law has to do with relying on it once the Messiah and faith (or faithfulness) have arrived and the written Law's function has ceased (3:23–24), then it is not impossible to think that Paul would allow for the existence of a reconfigured Law that is not the *basis* of justification but the *expression* of it, Law summarized in the words "faithfulness" issuing in "love" (5:6)— what we might call the "Law [*nomos*] of the Messiah" (as Paul does in 6:2) associated with the presence of the Spirit. We, of course, struggle with how to translate the *nomos* of 6:2 into English ("law," "principle," etc.), but Paul is not engaged in dealing with a source and a target language. Rather, his use of *nomos* in 6:2 indicates that there is continuity with his overall argument about *nomos* in Galatians, but his specific usage of the word—in connection with the Messiah and in the context of discussing the work of the Spirit—implies as well a certain discontinuity with previous understandings of *nomos*. Paul is singing *nomos* in a new key.

Accordingly, when Paul speaks of "the Law of the Messiah," he is likely once again speaking about the indwelling of Christ, not in terms of the internalized *Spirit* promised by Ezekiel, as in 4:6, but in terms of the internalized *Law* promised by Jeremiah. Yet for Paul, I would argue, these two promises and their fulfillments are one and the same. Richard Hays rightly suggests that we understand this "Law" as the "pattern" of Christ, a normative pattern (or "life-pattern") of self-giving love that gives expression to the faith, or faithfulness, of Christ.[37] It is important to stress that this is the pattern of both the dying and the indwelling Messiah, the latter continuous with the former. The primary point is that the presence of the living, crucified Son of

---

37. Hays, "Christology and Ethics in Galatians," esp. 273, 278, 280–83, 286–90.

God, the presence of "the Spirit of the Son," will shape people into Christ-like, faithful, and loving individuals and communities (5:6). This formational activity is clearly for Paul the work of the Spirit, as the context of 5:6 makes plain (5:16–6:8).[38]

I suggest, then, that Paul has interpreted the complementary prophetic promises that God would place "my" *pneuma* and "my" *nomos* (i.e., the Spirit and the Law of God) within the people of God as having been fulfilled in the indwelling presence of the *pneuma tou huiou autou* (4:6) and of the *nomos tou Christou* (6:2)—the Spirit and the Law of God's Son/the Messiah. To be sure, Paul only explicitly says that the *Spirit* of the Son—not the *Law* of the Son—has been sent "into our hearts" (4:6). Nonetheless, there is an implicit theological link between the indwelling Spirit and the indwelling Law: love.

The fruit of the Spirit's presence is love (5:22), which can only mean Christ-like, cruciform love (2:20).[39] But love is also connected to Law in Galatians. Those who, by the Spirit, practice Christlike servant-love (5:13) are, ironically, embodying the very *nomos* that could not justify them (3:11) because the whole Law is "fulfilled" in the love command (5:14). Furthermore, since the syntactically and semantically similar phrases about serving one another in love (*dia tēs agapēs douleuete allēlois*, 5:13) and bearing one another's burdens (*Allēlōn ta barē bastazete*, 6:2) have to do with the fulfillment of *nomos*—either "the" *nomos* (5:13) or "the Messiah's" *nomos* (6:2)[40]—it also stands to reason that, in some fundamental sense, the presence of the love-enabling *Spirit* of the Messiah implies the presence of the *Law* of the Messiah. Thus, Paul makes a tight connection between those who "have received the Spirit" (*hoi pneumatikoi*, 6:1) and those who practice the Law of the Messiah (6:2). Moreover, although Paul does not say that this *nomos* of the Messiah is inscribed on the Galatians' hearts, such a claim may be implied, for Paul can clearly conceive of a textually indwelt heart. In Romans, for instance, he will quote and interpret Deuteronomy 30 (which refers to heart-circumcision): "'The word is near you, on your lips and in your heart' (that is, the word of faith that we proclaim)" (Rom. 10:8). Kyle Wells has argued convincingly that this "eschatological Torah" written on people's hearts means, for Paul, the "presence and agency" of Christ that comes with union with him, to

38. The Spirit is mentioned ten times in these verses.

39. On this, see my "Holy Spirit and Cruciformity."

40. Gal. 5:13 is followed in 5:14 by the statement "For the whole law is summed up in a single commandment, 'You shall love your neighbor as yourself.'" Gal. 6:2 reads, "Bear one another's burdens, and in this way you will fulfill the law of the Messiah" (NRSV alt.). Interestingly, the reciprocal pronoun ("one another") appears repeatedly in chap. 5, starting with *allēlois* in v. 13 (followed by vv. 15 [2x], 17, 26 [2x]) and then for the final time in 6:2 (*Allēlōn*).

which Galatians 2:20 bears witness.[41] The Messiah and his *nomos* are, for Paul, inseparable.

With respect to 2:20, then, de Boer is partly right to say that *en emoi* means "in Paul's current apostolic ministry," which is public and visible.[42] But because Paul is not merely speaking autobiographically, this life of faithfulness and love is also meant for *all* who are inhabited by the Messiah (i.e., by the Spirit and the Law of the Messiah) and who live in him.[43] The *cosmic*, apocalyptic, new-world-creating and new-covenant-creating event must and does become an *intimate*, apocalyptic, and new-person-creating event. The knowledge that Christ gave himself for *our* sins to liberate *us* from the present evil age (Gal. 1:4) must also become the personal knowledge that he loved *me* by giving himself for *me* (Gal. 2:20).[44]

Moreover, the death of Paul and of all believers has a starting point but no ending point in this life. The perfect verb *synestaurōmai* ("I have been crucified") suggests an ongoing reality. The paradox is that the resurrected self is always also the crucified self, just as the resurrected Jesus remains the crucified Jesus. This ongoing crucifixion is not, however, something that kills but something that gives life, for it is nothing other than a life of Messiah-like faithfulness and love. It is *resurrectional* cruciformity—a death that brings about life for both self and others, as Paul says especially in 2 Corinthians 4:10: "[We are] always carrying in our body the dying of Jesus so that the life of Jesus may also be made visible [*phanerōthē*] in our bodies" (MJG). That is, Paul, speaking with and for others, has become the apocalypse that has claimed his life and set him free. Christ is being revealed in his body, his life. Paul likely implies the same thing in Galatians itself: in the apostle's ministry, "Jesus Christ was publicly exhibited as crucified" (*Iēsous Christos proegraphē estaurōmenos*, 3:1), and Paul "carr[ies] the marks of Jesus branded on [his] body" (*ta stigmata tou Iēsou en tō sōmati mou bastazō*, 6:17).

This discussion now points us back to Galatians 1:16 and Paul's claim that God was pleased to reveal his son *en emoi*.

41. Wells, *Grace and Agency*, 269–75, esp. 273–74. Wells (255–69) also finds connections between the promised Law-inscription in the heart, love, and moral transformation in Rom. 6; Rom. 8:3–16; and 1 Thess. 4:8–9.

42. De Boer, *Galatians*, 161–62.

43. As de Boer himself implies (*Galatians*, 161).

44. At the same time, because the Messiah's death is for "our" sins (1:4), in 2:20 Paul is implicitly speaking not just about himself or about individuals but also about communities, in whom the Messiah corporately dwells and who corporately live in the Messiah (cf. the more explicit formulation of this claim in Rom. 8:3–4). See the comment in n. 40 above about the close connection between the Spirit and community in Gal. 5 and 6.

Galatians 1:16 in Conversation with 2 Corinthians

As we have seen, there is significant debate about what Paul means when he speaks of God's pleasure in revealing his Son "in me." It seems clear, however, from our study of later texts in Galatians that Paul was convinced that, whatever precisely happened at that moment of revelation to or in him, its immediate impact could be narrated as an experience of death and resurrection, indeed a co-crucifixion and co-resurrection, and its long-term effect on him could be described in terms of ongoing Christlike dying and rising to new life enabled by the Spirit of Christ and shaped by the Law/pattern of Christ. This sort of language appears not only in Galatians but also in Romans 6 and 8.

Moreover, similar language appears in 2 Corinthians, and not far from the occurrence of the important terms "new covenant" (2 Cor. 3:6) and "new creation" (5:17). As we just saw in 2 Corinthians 4:10, the ministry of the new covenant/new creation is a ministry of paradoxical, Christlike, life-giving dying, enabled by the Spirit ("the Spirit gives life," 3:6), but conveyed through the agency of weak apostles such as Paul. They are powerless in themselves (4:7), and their difficult, deathlike existence is the manifestation of Jesus' life (*phanerōthē*, 4:11; NRSV, "made visible"), and thus the means of life for others (4:12), only by God's power.[45]

This is the paradoxical modus operandi of the apocalyptic new covenant: the power of God is revealed in the weakness of the cross (cf. 1 Cor. 1:18–25) and of those who enslave themselves to others for Jesus' sake (2 Cor. 4:5) and in the mode of Jesus (cf. Phil. 2:1–11). The glorious ministry of life comes through suffering and death—Christ's death on the cross, and the ongoing suffering and even dying of Paul and his team that constitute an ongoing revelation of the death of Jesus himself (2 Cor. 4:10; cf. Phil. 3:17). What we find developed at length in 2 Corinthians, we see also in Galatians: Paul's "crucifixion" and suffering are part of his participation in the new creation, and evidence of it (Gal. 6:12–17; cf. 5:11). At the same time, if, as it seems, the Galatian believers also suffered (*epathete*, Gal. 3:4; cf. 4:29), it was because of their apocalyptic participation in the new-covenant gifts of Messiah and Spirit (3:1–5).[46]

According to Paul, therefore, life in the Messiah, and specifically ministry, is a kind of revelation, or apocalypse. He does not use the verb *apokalyptō* and the noun *apokalypsis* to describe that ministry in 2 Corinthians, however, but the verb *phaneroō* and the noun *phanerōsis* (esp. 2:14; 4:10–11; cf.

---

45. See further the discussion of this passage in chap. 3 above.
46. See Dunne, "Suffering and Covenantal Hope in Galatians"; Dunne, "Suffering in Vain"; Dunne, *Persecution and Participation*.

4:2; 7:12; 11:6); this word-family signifies making manifest or visible. Paul explains and defends the peculiar narrative shape of his ministry to the Corinthians as one means by which the gospel is made visible or manifest to the world. Without such a revelation, the gospel cannot be known, for it must be proclaimed not only in word as *audition* but in life as *vision*—or even *incarnation* (cf. 1 John 1:1).

This is not to say that *apokalyptō* and *apokalypsis* are necessarily precise overlapping synonyms with *phaneroō* and *phanerōsis*. Contrary to the general thrust of scholarship on this question, Dominika Kurek-Chomycz has recently argued that they are not.[47] Instead, she contends, *phaneroō* and *phanerōsis* refer to *mediated* rather than unmediated revelation. Paul uses this word-family to represent himself as "the medium of divine revelation."[48] We might say that Paul is the necessary public face of his revelations, both initial (such as mentioned in Gal. 1:16) and ongoing (such as narrated in 2 Cor. 12:1–10), to which *apokalyptō* and *apokalypsis* refer.[49] *Revelation* becomes *manifestation*.[50]

If Kurek-Chomycz is right about the vocabulary of revelation, then that which occurred *en emoi* according to Galatians 1:16 should be understood as a direct, and perhaps even private, revelation *to* Paul, not *in* (or *through*) him in any public way. I am not convinced, however, that the verb alone should determine the force of *en emoi*. Paul's use of the same phrase in 2:20 suggests that the initial revelation of the Son "in" Paul was, or at least organically became, an ongoing mode of existence shaped by the Son/Messiah "in" him.[51] However, even if the revelation of Galatians 1:16 is not a specifically public event (because it is not described in terms of *phaneroō* or *phanerōsis*), my main contention remains intact: Paul's apocalypse is complete only when it is embodied, when it has a public ("mediated") manifestation. Christopher Rowland agrees: no matter the interpretation of 1:16, "there is other evidence in Paul's letters of an intimate link between the human medium (the apostle) and the message about, and even the person of, Christ."[52]

The medium, however, is greater than the apostle himself, even if (at times) he and his colleagues constitute the focal point of the Christ-medium for

47. Kurek-Chomycz, "Scent of (Mediated) Revelation?," 69–108.
48. Kurek-Chomycz, "Scent of (Mediated) Revelation?," 70.
49. See the word *apokalypsis*, in the plural, in 2 Cor. 12:1, 7.
50. Kurek-Chomycz suggests that "reveal" and "manifest" may sometimes best capture the distinction in the two semantic domains ("Scent of [Mediated] Revelation?," 106). She argues persuasively (90–100) that in 2 Corinthians Paul maintains a clear distinction between the two word-families (*apokalyptō/apokalypsis* and *phaneroō/phanerōsis*).
51. Ben Witherington (*Grace in Galatia*, 106) similarly interprets 1:16 in connection with 2:20.
52. Rowland, "Paul and the Apocalypse of Jesus Christ," 145.

rhetorical purposes.[53] The apocalyptically revealed new covenant is, and must be, revealed for what it is by being made visible in human lives and communities that are being transformed by the Spirit to bear testimony to the paradoxical reality of the nature of God's apocalypse and new creation in the crucified Messiah. To put it in new-covenant language, the new covenant, reception of the Spirit, and Spirit-enabled obedience are inseparable realities.

Our consideration of Galatians 1:16 in connection with parts of 2 Corinthians means that the divine apocalypse is that which inaugurates the new covenant, and the evidence of the presence of the new covenant is life and ministry that correspond to the apocalypse—to the death and resurrection of Jesus. The common factor in each (the apocalypse and the new covenant) is the activity of the Father and the Son by the Spirit. Our inquiry into 2 Corinthians reinforces precisely what we see, in less developed form, in Galatians itself.[54] The apocalypse of the apocalypse, according to Galatians, means the crucified Messiah alive and active (2:20); it consists of both the apostle who exhibits Christ crucified, bearing the marks of Jesus the crucified, and the community that shares in the faithfulness and love of the crucified and in all the "fruit" his Spirit produces. Of course, Paul also exemplifies faithfulness and love, and the community also, more than likely, suffers. Each manifestation of the new covenant/new creation is due to the activity of God in sending the Son and the Spirit (4:4–6).

"In the Spirit"

We have seen that it is absolutely critical for Paul that the Spirit of God that is sent into human hearts is the Spirit of the Son. This chapter's title, however, refers to the shape of life *in the Spirit—pneumati*, as Paul says in 5:16.[55] Yet our focus has been on the *Spirit within*. These two ways of looking at the "location" of the Spirit are not contradictory. It is significant for Paul that the Spirit is both internal and external to believers, reflecting, I would suggest, the "Spirit in" language (indwelling, internal) and the "Spirit on" language (anointing, external) of the biblical tradition, as well as the prophetic eschatological expectation that the Spirit would be both put *within* God's people and poured out *on* them.[56]

---

53. Even Rowland ("Paul and the Apocalypse of Jesus Christ," 145) notes that the medium is not limited to apostles. See, e.g., 2 Cor. 3:3, 18.

54. For further evidence that 2 Corinthians builds on Galatians, see chap. 7 below.

55. In the undisputed letters, there are more than twenty occurrences of *en pneumati* or a similar phrase (including *pneumati* alone) in which location "in" the Spirit is at least a plausible interpretation. For the apocalyptic/revelatory significance of the phrase *en pneumati*, see also Rev. 1:10.

56. E.g., Ezek. 11:9; 36:26–27; 37:14 (put within); Isa. 32:15; 44:3; Ezek. 39:29; Joel 2:28–29 (poured out on).

The result for Paul is the mutual indwelling, or reciprocal residence, of (a) both the Spirit and the Messiah, and (b) the community of believers (as Rom. 8:1–17 makes most clear)—by which Paul means the Messiah's dwelling by means of, or in the person of, the Spirit.[57] This intricate understanding of the Spirit is another aspect of the surprising newness of the new covenant. It is a development from the prophetic expectation, especially in the notion of the Spirit *of* the Messiah. Paul's use of the idiom of being "in" the Spirit may well be modeled on his language of being "in" the Messiah.[58] It is perhaps his way of saying that it is in fact the surprising messianic Spirit, the Spirit associated with anointing and thus with the Anointed One (cf. 2 Cor. 1:21),[59] that is revealed and given in the new covenant. In any event, to be in Christ is to be in the Spirit, and to be in the Spirit is simultaneously to have the Spirit within (individuals) and among (the community). This is the result of God's all-encompassing new-covenant incursion.

Conclusion

As noted earlier, it was J. Louis Martyn who wrote that God's apocalyptic invasion in Christ is analogous to the prophetic promise of a new, divinely given heart and spirit.[60] The argument of this chapter suggests that Martyn was absolutely right. We have encountered evidence from Paul's letters for the inseparability of apocalypse and new covenant, and have therefore contended that Paul should be described as a proponent of the apocalyptic new covenant, the coming of which is an event of disruptive continuity. Moreover, we have seen that inherent in this apocalyptic new covenant is the need for apostles and all believers to embody, and thus also to manifest, the revelation. *By means of the Spirit, the church is to be an apocalypse of the apocalypse, a living manifestation and exegesis of the surprising new covenant.*[61] Life in

---

57. In Rom. 8, note the use of "in" (*en*): "the law of the Spirit of life in Christ Jesus" (8:2); "⁹But you are not in the flesh; you are in the Spirit, since the Spirit of God dwells in you. Anyone who does not have the Spirit of Christ does not belong to him. ¹⁰But if Christ is in you, though the body is dead because of sin, the Spirit is life because of righteousness. ¹¹If the Spirit of him who raised Jesus from the dead dwells in you, he who raised Christ from the dead will give life to your mortal bodies also through his Spirit that dwells in you" (8:9–11).

58. I am not claiming that Paul invented the language of being in the Spirit but suggesting (part of) the reason for his attraction to it. The Spirit is of course "upon" the figure(s) in Isaiah (Isa. 11:2; 42:1; 61:1).

59. *Ho de . . . chrisas hēmas theos* ("But . . . it is God who has anointed us"). It is also likely that the Gospel tradition about Jesus' mission of baptizing in/with the Holy Spirit (Matt. 3:11; Mark 1:8; Luke 3:16; John 1:33; Acts 1:5; cf. 1 Cor. 12:13) is known to Paul.

60. Martyn, "Afterword: The Human Moral Dilemma," 164n13.

61. See further my *Becoming the Gospel*.

the Spirit of the crucified Messiah will therefore reflect the counterintuitive and countercultural ways of God revealed in that messianic apocalypse. Paul's own life is an attempt to bear witness to that apocalypse, empowered by the Spirit, and to encourage those who encounter him, whether in person or via his letters, to do the same.

six

Reading Galatians 2:15–21 Theologically

Beyond Old and New, West and East

The preceding chapter examined the Letter to the Galatians as a witness to the apocalyptic new covenant that was central to Paul's theology and lived experience (spirituality). Within that chapter we briefly considered the main theological claims of Galatians 2:15–21 before focusing on its connection to the apocalyptic new covenant. This is not the normal focus of interpreters of Galatians 2:15–21, which is a central text about justification.

In this and the following two chapters, therefore, we turn our attention to justification. These three chapters will argue that justification, according to Paul, is both *participatory* and *transformative*—so transformative that the apostle describes it as resurrection to new life. Moreover, justification for Paul can be understood in terms of what the later Christian tradition calls theosis, or transformative participation in the life of God.[1] The three chapters will contend for a "justification connection" or "justification trajectory"—a connection among three key texts in Paul, most likely constituting a trajectory from one to the next to the next: Galatians 2:15–21, 2 Corinthians 5:11–21, and Romans as a whole. This chapter is concerned with Galatians 2.

Hans Dieter Betz famously argued, rightly or wrongly, that Galatians 2:15–21 is the letter's *propositio*, or thesis statement.[2] This passage is often

---

1. I repeat my "mantra": the language of theosis is both helpful and appropriate, yet the main point is not the label "theosis" but the claim that justification is participatory and transformative.

2. Betz, *Galatians*, 18–19, 113–14.

considered to contain some of Paul's most important claims about both soteriology and spirituality. The purpose of this chapter is to offer various insights
about this important text that will not only enlighten us about Paul but also
cause us to think seriously about our topic in ways that may encourage some
theological agreement, some rapprochement, between old and new perspectives on Paul, and between West and East.[3] Of course, this chapter cannot
address every issue, fully justify every interpretive move, or interact with more
than a few of the many participants in the conversation.[4] But it will attempt,
at least, to open up some new and productive vistas.

We will be reading this Galatians passage theologically. By "theologically"
I have two primary senses in mind. First, it means reading Galatians 2 with
a focus on its theological claims. This focus will not exclude other concerns,
whether literary and rhetorical or social and historical, though such concerns
will be pursued not as ends in themselves but rather as means to the greater end
of understanding the text's theological claims. Second, it means reading Galatians 2 not merely as an ancient text, and not even merely as a text that makes
theological claims, but as a text that makes claims *on us*. Reading theologically
means listening to the text as divine address. Among many other things, this
approach will mean that our text *ought* to unite rather than divide the members
of the one universal body of Christ. This rather lofty goal should not suppress
debate or terminate difference. But it should create within us, and among us,
a generosity of spirit within our debates and our differences. Such generosity
has not always been the case, to put it mildly, concerning justification.

Galatians 2:15–21—Text and Tentative Translation

Table 6.1 on page 117 contains the Greek text, transliteration, and tentative
translation of Galatians 2:15–21.[5] (After this, we will discuss the text by using
only the transliteration of the Greek text.)

3. Issues of justification, participation, and conversion have recently been front and center in
Pauline studies. Sometimes the conversation has generated more heat than light, yet occasionally there has been progress and even the hope of reconciliation among differing traditions and
perspectives. Unfortunately, however, the voices of Orthodox scholars have not been given much
of a hearing, at least in American and British scholarship. The volume *Participation, Justification, and Conversion*, edited by Athanasios Despotis, is an important attempt to bring more
voices into the conversation and build additional, much-needed bridges. This chapter revises
an essay in that volume.

4. For an earlier close reading of this text, see my *Inhabiting the Cruciform God*, 63–72.

5. I include the Greek text of 2:15–21 here for the benefit of those who are especially interested in various grammatical and syntactical arguments presented in this chapter. At the end
of the chapter, I will offer a slightly revised translation. Unless indicated otherwise, the NRSV
is used in this chapter for the translation of texts other than Gal. 2:15–21.

Table 6.1. Text, Transliteration, and Translation of Gal. 2:15–21

Greek Text and Transliteration	Tentative Translation
[15]ἡμεῖς φύσει Ἰουδαῖοι καὶ οὐκ ἐξ ἐθνῶν ἁμαρτωλοί [15]hēmeis physei Ioudaioi kai ouk ex ethnōn hamartōloi	[15][But] we ourselves, by birth Jews and not sinners from the nations/gentiles,
[16]εἰδότες [δὲ] ὅτι οὐ δικαιοῦται ἄνθρωπος ἐξ ἔργων νόμου ἐὰν μὴ διὰ πίστεως Ἰησοῦ Χριστοῦ, καὶ ἡμεῖς εἰς Χριστὸν Ἰησοῦν ἐπιστεύσαμεν, ἵνα δικαιωθῶμεν ἐκ πίστεως Χριστοῦ καὶ οὐκ ἐξ ἔργων νόμου, ὅτι ἐξ ἔργων νόμου οὐ δικαιωθήσεται πᾶσα σάρξ. [16]eidotes [de] hoti ou dikaioutai anthrōpos ex ergōn nomou ean mē dia pisteōs Iēsou Christou, kai hēmeis eis Christon Iēsoun episteusamen, hina dikaiōthōmen ek pisteōs Christou kai ouk ex ergōn nomou, hoti ex ergōn nomou ou dikaiōthēsetai pasa sarx.	[16]because we know that no person is justified by virtue of works of the law but rather through the faithfulness of Jesus the Messiah, even we came to faith [that incorporates us] into the Messiah Jesus, so that we would be justified by virtue of the faithfulness of the Messiah and not by virtue of works of the law, for no human being will be justified by virtue of works of the law.
[17]εἰ δὲ ζητοῦντες δικαιωθῆναι ἐν Χριστῷ εὑρέθημεν καὶ αὐτοὶ ἁμαρτωλοί, ἆρα Χριστὸς ἁμαρτίας διάκονος; μὴ γένοιτο. [17]ei de zētountes dikaiōthēnai en Christō heurethēmen kai autoi hamartōloi, ara Christos hamartias diakonos? mē genoito.	[17]But if we, while seeking to be justified in the Messiah, are ourselves found to be sinners, then is the Messiah a servant of sin? May it never be!
[18]εἰ γὰρ ἃ κατέλυσα ταῦτα πάλιν οἰκοδομῶ, παραβάτην ἐμαυτὸν συνιστάνω. [18]ei gar ha katelysa tauta palin oikodomō, parabatēn emauton synistanō.	[18]For if I rebuild the things I tore down, then I prove myself to be a transgressor.
[19]ἐγὼ γὰρ διὰ νόμου νόμῳ ἀπέθανον, ἵνα θεῷ ζήσω. Χριστῷ συνεσταύρωμαι [19]egō gar dia nomou nomō apethanon, hina theō zēsō. Christō synestaurōmai;	[19]For I myself, through the law, died in relation to the law so that I could live in relation to God. I have been crucified with the Messiah;[a]
[20]ζῶ δὲ οὐκέτι ἐγώ, ζῇ δὲ ἐν ἐμοὶ Χριστός· ὃ δὲ νῦν ζῶ ἐν σαρκί, ἐν πίστει ζῶ τῇ τοῦ υἱοῦ τοῦ θεοῦ τοῦ ἀγαπήσαντός με καὶ παραδόντος ἑαυτὸν ὑπὲρ ἐμοῦ. [20]zō de ouketi egō, zē de en emoi Christos; ho de nyn zō en sarki, en pistei zō tē tou huiou tou theou tou agapēsantos me kai paradontos heauton hyper emou.	[20]thus I myself no longer live, but the Messiah lives in me; and the life I do now live in the flesh, I live by means of the faithfulness of the Son of God, who loved me by giving himself for me.
[21]οὐκ ἀθετῶ τὴν χάριν τοῦ θεοῦ· εἰ γὰρ διὰ νόμου δικαιοσύνη, ἄρα Χριστὸς δωρεὰν ἀπέθανεν. [21]ouk athetō tēn charin tou theou; ei gar dia nomou dikaiosynē, ara Christos dōrean apethanen.	[21]I do not annul the grace of God; for if justice/righteousness comes through the law, then the Messiah died for nothing.

a. I follow the versification found in most critical editions of the NT and in such translations as the NRSV and NAB.

A few initial comments about this translation. First of all, the traditional language of "justification" has been used for the *dikai-* family verb forms in verses 16–17 (*dikaioutai*, *dikaiōthōmen*, *dikaiōthēsetai*, and *dikaiōthēnai*), and the less traditional (in English) language of "justice" for the noun *dikaiosynē* in verse 21, though it has been combined with "righteousness." I leave open for the moment the actual sense of both the verb and the noun, but I stress that this translational decision is complex, highly significant, and frustratingly inadequate. It is all of these things especially because (a) few ways of rendering the Greek can capture the links among the various words in the *dikai-* family, (b) the inability to capture these links diminishes our understanding of what Paul means to convey when he uses this word-family, and (c) some common ways of translating the *dikai-* family into English are actually misleading.

Elsewhere I have argued that, in order to maintain the conceptual, theological link between justification and justice, the verb and the noun should both be translated with forms of the "*just-*" family (e.g., "be justified," "justice"),[6] but even this approach is not completely satisfactory. For one thing, E. P. Sanders contends that "justification" is a weak word in English when we need a "strong" one, and that it is misleading because it often signifies "sufficient reason" or even "adequate excuse."[7] Moreover, for many English-speaking people the word "justice" has no connections to its biblical, prophetic sense and often implies retributive justice. It is tempting to go with "rectification"— the notion of making things right. This, however, would completely eliminate the "justice" dimension of the passage in English and thus has its own set of problems.

As my argument unfolds, it will become clear that we could render the verb "to justify" as "to make just," but we will not add that controversial interpretation quite yet. Unfortunately, we are left with translational imperfection at best. As the French say, "Traduire, c'est trahire"—"To translate is to betray" or "All translation is treason."[8]

Second, I have retained the passive voice in the translation of the verb "justify," rather than rendering it with the implicit actor "God," as in "God justifies." Theologically, however, the repeated passive voice stresses divine initiative and grace, as we must do. As for the tenses of the verb in verse 16, present (*dikaioutai*) and future (*dikaiōthēsetai*), they both have a gnomic sense: they state a principle, and the future tense does not *necessarily* refer to a future justification.

---

6. Gorman, "Justification and Justice in Paul," revised in my *Becoming the Gospel*, 212–60.
7. Sanders, *Paul: The Apostle's Life, Letters, and Thought*, 505.
8. I was recently reminded of this French dictum by my student Jérémy Favrelière.

Third, as elsewhere, including earlier chapters of this book, I have followed Richard Hays and others, opting for "faith" or "faithfulness," and the so-called subjective genitive, in the translation of the famous *pistis* + genitive constructions in verses 16 and 20.[9]

Fourth, the arguments of scholars such as Matthew Novenson, N. T. Wright, and Joshua Jipp have led to the rendering of all occurrences of *Christos* as "Messiah," not "Christ."[10]

Fifth, specific Greek prepositions that suggest source, instrumentality, or means have been translated with some differentiation and consistency to indicate the possibility of both similarities and differences among them: *ek* = "by virtue of"; *dia* = "through"; and *en* = "by means of" before "the faithfulness of the Son of God," but "in" before "the Messiah" and "the flesh" (two spheres of existence).

Finally, the word *dikaiosynē* in verse 21 is an ethical rather than a legal term. Its presence suggests something more than, or even other than, a (narrow) forensic understanding of justification.[11]

This last point is suggestive of the direction this chapter will be going. We proceed, therefore, to the seven main claims, which will include some justifying and nuancing of the translation.

Galatians 2:15–21 as Paul's Interpretation of Justification

1. Galatians 2:15–21 is a self-contained rhetorical unit, the subject of this unit is "justification," and Paul is offering his own interpretation of justification.

This claim is really a thesis with three parts, or subtheses, though they are all closely connected.

It is important that we recognize the rhetorical unity of these seven verses. They are set off from what precedes and follows by an inclusio (a set of rhetorical bookends)—namely, the occurrence of words from the *dikai-* family in the unit's opening and closing sentences (vv. 15–16 and v. 21, respectively). The presence of three lexical items in verse 16 (*dikaioutai . . . dikaiōthōmen . . . dikaiōthēsetai*) is matched with only one in verse 21 (*dikaiosynē*), but both the repetition and the singularity have their separate and appropriate rhetorical effects. The first sentence both introduces Paul's topic and states his fundamental thesis with great emphasis: not *that* way of justification but

9. See, e.g., Hays, *Faith of Jesus Christ*.
10. Novenson, *Christ among the Messiahs*; Wright, *Paul and the Faithfulness of God*, esp. 815–36; Jipp, *Christ Is King*.
11. See also deSilva, *Galatians*, 42, 50–51.

this way. The final sentence names the material subject of the unit again, both reminding us that Paul has not changed topics along the way and stating the seriousness of his compact argument about the topic in very succinct, even stark terms. The subject of the passage is that to which the *dikai-* family of words gives expression.

That "justification" is the subject, indeed the sole subject (see further below), of this carefully constructed passage is further signaled by the absence of *dikai-* language from the preceding and following verses. The very first occurrence of the *dikai-* family is in 2:16, and it does not reappear in any form until 3:6 (*kathōs Abraam episteusen tō theō, kai elogisthē autō eis dikaiosynēn*),[12] which begins a unit in which justification is again directly addressed. The start of a new unit, between 2:21 and 3:6, at 3:1 is clear as Paul shifts from the predominantly first-person language of 2:15–21 (with some third-person language) to the forceful second-person direct address of 3:1–5. This, of course, does not mean that 3:1–5 is unrelated to 2:15–21—it is in fact related in significant ways—but simply that a new rhetorical unit with a different rhetorical agenda has been introduced.

Although everyone acknowledges this shift to 3:1–5 at the conclusion of our passage, some interpreters want to add to the front end of our text, considering 2:11–21 as a unit.[13] There is some justification for this move, since 2:11–14 does indeed narrate the events at Antioch that generated Paul's response to Cephas about the real "truth of the gospel" (2:14a). Paul's rebuke of Cephas, which begins in 2:14b, may also end there, but it may continue into 2:15 and beyond; interpreters and translators are divided.[14]

Whether or not Paul intended his Galatian audience to understand 2:15–21 as part of his rebuke of Peter—and I am inclined to think he did, in part[15]— there are two reasons, in addition to the introduction of *dikai-* language in 2:15–16, not to blur the divide between 2:11–14 and 2:15–21. First, 2:14b is addressed specifically to Cephas, but his name does not appear in 2:15–21. The primary audience of 2:15–21 is the "foolish Galatians" directly addressed in 3:1, not merely Cephas and others present at Antioch. Second, Paul's words in 2:14b are in the form of a rhetorical question, a rebuke based on behavior (Cephas's "liv[ing] like a Gentile"). The question does not mention the

---

12. NRSV: "Just as Abraham 'believed God, and it was reckoned to him as righteousness' . . ."
13. E.g., Oakes, *Galatians*, 75–98.
14. Most translations end the quotation after 2:15, but some extend it through v. 16 (e.g., NLT; Louis Segond 21 [French]) or even v. 21 (e.g., NIV). Sanders thinks the unit begins at 2:14, calling 2:14–21 the first section of the letter's main argument, though he thinks the quotation ends at 2:14 (*Paul*, 501–3).
15. That is, vv. 15–21 are also, and especially, directed at the Galatians. Theologically speaking, they are also addressed to all subsequent audiences.

specifically theological topic of justification, though in Paul's mind Cephas's (mis)behavior and the subject of justification are intimately connected, as we will see further below. But in the letter as we have it, Paul's rhetorical rebuke of Cephas in 2:14b functions as an introduction to the subject of 2:15–21, justification. Accordingly, it is best to see 2:15–21 as a distinct unit, but one that is also closely related to the events at Antioch and at Galatia that are narrated in 2:11–14 and 3:1–5, respectively.

If justification is recognized as the subject of the unit 2:15–21, it should also be recognized as its *sole* subject. By "sole subject" I do not mean that justification is unrelated to other topics, such as faith, works of the law, Jesus' death, and so on, but simply that Paul has not abandoned justification for a *different* topic, such as "dying to the law" or "being crucified with Christ," if such topics are understood as being about something other than justification. In other words, by "*sole* subject" I mean "*persistent* subject."

Recognizing or denying the legitimacy of this claim is one of the two most significant exegetical meta-decisions an interpreter can make about this passage as a whole. *If justification is the persistent subject, then the death and resurrection of the self and the new life with the Messiah's indwelling presence are integral aspects of Paul's theology of justification*—not supplements to it or different topics. We may debate the best way to articulate the various dimensions of justification and how they are related to one another, but we will not separate out justification from these other theological and spiritual realities to which the text refers.[16]

The second most significant exegetical meta-decision is a corollary of the first: whether we force a prior understanding of justification onto Paul or allow him to tell us what he means by justification. Many interpreters come to

16. Referring to my argument in *Inhabiting the Cruciform God* that interprets justification in terms of co-crucifixion and co-resurrection, Douglas J. Moo, writing from the "traditional" perspective on Paul, charges me with confusing proximity with identity (*Galatians*, 155, 172). In his view, justification and co-crucifixion/co-resurrection are syntactical neighbors rather than semantic twins, but my argument here is precisely that, because the subject of the passage is defined by Paul as that to which the *dikai-* family of words gives expression, we misread Paul if we see these two topics merely as being proximate to each other. (To Moo's credit [155], he suggests that union with Christ may be "the key" to the letter.) Beverly Gaventa, writing from an "apocalyptic" perspective, seems to both deny and partly affirm the argument I am making. She argues that in Gal. 2:19–20 Paul has "shifted his discourse," moving beyond "making things right (rectifying or justifying) and how that is done; instead, it concerns death and life." But she also says that in 2:19–20 "Paul's *interpretation* of the singular character of justification transforms it" because "rectification is necessary but not sufficient" (emphasis original). An interpretation is not a change of subject; it is the development of the same subject. In the end, therefore, Gaventa actually agrees with my view. See Gaventa, "Singularity of the Gospel Revisited," 194. For an "apocalyptic" view even more similar to mine, see D. Campbell, *Deliverance of God*, 838–52.

texts like this in Paul with hard-and-fast understandings of what justification means in Scripture and/or Second Temple Judaism and/or Paul. Such positions are generally justified by appeal to the alleged meaning of the *dikai-* family that is evident from the lexicons or the primary sources themselves. Far more often than not, the conclusion offered by proponents of a fixed sense for justification is that it had, and could only have had for Paul, a forensic sense: a declaration. This boxed-in approach to justification can be seen in both the traditional perspective on Paul and the New Perspective on Paul, with the former sometimes saying justification can only mean a declaration of acquittal (e.g., Thomas Schreiner), the latter sometimes saying it can only mean the declaration of covenant membership (e.g., N. T. Wright).[17]

Apart from any arguments that need to be made about the meaning(s) of the verb *dikaioō*, not to mention the noun *dikaiosynē*, this principle of assigning inviolable semantic significance to a term, and to the concept to which the term refers, without investigating context, contravenes a fundamental linguistic principle: that meaning is context-dependent. Moreover, it violates the commonsense axiom that creative people understand old concepts in new ways. Theologically, it underestimates the transformative power of the gospel on Paul's mind, as he is forced to rethink everything, including justification, in light of the apocalyptic event of the Messiah's death and resurrection and his experience of it.[18]

17. Thomas R. Schreiner (*Galatians*, 155) claims that the verb "justify" in Paul has a "forensic and legal character" derived from the Old Testament. It "refers to God's verdict of not guilty on the day of judgment (Rom. 2:13). God's eschatological verdict has now been announced in advance for those who believe in Jesus Christ." Furthermore, it does not "denote a righteousness that transforms or 'makes us' righteous" (156). To be sure, Schreiner makes arguments for his view here and elsewhere; my point is that this perspective will hardly allow a reading of Paul in Gal. 2:15–21 that challenges it. Similarly, Wright has consistently argued for justification as divine declaration, as in *Paul and the Faithfulness of God*: "'Justification' is the declaration of the one God" that one is "a member of Abraham's covenant family" (958–59; cf. 797–99). Wright's understanding seems so controlled by his reconstruction of what a Pharisee would mean by justification by works of the law (see 184–88) that he fails to allow Paul to break the bounds of that understanding. See further discussion in Gorman, "Wright about Much, but Questions about Justification."

18. Cf. Jonathan Linebaugh's comment on the phrase "the righteousness of God": "Paul does not look in the lexicon of apocalyptic Judaism to define" it because the "Pauline definition . . . is a christological *redefinition*" ("Righteousness Revealed," 236–37 [emphasis added]). As I have argued elsewhere, it is ironic that in N. T. Wright's magnum opus, *Paul and the Faithfulness of God*, Paul's governing hermeneutical principle is rightly said to be the reconfiguring of everything in light of the crucified and resurrected Messiah, and yet "justification" is said to mean only "declaration." See Gorman, "Wright about Much, but Questions about Justification," where I also argue that, implicitly, Wright actually sees justification as more than declaration. De Boer (*Galatians*, 165), on the other hand, relying on J. Louis Martyn (*Galatians*), thinks rightly that Paul is consumed by the language of apocalyptic deliverance and co-crucifixion in Galatians and

To summarize my first thesis: in Galatians 2:15–21, from beginning to end, Paul is offering his own understanding of justification. We turn now to several aspects of that understanding.

The Messiah's Death, Not the Law, as the *Means* of Justification

2. According to Galatians 2:15–21, there are two mutually exclusive approaches to the means of justification—namely, the (works of the) law and the Messiah's death—but because Messiah Jesus' faithful and loving death is the manifestation (apocalypse) of God's grace, it alone is the actual *means*, or objective basis, of justification.

One of the most striking features of our passage is the cluster of phrases indicating antithetical claims about the source, or means, of justification—how justification is accomplished. One source/means is firmly and repeatedly denied, the other affirmed. We may set these out in table 6.2 (p. 124).

Several phrases here are disputed as to their syntactical sense and therefore their translation. Chief among these are (1) "works of the law," which appears three times in verse 16—referring either to works in general or to a specialized set of works or practices (circumcision, etc.); (2) *ean mē* in verse 16b—meaning either "except" or "but rather"; and (3) *pisteōs [Iēsou] Christou*—meaning "by faith in" or "by the faith[fulness] of" the Messiah (Jesus), twice in verse 16. With respect to (1), my interpretation does not take, or need to take, a definitive position. Regarding (2), I opt for the "but rather" interpretation in light of the antithetical structure of the entire passage.[19] As for (3), the translation expresses the so-called subjective-genitive interpretation, meaning "faith[fulness] of," not "faith in." We shall return to the reasons for that momentarily.

We may refer to these two approaches to justification in general terms as "Torah-centric" and "Messiah-centric" without necessarily agreeing on the meaning of all the disputed phrases. The main issue that arises from an unresolved dispute about these phrases is whether Paul is pitting something about works of the law, or the law generally, over against *human faith* or *the Messiah's faithfulness* as the alternative means of justification (i.e., the alternative to the law).

Of course, this debate cannot be played out or settled definitively here. But the argument that table 6.2 implicitly makes is that verse 21 is key to

---

that such language "forces [justification] to take on a different meaning," though de Boer unnecessarily claims that Paul only uses justification language because the "new preachers" in Galatia do.

19. Both Schreiner (*Galatians*, 162–63) and Martyn (*Galatians*, 251), each also appealing to context, arrive at similar conclusions—though from very different overall perspectives.

understanding the whole set of antitheses about the means of justification. Verse 21 contains an absurd contrary-to-fact condition: "I do not annul the grace of God; for if justice/righteousness comes through the law [which it

Table 6.2. Source/Means/Basis of Justification Denied and Affirmed

Source/Means/Basis of Justification Denied	Source/Means/Basis of Justification Affirmed
ou dikaioutai anthrōpos ex ergōn nomou (v. 16a) no person is justified by virtue of works of the law	
	ean mē [dikaioutai anthrōpos] dia pisteōs Iēsou Christou (v. 16b)[a] but rather [a person is justified] through the faithfulness of Jesus the Messiah
	hina dikaiōthōmen ek pisteōs Christou (v. 16d) so that we would be justified by virtue of the faithfulness of the Messiah
kai ouk [dikaio-] ex ergōn nomou (v. 16e)[b] and not [justified] by virtue of works of the law	
ex ergōn nomou ou dikaiōthēsetai pasa sarx (v. 16f) no human being will be justified by virtue of works of the law[c]	
	zētountes dikaiōthēnai en Christō (v. 17a) seeking to be justified in the Messiah
	tēn charin tou theou (v. 21a) the grace of God
ei gar dia nomou dikaiosynē [contrary-to-fact condition] (v. 21b) for if justice/righteousness comes through the law	
	Christos . . . apethanen (v. 21c) the Messiah . . . died

a. The phrase in brackets is implied, and supplied by the previous clause.

b. Some form of the *dikai-* family is implied in this phrase.

c. An allusion to Ps. 143:2, which reads (142:2 LXX) *ou dikaiōthēsetai enōpion sou pas zōn*, translating a Hebrew *qal* imperfect meaning "no one is righteous" in contrast to the righteous God (vv. 1, 11).

does not do—the false premise], then the Messiah died for nothing [which he did not do—the false conclusion]." Stated differently, as a simple declarative rather than a conditional sentence, the verse claims, "I affirm the grace of God that was manifested for our justification and justice/righteousness in the saving death of the Messiah, not in the law." This bold statement about the inefficacy of the law sums up the same assessment of the works of the law in verse 16 (the left column of table 6.2), while simultaneously describing the alternative means of justification (the right column of table 6.2) as both the grace of God and the death of Jesus. Significantly, *no mention is made in verse 21 of human faith*. Instead, the death of the Messiah is presented as the means of justification.

Thus the parallelism between the phrase *Christos . . . apethanen* ("the Messiah died") in verse 21 and the two occurrences of the phrase *dia/ek pisteōs [Iēsou] Christou* ("the faith of [Jesus] the Messiah") in verse 16 strongly suggests that we should understand "the faith of the Messiah" as a reference to Jesus' death—that is, to his act of fidelity to God the Father in dying for the justification of sinners, both Jews and gentiles.

The equation of the Messiah's death with his faith (or at least the ultimate expression of it) is reinforced by verse 20. Here Paul is setting out the modus operandi of the life of the justified person. He does so with two parallel sets of phrases (table 6.3 below).

In the phrases marked (a) and (a'), Paul is affirming the paradox of being dead but alive (to which we shall return in considering the third and fourth claims below). In the phrases marked (b) and (b'), he is explaining how this is the case: the crucified-but-resurrected Messiah lives in him. As the resurrected Messiah, Jesus is able to indwell people such as Paul (b); as the resurrected *crucified* Messiah (b'), he indwells people in a certain way, as the one who retains his identity as the Crucified One. The significance of this for messianic, or "in the Messiah," existence will be explored below. But for now the crucial point is that in (b) and (b') Paul is characterizing the One who does the *inhabiting*, not the one *inhabited*, who is described, albeit briefly,

Table 6.3. The Modus Operandi of Life for the Justified

(a) *zō de ouketi egō*,	(b) *zē de en emoi Christos*
thus I myself no longer live,	but the Messiah lives in me;
(a') *ho de nyn zō en sarki*,	(b') *en pistei zō tē tou huiou tou theou tou*
and the life I do now live in the flesh,	*agapēsantos me kai paradontos heauton hyper emou.*
	I live by means of the faithfulness of the Son of God, who loved me by giving himself for me.

in (a) and (a′). In other words, the *pistis* (faith/faithfulness) to which verse 21 refers—(b′) in the display above—is predicated of the Son of God, not of Paul. As in verse 16, it is Jesus the Messiah who is characterized as having faith, or (better) faithfulness, and it is consequently by virtue or by means of his faithfulness that people are both justified and able to live out their justified existence "in the flesh"—in real life.

It is the last part of verse 20, the (b′) above, then, that succinctly but significantly reveals the fundamental character of Jesus' death—which was mentioned even more briefly, and only implicitly, in the reference to co-crucifixion in verse 19 (*synestaurōmai*). In his death by crucifixion, Jesus displayed both faithfulness and love, *pistis* and *agapē*, the former toward God and parallel to Paul's language of the Messiah's obedience (Rom. 5:12–21; Phil. 2:8),[20] and the latter toward humanity.[21] Since in Paul's theology the display of Jesus' love is not separate from, but expressed through, his death, it is best to treat the *kai* as an epexegetical (explanatory) marker, signaling a hendiadys (one item expressed in two ways) in the text, yielding the translation "who loved me by giving himself for me."

To summarize this second claim about our text: Paul delineates two possible means of justification, one involving the law and the other involving the death of the Messiah as the expression of his faithfulness and love and as the embodiment, the apocalypse (revelation), of God's grace. It is the latter means alone that actually justifies, argues Paul.

Participation in the Messiah's Death as the *Mode* of Justification

3. According to Galatians 2:15–21, justification is a *participatory* reality described explicitly as entailing co-crucifixion with the Messiah,[22] and this is what Paul means here by "faith"; it is this type of faith—a death *with* the Messiah, and both *to* the law and *to* the self—that brings a person into the realm of the Messiah. This is the *mode*, or subjective basis, of justification.

Since Paul sets out two possible but antithetical means of justification and contends that the only true means of justification is the faithful, loving death of Jesus that embodies and reveals the grace of God, the question naturally

20. Especially in light of the close connection between faith(fulness) and obedience in Rom. 1:5 and 16:26 as well as 6:17; 10:16.

21. For further development of this claim, see my *Inhabiting the Cruciform God*, 57–63, where I refer to this symbiosis of faithfulness and love in the Messiah's death as the quintessential act of covenant fulfillment—i.e., one act of devotion to God and to others.

22. It also entails resurrection with the Messiah, discussed in the next section.

arises, "How does one benefit from that death?"—which is actually equivalent to asking, "How is one justified?" If Jesus' death is the *means* of justification, its objective basis, what is the *mode* of justification, its subjective basis?[23] The text itself, as well as the immediate and larger contexts of our passage, makes it clear that this is a question with the same answer for both Jews and gentiles.

The universality of the means and thus the mode of justification is especially clear in the text at hand. Paul uses two generic references to humanity with a negated passive form of the verb "to justify"—*ou dikaioutai anthrōpos . . . ou dikaiōthēsetai pasa sarx* (v. 16; "no person . . . no human being")[24]—to stress the non-effective means of justification, the law. As a Jew, he then twice uses emphatic first-person-plural language to include his Jewish audience, whether those in Antioch or those in Galatia:

- "Even we came to faith [that incorporates us] into the Messiah Jesus" (v. 16b; *kai hēmeis eis Christon Iēsoun episteusamen*).
- "But if we, while seeking to be justified in the Messiah, are ourselves found to be sinners . . ." (v. 17a; *ei de zētountes dikaiōthēnai en Christō heurethēmen kai autoi hamartōloi*).

That is, this understanding of justification is not merely for "gentile sinners" (v. 15).[25] If justification for Jews has transpired apart from the law by faith, then surely it has happened in the same way for gentiles. Thus the acts—specifically, faith and baptism, as we will see—through which people have been transferred into the Messiah (2:16; 3:25–27) have created a level playing field, a unity of "no longer Jew or Greek" (3:28). Moreover, at the end of the passage Paul uses first-person-singular language to speak not only about himself, or even all Jewish believers, but generically about all who are in the Messiah (vv. 19b–20, and probably also vv. 18–19, 21).

If the Messiah's death is the unique and universal *means* of justification, how is the justifying grace of God that is manifested in Jesus' death appropriated? The short answer is by participation in that death: co-crucifixion. The form, or content, of that participation is delineated in several brief phrases. Just as recognizing various sorts of parallelism was critical to understanding the *means* of justification, so also now recognizing parallelism is critical to understanding its *mode*. Paul contends that the mode of justification is "faith,"

23. The helpful language of "means" and "mode" comes from Frick, "Means and Mode of Salvation."

24. Woodenly, "a person will not be justified . . . all flesh will not be justified."

25. The first-person-singular language in vv. 18–20 is parallel to the first-person-plural language of vv. 16–17; Paul is speaking representatively for and about Jewish believers.

or better "faith-ing" (the verb), and that this entails being crucified with the Messiah. Co-crucifixion with the Messiah, in turn, entails two corollary "deaths": death to the law as the means of justification, and the death of the self. The result is being transferred into the realm of the Messiah, which means a "resurrection" to new life. (Our focus in this part of the chapter is on dying, and in the next part on resurrection to life, but in reality they are inseparable.)

It is important at this point to recall what I have argued under the first claim above: that Paul does not change subjects as he moves from the beginning to the end of this passage. In other words, when Paul speaks in the first-person-singular about being crucified with the Messiah, he is speaking about justification. This is part of his creative contribution to the first-century "justification wars." But before Paul arrives at this innovative description of justification, he speaks first about faith and about being in the Messiah.

One of the major concerns people have voiced about the "faith of Christ" interpretation of this passage and other texts is that it allegedly downplays the human response of faith. This concern is unnecessary, for in all the Pauline passages in question, human faith is affirmed, including this text. What Paul does, however, is to redefine faith (as he does justification), and he does so at least partly in light of his characterization of Jesus' death itself as an act of faith, or faithfulness.

Accordingly, we find Paul's statement about human faith in the midst of his double mention of the faith of Jesus, in verse 16:

> *eidotes [de] hoti ou dikaioutai anthrōpos ex ergōn nomou ean mē dia **pisteōs Iēsou Christou, kai hēmeis** eis Christon Iēsoun **episteusamen**, hina dikaiōthōmen **ek pisteōs Christou** kai ouk ex ergōn nomou, hoti ex ergōn nomou ou dikaiōthēsetai pasa sarx.*

> because we know that no person is justified by virtue of works of the law but rather through **the faithfulness of Jesus the Messiah, even we came to faith** [that incorporates us] into the Messiah Jesus, so that we would be justified by virtue of **the faithfulness of the Messiah** and not by virtue of works of the law.

With respect to the mode of justification, the key phrase in this sentence is *kai hēmeis eis Christon Iēsoun episteusamen, hina dikaiōthōmen ek pisteōs Christou*: "Even we came to faith [that incorporates us] into the Messiah Jesus, so that we would be justified by virtue of the faithfulness of the Messiah." The linguistic challenge of English is again on vivid display here, with no good way to convey the profound theological point Paul makes about faith (Gk. *pistis*): the human act of *pistis* is a response to the *pistis* of Messiah Jesus. In some sense, then, human *pistis* must inherently include a fidelity, a commitment, that entails more (though not less) than either intellectual assent or affective trust.

This sense of faith as fidelity and commitment—which some might wrongly take as a reference to salvation by human effort—does not make the faith-ing person's *pistis* into the *means* of justification, which remains the faithfulness of Jesus in his death, but it is in fact the necessary *mode*.[26] This grace-enabled human act of faith (cf. Phil. 1:29) results in justification, then, but only on the basis of Jesus' faithful death. Means and mode belong together; in fact, they intersect, even overlap, since both involve death—a shared death (see further below).

Faith "into" Christ

The meaning of the "state" of justification, so to speak, is further clarified by the phrase that precedes (in Greek) the verb "we came to faith": *eis Christon Iēsoun*. Almost always translated "in" (so every translation consulted), the preposition *eis* ("into") in this phrase more likely indicates the direction toward which a dynamic act—namely, faith—propels the one who expresses such faith. That is, "we believed into Jesus the Messiah." This is the act of faithful response to the faithful death of Jesus that results in being "in" the Messiah; Matthew Bates calls this faithful response "giving allegiance" in response to the allegiance of Jesus.[27] In the language of E. P. Sanders, a "transfer" has occurred;[28] we might even say a transfer of allegiance. (Paul would no doubt attribute this movement into the Messiah to the work of the Spirit—see 3:1–5 too—but that is not his emphasis here.) Hence my translation's bracketed phrase "that incorporates us." Paul implies that this movement is in fact what has happened when he speaks in 2:17 of "seeking to be justified in the Messiah": *zētountes dikaiōthēnai en Christō*. This is not a statement about a search that might terminate with justification in the Messiah, but rather a statement about an assumed, existing state, the consequence of having *pistis*: being in the Messiah, and claiming that that is the place where justification occurs. Such a claim has probably been questioned by critics of Paul, who contend that his understanding of justification makes the Messiah into a "servant of sin."

The phrase "into the Messiah Jesus" (*eis Christon Iēsoun*) in verse 16 has an exact parallel at the beginning of 3:27: "For as many of you who were baptized

---

26. The aorist verb *episteusamen* is usually translated as "(have) believed" or "have come/came to believe," though NIV has "have put our faith" (Gal. 2:16). Whether the conjunction *hina* ("so that") is taken as indicating purpose or result, the relation between the faith of Jesus and of humans remains the same: means and mode, objective and subjective basis, source and appropriating response.

27. Bates, *Salvation by Allegiance Alone*, 81.

28. Sanders, *Paul and Palestinian Judaism*, 463–72, 503, 506, 545; Sanders, *Paul: The Apostle's Life, Letters, and Thought*, 506, 511, 569, 638–39.

into the Messiah" (*hosoi gar eis Christon ebaptisthēte*), with the verb again following the phrase. The parallel suggests a close relationship in Paul's mind between faith and baptism as acts of transfer into the (realm of the) Messiah. Immediately after 3:27, Paul famously affirms that all who have been baptized are one in the Messiah: "for all of you are one in Christ Jesus" (3:28; *pantes gar hymeis heis este en Christō Iēsou*), the phrase *en Christō Iēsou* being equivalent to *en Christō Iēsou* in 2:17. Theologically, Paul's close association of "faith-ing" and being baptized suggests that these two modes of transfer into the Messiah should not be separated.[29] For Paul they are two sides of the one coin of conversion/initiation that is a death-and-resurrection experience. Furthermore, the theme of unity in Galatians 3:28 indicates clearly that justification has a horizontal, or ecclesial, dimension, as its context also makes clear (especially 2:1–14); it is not simply about "me and Jesus." We will return to this below.

Faith as Co-crucifixion

If Paul has said that human faith is a response to the faith of Jesus, then it should come as no surprise that he develops this idea further, and with imaginative imagery, by depicting "justification by faith," to use the Reformers' language, in terms of participating in Jesus' faithful death, or co-crucifixion: "I have been crucified with the Messiah" (*Christō synestaurōmai*; v. 19b). The verb *systauroō* ("crucify with") occurs just five times in the New Testament, three times with a literal sense in the Gospels (Matt. 27:44; Mark 15:32; John 19:32) and twice metaphorically (though "metaphor" is insufficient to describe what Paul is doing with the word) in Paul's letters, here in Galatians 2:19 and in Romans 6:6.[30] We cite one of those Gospel texts and both of Paul's:

> *ho christos ho basileus Israēl katabatō nyn apo tou staurou, hina idōmen kai pisteusōmen. kai hoi* **synestaurōmenoi** *syn autō ōneidizon auton.*

> "Let the **Messiah**, the King of Israel, come down from the cross now, so that we may see and believe." Those who were **crucified with him** also taunted him. (Mark 15:32; cf. Matt. 27:43–44)

> *egō gar dia nomou nomō apethanon, hina theō zēsō.* **Christō synestaurōmai**

> For I myself, through the law, died in relation to the law so that I could live in relation to God. I have been **crucified with the Messiah**. (Gal. 2:19 MJG)

---

29. I have explored these connections in more detail, with reference also to Rom. 6, in *Inhabiting the Cruciform God*, 63–79.

30. De Boer (*Galatians*, 160) says that the ("nomistic") "I" has been "metaphorically yet truly crucified."

*touto ginōskontes hoti ho palaios hēmōn anthrōpos **synestaurōthē**, hina katargēthē to sōma tēs hamartias, tou mēketi douleuein hēmas tē hamartia*

We know that our old self **was crucified with him** so that the body of sin would be destroyed, and we might no longer be enslaved to sin. (Rom. 6:6 NRSV alt.)

Both Mark's and Matthew's combination of the verb *systauroō* ("co-crucify") with an explicit reference to the Messiah in the same breath (Messiah in Mark 15:32; Son of God in Matt. 27:40, 43) makes it rather likely that Paul knew at least an oral tradition similar to that which is preserved in these Gospels. So what is Paul doing theologically with this language?

For those like Paul who were not literally present with, much less crucified with, the Messiah, the literal co-crucifixion of those who insulted Jesus even as he was dying for them is paradigmatic in at least two ways. First, the connection emphasizes the great love (Gal. 2:20) that Jesus had, and that God displayed in Jesus, for his enemies (cf. Rom. 5:6–8). Justification means the justification of the ungodly (Rom. 4:5; 5:6). Amazingly, to be *crucified with* Jesus is to be *loved by* Jesus, loved to the uttermost, as the Fourth Gospel puts it (John 13:1). Second, the connection suggests that to have faith "into" Jesus is to so fully identify with his death that what happened to Jesus also happens to the "believer": a death, a termination of previous existence.

Despite the linguistic connection between the passion narrative(s) and Galatians, being crucified with the Messiah does not occur "when Christ died," as some have said.[31] It occurs, rather, at the time of initial faith and its public manifestation in baptism, as the parallels between 2:19–20 and Romans 6:1–11 indicate.[32] The effects of that co-crucifixion endure, as the perfect tense of the verb (*synestaurōmai*, "I have been crucified") suggests.

Death to the Law and the Death of the (Old) Self

Looking at 2:19–20 by itself, apart from the connection to the Gospel tradition, we find that crucifixion with the Messiah entails death to the law and the death of the (old) self.

31. E.g., from different interpretive perspectives, Schreiner (*Galatians*, 171) and Moo (*Galatians*, 171: "Believers are regarded by God as having hung on the cross with Christ"), on the one hand, and de Boer (*Galatians*, 160–61), on the other. This interpretation can effectively rule out a connection between co-crucifixion and justification (though it does not for de Boer).

32. Moreover, Gal. 3:1–5 indicates that receipt of the Spirit, part of the initiation into the Messiah through the death and resurrection described in 2:19–20, occurs in connection with a faith-filled response to the message of the crucified Messiah.

"I have died in relation to the law," or possibly "with respect to the law" (*nomō*; dative case), means a severance from reliance on the law for life.[33] This suggests that "life" and "justification" are overlapping terms, as 3:21 confirms, claiming that the law can effect neither: "For if a law had been given that could make alive, then righteousness would indeed come through the law" (*ei gar edothē nomos ho dynamenos zōopoiēsai, ontōs ek nomou an ēn hē dikaiosynē*). A "death" to the law was necessary for Paul "so that I could live in relation to/with respect to God" (*hina theō zēsō*; another, parallel instance of the dative case). The rather shocking assumption behind this claim in verse 19 is that the very thing the Scriptures said, and Jews believed, would bring them life—the law—did not and does not do so. In the words of Michael Wolter, with the gift of the Torah God had "given Israel the possibility of an abiding participation in God's sanctity."[34] Because of the Messiah, the means of such life-giving participation in God's holiness has now changed in Paul's view.

But although the "I" in 2:19–20 is certainly autobiographical—Paul's interpretation of his call (1:10–24) as a death (and new life), or a transformation/conversion—it also certainly applies beyond his own life.[35] As always when speaking autobiographically in his letters, Paul is here speaking paradigmatically as well. *Jews* who have accepted the death of the Messiah as the means of justification/life have ended, or should end, any dependence on the law for justification. They should also terminate any practices that, despite shared participation in the Messiah, would separate gentiles from them, for (as Paul will later say) the law's function has been completed (3:19–26). Moreover, *gentiles* who have accepted the death of the Messiah as the means of justification should not now pursue the law in any way, no matter who might encourage them to seek circumcision or whatever. Thus "I have died to the law" is a death that applies to all in the Messiah, Jews and gentiles alike. Theologically speaking, since the law is repeatedly named in this passage as the (false) alternative means of justification, we may say by extension—without at all discounting the specific reference to the Jewish law and its practices—that dying to the law means the renunciation of any and all alleged means of justification, of life in relation to God, and in fact of "righteousness" (2:21)

33. This dying to the law is not only a comment on the previous verse but also part of the entire rejection of the law as the means to life and justification.

34. Wolter, *Paul*, 17.

35. De Boer (*Galatians*, 159) calls 2:19–20 both "the theological high point" of Gal. 1–2 and "Paul's (further) interpretation of his conversion." Wolter responds to the debate about Paul's transformation—was it a call or a conversion?—with a strongly worded "both": "Anyone who gives up the category of 'conversion' or semantically analogous concepts . . . does not at all come close to the meaning of the vision of Christ for Pauline biography and theology" (*Paul*, 28).

other than the saving death of Jesus. There is no other way to participate in the holiness and life of God.

Furthermore, Paul's claim that "I myself no longer live" (*zō de ouketi egō*), with stress on the pronoun (*egō*) representing the "I," the self, expands the death motif beyond the notion of death with respect to the law; it entails the death of the person qua person. The "old person" or "former self" (*ho palaios hēmōn anthrōpos*—plural, and inclusive of all in the Messiah: "our old self/selves") has died, as Paul puts it in Romans in connection with baptism (Rom. 6:6, cited above). Such language, though it may spring from reflection on a "death" to the law, is not restricted to that context; it is language understandable by and applicable to all humans. Elsewhere Scripture speaks of new birth (John 3; 1 Pet. 1:23); Paul will soon employ the language of new creation (Gal. 6:15; cf. 2 Cor. 5:17). Entering the new creation requires forsaking the old, including the old self and old humanity that are determined by that old creation.

The larger context of Galatians further enlarges our understanding of co-crucifixion with the Messiah, and its applicability to all, as the verb *stauroō* ("crucify") appears two times in reference to believers (plus once in reference to Jesus [3:1]). In 5:24 Paul says those who belong to the Messiah have crucified "the flesh," together with its passions and desires (*hoi de tou Christou [Iēsou] tēn sarka estaurōsan syn tois pathēmasin kai tais epithymiais*). The presence of several words found also in 2:19–20—"Messiah" (Jesus), "flesh," and "crucify"—suggests that 5:24 is a brief commentary on 2:19–20. Those who belong to the Messiah *live in* the flesh, but they are not *governed by* the flesh—that is, by base passions and desires. The extension in 5:24 of the crucifixion metaphor to all who belong to the Messiah confirms the claim that 2:19 is also true of all who are in the Messiah. In 6:14, containing the second instance of *stauroō* ("crucify") referring to believers, Paul again employs first-person-singular language but certainly, once again, in a paradigmatic way. As he pronounces both circumcision and uncircumcision soteriologically irrelevant and denounces any pride in "the flesh," he also announces the focus of his own life and source of his own pride—"the cross of our Lord Jesus the Messiah"—as the fruit of his having been crucified to the world, and it to him (6:11–17).

Thus, to be co-crucified with the Messiah entails severing any attachment to normal human values, even the most religious ones, that in any way contradict the saving power of the crucified Messiah—"the cross." It alone is the means by which God has effected salvation, indeed the "new creation" (6:15). As such, as we saw in the previous chapter, the cross is an "apocalyptic" event, the definitive divine incursion into the human predicament that delivers people both from their sins and from the "present evil age" (1:4) into this new creation. We can also say, therefore, that to be crucified with the Messiah means to be personally "invaded" by this apocalyptic event of divine giving and messianic self-giving, and thereby to receive the benefits of the incursion named in 1:4 and elsewhere in the letter (e.g., the gift of the Spirit in 3:1–5; adoption as children in 4:4–6). It is not so much a decision made as an invasion experienced, a gift received—indicated by the passive voice: "I have been crucified."

Finally, although we must be careful not to make too much of the perfect tense of that passive voice, it does suggest, not a one-time reality, but an ongoing reality with a one-time starting point, a vocation with a specific start date but no termination date. Thus the death with Jesus of which Paul writes is not over; it continues into the present. And this ongoing reality of co-crucifixion with the Messiah leads us ineluctably to the conclusion that, in close connection with death, there has also been resurrection—the Messiah's and "mine."

That, in fact, is the subject to which we now turn. It follows directly from the discussion of this third claim, in which I have argued that when Paul speaks of justification, its mode is co-crucifixion with the Messiah, which is the faith by which a person is transferred into the realm of Jesus the Messiah, the "location" of justification.

Justification as Resurrection

4. According to Galatians 2:15–21, justification is participation not only in the Messiah's death but also in his resurrection, which means that justification entails resurrection to new life—that is, the emergence of a new self indwelt by the (Spirit of the) Messiah and living in proper relation to God.

Galatians 2:15–21 contains no specific reference to Jesus' resurrection; neither is there a specific word about believers sharing in that resurrection, whether now or later. Unlike the creed-like text in 1 Corinthians 15, the explicit language of our text says simply that the Messiah died, and nothing about his being raised. Unlike the participatory interpretation of baptism in Romans 6, which echoes that creed, the explicit claim of our text is simply that "I" died, "I" was crucified with him. Nevertheless, within these verses are strong implicit references to resurrection, both the resurrection of Jesus and the resurrection of believers to new life in him.[36] Indeed, the ultimate

---

36. Boakye (*Death and Life*, 87, 89) rightly sees a correspondence between the resurrection of Jesus (1:1) and the transformation of Paul narrated in 2:19. He interprets 2:19–20 (93–119) as

theological focus of 2:19–20 is life, living. Paul's supreme interest, as we see in 3:21 (noted above), is being made alive (indicated by the verb *zōopoiēsai*), glossed as *dikaiosynē* (cf. Rom. 5:17–21). In fact, Paul affirms throughout 2:15–21 both that justification means life and that such life comes, paradoxically, through death—both the Messiah's and "mine," or ours. We turn now to the rhetorical, theological, and spiritual telos of this death: life.

The verb *zaō* ("live") occurs five times in 2:19–20, once in verse 19 and four times in verse 20. The first instance, in verse 19, defines justification as having life, specifically living in relation to God:

*egō gar dia nomou nomō apethanon, **hina theō zēsō**.*

For I myself, through the law, died in relation to the law **so that I could live** in relation to God.

The *hina* ("so that"), or purpose, clause in which the verb "live" is located is parallel to the *hina* clause in the middle of verse 16:

hina dikaiōthōmen *ek pisteōs Christou kai ouk ex ergōn nomou*

so that we would be justified by virtue of the faithfulness of the Messiah and not by virtue of works of the law

According to both verses, the soteriological goal of life/justification is realized only apart from the law, as also in 3:21. That which was believed to give life did not. In verse 19, the way in which this soteriological goal is realized is paradoxical: it occurs only by a death that makes life possible.[37]

The four occurrences of the verb *zaō* ("live") in verse 20 speak of four interrelated realities that Paul narrates in the first person with implications for all who are in the Messiah: (a) the death of myself—that is, the end of my previous life, life in its default mode; (b) the presence of the Messiah living in me; (c) the affirmation that in spite of my death, I do in fact live; and (d) the claim that I now live by means of the faithfulness of God's Son. The dominance of the self in this verse is expressed in several ways, including the use of three first-person-singular verbs ("live" three times) and four first-person-singular pronouns ("I," "me"): *zō . . . egō* [I myself . . . live] . . . *emoi* [me] . . . *zō* [I

---

one of the key texts demonstrating that rectification in Galatians is resurrection, or (his preferred term) revivification. (Boakye, 20–21, prefers "rectification" to "justification," incorporating both forensic and, especially, participationist elements into his interpretation.)

37. De Boer refers to this dynamic as Paul's "negative soteriology" and "positive soteriology," which constitute "two sides of the same coin" ("Cross and Cosmos in Galatians"). On 3:21 and revivification, see Boakye, *Death and Life*, 120–58.

Table 6.4. The Role of the Messiah in the Self's Death and Life

The Self's Death and Life	The Role of the Messiah
(a) *zō de ouketi egō,* thus I myself no longer **live,**	(b) *zē de en emoi Christos* but the Messiah **lives** in me;
(a') *ho de nyn zō en sarki*	(b') *en pistei zō tē tou huiou tou theou tou agapēsantos me kai paradontos heauton hyper emou.*
and the life I do now **live** in the flesh,	I **live** by means of the faithfulness of the Son of God, who loved me by giving himself for me.

live] . . . *zō* [I live] . . . *me* [me] . . . *emou* [me]. But ultimately the stress is on the presence of the living Messiah; the whole point of the verse is that Paul's self is no longer determined by himself but by Another.

We can see this clearly by laying out once again the parallel phrases in verse 20, thus highlighting the four occurrences of *zaō* ("live") in verse 20 and the four realities to which they point in two pairs, one pair—(a) and (a')—focusing on the self's (death and) life, the other pair—(b) and (b')—focusing on the role of the Messiah in that life (table 6.4 above).

Taken together, these four statements point to the overarching reality of resurrection. Jesus the Messiah has obviously been raised from the dead or he would be unable to live "in me." At the same time, and in a highly paradoxical way, Paul's dead self has also been resurrected; he has died but is alive, enlivened by the presence of the living Messiah.[38] Paul is clearly speaking about participating in the Messiah's resurrection in the present, about co-resurrection with Jesus to new life. What he says by clear implication here, we find elsewhere in the Pauline letters more explicitly, using language that would have been completely appropriate here: *synegeirō* ("raise with") in the passive voice, as in Colossians and Ephesians (Col. 2:12; 3:1; Eph. 2:6); or *zōopoieō* ("make alive, give life to"), as in Romans 4:17 in describing God as the one who gives life to the dead (in the context of Abraham's justification: *theou tou zōopoiountos tous nekrous kai kalountos ta mē onta hōs onta*);[39] or perhaps the language of Romans 6:4:

> *synetaphēmen oun autō dia tou baptismatos eis ton thanaton, hina hōsper egerthē Christos ek nekrōn dia tēs doxēs tou patros, houtōs kai hēmeis en kainotēti zōēs peripatēsōmen.*

38. Boakye says that the text affirms that "God had effected in Paul, by virtue of Paul's faith, what he had effected in Jesus" (*Death and Life*, 114).

39. That is, "who gives life to the dead and calls into existence the things that do not exist" (NRSV). See the discussion of Abraham's justification/resurrection in chap. 8.

> Therefore we have been buried with him by baptism into his death, so that, just as the Messiah was raised from among the dead by the glory of the Father, so we too might walk in newness of life. (MJG)

The phrase "newness of life" (*kainotēti zōēs*) is another way of saying "I myself no longer live; well, I do live, but it's not me, it's the Messiah in me." Faith and baptism, again, are two sides of the one coin of entrance into the Messiah and into resurrection life.

We know from Romans 8, especially, that Paul identifies the indwelling Messiah with the indwelling Spirit. In that context, Paul lets the Romans know that they (individually and corporately, he implies) are inhabited by the Spirit of God, who is the Spirit of the Messiah, who is the source of their righteousness and life (Rom. 8:3–4, 9–11). The same spirituality is present here in Galatians, though less fully developed in a single passage. But Galatians 4 says specifically that the Spirit whom God "has sent . . . into our hearts"—an allusion to the promise of Ezekiel 36:26, as we saw in the previous chapter—is "the Spirit of his [God's] Son" (Gal. 4:6). This is the Spirit the Galatians received, not "by doing the works of the law," but by believing the message of the crucified Messiah (3:1–2).

That 3:1–2 follows directly after 2:15–21 implies that Paul integrates receiving the Spirit (as a consequence of believing the gospel of the crucified Messiah) with the singular experience of believing into the Messiah, dying and rising with the Messiah, and being initially indwelt by the Messiah. *These constitute not a series of events but different angles on one reality.* For Paul, the Spirit, not the law, was "the means by which Jewish and non-Jewish Christians received in one and the same way one and the same purity and participation in God's sanctity—the sanctity that characterized the people of God."[40] The result is what Paul will later in Galatians call "walking" in or by the Spirit (5:16)—the Spirit of the crucified and resurrected Messiah. Paradoxically (once again), therefore, the shape of this new, resurrection life in the Messiah/the Spirit, and with the Messiah/the Spirit within, is cruciform. Paul's spirituality, as we have seen again and again, is a resurrectional cruciformity—and both words are critical. Moreover, as noted earlier, co-crucifixion with the Messiah is an ongoing vocation, an ongoing sharing in the death of Jesus that is, paradoxically, life. More specifically, it is sharing in Jesus' faithfulness and love—to which we turn in the next section.

To summarize the fourth claim in this chapter: just as justification involves death to the law and the death of the former self, so also it entails resurrection to life with God and a new self, reconstituted by the crucified and

---

40. Wolter, *Paul*, 35.

resurrected Messiah Jesus, in whom believers live and who lives in them by his Spirit. This spirituality of mutual indwelling will mean that participation entails transformation; the substance of *dikaiōsis*/*dikaiousthai* ("being justified"/"justification") is *dikaiosynē* ("justice/righteousness"), which is the focus of the fifth claim.

Justification as Transformation into Justice/Righteousness (Faithfulness and Love)

5. According to Galatians 2:15–21, justification as participation in Jesus' death and resurrection means transformation into justice/righteousness, which will be exhibited fundamentally as cruciform faithfulness and love.

So far we have noted that the death of Jesus, not the law, is the means to justification (v. 16) and life (v. 19), and I have argued that justification and life are parallel—indeed, semantically overlapping—terms, two ways of referring to the same reality. We come, finally, in the last line of the passage (v. 21), to a third parallel term pointing to this one reality: *dikaiosynē*. The translation and interpretation of this word will have a significant impact on one's understanding of the passage as a whole. The argument made here is that either "righteousness" or "justice" (not "justification") is the best translation into English, for the point of verse 21 is that what the law fails to effect is the moral reality constitutive of being justified and of life in relation to God.[41]

The interpretation of verse 21 raises a theological question that has concerned and divided Christians for centuries: Does justification entail transformation? More specifically (and admittedly a bit oversimplified), does justification entail being counted righteous (having the righteousness of Christ imputed) or being made righteous (having the righteousness of Christ imparted)? Some proponents of the New Perspective might add yet another possibility: Does justification entail being regarded as a member of the community of the righteous? A related question is whether *dikaiosynē* even has any sense of morality or ethics; is it simply a term for some sort of status? (There are, of course, various permutations and combinations of these questions and perspectives.)

It is tempting, especially within certain theological traditions, to allow one's theological framework to determine the possible acceptable answers,

41. Justification and righteousness in Paul have at times been correctly described as "relational" but incorrectly as "relational rather than ethical"—a claim that makes no sense whatsoever in either a Jewish or Christian context, for biblical relationships are covenantal and thus inherently carry obligations.

or even the sole acceptable answer, to the concrete exegetical question about the meaning of *dikaiosynē* in the second half of verse 21. English translations are somewhat unpredictable in their renderings of this text:

> If righteousness could be gained through the law, Christ died for nothing! (NIV)

> If keeping the law could make us right with God, then there was no need for Christ to die. (NLT)

> If justification comes through the law, then Christ died for nothing. (NRSV, with a note that "righteousness" is an alternative translation; NAB)

> If saving justice comes through the Law, Christ died needlessly. (NJB)

> If we become righteous through the Law, then Christ died for no purpose. (CEB)

The major evangelical Protestant translation (NIV) uses "righteousness" but does not interpret its specific meaning. More predictably, another evangelical translation (NLT) seems to define righteousness or justification more definitively as "mak[ing] us right with God." The major mainline ecumenical (NRSV) and Catholic (NAB) translations employ, without specific interpretation, "justification." Another Catholic translation (NJB) goes in a very different direction and uses "saving justice." Only one recent major translation, the ecumenical CEB, renders the phrase in a way that explicitly conveys transformation: "if we become righteous."

How do we determine the significance of *dikaiosynē* here without being unduly influenced by our theological lenses? It will be useful to see how Paul uses the word later in Galatians. There are three additional occurrences in Galatians, plus the one instance of the cognate adjective *dikaios*.

Dikaiosynē *Elsewhere in Galatians*

In Galatians 3:6 Paul quotes Genesis 15:6 LXX: *kathōs Abraam episteusen tō theō, kai elogisthē autō eis dikaiosynēn* ("Just as Abraham 'believed God . . .'"). The standard translation of this verse is to render the second clause as follows: "and it was reckoned [or credited] to him as righteousness." Now there is no reason to deny Paul's use of the accounting metaphor here (as also in Rom. 4), because God's "accounting" is efficacious (see the next section). However, the contextual connection with both "life" (3:11) and the Spirit (3:14) suggests that Paul is thinking of life in the Spirit as the consequence of faith. Thus it would be better to understand the phrase *eis dikaiosynēn* not as "as righteousness," as if the act of faith were being counted as righteousness, but as "resulting in righteousness." That is, the outcome of faith is taking on the quality of righteousness (implicitly by an act of divine grace, not human effort).

In the same context, Galatians 3:11 seems to equate justification, indicated by the verb, and being just/righteous, indicated by the nominalized adjective: *hoti de en nomō oudeis **dikaioutai** para tō theō dēlon, hoti **ho dikaios** ek pisteōs zēsetai.* The NRSV translates this as "Now it is evident that no one is justified before God by the law; for 'The one who is righteous will live by faith.'"[42] Once again, the CEB alone among English translations captures the transformative sense: "But since no one **is made righteous** by the Law . . . , **the righteous one** will live on the basis of faith." Other translations have "no one is justified" (NJB: "reckoned as upright"). This standard sort of translation fails to show that justification means the creation of a just person and a just people. The "faith" that is the source of *ho dikaios* ("the righteous one") "living" could be either that of the person being justified (the *mode* of justification, over against keeping the law) or that of the Messiah (the *means* of justification, over against the law). In either case, the result is an actual *dikaios* (righteous/just) person.

Galatians 3:21b, as noted earlier, is a contrary-to-fact condition that restates the contrary-to-fact condition in 2:21. It also includes an important echo of 2:19–20 and of 3:11 with its motif of "life": *ei gar edothē nomos ho dynamenos **zōopoiēsai**, ontōs ek nomou an ēn hē **dikaiosynē**.* The NRSV renders this as "For if a law had been given that could **make alive**, then **righteousness** would indeed come through the law." Curiously, despite the similarity of 3:21 to 2:21, no major English translation renders *hē dikaiosynē* in 3:21 as "justification." With the exception of the NJB's "saving justice," they all, like the NRSV, use "righteousness." The *dikaiosynē* mentioned in this verse is the material substance of "life."

Taken together, these three verses in chapter 3—two using the noun *dikaiosynē* and one the related nominalized adjective *dikaios*—imply that whatever else being justified (*dikaiousthai*) means, it entails the transformation of people into those who possess the quality of righteousness/justice, those who are in fact righteous/just. This quality is the fundamental content of the "life" in the Spirit that justification effects.

Galatians 5:5 contains the final instance of *dikaiosynē* in the letter: *hēmeis gar pneumati ek pisteōs elpida **dikaiosynēs** apekdechometha*, rendered by the

---

42. Whether we translate the second clause as "for the one who is righteous by faith will live" or "for the one who is righteous will live by faith," the text indicates an actual state of righteousness, an actual righteous person. In addition, we again have a reference to justification as life.

NRSV as "For through the Spirit, by faith, we eagerly wait for the hope of **righteousness**." This text might appear to suggest that *dikaiosynē* is only a future reality—a positive divine verdict at the final judgment or an eschatological transformation. But the context suggests otherwise. Paul is once again denying that the law can justify and affirming that grace alone—an echo of "the grace of God" (2:21), and thus ultimately a reference to the Messiah's death—does so (5:4). Paul's immediate concern here is preventing gentiles from seeking circumcision (5:2–3). His rationale for this is not only that the law (and its associated practices) cannot justify but also that neither possessing nor lacking circumcision "counts for anything" (5:6a, NRSV, NAB) or "carries any weight" (NET).[43] What does matter, however, is *pistis di' agapēs energoumenē*: "faith working through love" (most English translations), or "faith expressing itself through love" (NIV), or even "faithfulness issuing in love" (MJG).

From Dikaiosynē *to* Dikaiosynē

The pregnant phrase about faithfulness and love in 5:6 takes us back to 2:15–21, and specifically to the earlier argument that the Messiah's death was an act of faith(fulness) and love. If it is the faithful and loving death of the Messiah that is the apocalypse of God's grace and the means of justification—of making people righteous—and if that crucified-but-resurrected Messiah now dwells in and among the people who have been justified, then their individual and corporate lives will be characterized by the Messiah's faithfulness and love.[44] That is, in anticipation of their hoped-for eschatological righteousness, those who are in the Messiah and thus already made righteous in him will practice righteousness now by embodying the Messiah-like qualities of faithfulness and love. To borrow from 2 Corinthians 3:18 ("transformed . . . from glory to glory," NAB), it is as if Paul is saying that those in the Messiah are being changed "from righteousness to righteousness."

We have already seen that Paul speaks in terms of being justified, living in relation to God, and possessing righteousness (*dikaiosynē*) as three ways of referring to the same reality, a reality made possible by Jesus' faithful and loving death. Righteousness, then, is not only *derived* from the Messiah's death but also *defined* by the Messiah's death. His faithful and loving death is both the source and the shape of righteousness. These two qualities, this fundamental meaning of *dikaiosynē*, further clarify what being crucified with the Messiah means: it entails sharing in his death by practicing faithfulness and love. Such practices

43. Gk. *ischyei*.
44. This connection between 2:15–21 and 5:6 is persuasively made by Richard B. Hays in his classic essay "Christology and Ethics in Galatians."

are made possible by means of the indwelling Messiah, as 2:20 tells us—the indwelling of the Spirit of the Son (4:6). Accordingly, we should understand the lengthy exposition of a life of walking in the Spirit, guided by the Spirit, in Galatians 5 and 6 as an elaboration of the basic claim that those made righteous in the Messiah (2:17; *en Christō*) embody Messiah-like faithfulness and love, the "vertical" and "horizontal" relational requirements of covenantal existence.

The Christian tradition has several terms for the process of taking on God-like qualities by virtue of the empowering activity and presence of Christ/the Spirit. But it may be most appropriate (though shocking to some), if we are going to allow Paul's thought and language of justification as actual transformation, in the Messiah, into God's righteousness to have its full theological impact, (1) to use the term "theosis" or "deification" in connection with justification, and (2) to say that such transformation into Godlikeness is constitutive of justification itself.[45] This would not, of course, mean that justification entails crossing the line that divides creature from Creator, but it would mean stressing what Paul himself stresses: that God's justifying action means the transformation of the unrighteous into the righteous, such that they take on something of God's righteousness that was displayed in Jesus' faithful and loving death (cf. Rom. 3:21–26), in anticipation of the final eschatological reality of full participation in the righteousness of God. This is what the law could not do—make people alive in this full sense of sharing in the very life of God.[46]

The objections of some to this claim will be forceful indeed, but in the next section I suggest that it is possible to maintain an understanding of justification as divine declaration and still hold to its transformative quality. Moreover, it is possible to place all of these claims within the corporate context of covenant membership. Transformation into righteousness—the main point of the present claim—is compatible with both declarative and incorporative understandings of justification.

Participatory, Transformative Justification as Inclusive of Covenantal and Forensic Dimensions

6. A participatory and transformative understanding of justification based on 2:15–21 does not rule out either (1) a covenantal, primarily "horizontal" understanding of justification as membership in the covenant community grounded in the context

---

45. I repeat, yet again, that the language of theosis is helpful and accurate, but not necessary—but only if other language can adequately convey this claim.

46. Betz (*Galatians*, 125) rightly says that believers receive the "'divine life'" and refers to parallel notions in antiquity. See also my *Inhabiting the Cruciform God*, esp. 40–104; Litwa, *We Are Being Transformed*, though his work needs some correcting; Blackwell, *Christosis*.

of gentile acceptance or (2) a declarative understanding of justification—if a divine declaration is rightly understood as effective.

I would anticipate at this point that, on the one hand, Pauline interpreters who lean toward a traditional Protestant perspective are happy with the focus on the individual person that has characterized this chapter thus far. On the other hand, many of them are likely highly dissatisfied with the thesis that justification is participatory and even transformative—much less theotic! This participatory and transformative interpretation may please certain members of the "apocalyptic" school of Pauline interpretation, however, as well as Catholics and Orthodox (and their "heirs" in other traditions) who are theologically predisposed to that point of view. What about those from the New Perspective? What appears to be an overemphasis on the individual and the "vertical" dimension of justification may leave them unhappy that the communal, ecclesial, "horizontal" dimension of justification has not received its due.

Justification is a polyvalent reality for Paul. What I have been doing thus far is arguing from Galatians 2:15–21 for some distinctive aspects of Paul's interpretation of justification that have sometimes been underappreciated, especially in the West and particularly among Protestants.[47] I turn now, briefly, to show how these distinctive dimensions do not exclude other aspects, and how they are, in fact, related to them. While it is important to see 2:15–21 as a distinct unit, this text is also closely related to the narratives of the events at Antioch and at Galatia (2:11–14 and 3:1–5, respectively), as well as the discussion of justification throughout Galatians 3.

Covenantal (Corporate) Justification

It is absolutely clear that the presenting problem that elicits Paul's interpretation of justification in 2:15–21 is the sudden apartheid that was created by Cephas and others when they stopped eating with gentiles out of fear of the "circumcision faction" (2:11–13). Accordingly, Paul's response, and thus the theology of justification he creatively articulates, are inherently corporate: horizontal and ecclesial. The overemphasis by some proponents of the New Perspective, especially early in the movement, on this aspect of justification does not invalidate the fundamental claim: justification is about who gets into the covenant people, now defined by the Messiah Jesus, and how.[48]

47. For a significant Roman Catholic perspective on justification in Paul, in conversation with the New Perspective (Wright) and others, see Stegman, "Paul's Use of *dikaio-* Terminology."

48. See the classic New Perspective exposition in Dunn, *Epistle to the Galatians*, 131–50. Cf. the essay introducing his collection of essays for his later, or clarified, emphasis on both the horizontal and the vertical: "New Perspective on Paul," esp. 32–33.

This corporate, horizontal aspect of justification is present in our passage in at least two principal ways. First, there is the presence of first-person-plural verbs and pronouns in 2:15–17, which Paul uses to remind his audience that, although justification occurs one person at a time (indicated by the first-person-singular verbs and pronouns signifying "I"/"me" in 2:18–21), it is ultimately about "us," about being together "in the Messiah," the locus of justification (2:17). Second, this "in the Messiah" language—and implicitly also the "Messiah in" language—is inherently communal, not merely individual. The "transfer" language ("into the Messiah") of faith and baptism (2:16 and 3:27, respectively) and the resulting "incorporative" language ("in the Messiah," 2:17; 3:28) refer to a communal reality—membership in the people of God reconfigured by the Messiah and ruled by his presence and power.

This corporate understanding of justification is manifest, then, in the discussion of baptism and unity in the Messiah at the end of Galatians 3, which is the culmination of everything Paul says about the Galatians' receiving the Spirit (3:1–5) and their being offspring of Abraham by virtue of their being in the Messiah (3:14), the one seed (*sperma*) of Abraham (3:16). The references to justification in Galatians 3 (some of which were considered in the previous section of this chapter) must be understood in this corporate way, as the presence of multiple first-person-*plural* verbs and pronouns ("we"/"us") confirms. As in 2:15–21, however, the communal character of justification does not rule out the need for each person to be justified, as the example of Abraham (3:6) and the first of two summary statements about justification using the verb *dikaioō* (3:11–12) indicate.[49]

Forensic (Effective) Justification

It seems evident that justification in this context is more than a divine declaration, as some have insisted over the centuries (or at least the kind of divine declaration they have proposed). Although there may be other texts where *dikaioō* means a divine pronouncement of acquittal or vindication, that simply does not seem to be the case in Galatians 3 any more than it does in Galatians 2. Rather, when justification occurs, something happens: people receive life, they become children of Abraham, they are clothed with the Messiah and incorporated into him, and so on.

It may, however, be the case that justification as divine declaration and justification as divine transformative action are actually not distinct and mutually exclusive understandings of justification for Paul, or for us. If we think

---

49. The second such statement, in 3:24, uses the first-person-plural verb.

of a divine declaration as an effective word, a performative utterance, then justification as divine declaration not only *permits* but also *requires* transformation. The neologism of Reformed theologian Peter Leithart is particularly helpful in articulating this truth; he understands justification as a "deliverdict," a verdict that effects deliverance.[50] Whether intentionally or not, with this term Leithart has brought together traditional Protestant approaches to Paul and apocalyptic approaches (which generally characterize justification as "deliverance" from apocalyptic powers), as well as other perspectives that stress justification's transformative element.[51] The theological stakes here are, in my view, quite high. The German Lutheran scholar Michael Wolter agrees; he breaks down the wall between "forensic justification" and "real participation," claiming that "if God's judgment about a person were not completely directly efficacious in reality and God's *pledge* of salvation were not a salvific *power* that changes the person, *God would not be God.*"[52]

A final example from Paul will help us see the close connection between the communal, the transformative, and (possibly) the declarative elements in justification according to the apostle. In 1 Corinthians 6:1–11 Paul attempts to persuade the Corinthian community that the practice of pursuing lawsuits against their siblings in the Messiah is a form of *adikia* ("injustice, unrighteousness"). Although this noun itself does not occur in the text (but see 1 Cor. 13:6), its cognate adjective *adikos* ("unjust, unrighteous"), used as a noun, occurs in verses 1 and 9, and its cognate verb *adikeō* ("commit injustice, harm") appears in verses 7 and 8. Paul's arguments against this injustice culminate in his claim that the unjust (*adikoi*)—implicitly including the Corinthian litigants—will not inherit the kingdom of God (v. 9). The Corinthians, he says, used to practice injustice and other evils disqualifying people from the kingdom, but then he says, "You [the Corinthians] were washed . . . sanctified . . . justified [*alla apelousasthe, alla hēgiasthēte, alla edikaiōthēte*] in the name of the Lord Jesus Christ and in the Spirit of our God" (v. 11 NRSV). That is, *something happened* to these Corinthians, including justification; the passive voice connotes an act from outside the self, an act of grace and of God. Whether or not we see in this third passive verb a

50. Leithart, *Baptized Body*, 75–76; Leithart, *Delivered from the Elements of the World*, esp. 180–214, 333–54.

51. Douglas Campbell (*Deliverance of God*, 852) calls the justification described in Gal. 2:15–21 "a forensic-liberative act of resurrection by God."

52. Wolter, *Paul*, 251 (emphasis original except for the last phrase). His entire succinct discussion of the issue on 250–51 is helpful. Even N. T. Wright acknowledges that justification is an "illocutionary speech-act of declaration and verdict" (*Paul and the Faithfulness of God*, 945), but it is not clear that this means anything more than the status of covenant membership declared is actually granted.

divine declaration, we cannot help but see a transformation. The unrighteous have become righteous; the unjust have been incorporated into the community of the just—the community of the Messiah and the Spirit where practices of justice have replaced practices of injustice.[53]

Our sixth and penultimate claim, then, is that even as justification is participatory and transformative, the participation it entails is inherently corporate, referring to gentiles and Jews together in the Messiah, and the transformation it entails can be understood as the result of a divine declaration, God's performative utterance.

Justification and Theological Rapprochement

7. The participatory and transformative understanding of justification presented in this chapter should contribute to theological rapprochement between old and new perspectives and between West and East.

A common element in recent discussions of justification in Paul has been the warning not to make Paul's theology of justification bear too much of a soteriological load. After all, it is not the fullness of Paul's soteriology, not the only metaphor or image he uses. But there is another caution to heed: we must be sure that we do not *limit* justification in Paul to our preconceived notions of what it can or must mean, and we must not let justification bear too *little* of a load. Instead, we must attempt to understand justification as fully as Paul understood it.

The perspective on justification articulated in this chapter contends that Paul had—and that we should have—a thick, robust theology of justification. In particular, I have argued for justification as a participatory and transformative event that may both expand our theological horizons and break down some of our theological walls. Justification entails death to an old existence and resurrection to new life. And perhaps so does rethinking justification.

The final dimension of Paul's theology of justification to note is that it is inherently an ecumenical theology; and this, I contend, is a highly important aspect of its contemporary theological significance. That significance can be summarized in the following four claims:

1. The interpretation offered in this chapter promotes an understanding of justification as entailing transformation and ethics—and even theosis— without thereby promoting "works-righteousness," an unhealthy syn-

---

53. See further my "Justification and Justice," 32–34, and *Becoming the Gospel*, 234–40.

ergism, or autosoterism (self-salvation). It therefore has the possibility of building bridges between Protestants and Catholics, between West and East, and among various schools of Pauline thought.

2. This interpretation, while stressing participation (the *mode* of justification), acknowledges that justification is God's gracious activity accomplished in the Messiah's death (the *means* of justification). If we say "justification by co-crucifixion,"[54] then we must acknowledge that this phrase implies the means (crucifixion) as well as the mode (co-crucifixion). It means the gift of life through the gift of death. In more traditional language, we should say "justification by grace through faith," not merely "justification by faith." The interpretation offered here should further close the door to any form of Pelagianism.

3. This interpretation, while stressing participation and transformation, does not rule out a more forensic approach to justification as long as any divine pronouncement is understood to be effective and thereby inherently transformative. It therefore acknowledges the contributions of forensic approaches while incorporating them into more participatory perspectives, again permitting rapprochement between Protestants and Catholics, between West and East, and among Pauline interpretive schools.[55]

4. The interpretation offered here also highlights the traditional Protestant emphasis on individual, personal, "vertical" justification as well as the concern of the New Perspective—namely, the issue of gentile inclusion, justification's "horizontal," ecclesial dimension. It therefore promotes a "both-and" approach to justification that can build bridges between so-called traditional (especially Protestant) and more recent emphases in the study of Paul.[56] To the modern question of whether justification is about soteriology or ecclesiology, the answer is a resounding yes. In fact, these two theological loci are inseparable in Paul's mind, for he is convinced (to paraphrase Cyprian, writing two centuries later) that outside the Messiah/the *ekklēsia* there is no salvation.

It is important to stress that these claims have not been the *motivation* or *purpose* of my study of justification, but rather the *fruit* of that study. It is ironic that a passage that was intended to end the Galatian "apartheid" has

---

54. See my *Inhabiting the Cruciform God*, 40–104.
55. See the similar approach of Veli-Matti Kärkkäinen in his "Deification View."
56. I say "so-called traditional" because, as Stephen Chester points out, Protestant Reformers such as Calvin and Luther put justification and union with Christ together; see Chester, *Reading Paul with the Reformers.*

been so divisive. Perhaps that situation can be ameliorated by ongoing careful studies and conversations.[57]

We come finally, in light of our study, to an attempt at a working definition of justification in Paul and then to a retranslation of Galatians 2:15–21. As noted early on, the words "justify" and "justification" themselves are problematic in English. But I have not yet found a suitable substitute, although I am drawn—despite my favoring terms from the "*just-*" family—to words like "rightwise/rightwising" and "rectify/rectification" because they imply that God is actually fixing the human condition and because one can make fairly easy connections in English between verbs and nouns in the word-family (although the resulting words are not always commonly used in English). At the same time, despite its problems, "justify/justification" is appealing because it retains the connection to the theological tradition and because "justice" and "just" are part of the word-family. On the other hand, a neologism like "righteousification" might be helpful, if clumsy.[58]

There is no perfect solution. But here is my extended working definition of justification according to Galatians 2:15–21:

> Justification/righteousification is God's gracious act of delivering people from the power of Sin and restoring them to a right covenant relationship with himself, the righteous/just God, through the Messiah's faithful, loving death and resurrection, giving them new life and incorporating them into the righteous/just people of God who share in God's righteousness/justice, both Jews and gentiles, "in" the Messiah, as by God's grace they participate in the Messiah's death and resurrection, dying to their past lives and rising to lives of righteousness/justice marked by faithfulness to God and love for others—resurrectional cruciformity.

In brief: God makes people right. A bit longer: In the Messiah, God allows people to share in his own righteousness. It is all—past righteousification and present life/righteousness—by grace, by a means other than the law or the self.[59]

How might this come across in a translation? There is no perfect way, thanks to the limitations of the English language and of the process of translation, but perhaps as follows, in which I add a gloss to the main verb and its cognate nouns. (Changes from the earlier translation are in boldface.)

57. On the importance of 2:15–21 in light of what precedes it, and thus as an instrument of communal unity, see W. Campbell, "Unity in the Community."

58. Sanders (*Paul*, 504–16) uses "to righteous/be righteoused," calling this verb both a revival of an older English verb and a neologism. (The actual Old/Middle English verb [515] would today be "to rightwise.")

59. Hence, in the following translation, I render *ek*, *dia*, and *en* (except when *en* means "in"—i.e., "in the sphere of") as "by means of." They differ only stylistically, not substantively.

[15][But] we, by birth Jews and not sinners from the nations, [16]because we know that no person is **made right/just—alive to God and transformed from "sin" to "righteousness" by being delivered from this present evil age into the community of the righteous/just—**by means of works of the law but rather by **means** of the faithfulness of Jesus the Messiah, even we came to faith **and so entered** into the Messiah Jesus, so that we would **be made right/just** by **means** of the faithfulness of the Messiah and not by **means** of works of the law, for no human being **will be made right/just** by **means** of works of the law. [17]But if we, while seeking to be **made right/just** in the Messiah, are ourselves found to be sinners, then is the Messiah a servant of sin? May it never be! [18]For if I rebuild the things I tore down, then I prove myself to be a transgressor. [19]For I myself, through the law, died in relation to the law so that I could live in relation to God. I have been crucified with the Messiah; [20]thus I myself no longer live, but the Messiah lives in me; and the life I do now live in the flesh, I live by means of the faithfulness of the Son of God, who loved me by giving himself for me. [21]I do not annul the grace of God; for if righteousness—**the life of right covenant relations with God and others (namely, faithfulness and love) that is the substance of being made right—**has its source in the law, then the Messiah **died for no reason and to no effect.**

New Creation!

Justification and Participation from Galatians to 2 Corinthians

In the previous chapter I argued that in the theologically rich passage Galatians 2:15–21 we find a theology of justification as participatory and transformative. This overarching thesis was developed in the form of seven exegetical and theological claims. In this and the next chapter, the "justification connection" or "justification trajectory" noted at the start of the previous chapter is pursued in the form of two basic propositions. First, the equally theologically rich passage 2 Corinthians 5:14–21 is also a text about justification, and it is a *restatement* of Galatians 2:15–21 (in connection with some related texts in Galatians) for a new audience.[1] This is the focus of the present chapter. Second, and the concern of the next chapter, 2 Corinthians 5:14–21 is also a *foreshadowing* of the central affirmations of Romans on justification. That is, in these two chapters, building on the last chapter, we will trace Paul's understanding of participatory, transformative justification from Galatians to 2 Corinthians to Romans.

I contend in these two chapters that justification is so transformative that Paul describes it as new creation and resurrection to new life. Moreover, therefore, justification for Paul can be understood in terms of what the later Christian tradition calls theosis, or transformative participation in the life of God. As I have stated repeatedly in this book and beyond, however, it is not necessary to

---

1. With respect to its theological richness, Edith Humphrey lists (some of) the various themes of this section of 2 Cor. 5: "physicality and new creation, substitution and participation, sin and righteousness, apostolic and ecclesial action, transformation and theosis." See her "Becoming the Righteousness of God," 125.

utilize the term "theosis," though I contend that it is both accurate and useful.[2] The main point, however, is that justification entails resurrection to new life.

It is a commonplace among interpreters of Paul to say that Romans develops some of the claims and themes of Galatians for a new context. Less common, but no less correct, is the claim that Romans builds on 2 Corinthians. This thesis was argued convincingly some years ago by Frances Young.[3] (I note in passing the remark of one of my students that Romans is Paul's "greatest hits.")[4] The claim of this chapter, going from Galatians to 2 Corinthians, depends in part on an assumption about the order of composition of these two letters. For those who propose another chronological order, such as placing Galatians after 2 Corinthians, my argument will still be useful. The results would then be an exercise in comparing letters or in showing a different sort of chronological development. At the very least, no matter one's theory about dating Paul's correspondence, these two letters will be placed in meaningful conversation with each other and then, in the next chapter, with Romans—which is clearly later than both Galatians and 2 Corinthians, whichever of those two letters was written first.[5] In fact, if Benj Petroelje is right about how to read an ancient corpus—in our case, "the Pauline book"—reading the letters in such conversation with one another is certainly legitimate and perhaps preferable to reading them one at a time.[6] In any event, the main claim I am making in chapters 6–8 is that *Paul has a consistent view of justification as participatory, transformative, and resurrectional.*

We begin this chapter with a brief review of Galatians 2:15–21.

Galatians 2:15–21: A Theological Summary

Following are the seven theses about Galatians 2:15–21 from the preceding chapter:

1. Galatians 2:15–21 is a self-contained rhetorical unit, the subject of this unit is "justification," and Paul is offering his own interpretation of justification.

2. See, e.g., my *Becoming the Gospel*, 7–8.
3. Young, "Understanding Romans in the Light of 2 Corinthians."
4. The student is Andrew Lacovara. Romans is indebted not only to Galatians and 2 Corinthians but also to 1 Corinthians and perhaps Philippians, or at least the content of the Christ-poem in Phil. 2:6–11.
5. In my *Inhabiting the Cruciform God*, 63–86, I already show the similarities between justification in Gal. 2:15–21 and baptism in Rom. 6. This chapter and the next focus primarily on justification itself.
6. See Petroelje, "What to Do with the Pauline Book?"

2. There are two mutually exclusive approaches to the means of justification—namely, the (works of the) law and the Messiah's death—but because Messiah Jesus' faithful and loving death is the manifestation (or apocalypse) of God's grace, it alone is the actual *means*, or objective basis, of justification.

3. Justification is a *participatory* reality described explicitly as entailing co-crucifixion with the Messiah, and this is what Paul means here by "faith"; it is this type of faith—a death *with* the Messiah, and both *to* the law and *to* the self—that brings a person into the realm of the Messiah. This is the *mode*, or subjective basis, of justification.

4. Justification is participation not only in the Messiah's death but also in his resurrection, which means that justification entails resurrection to new life—that is, the emergence of a new self indwelt by the (Spirit of the) Messiah and living in proper relation to God.

Before moving on to the last three summary points from the preceding chapter, we should pause to stress the significance of claims 3 and 4 together: *justification is a participatory reality entailing both co-crucifixion with the Messiah and co-resurrection with the Messiah.*

5. Justification as participation in Jesus' death and resurrection means transformation into righteousness, which will be exhibited fundamentally as cruciform faithfulness and love.

6. A participatory and transformative understanding of justification based on 2:15–21 does not rule out either (1) a covenantal, primarily "horizontal" understanding of justification as membership in the covenant community grounded in the context of gentile acceptance or (2) a declarative understanding of justification—if a divine declaration is rightly understood as effective.

7. The participatory and transformative understanding of justification presented in chapter 6 should contribute to theological rapprochement between old and new perspectives and between West and East.

With this review, we turn now to 2 Corinthians 5:14–21 and to its roots in Galatians 2:15–21.

The *Crux Interpretum*: 2 Corinthians 5:21

Is 2 Corinthians 5:14–21 also about justification? There is only one occurrence of the *dikai*- word-family in this passage, and it is in verse 21: a reference to the righteousness/justice (*dikaiosynē*) of God. Therefore, the central interpretive problem, or *crux interpretum*, in 2 Corinthians 5 is for our purposes verse 21. It reads as follows in the NRSV: "For our sake he made him to be sin who knew no sin, so that in him we might become the righteousness of God." The first thing to be said about this text is that it is consistent with the preceding verses (esp. vv. 18–20) in stressing the divine initiative in the whole matter of participation: God participates in our humanity before we participate in Christ, and in order that we might do so. This divine participation ("made him to be sin") no doubt refers to Jesus' crucifixion, but also probably to the incarnation.[7] As with many texts in 2 Corinthians, it is important to consider the identity of the "we" in verse 21—does it refer to all or only to Paul and his apostolic colleagues?[8] Although some interpreters, especially N. T. Wright, take the latter view, this interpretation would almost require the impossible restriction of God's saving, reconciling work in this verse, in verse 18, and elsewhere in the context to Paul and colleagues. It is best, therefore, to interpret the "we" broadly rather than narrowly.[9]

The second thing to be said, with the majority of interpreters, is that we should understand verse 21 (at least) also to be about justification. But what sort of justification? Many say that 2 Corinthians is about a change of status or condition. This can be expressed in the language of imputed or credited righteousness, as in the case of Stephen Westerholm: "The dramatic exchange . . . is perhaps the closest Paul comes to the traditional understanding that Christ's righteousness is 'imputed' to believers."[10] F. F. Bruce writes of believers being given "a righteous status before God" in this "statement about justification."[11] C. K. Barrett speaks of their being "acquitted in his [God's] court."[12] These interpreters cling to a forensic, or juridical, understanding of justification, one that understands justification in terms of a law-court metaphor. Justification is thus a change in status. Many Protestants read Paul this way.

7. Since our chief concern is our participation in Christ/God, we will not explore this christological question in any depth here. But see Hooker, *From Adam to Christ*, 17: we should be "wary of driving a wedge between incarnation and crucifixion."

8. Humphrey ("Becoming the Righteousness of God," 132) helpfully uses the labels "ecclesial" and "apostolic" for these two interpretations.

9. For the apostolic, rather than ecclesial, interpretation, see Wright, "On Becoming the Righteousness of God"; Wright, *Paul and the Faithfulness of God*, 880–84. See as well Keener, *1–2 Corinthians*, 187; Hooker, "On Becoming the Righteousness of God." Hooker allows for the application of the text beyond the apostles (similarly, Stegman, "Paul's Use of *dikaio-* Terminology," 500n12; cf. 504). The view proposed here is similar to that of Grieb, "'So That in Him'"; see also Ellington, "So That We Might Become."

10. Westerholm, *Justification Reconsidered*, 70.

11. Bruce, *1 and 2 Corinthians*, 211.

12. Barrett, *Second Epistle to the Corinthians*, 180–81.

Such an approach, however, is not limited to recent and contemporary Protestant interpreters. Raymond Collins, a Roman Catholic, also emphasizes a change in status, or condition, though he stresses the relational dimension of justification:

> The "righteousness of God" is an abstract concept that Paul uses in place of more concrete and personal language. He is saying that we are justified by God. We are in a right relationship with God; our justification comes from God. Hence we are a manifestation of the righteousness of God. When Paul says that "in him" we might become the righteousness of God, he is affirming that Christ is the means of our justification. Because of Christ's death and resurrection, humanity's state of sin has been exchanged for a condition of justification.[13]

Although N. T. Wright's interpretation of justification has been criticized by "traditional" Protestants, it too is basically a forensic model in which justification entails a divine declaration about membership in the covenant community.[14]

Others, such as Calvin, echoed more recently by Michael Bird, use the language of imputation (see Westerholm above) but also speak of union with Christ, of "incorporated righteousness." Here is a comment from Calvin:

> For these two things are equivalent—that we are acceptable to God, and that we are regarded by him as righteous. . . . *Righteousness*, here, is not taken to denote a quality or habit, but by way of imputation, on the ground of Christ's righteousness being reckoned to have been received by us. . . . How are we righteous in the sight of God? . . . It is in the same manner, assuredly, that we are now *righteous in him*—not in respect of our rendering satisfaction to the justice of God by our own works, but because we are judged of in connection with Christ's righteousness, which we have put on by faith, that it might become ours. On this account I have preferred to retain the particle ἐν [*en*] (*in*), rather than substitute in its place *per* (*through*), for that signification corresponds better with Paul's intention.[15]

Margaret Thrall has yet a different approach. Because of Paul's emphasis on union with Christ, she denies that justification here means imputation of Christ's alien righteousness. She speaks instead of innocence replacing guilt, but she rejects the suggestion that this implies *moral* righteousness.[16]

13. Collins, *Second Corinthians*, 126–27. Collins goes on to say (127) that because justification is about relationship, it has ethical consequences. But for him it is not about transformation per se.

14. For discussion and critique, see Stegman, "Paul's Use of *dikaio-* Terminology." Stegman is responding to Wright, *Justification*. See also my comments on Wright's understanding of justification in my "Wright about Much, but Questions about Justification."

15. Calvin, *Commentary on Corinthians*, vol. 2 (2 Cor. 5:18–21). For Bird, see *Saving Righteousness of God*.

16. Thrall, *2 Corinthians 1–7*, 443–44.

Many other interpretations of this text regarding change in status or condition, and regarding imputation and/or incorporation, could be discussed. We turn instead to another view of the text.

Several significant recent commentators agree that something different is going on in 2 Corinthians 5:21. They, like I, understand justification here as participatory transformation. George Guthrie, for instance, does not think "imputation" (or "transference") is specifically at play here, though he thinks 5:21 "plays a part in a broader theology of imputation."[17] Guthrie's preferred term with respect to 5:21 is "transformational interchange,"[18] which develops Morna Hooker's language of "interchange" and echoes the patristic language of Christ's becoming what we are so that we could become what he is.[19] Some interpreters wish to hold on to a forensic element while also admitting the presence of participatory and transformative dimensions; for example, Murray Harris speaks of both the forensic and the mystical dimensions of this text.[20] Others, such as Katherine Grieb and Thomas Stegman, argue that a forensic interpretation of this text actually misses Paul's main point, which is transformation—and the continuity between God's righteousness displayed in Christ and the righteousness that people can embody in Christ.[21] At the end of this chapter, I will mention additional scholars who hold similar views.

My contention, in this vein, is the following: significant similarities between 2 Corinthians 5:14–21 and Galatians 2:15–21 confirm that the text from 2 Corinthians is indeed about justification, and about justification understood in terms of participation and transformation.

A Translation of 2 Corinthians 5:14–21 as a Rhetorical Unit

Following is my translation of 2 Corinthians 5:14–21 for our use in this chapter:[22]

[14]For the Messiah's love compels us, since we have concluded this: that one died for all, and therefore all died. [15]And he died for all so that those who live would live no longer for themselves, but for the one who died for them and was

17. Guthrie, *2 Corinthians*, 315.

18. Guthrie, *2 Corinthians*, 315. However, Guthrie unfortunately misses the thick nature of the participatory dimension of this interchange by maintaining the rather thin label "positional" for the sense of "in him."

19. Recently, Ben Blackwell has explored this similarity in his important book *Christosis*.

20. Harris, *Second Epistle to the Corinthians*, 454–55.

21. Grieb, "'So That in Him'"; Stegman, "Paul's Use of *dikaio-* Terminology," 500–504.

22. Unless otherwise indicated, the NRSV is used for the translation of texts other than 2 Cor. 5:14–21 and Gal. 2:15–21, which are my own translation.

raised. [16]Thus from now on we regard no one according to human standards; even though we used to regard the Messiah according to human standards, we now no longer know him in that way. [17]Therefore, if anyone is in the Messiah, new creation! The old things have passed away; look!—new things have arrived! [18]And all these things are from the God who reconciled us to himself through the Messiah and who gave us the ministry of reconciliation; [19]that is, God was in the Messiah reconciling the world to himself, not counting their trespasses against them, and entrusting to us the message of reconciliation. [20]Therefore, we are the Messiah's ambassadors, with God making his appeal through us. We entreat you on behalf of the Messiah: be reconciled to God. [21]For us [or "For our sake"] God made the one who did not know sin [the Messiah Jesus] to be sin so that we ourselves would become the justice [or "righteousness"] of God in him.

Before launching our investigation, we need to briefly consider the first issue with respect to this passage: Is this a self-contained unit?[23] Should we not consider the unit to start at 5:11 ("Therefore, knowing the fear of the Lord, we try to persuade others"), which follows 5:10 ("For all of us must appear before the judgment seat of Christ, so that each may receive recompense for what has been done in the body, whether good or evil") and introduces Paul's ministry of reconciliation? Or perhaps the unit begins at 5:16 ("Thus from now on we regard no one according to human standards"), following 5:15 ("And he died for all so that those who live would live no longer for themselves, but for him who died and was raised for them"). As for the unit's conclusion, perhaps the terminus should be found at 6:2 ("For he says, 'At an acceptable time I have listened to you, and on a day of salvation I have helped you.' See, now is the acceptable time; see, now is the day of salvation!"), which is a sort of peroration, or even at 6:10, which concludes Paul's description of his ministry of reconciliation.

As we saw in considering Galatians 2, there are also multiple ways of perceiving the structure of this part of 2 Corinthians, and there are units within units.[24] Regarding 5:14–21 as a discrete unit, there is an immediate issue: the postpositive *gar* ("for")[25] of 5:14 clearly links that verse to what precedes, specifically 5:11–13, and sounds like a continuation of the thought contained in those verses. At the same time, however, 5:14 signals a shift in *focus* away

23. The same question was asked about Gal. 2:15–21 in the previous chapter.

24. Two examples from other scholars will suffice, one perceiving a broader and one a narrower unit: Raymond Collins (*Second Corinthians*, 114–40) sees 5:11 to 6:10 as a single passage, while Edith Humphrey ("Becoming the Righteousness of God") works with 5:16–21.

25. A postpositive word in Greek cannot be the first word in a clause, even though it may be translated into English as the first word.

from the apostle and his colleagues and onto Christ and God. (The apostolic ministry is still mentioned in vv. 18–20, but it is literally surrounded by the witness to God's saving activity in the Messiah.) Moreover, a verbal and thematic inclusio appears in verse 14 (echoed twice in v. 15) and verse 21, focusing on the critical word *hyper* ("for," "for the sake of," "in the place of"):

[one] died **for** all (v. 14)

hyper pantōn apethanen

died **for** all . . . for the one who died **for** them and was raised (v. 15)

hyper pantōn apethanen . . . hyper autōn apothanonti kai egerthenti

For us God made the one who did not know sin to be sin (v. 21)

hyper hēmōn hamartian epoiēsen

This *verbal* echo of verses 14 and 15 in verse 21 suggests a *semantic* echo— that the Messiah's being made sin is a reference to his death. Furthermore, the shift from "died for all" to, essentially, "died for us," makes the generic theological claim personal and prepares the way for the invitation to reconciliation in 6:1–2. (This invitation is anticipated in 5:20b.) Thus we have a self-contained unit in 5:14–21—and the first echo of Galatians 2:15–21 to be explored: the Messiah's death for us. We will examine that echo as part of a cluster of echoes—the first of two clusters. (Note: all parallels/echoes are summarized in a table included as the appendix to this chapter: "Echoes of Galatians 2:15–21 (and Beyond) in 2 Corinthians 5:14–21.")

The First Cluster of Echoes: Death, Love, Life, Resurrection, New Creation

Several crucial dimensions of Galatians 2:15–21 appear also in 2 Corinthians 5:14–21. The first cluster of links, or echoes, includes the themes of death, love, life, resurrection, and new creation; we begin with death.

Death

There is a clear echo of Galatians 2:15–21 in 2 Corinthians 5:14–21 in the language of death. The first aspect of this echo occurs in the verb *apethanen* ("died"), from *apothnēskō*, which appears on the front end of the inclusio framing the passage (2 Cor. 5:14). Two forms of the same verb (*apothnēskō*) immediately recur in the following verse, where Christ is described as the one who "died [*apethanen*] for all" and who "died [*apothanonti*] for them" (5:15). Both *apethanen* (the third-person-singular form) and *apethanon* (the first-person-singular form) also appear in Galatians 2, the former in reference to Christ (2:21) and the latter in reference to Paul (2:19):[26]

Table 7.1. Death in Gal. 2:19, 21

the Messiah died for nothing	I . . . died in relation to the law
Christos dōrean apethanen (Gal. 2:21)	*egō . . . nomō apethanon* (Gal. 2:19)

Furthermore, as in 2 Corinthians 5 (at least 5:21, and perhaps also 5:18–19), in Galatians 2 Paul makes additional note of Christ's death, though without using the verb *apothnēskō*. In fact, there are two such references: "by giving himself for me" (*paradontos heauton hyper emou*, 2:20) and "I have been crucified with the Messiah" (*Christō synestaurōmai*, 2:19), which implies Christ's death by crucifixion even if it focuses on Paul's co-crucifixion. Thus begins our first cluster of connections between 2 Corinthians 5 and Galatians 2: the language of death.

There are additional connections in the various ways this language of death is interpreted. The phrase *hyper emou* ("for me") in Galatians 2:20 is obviously similar to the *hyper* phrases of 2 Corinthians 5, where (as noted above) there are four *hyper* formulae:

- *hyper pantōn* ("for all," 5:14, 15)
- *hyper autōn* ("for them," 5:15)
- *hyper hēmōn* ("for us," 5:21)[27]

If we combine Galatians 2 and 2 Corinthians 5, then, Paul affirms that the Messiah died for *me* (Gal. 2:20), for *all* (2 Cor. 5:14), for *them* (2 Cor. 5:15), and for *us* (2 Cor. 5:21).

Furthermore, Paul affirms that Jesus the Messiah's death *for* me (or us) entails my (or our) death too: two references to the Messiah's death in Galatians 2:19, 21 are connected to a reference to the apostle's co-crucifixion with the Messiah ("I have been crucified," 2:19). Similarly, the multiple references in

26. The translation of Gal. 2:15–21 used here is that offered at the beginning of the previous chapter. (Note: for some stylistic relief from the repetition of Gal. 2:15–21 and 2 Cor. 5:14–21, this chapter will sometimes refer to the former simply as Gal. 2 and the latter as 2 Cor. 5.)

27. Cf. similar uses of *hyper* in Gal. 1:4; 3:13 as well as in 1 Cor. 11:24; 15:3. Uses in Romans will be noted in the next chapter.

2 Corinthians 5 to Christ's death "for" others are combined with a reference to their death ("all died," 5:14). In 2 Corinthians 5, writes Edith Humphrey, Paul "sets substitutionary (or perhaps representative) language in juxtaposition with participation."[28] Although the *explicit* notion of co-crucifixion found in Galatians is absent from 2 Corinthians, it is nonetheless clear in 2 Corinthians 5:14 that there is a very close connection between Christ's death and the death of "all": "*Therefore* [Gk. *ara*] all died" (2 Cor. 5:14). The death of Jesus means our death too.

We do not need to settle the question of the referent of the word "all": does it signify all people or all believers/holy ones (those in the Messiah)? Nor do we need to decide whether the word "therefore" indicates a chronologically simultaneous, a chronologically subsequent, or simply a logically consequent "death" of all people or people in Christ. Whatever the precise sense of this verse, the tight relationship between the death of the Messiah and the death of "all" is evident. Some interpreters have connected this verse to the discussion of Adam in Romans 5:12–21 or 1 Corinthians 15:22 or both.[29] However, although there is a faint echo of Adam in 2 Corinthians 5:21, Paul's primary point seems to be something resembling a *corporate* co-crucifixion that is similar to the *individual* co-crucifixion ("I have been crucified with the Messiah") of Galatians 2.[30] This interpretation is strengthened by what is associated with this corporate death: not the negative result of condemnation (as in Rom. 5) but the positive result of a new and reoriented life (2 Cor. 5:15), as in Galatians 2:19–20.[31]

Clearly Paul does not mean, in Galatians, that he *alone* was crucified with Christ; he is speaking personally but also representatively. Nor is it likely, in 2 Corinthians, that he thinks a death for *all* is so generic that it does not also mean that individuals, in some sense, die. What seems to be happening, then, is that Paul sometimes looks at the *group* through the lens of the *individual* (so Galatians), and sometimes at the *individual* through the lens of the *group* (so 2 Corinthians). In Galatians he is articulating a strong emphasis on

28. Humphrey, "Becoming the Righteousness of God," 131. Collins (*Second Corinthians*, 119) says that Paul implies that "all of us somehow participate" in Christ's death, but our death is "metaphorical" rather than literal. He connects the idea to the "Adam-Christ typology" of Rom. 5:15, however, rather than to Galatians.

29. E.g., Collins, *Second Corinthians*, 119, referring to Rom. 5:19.

30. Cf. Boakye, *Death and Life*, 65: "For Paul, corporate death evokes union with Christ," referring to Gal. 2:19 and 2 Cor. 5:14 as well as Rom. 6:8, with which Col. 2:20 and 2 Tim. 2:11 should be compared. Frank Matera (*2 Corinthians*, 134) also connects this verse to Gal. 2 and Rom. 6.

31. To be sure, as we will see in the next chapter, Paul's discussion of Adam and Christ will include a focus on the life that comes from Christ's death, but the death associated with Adam is certainly not life-giving.

the individual (himself) as beneficiary of, and participant in, Christ's death, yet in a representative capacity. In 2 Corinthians he is articulating the same fundamental claim about the group, with the clear implication that every individual is affected. In fact, the phrase "if anyone [a singular rather than a plural pronoun: Gk. *tis*] is in the Messiah" in 2 Corinthians 5:17 makes explicit this corporate-individual dynamic in that letter, while the presence of multiple first-person-plural pronouns and verbs in Galatians 2:15–17 does the same sort of balancing work for Galatians.[32]

Death and Love

Yet another link between Galatians 2 and 2 Corinthians 5 emerges in the characterization of Jesus' death. Explicitly in Galatians and implicitly—but very clearly—in 2 Corinthians, Jesus' death is described as his act of love. In Galatians the Messiah is the Son of God who "loved me and gave himself for me" (Gal. 2:20 NRSV). As discussed in the previous chapter, we should translate the *kai* ("and") epexegetically: "loved me by giving himself for me." Paul begins 2 Corinthians 5:14–21 with a reference to "the love of Christ/the Messiah" (*hē . . . agapē tou Christou*). Although the genitive construction ("of . . .") could be either objective or subjective ("our love for the Messiah" or "the Messiah's love for us," respectively), the latter interpretation is almost certainly preferable since 5:14–15 includes three references to the Messiah's death. The implication is that Christ's death was the act that manifested Christ's love.[33]

However, there is more to this "love of the Messiah" than its manifestation on the cross. In fact, even if Christ's death is the primary meaning and manifestation of his love, its ongoing manifestation in the ministry of Paul and his colleagues is the main concern of 2 Corinthians 5:14. It is this love that "compels" or even "controls" (so CEB, ESV, NET, RSV) the apostle, his coworkers, and (implicitly) all who are in Christ. This sort of governing compulsion, this loving power, is not far from what Paul says about himself—and, by implication, all believers—in Galatians 2:20a: "I myself no longer live, but the Messiah lives in me." And what is the nature of this indwelling personal power? Paul answers that question in Galatians 2:20b: this indwelling Messiah is none other than the faithful, loving, self-giving Son of God who died on the cross.

32. "We ourselves . . . we know. . . . Even we came to faith . . . so that we would be justified. . . . But if we, while seeking to be justified in the Messiah are ourselves found to be sinners . . ." (Gal. 2:15–17).

33. So also Furnish, *II Corinthians*, 309, and many others.

Death and Life/Resurrection

These observations about death lead to still another, related similarity between our two passages: the presence of the Greek conjunction *hina* ("so that," "in order that"). In 2 Corinthians 5 there are two *hina*, or purpose, clauses describing the purpose of Jesus the Messiah's death:

> And he died for all so that [*hina*] those who live would live no longer for themselves, but for the one who died for them and was raised. (2 Cor. 5:15)
>
> *kai hyper pantōn apethanen, hina hoi zōntes mēketi heautois zōsin alla tō hyper autōn apothanonti kai egerthenti.*

> For us [or "For our sake"] God made the one who did not know sin [the Messiah] to be sin so that [*hina*] we ourselves would become the justice [or "righteousness"] of God in him. (2 Cor. 5:21)
>
> *ton mē gnonta hamartian hyper hēmōn hamartian epoiēsen, hina hēmeis genōmetha dikaiosynē theou en autō.*

We should read these two purpose clauses as containing parallel, mutually interpreting claims about the purpose of the Messiah's death. Verse 15 says that the purpose was to redirect living persons' mode of existence away from *themselves* as their life's focus and beneficiary, and to *Christ* as their life's orientation. The two antithetical constructions in verse 15, "no longer for themselves . . . but for the one who died" (*mēketi heautois . . . alla tō . . . apothanonti*), should be taken as datives signifying advantage, respect, beneficiary, or even direction. Christ's death makes this existential reorientation and recentering possible; it is a new way of being, a transformation (cf. *genōmetha*, "become," v. 21) into something Paul calls the righteousness, or justice, of God (*dikaiosynē theou*, v. 21).

Whatever else this transformation into God's justice means—and we will return to this question later—it is implicitly both the opposite of an existence characterized by sin (*hamartian*, v. 21) and the opposite of a life lived for self (v. 15). It is thus, implicitly but certainly, intimately related to living "for" or "toward" Christ, which certainly includes embodying his sort of love for others.[34] The language of transformation, of "becoming" (*genōmetha*), in verse 21 is paralleled by the adverb "no longer" (*mēketi*) in verse 15. To put it in the transformative language of verse 17: "Therefore, if anyone is in the

---

34. Stegman ("Paul's Use of *dikaio-* Terminology," 503) writes, "Implicit here is that living for the sake of Jesus entails living as he did by loving and giving himself for others (see Gal 2:20; Eph 5:2)."

Messiah, new creation! The old things have passed away; look!—new things have arrived!" We will return to this verse later too.[35]

Similarly, in Galatians 2:19 Paul gives us a purpose (*hina*) clause, in which he both uses the verb "live" (*zaō*), as in 2 Corinthians 5, and speaks of radical transformation from one way of living to another: "For I myself, through the law, died in relation to the law so that I could live in relation to [or "for"] God" (*egō gar dia nomou nomō apethanon, hina theō zēsō*). The paradox here is that a form of death is necessary in order to experience life. As in 2 Corinthians 5, there is a radical reorientation of focus and direction, expressed— once again—in terms of terminating one relationship and modus vivendi and beginning a new one. And, as in 2 Corinthians 5, the new and old relationships are articulated by means of dative constructions indicating advantage and/ or respect: "in relation to/for the law . . . to/for God" (*nomō . . . theō*, 2:19).[36] Moreover, Paul's claim that he no longer lives (2:20) really means that he no longer lives in his old way and in his own power; rather, he lives by means of faith in, or (more likely) by the faithfulness of, the resurrected indwelling Christ. Paul's dying *to* (or "with respect to") the law and *with* Christ has led to life. Implicitly, Paul—speaking representatively—sees justification, the subject of Galatians 2:15–21, as an experience of death and resurrection. (See the previous chapter, especially claims 3–5, for elaboration of this point.)

The theological grammar of this transformation, then, is that of a death-to-life dynamic. This dynamic is grounded in the Messiah's death and resurrection. In Galatians 2 the Messiah's *death* is prominent, the resurrection more implicit, subdued. But of course the crucified Messiah cannot live in Paul unless he has been raised from the dead.[37] In 2 Corinthians 5 the Messiah's *resurrection* is more explicit: Paul names Christ as "him who died for them and was raised [by God]" (v. 15). But the same existential, participatory dynamic is at work: to have died and to have become a new creation, or part of the new creation, is an event of such transformation that it can also be

---

35. My emphasis on the individual here is not meant to suggest that individual transformation is the only meaning of new creation; in fact, such individual transformation is actually part of a communal transformation, indicated by the present of first-person-plural language (2 Cor. 5:21; cf. 3:18), which is in turn part of the larger, even cosmic transformation expected by the prophets and noted by Paul elsewhere (Rom. 8; Col. 1:15–20). "It is not simply that the believer has been declared to be a 'new creation' . . . ; besides this, there is a new creation, visible for those with eyes to see," which will entail "solid and permanent glory" (Humphrey, "Becoming the Righteousness of God," 130).

36. The mention of the law rather than the self as the focus of the old way of living is of course a major difference from 2 Corinthians, which should be explained in terms of different contexts for the letters. Our focus here is on the similarities.

37. On the importance of resurrection and revivification in Galatians, see Boakye, *Death and Life*.

interpreted, if more subtly, as an event of death and resurrection. This transformation pivots, so to speak, on the notion of "no longer," which appears in both of our texts, expressed in the synonymous words *ouketi* and *mēketi*:

> Thus I myself **no longer** live, but the Messiah lives in me. (Gal. 2:20)
>
> *zō de **ouketi** egō, zē de en emoi Christos.*

> so that those who live would live **no longer** for themselves (2 Cor. 5:15; cf. 5:16, "We now **no longer** know")
>
> *hina hoi zōntes **mēketi** heautois zōsin* (cf. 5:16, *nyn **ouketi** ginōskomen*)

The uses of "no longer" are strikingly similar in Galatians 2:20 and 2 Corinthians 5:15, both implying radical life transformations in the most comprehensive sense. As Calvin said in commenting on 2 Corinthians 5:14, "This design is to be carefully kept in view—that *Christ died for us, that we might die to ourselves.*"[38] Second Corinthians 5:16 is about no less a transformation, though couched, at least primarily, in the language of epistemology and perception.[39] This language about knowledge is yet another point of contact between our two passages, as two verbs meaning "to know" (*oida*, from *eidō*; *ginōskō*) appear three times in 2 Corinthians 5:16 and once in Galatians 2:16.[40] That is, both passages are concerned with what is known and experienced among those who encounter the resurrected crucified Messiah.

New Creation

This transformation from sin and death into God's life and righteousness, Paul says, takes place in the Messiah (*en autō*, "in him," 2 Cor. 5:21). Although it might be tempting, in light of the similar prepositional phrase in 2 Corinthians 5:19 (*theos ēn en Christō kosmon katallassōn heautō*, "God was in the Messiah reconciling the world to himself"), to interpret the phrase *en Christō* in 5:21 instrumentally ("by means of the Messiah," rather than "in the Messiah"), the locative meaning makes much more sense of both *en* ("in") phrases.[41] In Christ, God did something (reconciliation) so that we might, in

---

38. Calvin, *Commentary on Corinthians*, vol. 2 (2 Cor. 5:13–17).

39. Edith Humphrey ("Becoming the Righteousness of God," 131) rightly insists that the claims of 5:16–17 "entail more than perception or epistemology: they instead also indicate ontological realities to be played out in the reclaimed world of space and time: perception is changed for those who are in Christ, as has actual reality."

40. In 2 Cor. 5:16 we find *oidamen . . . egnōkamen . . . ginōskomen*; in Gal. 2:16, *eidotes*.

41. *Pace* C. Campbell, *Paul and Union with Christ*, 79–80, with respect to 5:19. It is exegetically possible that *en Christō* ("in/by Christ") is simply parallel to *dia Christou* ("through

an analogous way, come to be in Christ and thus become something (God's justice/righteousness) that also implies doing something. The appearance of the same sort of "in" idiom in 5:17—"If anyone is in the Messiah, new creation! [*ei tis en Christō, kainē ktisis*]"—supports the locative interpretation of both 5:19 and 5:21 as well. Location is everything: where God acts, and where beneficiaries of that action find themselves by grace.

The prophetic language of "new creation" (e.g., Isa. 65:17; 66:22; cf. 43:18–19[42]) appears in precisely the same phraseology (*kainē ktisis*) in Galatians 6:15: "For neither circumcision nor uncircumcision is anything; but a new creation is everything!" One can hardly imagine a more robust image of transformation in Christ. Indeed, *kainē ktisis* in Galatians 6:15 should be understood as an exclamatory summary of the letter's message and of its major sections that contribute to that overall message. In other words, Galatians 2:15–21, certainly a key component of the letter, and Galatians 6:15 are mutually interpreting. Galatians 2:15–21 means that neither circumcision nor uncircumcision is anything (cf. Gal. 5:6), because what that passage is describing is a new creation.[43] "New creation," writes Frank Matera, "is a summary of his [Paul's] doctrine of justification," which is further explained, he adds, in 2 Corinthians 5:21.[44] This connection between new creation in Galatians 6:15 and justification in 2:15–21 is reinforced by the language of 6:14, which has echoes of 2:15–21 in its focus on the crucifixion of the self: "May I never boast of anything except the cross of our Lord Jesus Christ, by which the world has been crucified to me, and I to the world [*emoi kosmos estaurōtai kagō kosmō*]."

Similarly, we should follow Matera's lead and take "new creation" in 2 Corinthians 5:17 as a summary of Paul's understanding of justification in

---

Christ," 5:18) and that Christ is the instrument of God's reconciliation. But it is more likely, especially in light of the *en* phrase in 5:21, that Paul intends something more personal with "in Christ God . . ." (to follow the Greek sentence structure). That is, Christ is more than the instrument of God's reconciliation; he is the location of that reconciliation. Whether we translate this verse as "in Christ God was reconciling . . ." (a periphrastic construction) or "God was in Christ reconciling . . . ," the main point is the same: God's participation in humanity's situation, indeed in humanity's sinful situation (implied by 5:21a). And the ultimate goal of God's participation in our life, in all its sinful and inglorious character, is that we might participate in God's life, in all its righteous and glorious character (5:21b). I agree with Campbell (185–87) that 5:21 is not instrumental, but his reading of 5:21 unnecessarily sets a locative and a "union with Christ" interpretation (settling on the latter) in opposition to each other.

42. Oropeza (*Exploring Second Corinthians*, 356) shows the verbal similarities between 2 Cor. 5:16b–17, 19 and Isa. 43:18–19 LXX.

43. De Boer (*Galatians*, 403) similarly sees 6:15 as a gloss on 2:20. With de Boer, I would see this new creation as an "apocalyptic" event that entails both individual transformation and community formation—in anticipation of the eschatological new creation.

44. Matera, *Galatians*, 231.

2 Corinthians 5:17–21. As with Galatians 6:14–15 and 2:15–21 on new creation and justification, we should therefore read 2 Corinthians 5:17 and 5:21
as mutually interpreting: in the Messiah, people experience a new creation that
consists of being transformed into the righteousness of God. Jason Maston
rightly observes that the verb "become" (as well as the verb "made") in 5:21
recalls the "new creation" language of 5:17—and that "the process being
described in verse 17 and verse 21 is the same."[45] Here is the key point: *new
creation as transformation into God's justice/righteousness is justification.*

While Galatians 2:15–21 begins with explicit "justification" (*dikai-*) language
in verses 15–16 and ends with transformation language in verses 19–20, 2 Corinthians 5:14–21 begins with transformation language in verses 14–16 and ends in
verse 21 with justification (*dikai-*) language, while also resuming the language
of transformation. In other words, both passages, as distinct rhetorical units,
consider justification and transformation/new creation as two different but
ultimately inseparable ways of speaking of one reality. And this reality means
"a serious change in the convert's biography" that is both "relational" and
"ontological" while being socially embedded; it entails "overcoming 'normal'
social and religious borders, following an alternative way of life and religiosity
by voluntarily accepting the community's counter-intuitive faith and ethics."[46]

In each passage the final words about transformation suggest that justification is a lived, incarnated reality. In Galatians 2 the reality is a new life—I no
longer live, and yet I *do* live. In 2 Corinthians 5 it is a life lived no longer for
self but for Christ, expressing divine justice/righteousness. In the words of
Edith Humphrey, 2 Corinthians 5:21 manifests "a surprising emphasis upon
the tangible, embodied nature of the δικαιοσύνη θεοῦ [*dikaiosynē theou*], a
phrase used exceptionally here to indicate the outward display of the new
creation in the mediating body of Christ, the church."[47] Something very similar could be said about Galatians 2: the faithfulness and love of the Messiah
that effected the new person, the new creation, must be embodied in that new
person/new creation.

Michael Wolter finds the overlap between Galatians 2:19–20 and 2 Corinthians 5:14–17 "palpable"; in Galatians Paul "describes his own becoming
the same 'new creation.'"[48] Or, to put it differently, in both Galatians and
2 Corinthians, Paul is speaking of participatory, transformative justification.

---

45. Maston, "Plight and Solution in Paul's Apocalyptic Perspective," 312.
46. Despotis, "From Conversion according to Paul and 'John' to Theosis," 96–97. Despotis
rightly suggests that many Pauline terms and expressions reflect a conversionist/transformation
theological understanding.
47. Humphrey, "Becoming the Righteousness of God," 125.
48. Wolter, *Paul*, 90.

Summary

Thus far we have examined numerous aspects of 2 Corinthians 5:14–21 that are echoes of Galatians 2:15–21. Themes of death, love, life, resurrection, and new creation appear in various but similar ways in both passages, suggesting not only the existence of links between them but also, and more importantly, aspects of their similar understanding of justification.

The Second Cluster of Echoes: Interchange, Participation, Transformation

We turn now in a more focused way to a subject that has already inevitably emerged: participation and transformation. More specifically, the subject is Paul's "in the Messiah/in Christ" language and its relationship to the language of (God's) *dikaiosynē*—whether that should be translated "justification" or "righteousness" or something else. We will be considering an additional cluster of links between Galatians and 2 Corinthians, or echoes of the former in the latter. Our discussion focuses on the similar "interchange" texts in the two letters.

Interchange

Before we consider the "in Christ" language in both of our letters more thoroughly, we need to note the character of the climax of 2 Corinthians 5— that is, verse 21:

> For us [or "For our sake"] God made the one who did not know sin [the Messiah Jesus] to be sin so that we ourselves would become the justice [or "righteousness"] of God in him.

> *ton mē gnonta hamartian hyper hēmōn hamartian epoiēsen, hina hēmeis genōmetha dikaiosynē theou en autō.*

Morna Hooker has referred to this as one of Paul's "interchange texts."[49] The "basic pattern" of such texts, says Hooker, is that "Christ is identified with the human condition in order that we might be identified with his."[50] As Hooker acknowledges, such texts are, in important ways, predecessors of texts in Irenaeus, Athanasius, and many others after them—Augustine,

49. Hooker, *From Adam to Christ*, esp. 13–69; Hooker, "On Becoming the Righteousness of God."
50. Hooker, *From Adam to Christ*, 26. Another interchange text in this letter is 8:9, discussed in chap. 9.

Luther, Calvin, Bonhoeffer, Barth, Torrance, and so on—that speak of God or Christ becoming what we are so that we could become what he is. In the Christian tradition, such texts have been associated with theological claims about the "marvelous exchange" and also about deification, or theosis. The language of interchange incorporates both substitution (or representation), on the one hand, and participation (or union) and transformation, on the other.[51]

We find a similar interchange text also in Galatians—this time not in chapter 2 but in Galatians 3:13–14:

> [13]The Messiah redeemed us from the curse of the law by becoming a curse for us [*hyper hēmōn*]—for it is written, "Cursed is everyone who hangs on a tree"—[14]in order that [*hina*] in the Messiah Jesus the blessing of Abraham might come [*genētai*] to the Gentiles, so that [*hina*] we might receive the promise of the Spirit through faith. (NRSV alt.)

> [13]*Christos hēmas exēgorasen ek tēs kataras tou nomou genomenos hyper hēmōn katara, hoti gegraptai; epikataratos pas ho kremamenos epi xylou,* [14]*hina eis ta ethnē hē eulogia tou Abraam genētai en Christō Iēsou, hina tēn epangelian tou pneumatos labōmen dia tēs pisteōs.*

Interchange: Further Echoes and Their Significance

In addition to the parallelism of Galatians 3:13 with 2 Corinthians 5:21 as an interchange text, this passage resonates with at least four other aspects of 2 Corinthians 5:14–21:

1. the presence of two purpose (*hina*) clauses in 3:14[52]
2. the "in the Messiah" language of 3:14 (*en Christō Iēsou*), which is best interpreted locatively[53]

---

51. Cf. Humphrey, "Becoming the Righteousness of God," 132, though she assumes, rather than demonstrates, the presence of "forensic" language in 5:21. Such language is more clearly present (as she also notes) in 5:19, yet the claim that God does not reckon or count trespasses against people does not necessarily imply the corollary that God counts something else (e.g., Christ's righteousness) in their favor. In fact, the language of reconciliation (5:19) and of transformation (5:21) suggests something more relational and participatory than forensic as the divine solution to human sin, and thus as the corollary to God's not reckoning trespasses. (Humphrey herself makes a similar point.)

52. Jan Lambrecht (*Second Corinthians*, 101) also points to this similarity.

53. *Pace* C. Campbell, *Paul and Union with Christ*, 81–82. Frederick S. Tappenden (*Resurrection in Paul*, esp. 177–81) makes a convincing case from the perspective of cognitive linguistics that Paul's "in" (Gk. *en*) language is fundamentally locative (using the image of a container) even when it suggests an instrumental function. Tappenden's cognitive-linguistics approach argues that prepositional meaning is grounded in embodied experience.

3. the language of transformation expressed in forms of the double appearance of the verb "become" in 3:13 (*genomenos*, of Christ) and in 3:14 (*genētai*, of the promise coming to gentiles)
4. the occurrence of the phrase *hyper hēmōn*, "for us," in 3:13

Given these several parallels between Galatians 3:13–14 and 2 Corinthians 5:21, two important things seem clear. First, whether Paul is using the language of redemption (Gal. 3:13) or of justification (2 Cor. 5:21), the objective basis of salvation is "the marvelous exchange"—Christ's becoming sin and a curse for us. Second, the purpose of this exchange—the meaning of salvation—is to be found in the parallel statements "in the Messiah Jesus . . . we might receive the promise of the Spirit through faith" (Gal. 3:14) and "we ourselves would become the justice [or "righteousness"] of God in him" (2 Cor. 5:21). That is (putting the two together), becoming the new creation in Christ that embodies God's justice is precisely what the gift of the Spirit effects. And, vice versa, it is the case for Paul that becoming God's justice is dependent on receiving the gift of the Spirit. Furthermore, since the Spirit believers receive is the Spirit of the Son (Gal. 4:6), to be in Christ (2 Cor. 5:17, 21) is to be in the Spirit, and to have Christ within (Gal. 2:20) is to have received the Spirit (Gal. 3:14). (Paul will bring all this together in Rom. 8.)

Still further, we can string together the various purposes of the Messiah's death, the marvelous exchange, in our texts as follows:

> For I myself, through the law, died in relation to the law so that [*hina*] I could live in relation to [or "for"] God. (Gal. 2:19)

> [13]The Messiah redeemed us from the curse of the law by becoming a curse for us—for it is written, "Cursed is everyone who hangs on a tree"—[14]in order that [*hina*] in the Messiah Jesus the blessing of Abraham might come to the Gentiles, so that [*hina*] we might receive the promise of the Spirit through faith. (Gal. 3:13–14 NRSV alt.)

> And he died for all so that [*hina*] those who live would live no longer for themselves, but for the one who died for them and was raised. (2 Cor. 5:15)

> For us [or "For our sake"] God made the one who did not know sin [the Messiah Jesus] to be sin so that [*hina*] we ourselves would become the justice [or "righteousness"] of God in him. (2 Cor. 5:21)

We arrive, then, at the following synthesis: the interchange of which Paul writes has as its purpose the reconfiguration of human existence in relation to

God (the Father), the Son, and the Spirit (i.e., the Spirit of God/the Son). Since in both Galatians 2 and 2 Corinthians 5 this divine activity is depicted in the language of justification (in addition to other language), we are compelled to conclude that justification in 2 Corinthians, as in Galatians, is participatory and transformative. Moreover, as we have seen in other chapters, the reality of salvation is clearly trinitarian in character.

Justification as Participation and Transformation: Revisiting the Translation of Galatians 2:15–21

This consideration of interchange texts has been directing us to understand justification as both participatory and transformative. It is appropriate, therefore, to return briefly to the translation of part of Galatians 2:15–21 offered at the end of the previous chapter. In Galatians 2:16–17 we find forms of the verb from the *dikai-* word-family:

> [16]because we know that no person **is made right/just** [*dikaioutai*]—alive to God and transformed from "sin" to "righteousness" by being delivered from this present evil age into the community of the righteous/just—by means of works of the law but rather by means of the faithfulness of Jesus the Messiah, even we came to faith and so entered into the Messiah Jesus, so that we **would be made right/just** [*dikaiōthōmen*] by means of the faithfulness of the Messiah and not by means of works of the law, for no human being **will be made right/just** [*dikaiōthēsetai*] by means of works of the law. [17]But if we, while seeking **to be made right/just** [*dikaiōthēnai*] in the Messiah, are ourselves found to be sinners, then is the Messiah a servant of sin? May it never be!

The key issue here is the rendering of the verb *dikaioō*: Does it mean (1) "justify" only in a (narrow) declarative or forensic sense, or does it mean (2) "make right" or even "make just"? The text's relationship with 2 Corinthians 5:14–21 and its theology of transformation, using the noun *dikaiosynē* with the verb "become," strongly suggests (2), and that sense is reflected in this translation.[54]

This connection confirms the translation of *dikaiosynē* in Galatians 2:21, offered at both the beginning and the end of the previous chapter, as "justice/righteousness" rather than "justification" (NRSV: "if justification comes through the law"). The noun functions as a sort of gloss on the multiple occurrences of the verb *dikaioō* in verses 16–17. Paul's use of *dikaiosynē* after several appearances of the verb suggests that the noun *dikaiosynē* indicates

---

54. For the initial translation of Gal. 2:15–21 at the start of the last chapter, I translated the *dikai-* verb forms simply with forms of "justify."

the result of the action signified by the verb *dikaioō*. That is, the result of the verb *dikaioō* is the state of affairs Paul calls *dikaiosynē*. The CEB is one translation that implicitly agrees with this claim, interpreting both *dikaioō* in verses 16–17 and *dikaiosynē* in verse 21 as signifying becoming righteous:

> [16]However, we know that a person isn't **made righteous** by the works of the Law but rather through the faithfulness of Jesus Christ. We ourselves believed in Christ Jesus so that we could be **made righteous** by the faithfulness of Christ and not by the works of the Law—because no one will be **made righteous** by the works of the Law. [17]But if it is discovered that we ourselves are sinners while we are trying to be made righteous in Christ, then is Christ a servant of sin? Absolutely not! . . . . [21]I don't ignore the grace of God, because **if we become righteous** through the Law, then Christ died for no purpose. (Gal. 2:16–17, 21 CEB)

In other words, as at least one translation recognizes, the verb *dikaioō* signifies transformation, specifically transformation of people implicitly characterized by unrighteousness (or injustice) into people characterized by *dikaiosynē*. Or, if we were to use an adjective, the action signified by the verb *dikaioō* transforms unrighteous/unjust people into righteous/just people. In context, becoming and being such people would be what it means to "live to/for/in relation to God" (2:19), a transformation effected by means of Christ's death (2:21) and enabled existentially by his present indwelling (2:20). As Thomas Stegman puts it, "God's saving action brings not only a new status but also a Spirit-enabled transformation by which Paul embodies the pattern of Jesus' self-giving love. . . . The Spirit-empowered transformation indicated here is an essential aspect of Paul's use of *dikaio*-terminology."[55] Of course, the Spirit is not explicitly named in this passage, but in Galatians 4:6 Paul speaks about God's having sent "the Spirit of his Son into our hearts," and most interpreters rightly equate the indwelling Christ with the indwelling Spirit.

Moreover, the reality of the indwelling Christ is matched by the reality of being in Christ; justification, or being made righteous/just, takes place "in Christ": *dikaiōthēnai en Christō* (Gal. 2:17). Although this could be translated instrumentally ("by means of Christ"), the context and the parallel in Philippians 3:9 (not to mention 2 Cor. 5:21) argue strongly for a locative sense.[56] The existential reality of *dikaiōthēnai* (being made right/just) is pos-

---

55. Stegman, "Paul's Use of *dikaio*- Terminology," 509.
56. *Pace* C. Campbell, *Paul and Union with Christ*, 114–15. Although the verb *dikaioō* does not occur in Phil. 3:9, both *dikaiosynē* ("righteousness/justice") and *en autō* ("in him") do: *kai heurethō en autō, mē echōn emēn dikaiosynēn tēn ek nomou alla tēn dia pisteōs Christou, tēn ek theou dikaiosynēn epi tē pistei* ("and be found in him, not having my own righteousness that

sible only because of this reality of mutual indwelling, or reciprocal residence. The one whose death effects the transformation (i.e., the *objective* means of *dikaiōthēnai*) brings it about in actual human lives through their intimate identification with that Crucified One, or union with Christ, which is to say through human participation—what Paul calls co-crucifixion (the *subjective* mode of justification/transformation—*dikaiōthēnai*).

The claims of 2 Corinthians 5:14–21 echo and substantiate this interpretation.[57] The verb *dikaioō* does not appear in 2 Corinthians, but the related noun *dikaiosynē* does (in 2 Cor. 5:21), as in Galatians 2:21. In 2 Corinthians 5:21, as we have noted, *dikaiosynē* appears as the purpose of what God has done in Christ, specifically in his death: *hina hēmeis genōmetha dikaiosynē theou en autō*—"so that we ourselves would become the justice [or "righteousness"] of God in him." The echo of, and parallel to, Galatians 2:17 is obvious, the main difference being whether the *dikai-* verbal infinitive or the *dikai-* noun is used:[58]

while seeking **to be made right/just** in the Messiah

ei de zētountes dikaiōthēnai en Christō (Gal. 2:17)

so that we would **become the justice [or "righteousness"]** of God in him

hina hēmeis genōmetha dikaiosynē theou en autō (2 Cor. 5:21)

Justification, then, is locative—it is based on location (being in the Messiah)—and hence participatory.

In addition to the presence of the *en* prepositional phrase (*en Christō; en autō*) indicating location, it is worth noting that in both sentences the subject of this justification in Christ is "we," with some degree of emphasis added: "But if **we**, while seeking to be made right/just in the Messiah, are **ourselves** [*autoi*] found to be sinners" (Gal. 2:17) and "so that **we ourselves** [*hēmeis*]

---

comes from the law, but one that comes through the faithfulness of Christ, the righteousness of God grounded in faith" [MJG]).

57. Humphrey ("Becoming the Righteousness of God," 127) says that "whether this passage [for her, 5:16–21] actually concerns 'justification' can be decided only by means of a close reading of a text which ends with a mysterious reference to God's righteousness (5:21)." Without disagreeing, I would suggest that the larger context of Paul's writing also bears on the question, as I am arguing in this chapter.

58. An additional difference, though minor for the point at hand, is whether *dikaiōthēnai/ dikaiosynē* is being sought (Galatians) and is thus perhaps the grammatical "content" of the search (which is still, semantically, the goal), or is the grammatical as well as semantic purpose of a divine action (2 Corinthians). Thrall (*2 Corinthians 1–7*, 443) thinks the subject here is justification, understood rather traditionally, and the strange use of *dikaiosynē* is "for the sake of literary symmetry" with *hamartia*.

would become the righteousness of God in him" (2 Cor. 5:21).[59] Both of our texts, then, bear witness to corporate participatory transformation. As Richard Hays has put it, in 2 Corinthians 5:21

> [Paul] does not say "that we might *know about* the righteousness of God," nor "that we might *believe in* the righteousness of God," nor even "that we might *receive* the righteousness of God." Instead, the church is to *become* the righteousness of God: where the church embodies in its life together the world-reconciling love of Jesus Christ, the new creation is manifest. The church incarnates the righteousness of God.[60]

Similarly, Mark Seifrid, commenting on 2 Corinthians 5:21, rejects justification as a "bare imputation or declaration" and calls it a "forensic *event*" that is "irreducibly ontological."[61] That is, believers share in the righteous character of God, the character manifested in Christ. Put differently, there is great continuity between the righteousness of God in Christ and the human righteousness that is the result of participation in that same Christ.[62]

The full meaning of this transformation is not given to us in 2 Corinthians 5:14–21, but it will be spelled out in some detail with respect to financial obligations to the church in Jerusalem in 2 Corinthians 8–9. (We will return to this passage in chap. 9.)[63] As we have seen throughout the present chapter, this transformation is not merely for individuals but for the community—for "us." As Katherine Grieb comments,

> The "new creation/new creature" that God has accomplished in Christ belongs to a spiritually empowered reality that was previously as inconceivable as it was impossible: God's own covenant righteousness enacted in community—in Corinth.[64]

59. The presence of the pronoun *hēmeis* ("we") in 2 Cor. 5:16—which is not necessary because the verb form indicates person and number—likely suggests emphasis there too.

60. Hays, *Moral Vision of the New Testament*, 24. On the importance of "becoming," see further Grieb, "'So That in Him'"; Aernie, "Participation in Christ," esp. 61; Maston, "Plight and Solution in Paul's Apocalyptic Perspective," 311–12.

61. Seifrid, *Second Letter to the Corinthians*, 265, 260. See also Stegman, "Paul's Use of *dikaio-* Terminology."

62. For similar language of continuity between divine and human righteousness, see Stegman, "Paul's Use of *dikaio-* Terminology," 503, 523; Ellington, "So That We Might Become," 176–77.

63. In that chapter we will also see, in depth, the connection between divine and human righteousness/justice. Grieb ("'So That in Him,'" 68–72) connects 2 Cor. 5:21 to other Pauline texts, especially 2 Cor. 8–9, that mention the righteousness/justice of God, arguing that the Pauline themes of "the generosity of God's justice" (68–72) and "the harvest of righteousness/justice" mean that God's justice overflows, or should overflow, into human justice, as the prophetic books like Isaiah make clear (72–73).

64. Grieb, "'So That in Him,'" 66.

Edith Humphrey echoes Grieb's sentiments:

> As an early foreshadowing of the patristic exchange formulae, it [2 Cor. 5:21] can hardly be more striking: the faithful community is to become God's very own justice or righteousness in the world.[65]

Though outside the focus of this chapter, it is worth noting that we could trace Paul's thinking about justification, righteousness, and atonement "backward," through Galatians, through the Christ-event (or Paschal Mystery) and his experience of it, to the book of Isaiah. It is likely that Isaiah is a main source for Paul's thinking about divine and human righteousness, new creation, and other themes in 2 Corinthians.[66] I suspect that Paul's understanding of the connection between atonement and justice is greatly indebted to Isaiah's fourth servant poem (Isa. 52:13–53:12) and particularly to Isaiah 53:11 in some form.[67]

A Final Link: Reconciliation

One final connection between Galatians and 2 Corinthians 5 needs to be mentioned, though it is implicit rather than explicit: reconciliation. One could reasonably argue that Galatians is ultimately about reconciliation, even though the words "reconcile" and "reconciliation" do not appear in the letter.[68] In fact, those two words occur in the undisputed Pauline letters only in the Corinthian correspondence and Romans, a total of ten times, half of them in 2 Corinthians 5:18–20.[69]

But in Galatians Paul articulates his understanding of justification, as the New Perspective rightly observed, in the midst of a controversy about table fellowship, about the equality of Jews and gentiles (and males and females,

65. Humphrey, "Becoming the Righteousness of God," 151.

66. See also Seifrid, *Second Letter to the Corinthians*, 263; Ellington, "So That We Might Become," 185–87; Stegman, "Paul's Use of *dikaio*- Terminology," 504, 523–24; Grieb, "'So That in Him,'" 72–73.

67. NRSV (translating the OT [Hebrew]): "Out of his anguish he shall see light; / he shall find satisfaction through his knowledge. / The righteous one, my servant, shall make many righteous, / and he shall bear their iniquities." NETS (translating the LXX [Greek]): "from the pain of his soul, to show him light and fill him with understanding, to justify a righteous one who is well subject to many, and he himself shall bear their sins."

68. See esp. the discussion of Paul's "mission of participatory reconciliation" in Kok and Dunne, "Participation in Christ and Missional Dynamics," esp. 64–73.

69. "Reconcile" (*katalassō*) in Rom. 5:10 (2x); 1 Cor. 7:11; 2 Cor. 5:18, 19, 20; "reconciliation" (*katallagē*) in Rom. 5:11; 11:15; 2 Cor. 5:18, 19. In addition, *apokatalassō* ("reconcile") occurs in Eph. 2:16; Col. 1:20, 22.

slaves and free; Gal. 3:28) in the Messiah (cf. 3:26). Justification, for Paul, both implies and requires reconciliation, not only with God, but also with one another. It is a "doctrine" with social consequences.[70] Both justification and reconciliation are inherent to the reality of new creation: "For neither circumcision nor uncircumcision is anything; but a new creation is everything!" (Gal. 6:15); "In Christ Jesus neither circumcision nor uncircumcision carry any weight, but rather faithfulness being worked out through love" (5:6 MJG). Yet as a doctrine about "horizontal" relations (love: human-human), justification/reconciliation never stops being a doctrine about "vertical" relations (faith: human-God). Indeed, the horizontal is grounded in the vertical.

Perhaps the most interesting theological innovation Paul introduces in 2 Corinthians 5:14–21 to his theology of justification developed from Galatians is the explicit articulation of reconciliation. In fact, most interpreters of 2 Corinthians designate this part of the letter with a heading that includes the word "reconciliation." My point is not to dispute the centrality or significance of reconciliation but to stress its link to justification. In Romans this connection will be taken up even more explicitly. To be precise: reconciliation is, for Paul, not something different from justification, or simply another metaphor in personal rather than forensic terms. Rather, reconciliation is at the very core of the meaning of justification for Paul. In other words, Paul's vision of justification includes, along with the concept of transformation expressed in the language of new creation and becoming the justice of God, the notion of reconciliation, which entails both the forgiveness of trespasses and the creation of a reconciled community. A transformative understanding of justification does not ignore or eliminate forgiveness and reconciliation with God, but it does expand them.

Conclusion

A growing chorus of voices, from various Christian traditions, sees in 2 Corinthians 5:14–21, especially in its *crux interpretum* (v. 21), an understanding of justification that includes participation and transformation, without discounting other aspects of justification: its forensic, liberative, and "horizontal" (or ecclesial) dimensions.

Edith Humphrey, an Orthodox scholar, declares that verse 21 is properly characterized as "a transformational statement that borders on theosis."[71] Thomas Stegman cites with approval his Roman Catholic colleague Jean-Noël

---

70. See the classic essay of Markus Barth, "Jews and Gentiles: The Social Character of Justification in Paul."

71. Humphrey, "Becoming the Righteousness of God," 152.

Aletti: "The 'we might become' signals that we have been transformed: our righteousness is not a pure forensic declaration, but a real new human nature."[72] And the Protestant Mark Seifrid maintains the language of alien righteousness but speaks as well of "a change of being" brought about by God, who "sweeps us into Christ's life." "What the apostle says," Seifrid avers, "cannot rightly be reduced to the idea of an imputed righteousness," for Paul "speaks of the human being created anew in Christ."[73]

Second Corinthians, then, confirms the claims made about Galatians in the previous chapter: that justification is thoroughly participatory ("in him" [en autō]), transformative ("become" [genōmetha]), and ethical ("the justice/ righteousness [dikaiosynē] of God").[74]

The argument of this chapter leads us to three major conclusions:

1. There are many echoes of Galatians 2:15–21 in 2 Corinthians 5:14–21, such that *the latter should be seen as a restatement of the former* for a different audience. (Or, in the unlikely event that Galatians was written later, vice versa.)

2. *Both texts understand justification as an event of participation and transformation, such that the wall between justification and sanctification is in many ways collapsed.* Each text, Galatians 2 and 2 Corinthians 5, proclaims that justification is an *experience of death and resurrection, indeed an event of new creation.*

3. Since Paul builds on these two letters when writing Romans, we can assume that he carries forward this participatory, transformative, death-and-resurrection, new-creational understanding of justification when he composes that letter.

And it is to Romans that we turn in the next chapter.

Appendix

Table 7.2 (pp. 176–77) displays the echoes between Galatians 2:15–21 and 2 Corinthians 5:14–21 discussed in this chapter.

72. Stegman, "Paul's Use of *dikaio-* Terminology," 502n21, citing Aletti, "God Made Christ to Be Sin," 117.

73. Seifrid, *Second Letter to the Corinthians*, 263. For an understanding of justification similar to the one presented here and throughout this book, from a proponent of the "Paul within Judaism" perspective, see Fredriksen, "Question of Worship," esp. 189–94.

74. For Gal. 2:15–21, see not only the previous chapter but also my *Inhabiting the Cruciform God*, 63–72.

Table 7.2. Echoes of Galatians 2:15–21 (and Beyond) in 2 Corinthians 5:14–21

Galatians 2:15–21 (trans. MJG; in sequence)	2 Corinthians 5:14–21 (trans. MJG; echoes of Galatians)
• sinners (*hamartōloi*) (2:15) • if we . . . are ourselves found to be sinners (*ei . . . heurethēmen kai autoi hamartōloi*) (2:17)	• the one who did not know sin . . . [God] made to be sin (*ton mē gnonta hamartian . . . hamartian epoiēsen*) (5:21)
• is justified (*dikaioutai*) (2:16)	• justice [or "righteousness"] of God (*dikaiosynē theou*) (5:21)
• we would be justified (*dikaiōthōmen*) (2:16)	
• will be justified (*dikaiōthēsetai*) (2:16)	
• to be justified (*dikaiōthēnai*) (2:17)	
• justice/righteousness (*dikaiosynē*) (2:21)	
• in the Messiah (*en Christō*) (2:17)	• in the Messiah (*en Christō*) (5:17)
	• in him [the Messiah] (*en autō*) (5:21)
• I myself . . . died (*egō . . . apethanon*) (2:19)	• all died (*hoi pantes apethanon*) (5:14)
Cf.: • I have been crucified with the Messiah (*Christō synestaurōmai*) (2:19)	
• thus I myself no longer live (*zō de ouketi egō*) (2:20)	
• so that I could live in relation to God (*hina theō zēsō*) (2:19)	• so that those who live would live no longer for themselves, but for the one who died for them and was raised (*hina hoi zōntes mēketi heautois zōsin alla tō hyper autōn apothanonti kai egerthenti*) (5:15)
	• so that we ourselves would become the justice [or "righteousness"] of God in him (*hina hēmeis genōmetha dikaiosynē theou en autō*) (5:21)
• I could live (*zēsō*) (2:19)	• those who live . . . would live (*hoi zōntes . . . zōsin*) (5:15)
• thus I myself no longer live, but the Messiah lives in me; and the life I do now live in the flesh, I live by means of the faithfulness [of the Son of God] (*zō de ouketi egō, zē de en emoi Christos; ho de nyn zō en sarki, en pistei zō*) (2:20)	

Galatians 2:15–21 (trans. MJG; in sequence)	2 Corinthians 5:14–21 (trans. MJG; echoes of Galatians)
• no longer (*ouketi*) (2:20)	• no longer (*mēketi*) (5:15)
	• no longer (*ouketi*) (5:16)
• the Messiah lives (*zē . . . Christos*) (2:20)	• would live . . . for . . . the one who was raised (*zōsin . . . tō . . . egerthenti*) (5:15)
• the Son of God, who loved me by giving himself for me (*tou huiou tou theou tou agapēsantos me kai paradontos heauton hyper emou*) (2:20)	• For the Messiah's love compels us (*hē gar agapē tou Christou synechei hēmas*) (5:14)
• for me (*hyper emou*) (2:20)	• for all (*hyper pantōn*) (5:14)
	• for all (*hyper pantōn*) (5:15)
	• for them (*hyper autōn*) (5:15)
	• For us [or "For our sake"] (*hyper hēmōn*) (5:21)
• the Messiah died (*Christos . . . apethanen*) (2:21); cf. by giving himself (*paradontos heauton*) (2:20)	• one died (*heis . . . apethanen*) (5:14)
	• he died (*apethanen*) (5:15)
• I have been crucified with the Messiah (*Christō synestaurōmai*) (2:19)	• for . . . the one who died (*tō . . . apothanonti*) (5:15)

Beyond Galatians 2	2 Corinthians 5:14–21 (trans. MJG; echoes of Galatians)
• new creation (*kainē ktisis*) (6:15)	• new creation (*kainē ktisis*) (5:17)
• Christ redeemed us from the curse of the law by becoming a curse for us . . . in order that in Christ Jesus the blessing of Abraham might come to the Gentiles (*Christos hēmas exēgorasen ek tēs kataras tou nomou genomenos hyper hēmōn katara . . . hina eis ta ethnē hē eulogia tou Abraam genētai en Christō Iēsou*) (3:13–14a)	• For us [or "For our sake"] God made the one who did not know sin to be sin [the Messiah Jesus] so that we ourselves would become the justice [or "righteousness"] of God in him (*ton mē gnonta hamartian hyper hēmōn hamartian epoiēsen, hina hēmeis genōmetha dikaiosynē theou en autō*) (5:21)
• one in the Messiah Jesus (*heis . . . en Christō Iēsou*) (3:28)	• reconciliation (*katallassō*) (5:18–20)
• neither circumcision . . . nor uncircumcision (*oute gar peritomē . . . oute akrobystia*) (6:15)	

eight

Righteousness, Resurrection, Reconciliation

From 2 Corinthians to Romans

We transition now to Romans. This chapter and the two preceding chapters should be read together as a unit. In these three chapters I am tracing Paul's understanding of participatory, transformative justification from Galatians to 2 Corinthians to Romans.

In the previous chapter we saw the way in which numerous aspects of Galatians 2:15–21 appear also in 2 Corinthians 5:14–21. The chapter concluded by saying that Paul's theology of participatory, transformative justification in Galatians and 2 Corinthians would be brought forward to Romans. It is now time to test that hypothesis. The question before us, then, is whether and how aspects of 2 Corinthians 5:14–21 and therefore—either directly or indirectly—Galatians 2:15–21 reappear in Romans.

We will find that Galatians 2:15–21 has numerous parallels in one particular text (Rom. 6), but also that elements of 2 Corinthians 5:14–21 and, by extension, Galatians 2:15–21 are scattered throughout Romans. Romans, in other words, continues the understanding of participation, justification, and transformation we have found in Galatians 2:15–21 and 2 Corinthians 5:14–21. This understanding may be summarized in the words "righteousness," "resurrection," and "reconciliation." All of this occurs through, because of, and indeed in Christ. This does not mean, however, that Romans merely repeats what we have seen in Galatians and 2 Corinthians, for there are new twists and turns in the participatory justification plot.

Swimming against the Tide

We have noted, at various points, resistance to the claim that Paul sees justification in participatory terms. An example of this situation can be found even in the brilliant, magisterial commentary on Romans by Richard Longenecker. Longenecker contends that the "spiritual gift" (Rom. 1:11) Paul seeks to impart to the Roman house churches is the distinctive version of the gospel he preaches, which is found especially in Romans 5–8. In those chapters, Longenecker claims, Paul has transitioned from the more Jewish form of the gospel presented in chapters 1–4 and rooted in the Scriptures of Israel. It is this version of the gospel preserved in Romans 1–4 that the Roman believers first heard from Jewish Christ-following missionaries, according to Longenecker. That account of the gospel focused on justification, redemption, propitiation/expiation, and related concerns, while Paul's version focuses on reconciliation, life in Christ/the Spirit, participation, and related themes.[1] That is, in Romans 5–8 Paul uses "much more personal, relational, and participatory language."[2] This theology is, according to Longenecker, what Paul calls the heart of "my gospel" (2:16; 16:25), Paul's distinctive rendering of the gospel for gentile audiences.[3]

The claim of this chapter is quite different. For Paul in Romans, I contend, justification is itself participatory, transformative, and ethical because it is a resurrection from the dead—resurrection to new life—and a participation in the righteousness of God, God's justice-making, reconciling work. To be sure, Longenecker is right to say that in Romans 5–8 Paul "continues to proclaim his understanding of God's righteousness."[4] He also correctly argues against a common misinterpretation of Romans: that chapters 1–4 are about justification and chapters 5–8 are about sanctification. Rather, says Longenecker,

> these two sections could also be viewed as setting out somewhat parallel lines of thought, though with differing emphases and different modes of expression: the first in 1:16–4:25 using judicial and forensic language; the second in 5:1–8:39 using relational, personal, and participatory language—though with both sections speaking of much the same things.[5]

1. R. Longenecker, *Epistle to the Romans*, 538–39. An extreme version of Longenecker's view appears in the work of his student Douglas Campbell (*Deliverance of God*), for whom much of Rom. 1–4 represents the antithesis of Paul's gospel, and Rom. 5–8 represents, for all practical purposes, the totality of Paul's gospel.
2. R. Longenecker, *Epistle to the Romans*, 539.
3. R. Longenecker, *Epistle to the Romans*, 10, 16–20.
4. R. Longenecker, *Epistle to the Romans*, 538.
5. R. Longenecker, *Epistle to the Romans*, 539.

If pushed just a bit further, Longenecker's argument for "much the same things" could be transformed into the contention of this chapter: the two sections of Romans speak of the *same* thing. That is, as I have argued elsewhere,

> principally, Romans 5–8 functions to spell out the meaning and character of justification. Building on 3:21–4:25, Paul constructs an extended definition of justification as new life through a series of antithetical narratives [5:12–21; 6:1–7:6; 7:7–8:39] that echo the "but now" of 3:21.[6]

In this chapter we look at this claim from a different angle and develop it in some new directions. We begin with the general motif of participation, which explodes in Romans. Then we look at some overarching similarities between parts of Galatians and 2 Corinthians, on the one hand, and Romans, on the other. Then we consider justification as entailing righteousness, resurrection, and reconciliation—three of the principal themes we saw in 2 Corinthians 5:14–21. These are the "three Rs" of justification.

We begin with a brief overview of the central reality of participation in the Letter to the Romans.

Participation in Romans

If we have read Galatians 2 and 2 Corinthians 5, it comes as no surprise that a theology of participation permeates Romans. We find this phenomenon in two main forms, as we noted in chapter 1:[7]

- First, there is the language of "in Christ Jesus" (that is, "in the Messiah Jesus"; also, "in the Lord [Jesus]") and "in the Spirit," as well as the corollary language of Christ and the Spirit being in believers. This language employs the preposition "in" (Gk. *en*); we have already seen it in 2 Corinthians 5:17 and 5:21 as well as Galatians 2:17 and 3:14—to which a few other texts from those two letters could be added.[8]
- Second, there is the language of doing something "with" Christ or the Spirit. This language uses the preposition "with" (Gk. *syn*), which often appears as a prefix (*syn*- and alternative spellings)[9] that is sometimes translated into English as "co-" or "con-" but also as "with."

6. Gorman, *Apostle of the Crucified Lord*, 425. N. T. Wright also contends that we must see Rom. 5–8 as continuing the discussion of justification (see, e.g., *Paul and the Faithfulness of God*, 1024).

7. See the discussion and list of occurrences there.

8. 2 Cor. 1:21; 2:17; 12:2, 9; Gal. 1:22; 2:4; 3:26, 28; 5:6.

9. Other forms include *syg*-, *sym*-, and *sys*-.

Life *in* Christ is also life *with* Christ. And life in and with *Christ* is also life in and with *the Spirit*. This language is especially prominent in Romans 6 and 8, which means that understanding these two chapters is critical to grasping Paul's theology and spirituality of participation.

"In" Forms of Participation

We find "in Christ" language scattered throughout Romans, beginning in chapter 6, with some especially important occurrences in chapter 8 and a significant cluster in chapter 16. A few examples follow:

> So you also must consider yourselves dead to sin and alive to God **in Christ Jesus.** (6:11)

> For the wages of sin is death, but the free gift of God is eternal life **in Christ Jesus our Lord.** (6:23)

> [1]There is therefore now no condemnation for those who are **in Christ Jesus.** [2]For the law of the Spirit of life **in Christ Jesus** has set you free from the law of sin and of death. (8:1–2)

> [1]I commend to you our sister Phoebe . . . [2]so that you may welcome her **in the Lord** as is fitting for the saints. . . . [3]Greet Prisca and Aquila, who work with me **in Christ Jesus.** . . . [7]Greet Andronicus and Junia . . . ; they were **in Christ** before I was. [8]Greet Ampliatus, my beloved **in the Lord.** [9]Greet Urbanus, our co-worker **in Christ.** . . . [10]Greet Apelles, who is approved **in Christ.** . . . [11]Greet those **in the Lord** who belong to the family of Narcissus. [12]Greet those workers **in the Lord,** Tryphaena and Tryphosa. Greet the beloved Persis, who has worked hard **in the Lord.** [13]Greet Rufus, chosen **in the Lord.** . . . [22]I Tertius, the writer of this letter, greet you **in the Lord.** (16:1–3; 7–13, 22)

In addition to Paul's "in Christ" language, there is also "in the Spirit" language and, because Paul sees participation as reciprocal, also "Christ in" and "the Spirit in" language. All of this comes together in Romans 8, where the entire participatory experience, with both the Messiah and the Spirit, is most fully articulated. (As we will see below, there is also much "with" language in this chapter.) We have just noted the "in Christ" language of Romans 8:1–2, which should be read in connection with the following lines that speak of both "Christ in you" and the reciprocal residence of the Spirit and believers:

> [9]But you are not in the flesh; you are **in the Spirit,** since **the Spirit of God dwells in you.** Anyone who does not **have the Spirit of Christ** does not belong to him.

¹⁰But if **Christ is in you**, though the body is dead because of sin, the Spirit is life because of righteousness. ¹¹If **the Spirit of him who raised Jesus from the dead dwells in you**, he who raised Christ from the dead will give life to your mortal bodies also through **his Spirit that dwells in you**. (Rom. 8:9–11)

Significantly, being "in Christ/the Spirit" is the opposite of being "in Sin" (Rom. 6:1–2) or "in the flesh" (Rom. 8:8–9).¹⁰

While it is true that Paul's "in Christ/the Spirit" language appears in Romans only in chapters 6–16, with an in-depth theological analysis only in chapter 8, we should not conclude, with Longenecker, that participatory (or mutual indwelling) language is appropriate only for certain theological contexts. Such language is not opposed to or essentially different from speaking of the same people as those who believe/obey ("believers") or as those who are justified ("the just/righteous"). In fact, the idiom of being in Christ is so fundamental to Paul's understanding of "being a Christian" (to use our language) that it repeatedly rolls off his tongue in Romans 16, as we just heard. Its absence from a particular context is not an indication of its being inappropriate there. "In Christ" language is always *appropriate*, but not always *utilized*.

Some of the many ways to describe "Christians" are indicated already in both Galatians 2 and 2 Corinthians 5—they are the justified, the (participants in the) new creation, those who believe, those who are in Christ, the righteousness/justice of God, and so forth—and these are also scattered throughout Romans, combined as well with new images. But the most basic way to describe the Christian and the Christian community is as those who are "in Christ." The justified are participants, and their participation began in the very event of justification and its public expression in baptism.

"With" Forms of Participation

"With" forms of participation in Romans are concentrated in clusters in chapters 6 and 8. In Romans 6 Paul says the following:

⁴Therefore we have been **buried with him** [*synetaphēmen oun autō*] by baptism into death, so that, just as Christ was raised from the dead by the glory of the Father, so we too might walk in newness of life.
⁵For if we have been **united with him** [*symphytoi*] **in a death like his**, we will certainly be united with him [implied in Gk.] in a **resurrection like his**. ⁶We know that **our old self was crucified with him** [*ho palaios hēmōn anthrōpos*

10. Like most other interpreters, I understand "sin" (singular) in Paul as a power that Paul treats as a dramatic, personified figure in the story of the human predicament and the divine solution. I have therefore altered the NRSV text from "sin" to "Sin" (uppercase *S*).

synestaurōthē] so that the body of sin might be destroyed, and we might no longer be enslaved to sin. [7]For whoever has died is freed from sin. [8]But if **we have died with Christ** [*apethanomen syn Christō*], we believe that **we will also live with him** [*syzēsomen autō*]. (Rom. 6:4–8)

The context here is Paul's description of the significance of baptism. The question he raises is "What happened in baptism, and what does that mean, existentially, now?" The answer is that those who are baptized have entered into the story of Christ or, to be more precise, into the reality that the story narrates. The language of Romans 6 echoes that of 1 Corinthians 15:

[3]For I handed on to you as of first importance what I in turn had received: that **Christ died** for our sins in accordance with the scriptures, [4]and that **he was buried**, and that **he was raised** on the third day in accordance with the scriptures, [5]and that **he appeared** to Cephas, then to the twelve. [6]Then **he appeared** to more than five hundred brothers and sisters at one time. . . . [7]Then he **appeared** to James, then to all the apostles. [8]Last of all, as to one untimely born, he **appeared** also to me. (1 Cor. 15:3–8)

The sequence of four main verbs in 1 Corinthians 15:3–8 that are predicated of Christ—died, was buried, was raised, appeared—is essentially reproduced in Romans 6:4–8 as acts in which the baptized participate *with* Christ: death, burial, resurrection. The only missing element is "appeared," and that may be implied in the language of "presenting" oneself and one's members (six times in 6:13, 16, 19). Baptism is participational through and through, with weighty implications for both present and eschatological existence.[11]

We will return below to additional "with Christ" language in Romans 8. As we will now see, however, there are also significant parallels between Romans 6 and Galatians 2. These parallels mean that what Paul says about *baptism* he has also already said about *justification*. So we could say as well that the question here in Romans 6 is "What happened in *justification*, and what does that mean, existentially, now?"

Galatians 2:15–21 and Romans 6

In my book *Inhabiting the Cruciform God*, I noted significant similarities between Galatians 2:15–21 and Romans 6:1–7:6. The comparison came in a chapter entitled "Justification by Co-Crucifixion: The Logic of Paul's Soteriology," and in a subsection called "Justification by Co-Crucifixion (JCC)."[12]

11. For a helpful, extended discussion, see I. Morales, "Baptism and Union with Christ."
12. Gorman, *Inhabiting the Cruciform God*, 63–86.

Reproduced here, with minor changes, is a table from that book showing the parallels between the two texts (table 8.1, p. 185).

The conclusion I have drawn from the analysis summarized in table 8.1 is, essentially, that justification and baptism are two sides of the same coin, and that "coin" is entrance *into* Christ by means of an experience of co-crucifixion and co-resurrection *with* Christ. Moreover, although Galatians 2 is about faith while Romans 6 is about baptism, this is a "superfluous difference."[13] For Paul, "faith and baptism are theologically coterminous," such that "what Paul predicates of faith he can also predicate of baptism, and vice versa."[14] The comparative table for Galatians 2 and Romans 6 reveals that what Paul says of faith he says of baptism, and vice versa. It is the language of conversion/transfer/identity transformation, and it is *participatory*.

In light of the previous chapter, this sort of conclusion should come as no surprise: Paul "remixed" Galatians 2 in 2 Corinthians 5, and he appears to have done so again in Romans 6. As we will see below, Romans 6 has explicit echoes of 2 Corinthians 5. But for now we can first make this observation: even though baptism per se is not mentioned in 2 Corinthians 5:14–21, the claim that baptism, like justification, is about death and resurrection to new life—that is, that justification language is baptismal language (and vice versa)—is certainly compatible with the connections we saw in chapter 7 between Galatians 2 and 2 Corinthians 5.

We find additional participatory language in Romans 8, where the essential status and existential shape of the baptized/justified community is described not only as *in* Christ/the Spirit (as noted above) but also as *with* Christ/the Spirit.

> [16]It is that very Spirit **bearing witness with** [*symmartyrei*] our spirit that we are children of God, [17]and if children, then heirs, heirs of God and **joint heirs with** [*synklēronomoi*] Christ—if, in fact, we **suffer with** [*sympaschomen*] him so that we may also **be glorified with** [*syndoxasthōmen*] him. . . . [22]We know that the whole creation has been **groaning in labor pains** [*systenazei kai synōdinei*] until now. . . . [26]Likewise the Spirit helps us in our weakness; for we do not know how to pray as we ought, but that very Spirit **intercedes with** [*synantilambanetai*] sighs too deep for words. . . . [28]We know that all things **work together** [*synergei*] for good [or "God works all things together for good"] for those who love God, who are called according to his purpose. [29]For those whom he foreknew he also predestined to be **conformed** [*symmorphous*] to the image of his Son, in order that he might be the firstborn within a large family. (Rom. 8:16–17, 22, 26, 28–29)

13. Gorman, *Inhabiting the Cruciform God*, 78.
14. Gorman, *Inhabiting the Cruciform God*, 79.

Table 8.1. Similarities between Gal. 2:15–21 and Rom. 6:1–7:6[a]

Features	Galatians 2:15–21 NRSV (justification)	Romans 6:1–7:6 MJG (baptism)
Transfer into Christ	• even we came to faith [that incorporates us] into [eis] the Messiah Jesus (2:16) • justified in the Messiah (2:17); cf. 3:27	• baptized into [eis] Christ Jesus (6:3) • alive to God in Christ Jesus (6:11) • eternal life in Christ Jesus our Lord (6:23)
Death to the law/law and sin	• I myself, through the law, died in relation to the law (2:19)	• you have died to the law through the body of Christ (7:4); cf. died to sin (6:2) • so that the body of sin might be destroyed, and we might no longer be enslaved to sin (6:6) • dead to sin (6:11)
Co-crucifixion (expressed in passive voice), death of self	• I have been crucified with the Messiah; thus I myself no longer live (2:19–20)	• baptized into his death (6:3) • buried with him by baptism into death (6:4) • united with him in a death like his (6:5) • our old self was crucified with him (6:6) • we have died with Christ (6:8)
Resurrection to new life in the present	• so that I could live in relation to God . . . and the life I do now live in the flesh (2:19–20)	• just as Christ was raised from the dead . . . so we too might walk in newness of life (6:4) • alive to God in Christ Jesus (6:11) • those who have been brought from death to life (6:13) • died to the law . . . the new life of the Spirit (7:4, 6)
Participation with Christ and to God	• so that I could live in relation to God . . . the Messiah lives in me (2:19–20)	• alive to God in Christ Jesus (6:11) • so that you may belong to another, to him who has been raised from the dead in order that we may bear fruit for God (7:4)
Faith and love (Christ's and ours); i.e., proper covenantal relations with God and others ("resurrectional cruciformity")	• the faithfulness of Jesus the Messiah . . . the faithfulness of the Messiah (2:16) • we came to faith [that incorporates us] into [eis] the Messiah Jesus (2:16) • I live by means of the faithfulness of the Son of God, who loved me by giving himself for me (2:20) • Cf. 5:6 for believers' faith and love explicitly	• No longer present your members to sin as instruments of wickedness, but present yourselves to God as those who have been brought from death to life, and present your members to God as instruments of righteousness (6:13) • you . . . have become slaves of righteousness (6:18; cf. 6:19b) • the advantage you get is sanctification (6:22) • Cf. 5:19; 8:34–35 for Christ's faith/obedience and love explicitly

a. Adapted from *Inhabiting the Cruciform God*, 76–77. I have omitted a row that suggested that both texts have a future as well as a present dimension to resurrection and life. This no longer seems to me to be the case for Gal. 2, but it is for Rom. 6 (vv. 5b, 8, 22–23). Note: throughout this chapter I again use my own translations of Gal. 2:15–21 and 2 Cor. 5:14–21 (from chaps. 6 and 7) and the NRSV for other texts, including all of Romans, unless otherwise indicated. For Gal. 2:15–21, I have used the shorter translation from p. 117.

This passage from Romans 8 contains a cluster of nine compound *syn-* ("co-") words, as follows:[15]

- *symmartyrei* (8:16; "cowitness")
- *synklēronomoi* (8:17; "coheirs")
- *sympaschomen* (8:17; "cosuffer")
- *syndoxasthōmen* (8:17; "be coglorified")
- *systenazei* (8:22; "cogroan")
- *synōdinei* (8:22; "co-agonize")
- *synantilambanetai* (8:26; "co-take hold of"; i.e., "help")
- *synergei* (8:28; "coworks")
- *symmorphous* (8:29; "coformed")

This cluster emphatically indicates the participatory character of Christian existence. To repeat: life in Christ/the Spirit is life *with* Christ/the Spirit. Its essential shape includes present suffering with Christ, sustained in solidarity with the Spirit, to be followed by future glory with Christ, all as a process of being conformed to the image of Christ.

This participatory mode of Christian existence is in fact life itself, as Romans 8 also tells us: "To set the mind on the Spirit is life and peace" (Rom. 8:6b). The noun "life" and its cognate verb "to live" occur a total of seven times in Romans 8.[16] Such existence, such life, has already been referred to as "newness of life" in Romans 6:4. The combination of "new" and "life" is reminiscent of 2 Corinthians 5:14–21—new creation (v. 17), living for Christ rather than self (v. 15). We turn now, then, to 2 Corinthians 5:14–21 itself to see its connections with Romans.

2 Corinthians 5:14–21 in Romans

As noted in the previous chapter, Frances Young has argued that 2 Corinthians influenced Romans.[17] When we look specifically at 2 Corinthians 5:14–21, we will certainly find parallels with Romans 6, since 2 Corinthians 5:14–21, as I have demonstrated, is dependent on (or at least greatly similar to) Galatians

---

15. Translations seldom convey the presence or force of these many "co-" words.

16. "Life" (*zoē*) in 8:2, 6, 10, 38; "to live" (*zaō*) in 8:12, 13 (2x).

17. Young, "Understanding Romans in the Light of 2 Corinthians." While I agree with the several connections Young finds between the two letters, especially her emphasis on the new-covenant and Spirit motifs in each letter, it is ironic that she finds justification to be "more incidental to Paul's argument than has generally been assumed" (442).

2:15–21. But what is more significant for our purposes here is that elements of 2 Corinthians 5:14–21 are *scattered throughout much of Romans*; this key text of Pauline theology and spirituality permeates the letter, with bits and pieces located here and there from at least chapter 4 to at least chapter 14. That is, this 2 Corinthians text about justification as entailing reconciliation, participation, resurrection to new life, and transformation into God's righteousness, all grounded in Christ's loving death, is one of the chief sources of Romans. Accordingly, *Romans is, in part, an extended commentary on 2 Corinthians 5:14–21.*

Table 8.2 (pp. 188–90) shows the many echoes of 2 Corinthians 5:14–21 in Romans. We cannot possibly undertake a full analysis of all these parallels; rather, we will consider some of the most significant.

Yet one more table is worthy of consideration before doing so—one that presents the occurrences of the *dikai-* word-family in Romans. The *dikai-* word-family—meaning words translated into English as "justify," "justification," "justice," "just," "rectify," "righteousness," and "righteous"—is central to the theology of Romans. If Paul had truly left justification behind at the beginning of chapter 5 (so, e.g., R. Longenecker), then we would expect this word-family to disappear, or at least drop off, after chapter 4. But as table 8.3 demonstrates (p. 191), that is not the case.

Of the sixty-three occurrences of this word-family in Romans, more than half—thirty-three, to be exact—are found after chapter 4. To be sure, the verb *dikaioō* is concentrated in chapter 3, but it does occur six times in chapters 5 through 8. Moreover, the noun *dikaiosynē* has high concentrations not only in chapters 4 and 5 but also in chapters 9 and 10. Although one might argue that certain words or certain uses of certain words do not relate specifically to justification per se, that argument puts more weight on English translations than on the actual Greek word-family. One might also argue that certain occurrences of the *dikai-* word-family simply summarize or refer back to the content of earlier chapters, but at the very least such an argument proves that Paul has not left justification—or, more precisely, the *dikai-* word-family and whatever it signifies—behind.[18] Furthermore, as we will see momentarily, since elements of 2 Corinthians 5 and its theology of justification are especially found in Romans 5–8, *the contention that Paul leaves justification behind in those chapters is mistaken.*

As noted earlier, justification is often defined as acquittal, the argument being that it is an image drawn from the law court. In fact, however, justification

---

18. On this point Richard Longenecker and I might actually agree, since he rightly notes (*Epistle to the Romans*, 538) that after chap. 4 Paul is still unpacking the significance of God's righteousness.

Table 8.2. Echoes of 2 Cor. 5:14–21 in Romans

Subject	2 Corinthians 5:14–21 (MJG; in sequence)	Romans (NRSV alt.; echoes in selected texts)
Christ's love	• For the Messiah's love (hē gar agapē tou Christou) (v. 14)	• the love of the Messiah (tēs agapēs tou Christou) (8:35); cf. 8:39
Christ died for us	• one died for all (heis hyper pantōn apethanen) (v. 14) • he died for all (hyper pantōn apethanen) (v. 15) • died for them (hyper autōn apothanonti) (v. 15)	• the Messiah died for the ungodly (Christos . . . hyper asebōn apethanen) (5:6) • the Messiah died for us (Christos hyper hēmōn apethanen) (5:8) • the Messiah Jesus, who died (Christos [Iēsous] ho apothanōn) (8:34) • for whom the Messiah died (hyper hou Christos apethanen) (14:15)
Death → new life, redirected life	• one died for all, and therefore all died. And he died for all so that those who live would live no longer for themselves, but for the one who died for them and was raised (heis hyper pantōn apethanen, ara hoi pantes apethanon; kai hyper pantōn apethanen, hina hoi zōntes mēketi heautois zōsin alla tō hyper autōn apothanonti kai egerthenti) (vv. 14–15)	• our old self was crucified with him so that the body of sin might be destroyed, and we might no longer be enslaved to sin (ho palaios hēmōn anthrōpos synestaurōthē, hina katargēthē to sōma tēs hamartias, tou mēketi douleuein hēmas tē hamartia) (6:6) • No longer present your members to sin as instruments of wickedness [unrighteousness/injustice], but present yourselves to God as those who have been brought from death to life, and present your members to God as instruments of righteousness [righteousness/justice]. (mēde paristanete ta melē hymōn hopla adikias tē hamartia, alla parastēsate heautous tō theō hōsei ek nekrōn zōntas kai ta melē hymōn hopla dikaiosynēs tō theō) (6:13)
No longer (cf. new creation below)	• No longer (ouketi) (v. 16)	• what will their acceptance be but life from the dead! (tis hē proslēmpsis ei mē zōē ek nekrōn) (11:15)
Purpose: Christ-directed life	• so that those who live would live no longer for themselves, but for the one who died for them and was raised (hina hoi zōntes mēketi heautois zōsin alla tō hyper autōn apothanonti kai egerthenti) (v. 15)	• We do not live to ourselves, and we do not die to ourselves. If we live, we live to the Lord, and if we die, we die to the Lord; so then, whether we live or whether we die, we are the Lord's. For to this end the Messiah died and lived again, so that he might be Lord of both the dead and the living. (oudeis gar hēmōn heautō zē kai oudeis heautō apothnēskei; ean te gar zōmen, tō kyriō zōmen, ean te apothnēskōmen, tō kyriō apothnēskomen. ean te oun zōmen ean te apothnēskōmen, tou kyriou esmen. eis touto gar Christos apethanen kai ezēsen, hina kai nekrōn kai zōntōn kyrieusē) (14:7–9)
Christ's death and resurrection together	• for the one who died for them and was raised (tō hyper autōn apothanonti kai egerthenti) (v. 15)	• who was handed over to death for our trespasses and was raised for our justification (hos paredothē dia ta paraptōmata hēmōn kai ēgerthē dia tēn dikaiōsin hēmōn) (4:25) • the Messiah Jesus, who died, yes, who was raised (Christos [Iēsous] ho apothanōn, mallon de egertheis) (8:34) • the Messiah died and lived again (Christos apethanen kai ezēsen) (14:9)

Subject	2 Corinthians 5:14–21 (MJG; in sequence)	Romans (NRSV alt.; echoes in selected texts)
According to the flesh[a]	• according to human standards [the flesh] (*kata sarka*) (v. 16) • according to human standards [the flesh] (*kata sarka*) (v. 16)	• according to the flesh (*kata sarka*) (4:1) • according to the flesh (*kata sarka*) (8:4, 5, 12, 13)
In Christ (believers)	• if anyone is in Christ, new creation! (*ei tis en Christō, kainē ktisis*) (v. 17) • we ourselves would become the justice [or "righteousness"] of God in him (*genōmetha dikaiosynē theou en autō*) (v. 21)	• the God . . . who gives life to the dead and calls into existence the things that do not exist (*theou tou zōopoiountos tous nekrous kai kaloumtos ta mē onta hōs onta*) (4:17)
New creation		• so we too might walk in newness of life (*houtōs kai hēmeis en kainotēti zōēs peripatēsōmen*) (6:4) • alive to God in the Messiah Jesus (*zōntas de tō theō en Christō Iēsou*) (6:11) • There is therefore now no condemnation for those who are in the Messiah Jesus. For the law of the Spirit of life in the Messiah Jesus has set you free from the law of sin and of death. (*Ouden ara nyn katakrima tois en Christō Iēsou. ho gar nomos tou pneumatos tēs zōēs en Christō Iēsou ēleutherōsen se apo tou nomou tēs hamartias kai tou thanatou.*) (8:1–2)
Reconciliation	• the God who reconciled us to himself through the Messiah (*tou theou tou katallaxantos hēmas heautō dia Christou*) (v. 18)	• they are now justified by his grace as a gift, through the redemption that is in the Messiah Jesus (*dikaioumenoi dōrean tē autou chariti dia tēs apolytrōseōs tēs en Christō Iēsou*) (3:24)
In Christ (God's action)	• God was in the Messiah reconciling the world to himself (*theos ēn en Christō kosmon katallassōn heautō*) (v. 19) • be reconciled to God (*katallagēte tō theō*) (v. 20) Cf. • the ministry of reconciliation (*tēn diakonian tēs katallagēs*) (v. 18) • the message of reconciliation (*ton logon tēs katallagēs*) (v. 19)	• For if while we were enemies, we were reconciled to God through the death of his Son . . . We even boast in God through our Lord Jesus the Messiah, through whom we have now received reconciliation. (*echthroi ontes katēllagēmen tō theō dia tou thanatou tou huiou autou . . . katallagentes . . . kauchōmenoi en tō theō dia tou kyriou hēmōn Iēsou Christou di' hou nyn tēn katallagēn elabomen*) (5:10–11) • the love of God in Christ Jesus our Lord (*tēs agapēs tou theou en Christō Iēsou tō kyriō hēmōn*) (8:39) • the reconciliation of the world (*katallagē kosmou*) (11:15)
Reckoning (counting) vis-à-vis trespasses	• not counting their trespasses against them (*mē logizomenos autois ta paraptōmata autōn*) (v. 19)	• "blessed is the one against whom the Lord will not reckon sin" (*makarios anēr hou ou mē logisētai kyrios hamartian*) (4:8) • who was handed over to death for our trespasses (*hos paredothē dia ta paraptōmata hēmōn*) (4:25a)[b]

Subject	2 Corinthians 5:14–21 (MJG; in sequence)	Romans (NRSV alt.; echoes in selected texts)
Interchange and transformation into the justice/righteousness of God in Christ	• the one who did not know sin [the Messiah Jesus] to be sin so that we would become the justice [or "righteousness"] of God in him (ton mē gnonta hamartian hyper hēmōn hamartian epoiēsen, hina hēmeis genōmetha dikaiosynē theou en autō) (v. 21)	• But now, apart from law, the righteousness of God has been disclosed . . . . , the righteousness of God through faith in Jesus the Messiah [or "the faith of Jesus the Messiah"] for all who believe. (Nyni de chōris nomou dikaiosynē theou . . . , dikaiosynē de theou dia pisteōs Iēsou Christou eis pantas tous pisteuontas) (3:21–22)[c]
		• who was handed over to death for our trespasses and was raised for our justification (hos paredothē dia ta paraptōmata hēmōn kai ēgerthē dia tēn dikaiōsin hēmōn) (4:25)
		• For just as by the one man's disobedience the many were made sinners, so by the one man's obedience the many will be made righteous. (hōsper gar dia tēs parakoēs tou henos anthrōpou hamartōloi katestathēsan hoi polloi, houtōs kai dia tēs hypakoēs tou henos dikaioi katastathēsontai hoi polloi) (5:19)
		• No longer present your members to sin as instruments of wickedness [unrighteousness/injustice], but present yourselves to God as those who have been brought from death to life, and present your members to God as instruments of righteousness [righteousness/justice]. (mēde paristanete ta melē hymōn hopla adikias tē hamartia, alla parastēsate heautous tō theō hōsei ek nekrōn zōntas kai ta melē hymōn hopla dikaiosynēs tō theō) (6:13)
		• you, having been set free from sin, have become slaves of righteousness (eleutherōthentes de apo tēs hamartias edoulōthēte tē dikaiosynē) (6:18)[d]
		• For God has done what the law, weakened by the flesh, could not do: by sending his own Son in the likeness of sinful flesh, and to deal with sin, he condemned sin in the flesh, so that the just requirement of the law might be fulfilled in us, who walk not according to the flesh but according to the Spirit. (nomou en hō esthenei dia tēs sarkos, ho theos ton heautou huion pempsas en homoiōmati sarkos hamartias kai peri hamartias katekrinen tēn hamartian en tē sarki, hina to dikaiōma tou nomou plērōthē en hēmin tois mē kata sarka peripatousin alla kata pneuma) (8:3–4)
		• For the kingdom of God is not food and drink but righteousness and peace and joy in the Holy Spirit. (ou gar estin hē basileia tou theou brōsis kai posis alla dikaiosynē kai eirēnē kai chara en pneumati hagiō) (14:17)[e]

a. I do not mean to imply that the occurrences of *kata sarka* could come only from 2 Corinthians; the phrase occurs seventeen times in the undisputed letters and another two in the disputed.

b. The verb *logizomai* occurs nineteen times in Romans, eleven of them in chap. 4. The noun *paraptōma* appears nine times in Romans, six of them in 5:15–20.

c. Cf. Rom. 1:17; 10:3 for "the righteousness [justice] of God."

d. Cf. the uses of *dikaiosynē* also in 6:16, 19, 20.

e. As table 8.3 below indicates (p. 191), there are many other occurrences of the *dikai-* word-family in Romans.

Table 8.3. The *dikai-* Word-Family in Romans

Chapter	*dikaioō* (justify, make/declare righteous/just, rectify)	*dikaiosynē* (justice, righteousness, justification, rectification)	*dikaios* (just, righteous)	*dikaiōma* (just/righteous requirement)	*dikaiōsis* (justification, rectification)
1		1	1	1	
2	1		1	1	
3	6	5	2		
4	2	8			1
5	2	2	2	2	1
6	1	5			
7			1		
8	3	1		1	
9		4			
10		7			
11					
12					
13					
14		1			
15					
16					
TOTAL (# after chap. 4)	15 (6)	34 (20)	7 (3)	5 (3)	2 (1)

language has a more complex family of origin and, more importantly for our purposes, as tables 8.1–3 suggest, it is defined and described by Paul in new and creative ways. Paul cannot simply put new wine into old wineskins. Justification, as we will now see once again, is *a transformative death-and-resurrection event.* This is not to say that justification has nothing to do with acquittal and forgiveness, simply that it entails *more* than acquittal and forgiveness.

Participation, Justification, and Transformation into the Righteousness of God

The connection between baptism and justification implied by the parallels indicated in table 8.1 above are made explicit and clear in Romans 6, as Paul uses the verb *dikaioō* ("justify") in verse 7: "For whoever has died is freed from sin [*dedikaiōtai apo tēs hamartias*]." What does it mean to be "justified" from sin? This use of *dikaioō* has caused no small amount of consternation among interpreters of Romans, but in the present context, especially in light of both Galatians 2 and 2 Corinthians 5, it makes perfect sense: justification as the liberative and thus transformative work of God.[19] It entails liberation from the power of Sin (uppercase *S* to indicate that sin is a personified, cosmic power; cf. esp. 3:9) and transferal of the liberated person(s) from Sin into a life-giving "slavery" to God and to justice/righteousness: "You [plural], having been set free from sin, have become slaves of righteousness [*eleutherōthentes de apo tēs hamartias edoulōthēte tē dikaiosynē*]" (6:18, summarizing much of Rom. 6).[20]

A cluster of occurrences of *dikaiosynē* ("justice/righteousness") in Romans 6 reinforces this connection between baptism and justification (which is expressed with the cognate verb *dikaioō* and other cognates throughout Romans). But those occurrences of *dikaiosynē* also echo the claim of 2 Corinthians 5:21 that the purpose of justification is transformation into the justice/righteousness of God (*dikaiosynē theou*). That is, in the language of Romans 6, Christ died, and we died with Christ, so that our bodies that have embodied injustice/unrighteousness (*adikia*; see Rom. 1:18 [2x], 29; 2:8; 3:5; 6:13) would henceforth embody justice/righteousness:

> [13]No longer present your members [i.e., the members of your body] to Sin as weapons of **injustice/unrighteousness** [*adikias*], but present yourselves to God as those who have been brought from death to life, and present your members to God as weapons of **justice/righteousness** [*dikaiosynēs*]. [14]For Sin will have no dominion over you, since you are not under law but under grace.
>
> [15]What then? Should we sin because we are not under law but under grace? By no means! [16]Do you not know that if you present yourselves to anyone as obedient slaves, you are slaves of the one whom you obey, either of Sin, which leads to death, or of obedience, which leads to **justice/righteousness** [*dikaiosynēn*]? [17]But thanks be to God that you, having once been slaves of Sin, have become obedient from the heart to the form of teaching to which you were entrusted, [18]and that you, having been set free from Sin, have become slaves of **justice/righteousness** [*dikaiosynē*]. [19]I am speaking in human terms because of your natural limitations. For just as you once presented your members as slaves to impurity and to greater and greater iniquity, so now present your members as slaves to **justice/righteousness** [*dikaiosynē*] for sanctification.
>
> [20]When you were slaves of Sin, you were free in regard to **justice/righteousness** [*dikaiosynē*]. (Rom. 6:13–20 NRSV alt.)[21]

19. The passive voice implies divine action.

20. For the liberative, transformative interpretation of justification here and elsewhere, see esp. D. Campbell, *Deliverance of God*. Despite its polemical tone and its unconvincing reading of the early chapters of Romans (as containing a lot of non-Paul theology), Campbell's constructive work on justification is brilliant. See my review of the book in Gorman, "Douglas Campbell's *The Deliverance of God*." See also Despotis, "ὁ γὰρ ἀποθανὼν δεδικαίωται ἀπὸ τῆς ἁμαρτίας."

21. I have made the following adjustments to the NRSV: the noun "sin" is spelled "Sin," the *dikai-* family is consistently translated in terms of (in)justice/(un)righteousness, and "instruments" (*hopla*) is instead rendered as "weapons."

These five clustered instances of justice/righteousness, along with one of in-justice/unrighteousness, demonstrate that Paul sees an intimate connection between justification and justice/righteousness, and that this involves a radical transformation in people. This transformation is the content and the ongoing consequence of participation in Christ's death and resurrection. Justification, expressed in baptism and theologically inseparable from baptism, is partici-patory, transformative, and ethical. Those who have experienced the justice/righteousness of God (Rom. 3:21–22) in justification/baptism, through dying and rising with Christ, will embody justice/righteousness in daily life. More specifics about the content of that embodiment will be given in Romans 12–15.

Romans and 2 Corinthians 5:21

All of this suggests that Romans 6 is not only a relecture, or remix, of Galatians 2:15–21 (as suggested in table 8.1 above) but also an extended com-mentary on the second half of 2 Corinthians 5:21—"so that we ourselves would become the justice [or "righteousness"] of God in him [Christ]." This sug-gestion raises the question of the connection between the phrase "the justice/righteousness of God" (*dikaiosynē theou*) in 2 Corinthians and in Romans, and the corollary question of the connection between its referring both to God and to believers in Romans.

Romans 1 and 3: God's Justice

It is interesting that the phrase *dikaiosynē theou* occurs in the Pauline cor-respondence only in 2 Corinthians and in Romans. It is likewise interesting that the phrase refers explicitly in 2 Corinthians only to believers and refers explicitly in Romans only to God. What connects the reality of the *divine* "righteousness/justice of God" per se to a *human* "righteousness/justice of God"? The answer, the common denominator, is Christ, as Paul says in 1 Corinthians 1:30: "He [God] is the source of your life in Christ Jesus, who became for us wisdom from God, and righteousness [or "justice"; *dikaiosynē*] and sanctification and redemption." This is similar to what Paul says in Ro-mans 1:16–17 and 3:21–26, passages in which, according to Luke Johnson, we find the thesis of Romans and then its restatement:[22]

> For in it [the gospel] the righteousness of God is revealed through faith for faith. (Rom. 1:17a)

22. L. T. Johnson, *Reading Romans*, 13, 19–30, 47, 52–62. While some interpreters contend, with good reason, that 1:3–4 is also part of the thesis (or even the main thesis), in terms of vocabulary and theological content, 1:16–17 and its expansion in 3:21–26 undoubtedly lie at the heart of Paul's theology in the letter.

This verse may also be translated in the following way, as containing a reference to Christ and conveying particular understandings of the Greek phrase *dikaiosynē theou* and the Greek word *pistis* (translated as "faith" above):

> For in it [the gospel] the saving justice/righteousness of God is revealed through [Christ's] faith(fulness) in order to elicit our faith(fulness). (MJG)[23]

The righteousness-faithfulness link recurs in Romans 3 (again, MJG):[24]

> [21]But now, apart from law, the saving justice/righteousness of God has been disclosed, and is attested by the law and the prophets; [22]the saving justice/righteousness of God through the faithfulness of Jesus Christ for all who respond to it in faith(fulness).[25] (Rom. 3:21–22a)[26]

As in real estate, so also in soteriology: location is everything. Jesus the Messiah became, for us, God's righteousness and thus was the "location" of God's righteousness, God's saving act of restorative justice; he is now the location of believers, who are "in" the Messiah. For that reason, those who are in Christ can "become," or embody (realistically, we might say "approximate"), the sort of justice/righteousness that is characteristic of the God who has acted in Jesus Christ.

Romans 5:12–21: Justification and Transformative Justice

A similar conclusion is indicated by Romans 5:12–21, where Christ's death as an act of grace, obedience, and justice/righteousness (*dikaiōmatos*, 5:18) leads to righteousness (*dikaiōsin*, Rom. 5:18),[27] an act that also effects the transformation of sinners into righteous, or just, ones (*dikaioi*, 5:19). Although

23. Similarly, e.g., L. T. Johnson, *Reading Romans*, 29.

24. Cf. NRSV: "But now, apart from law, the righteousness of God has been disclosed, and is attested by the law and the prophets; the righteousness of God through faith in Jesus Christ for all who believe."

25. As in Gal. 2:15–21 (see chap. 6), we may speak of Christ's faith(fulness) and ours as the means and the mode of justification, or its objective and subjective basis, respectively.

26. See Talbert, *Romans*, 35–47, for a thorough reading of 1:16–17 along these lines. A similar reading, with emphasis on God's faithfulness, is R. Longenecker, *Epistle to the Romans*, 154–88. See also the classic statements of this sort of interpretation in Hays, *Faith of Jesus Christ*, 156–61; cf. L. T. Johnson, *Reading Romans*, 59–62.

27. The NRSV and many other translations here have "justification" rather than "righteousness" for *dikaiōsin*, while some others have "acquittal" (so also BDAG). Robert Jewett (*Romans*, 385–86) translates *dikaiōsin* as "rightness" because it is followed by the phrase "of life," implying that "the state of righteousness produced by Christ's grace . . . will assure the new form of life." But even if 5:18 connotes primarily acquittal, 5:19 is clearly about transformation. See further below.

Paul does not explicitly use the language of being "in Christ" versus being "in Adam" in this passage, as he does in 1 Corinthians 15:22, he certainly could have done so. To be in Christ is to benefit from his singular act of justice/righteousness and to become a people that is also characterized by similar justice/righteousness. In fact, Romans 5:19 is like 2 Corinthians 5:21; it is an interchange text—one that looks like a reinterpretation of 2 Corinthians 5:21 in light of the Adam-Christ antithesis that is the fundamental theological framework of Romans 5:12–21:

> For us [or "For our sake"] God made the one who did not know sin [the Messiah Jesus] to be sin so that we ourselves **would become** the justice [or "righteousness"] of God in him. (2 Cor. 5:21)
>
> *ton mē gnonta hamartian hyper hēmōn hamartian epoiēsen, hina hēmeis* **genōmetha** *dikaiosynē theou en autō.*
>
> For just as by the one man's disobedience the many **were made** sinners, so by the one man's obedience the many **will be made** righteous. (Rom. 5:19)
>
> *hōsper gar dia tēs parakoēs tou henos anthrōpou hamartōloi* **katestathēsan** *hoi polloi, houtōs kai dia tēs hypakoēs tou henos* dikaioi **katastathēsontai** *hoi polloi.*

The verb Paul uses twice in Romans 5:19, *kathistēmi/kathistanō* (boldfaced in English translation and in Greek above), here means "to make" or "to cause to become."[28] It is the functional equivalent of *ginomai,* "become" (*genōmetha;* also boldfaced), in 2 Corinthians 5:21. Similarly, the word *dikaioi* ("righteous") in Romans 5:19 is the functional equivalent of "the justice [or "righteousness"] of God" in 2 Corinthians 5:21 (both underlined in English translation and Greek).

Despite the future tense of the second verb ("will be made," *katastathēsontai*), I would contend (contra some interpreters) that Paul is almost certainly not referring primarily to a future, eschatological transformation or verdict. The context makes it highly probable that since he is referring to the actual, present effects of Adam's unrighteous act, he is also referring to the actual, present effects of Christ's righteous deed. The future tense likely reflects the sense of the Hebrew of Isaiah 53:11, to which Paul seems to be alluding: "The righteous one, my servant, shall make many righteous, and he shall bear their iniquities."[29] The future tense may also suggest that the work of God effected through Christ's obedience is not over; it continues in Rome and beyond.

The righteous, justice-making, transformative work of God in Christ's death is to create communities of righteous/just persons out of people who

---

28. BDAG, s.v. καθίστημι/καθιστάνω (*kathistēmi/kathistanō*) 3.
29. Similarly, Jewett, *Romans,* 386–87.

were unrighteous/unjust sinners. (Paul makes the same claim in more detail in 1 Cor. 6:1–11.)[30] This is what it means to be transferred out of Adam and into Christ. Romans 5:19 is part of the theological foundation for the concrete descriptions of, and calls for, justice/righteousness in Romans 6 that we have already considered. As in 2 Corinthians 5:21, Isaiah 53:11 is once again probably Paul's source. The book of Isaiah, like Paul, is interested in the creation of a transformed people. "Justification here [in Rom. 5:17, 19], then, means more than forgiveness," writes Charles Talbert. "It means divine enablement to be righteous (= faithful to God)."[31]

Furthermore, as also in both 2 Corinthians 5 and Galatians 2, this transformation is expressed with the use of the adverb "no longer" (Gk. *ouketi, mēketi*):

> And he died for all so that those who live would live no longer [*mēketi*] for themselves, but for the one who died for them and was raised. (2 Cor. 5:15 MJG)

> I myself no longer [*ouketi*] live, but the Messiah lives in me. (Gal. 2:20a MJG)

> We know that our old self was crucified with him so that the body dominated by Sin would be incapacitated [NRSV: destroyed], and we would no longer [*mēketi*] be enslaved to sin. (Rom. 6:6 MJG)

Does this transformative event of being made righteous involve forgiveness and acquittal? Of course! Is it limited to forgiveness and acquittal? *Mē genoito!* (May it never be!) In fact, Romans 5:12–21 seems to depict justification as involving both acquittal (implying forgiveness) and transformation, which is also the case in 2 Corinthians 5:14–21 (trespasses not counted, v. 19; transformation effected, vv. 14, 17, 21).[32] Romans 5:12–21 is also quite similar to the claim of Romans 3:21–26 that justification involves both the expiation of sins and redemption, or liberation, from the power of Sin:

> [24]They are now justified by his grace as a gift, through the redemption [liberation] that is in the Messiah Jesus, [25]whom God put forward as a sacrifice of atonement by his blood [expiation/forgiveness]. (Rom. 3:24–25a MJG)[33]

Furthermore, as we will see below, both forgiveness and transformation are also present in Romans 4. All of this is an event of grace, an act of both God's

---

30. The Corinthians should not be practicing injustice because, as justified people, they are part of the just, not the unjust. See the discussion in my *Becoming the Gospel*, 234–40.

31. Talbert, *Romans*, 153.

32. It also involves life, as we will see when we return to Rom. 5:12–21 below.

33. See further discussion in Gorman, *Apostle of the Crucified Lord*, 419–21.

grace and Christ's: "the grace [*charis*] of God and the free gift in the grace [*chariti*] of the one man, Jesus Christ" (Rom. 5:15).

Romans 12–16: The Kingdom of God's Justice and Peace

Thus the gracious justice/righteousness of God in Christ corresponds in location and in substance to its telos: the making of a people of justice/righteousness in Christ. As we will see more fully in the next chapter, Paul speaks of this similarity between divine and human justice in Christ in 2 Corinthians 9, where he employs Psalms 111 and 112 together to show the parallel between God's justice/righteousness (*dikaiosynē*) and that of God's people. In Romans itself, beyond the numerous references to *dikaiosynē* in Romans 6 that we have already examined, Paul summarizes the essence of life in Christ with these words, in a rare reference to God's kingdom:

> For the kingdom of God is not food and drink but righteousness and peace [*dikaiosynē kai eirēnē*] and joy in the Holy Spirit. (Rom. 14:17)

Paul may well be alluding here to a well-known text from Psalm 85 (84 LXX):

> Mercy and truth met; righteousness and peace [*dikaiosynē kai eirēnē*] kissed. (Ps. 85:10 [84:11 LXX] MJG)

As a summary of Paul's argument in Romans 14:1–15:13 about what does and does not matter in the body of Christ—cultural differences falling in the latter category, lovingly welcoming the culturally "other" in the former—this text serves also as an excellent summary of the "marks" of the church according to Paul in Romans. It functions also, therefore, as a brief synthesis of the entirety of the last quarter of the letter, chapters 12–16, in which Paul unpacks what it means for the justified, baptized, graced community in Christ to "by the mercies of God . . . present your bodies as a living sacrifice, holy and acceptable to God" (Rom. 12:1).

Accordingly, although the *dikai-* word-family may not occur frequently in the latter part of Romans, its appearance in 14:17 is weighty indeed. Those who have received the peace of God in justification (Rom. 5:1) are called to be a community of peace and justice. They are summoned and enabled, in other words, to participate in the peace and justice of God—indeed to become God's *shalom* (cf. 2 Cor. 5:21).

To be sure, Paul does not use the precise language of "becoming" the righteousness/justice of God in Romans. But the net effect of everything he says is precisely that: justification means transformation; it is becoming a just person, becoming incorporated into a just people, participating in the justice of God that was and is present in Jesus the Messiah.

This is, to be sure, resurrection to new life.

Justification as Resurrection from the Dead, New Creation, and Transformation

As we saw above, those who have died and been raised with Christ in baptism (and thus also in justification) are instructed to "present [themselves] to God as those who have been brought from death to life" (Rom. 6:13), and they are to "walk in newness of life" (6:4). They have undergone a resurrection. In the language of 2 Corinthians 5, those in Christ are a (or are a part of the) new creation. We can trace this baptismal language in Romans 6 back through chapter 5 to its roots in chapter 4.

Romans 6: Resurrection and Life Now

We have noted on several occasions the claim that Romans 6, specifically Romans 6:4, depicts those who have been crucified with Christ in baptism as those who have also been raised with him to new life. Although the resurrection *of* the body is future, resurrection *in* the body is present. We may wish to label this a "metaphorical" or an "ethical" resurrection, but whatever we call it, we must not underestimate its significance for Paul: the justified/baptized participate in Jesus' resurrection *now*.[34] Without a present resurrection, both baptism and justification would be events of only partial participation in the Messiah's saving event of crucifixion and resurrection. Baptism into Christ's death would be, in fact, a dead end. But it is not; it is full of resurrection life:

> [11]So you also must consider yourselves dead to sin and **alive to God in Christ Jesus**. . . . [13]No longer present your members to sin as instruments of wickedness, but present yourselves to God **as those who have been brought from death to life**, and present your members to God as instruments of righteousness. (Rom. 6:11, 13)

34. For a defense of believers' present participation in Jesus' resurrection in Rom. 6, see Kirk, *Unlocking Romans*, esp. 107–23. See also Tappenden, *Resurrection in Paul*. It is unfortunate that Thomas Tobin (*Paul's Rhetoric in Its Contexts*), who rightly emphasizes the ethical implications of baptism and correctly perceives that in Rom. 6 Paul is drawing on the narratival "creed" at the beginning of 1 Cor. 15 (193–94), for various reasons claims that Paul "refrain[s] from connecting Christ's resurrection directly with what happens to believers in baptism" (194). Yet even Tobin admits that there is a "present living from the dead . . . in a qualified sense" (197).

It is precisely this sort of resurrection—to (new) life—that we have seen in Galatians 2 and 2 Corinthians 5. To be sure, the new life is a life of ongoing participation in Christ's death too, a life of cruciformity. But it is *resurrectional* cruciformity.

Romans 5–8: Righteousness and Life

The theme of life is not restricted to Romans 6 or to baptism. It permeates Paul's letters, including Romans 5–8 in a significant way, where "Paul describes the work of God in Christ bringing about the very things that the law itself held out and promised: righteousness and life."[35] Of particular importance for Paul, especially in Romans, is the association of justification with life.[36] In Romans 5, for example, he says:

> [17]If, because of the one man's trespass, **death** exercised dominion through that one, much more surely will those who receive the abundance of grace and the free gift of righteousness exercise dominion in **life** through the one man, Jesus the Messiah. [18]Therefore just as one man's trespass led to condemnation for all, so one man's act of righteousness leads to **justification and life [*dikaiōsin zōēs*]** for all. [19]For just as by the one man's disobedience the many were made sinners, so by the one man's obedience the many will be made righteous. [20]But law came in, with the result that the trespass multiplied; but where sin increased, grace abounded all the more, [21]so that, just as sin exercised dominion in **death**, so grace might also exercise dominion through justification leading to **eternal life** through the Messiah Jesus our Lord. (Rom. 5:17–21 NRSV alt.)

What is particularly striking in Romans 5:12–21, which is full of antitheses,[37] as we have seen, is the antithetical language of death and life. This death-life antithesis is stated succinctly in verse 21, but it permeates the entire passage, all the way back to verse 12. Death, like Sin, is a cosmic power. Release, or liberation, from Sin and Death occurs in justification/baptism, when a person is moved from being in Adam to being in Christ. To go from death to life is, in Christian parlance, a resurrection, as we have already noted in considering Romans 6, and as we shall see again, momentarily, in looking at Romans 8 and then Romans 4.

The unusual Greek phrase *dikaiōsin zōēs* in 5:18, which the NRSV translates as "justification and life," should probably be rendered as something

---

35. Kirk, *Unlocking Romans*, 99.
36. On life, righteousness, and glory in Romans, see Blackwell, "Immortal Glory."
37. Free gift/grace vs. trespass/sin, condemnation vs. justification, death vs. life, trespass vs. act of righteousness, disobedience vs. obedience, sinners vs. righteous, all in the context of Adam vs. Christ.

like "the justification that consists in life" or the "righteousness that is full of life." To be sure, Paul has *eternal* life in view here, but not *only* future, eternal life. Rather, in reading Romans 5–6 we see a seamless connection between justification, new life in the present, and eternal (future, eschatological) life. Justification entails the reality of resurrection as new life now (cf., again, Rom. 6:4) as well as the promise of eternal life in the future. As elsewhere in Romans, Paul probably has the covenant-renewal language of Deuteronomy 30 in mind:

> [19]I call heaven and earth to witness against you today that I have set before you life and death, blessings and curses. Choose life so that you and your descendants may live, [20]loving the LORD your God, obeying him, and holding fast to him; for that means life to you and length of days, so that you may live in the land that the Lord swore to give to your ancestors, to Abraham, to Isaac, and to Jacob. (Deut. 30:19–20)[38]

The covenant renewal and its gift of life have been provided, according to Paul, in the death and resurrection of the Son of God.

In Romans 8 there is also a close connection between justification/justice/ righteousness and life: "But if Christ is in you, though the body is dead because of sin, the Spirit is life because of righteousness [*dikaiosynēn*]" (Rom. 8:10). That is, the gift of the prophetically promised Spirit[39] has brought life to those who have been made righteous by the righteousness of God in Christ and have been transferred into Christ; this is "the law of the Spirit of life in Christ Jesus" (Rom. 8:2; cf. all of 8:1–13). Ezekiel pictured the renewal of Israel as a Spirit-effected resurrection (Ezek. 37); so also does Paul.[40]

This sort of relationship between justification and life obtains also in Galatians, which is likely also behind Paul's claims in Romans, as Paul argues for the faithfulness of the Messiah and the response of faith as the basis of justification:

> [21]For if a law had been given that could make alive [*zōopoiēsai*], then righteousness [*hē dikaiosynē*] would indeed come through the law. [22]But the scripture has imprisoned all things under the power of sin, so that what was promised through faith in Jesus the Messiah [or "the faith(fulness) of Jesus the Messiah"] might be given to those who believe [or "respond in faith(fulness)"]. (Gal. 3:21b–22 NRSV alt.)[41]

---

38. On covenant renewal in Romans, see Whittle, *Covenant Renewal and the Consecration of the Gentiles.*

39. See, e.g., Isa. 44:1–8; Ezek. 11:14–21; 36:21–31; 37:9–14; 39:24–29; Joel 2:28–32.

40. Some (e.g., Boakye, writing about Galatians in *Death and Life*) prefer the term "revivification" to "resurrection."

41. As with Gal. 2:15–21 and Rom. 3:21–26, we may again speak of Christ's faith(fulness) and ours as the means and the mode of justification, or its objective and subjective basis, respectively.

The association of justification with life reinforces the claim that justification and baptism are two aspects of one participatory, life-giving event: resurrection from death into life, by faith—that is, by dying and rising with Christ.[42]

Romans 4, we will now see, sustains the claim with respect to justification: justification is resurrection to new life.

Romans 4: Abraham, the Prototype of Justification as Resurrection

Abraham, especially as portrayed in Romans 4, is highly significant for any interpretation of justification. Indeed, he constitutes a "critical test case" of justification.[43] Abraham has several functions—he wears many hats—in Romans 4.[44]

Some of Abraham's Functions in Romans 4

Interpreters often focus their attention on the first half of Romans 4. Abraham is generally, and rightly, portrayed as a scriptural demonstration of the claims of Romans 3:21–31, the justification of the ungodly by grace through faith, apart from circumcision. As such, Abraham is interpreted as a "believer" rather than a "doer," and thus as an exemplum of justifying faith, faith that is "reckoned" (or "counted") as righteousness.[45] In fact, Paul implicitly invites all to "share the faith of Abraham" (4:16). However, the language of 4:16 is parallel to the language in the latter half of 3:26, which should be translated as "[God] justifies the one who shares the faith(fulness) of Jesus." Accordingly, Paul is probably implying—to the chagrin of some interpreters—that Abraham's faith consisted of faithfulness as well as belief or trust, and he is implicitly calling his audience to share in that faithfulness.[46] Paul sees Abraham's persistence in hope—his faithfulness, if you will—as synonymous with his faith and as the basis for his justification (4:18–22). This faithfulness is not "works," but it is certainly a thick, rather than a thin, understanding of faith.

But there is more to Paul's interpretation of Abraham in Romans 4, especially in the second half of the chapter.[47] For one thing, Abraham also clearly

---

42. Note also that in Gal. 3 Paul speaks of baptism in 3:27, right after the discussion of justification and faith(fulness) in 3:21–26.

43. Dunn, *Romans 1–8*, 196.

44. See my discussion in *Apostle of the Crucified Lord*, 422–24.

45. This accounting metaphor, taken from Gen. 15:6 and Ps. 32:1–2, occurs eleven times in the chapter: vv. 3, 4, 5, 6, 8, 9, 10, 11, 22, 23, 24.

46. For Abraham's faith as both trust and faithfulness, see also D. Campbell, *Deliverance of God*, 381–95, 750–54. Joshua Jipp ("Rereading the Story of Abraham, Isaac, and 'Us,'" esp. 226–39) argues persuasively that in 4:16–25 Paul narrates Abraham's "heroic fidelity," which has been configured in light of the faithfulness of Jesus.

47. Jipp ("Rereading the Story of Abraham, Isaac, and 'Us'") argues that Abraham serves not one but multiple purposes; that there is more to Rom. 4 than justification by faith, gentile

functions as an example of one who believes in the God who "gives life to the dead and calls into existence the things that do not exist" (4:17). Abraham has a kind of proto-Christian faith, for justification today is for those who "believe in him who raised Jesus our Lord from the dead" (4:24). "It appears likely," writes Joshua Jipp, "that Paul's interpretation of the Abraham story is being construed according to his Christological presuppositions."[48] Furthermore, as Jipp argues, "Paul's portrait of the faith of Abraham is generated by his commitment to the revelation of God's saving act through the faithful Jesus who trusted God for his own resurrection in the face of death."[49]

Jipp's claim about Jesus' trust concerning "his own resurrection" and the parallel with Abraham means that there is still more to Paul's interpretation of Abraham. In 4:17–25 Abraham also serves as an exemplum, or (better) a prototype, of Paul's unique participatory understanding of justification by faith as an event of *resurrection from the dead*: as co-crucifixion and co-resurrection with Christ.[50]

Abraham's Resurrection from the Dead

Abraham's faith, as portrayed in 4:17–22 and further interpreted in 4:23–25, was not merely an attitude of faith, or trust, versus the doing of deeds (so the "traditional perspective" on Paul), or of nonconfidence in possession of the "boundary marker" circumcision (so, at times, the "New Perspective"). It was not even limited to faithfulness, as "thick" a description of faith as that may be. Nor was Abraham's faith merely a general theological belief in, or even a trusting posture toward, God as the one who can raise the dead or bring life out of death. All of this is true, but the story of Abraham has still not been fully told.

According to Paul the interpreter of his Jewish scriptures, Abraham was *dead*. He was not merely "as good as dead" (so the NRSV, Rom. 4:19a) but, as James Dunn says, "already dead."[51] Also dead was his wife's womb (4:19b); Paul uses a term indicating the condition of a corpse (*nekrōsis*, as in 2 Cor. 4:10).[52] They were dead because they were the end of the line: no children, no

---

inclusion, and similar concerns; and that 4:16–25 is more important than normally recognized. Edward Adams ("Abraham's Faith and Gentile Disobedience") argues convincingly that Paul depicts Abraham's faith and justification as the antithesis of the gentile (I would say human) sinfulness portrayed in Rom. 1:18–32.

48. Jipp, "Rereading the Story of Abraham, Isaac, and 'Us,'" 236 (so also many other commentators).

49. Jipp, "Rereading the Story of Abraham, Isaac, and 'Us,'" 237.

50. This section borrows from and builds on my *Becoming the Gospel*, 278–79.

51. Dunn, *Romans 1–8*, 219–20; cf. 238.

52. Jipp, "Rereading the Story of Abraham, Isaac, and 'Us,'" 235.

heirs, no life. Thus Abraham's faith was that God could bring life out of *his* death, *their* death. He was certain that God could transform *his* deadness, their shared deadness, into life. In other words, his faith was completely *self-involving* and *participatory*. God was, for Abraham, not merely the God who raises the dead in general but the God who would raise *him*—and who did so.

That Abraham was justified by *faith* means that he trusted the promise of life-out-of-death given to him. That he was *justified* by faith means not that he was fictitiously considered just or righteous (so some traditional interpretations of justification by faith), nor merely that he was included in God's covenant people (so some New Perspective interpretations), but that he was granted the gracious gift of new life out of death. This new life out of death, this resurrection, came to pass in the birth of a descendant, the unnamed (in Rom. 4) son Isaac.

Kevin Madigan and Jon Levenson have shown that this is a very Jewish notion of life and resurrection rooted in biblical stories like the one to which Paul appeals in Romans 4.[53] They use such stories to show how, for ancient Jews, the barren womb and the privation of progeny were the functional equivalent of death.[54] Birth and progeny, on the other hand, are "the reversal of death" and thus "to a large degree the functional equivalent of resurrection (or afterlife in general). . . . In these stories, it is not death but birth that is God's last word."[55] In Romans 4 this resurrection life is actualized, not merely in the birth of Isaac, but in the subsequent reality of many descendants (4:16–18).[56]

But the key aspect of the story that is almost universally missed is that *Abraham himself has experienced resurrection from death.* (Of course, both Abraham and Sarah have had that experience, though Paul focuses on Abraham for a variety of reasons.) Accordingly, Abraham foreshadows and embodies not only the *focus* of justifying, Christian faith (as trust in the God who raised the dead Jesus) but also the content and the *experiential character* of justification. Indeed, Jesus "was raised for our justification" (Rom. 4:25),[57]

---

53. Madigan and Levenson, *Resurrection*, 107–20.

54. Madigan and Levenson, *Resurrection*, 112.

55. Madigan and Levenson, *Resurrection*, 113.

56. David Burnett ("'So Shall Your Seed Be'") argues that Paul sees deification (quality of descendants, not merely quantity) in this passage. If he is right, it would further strengthen the argument of this section of the chapter.

57. The argument of Rom. 4 strongly suggests that the noun *dikaiōsis* in 4:25 is rightly rendered by most translations as "justification," not "acquittal." Paul's theology of justification expressed here includes, but is not limited to, acquittal. Indeed, if Rom. 4:25 is an echo of Isa. 53:11b (as many interpreters think), then for Paul in this verse "justification" likely includes both being forgiven and being made righteous/just: "The righteous one, my servant, shall make many righteous [Heb. *yaṣdîq*; LXX *dikaiōsai*], and he shall bear their iniquities" (so also CEB; other translations of the Hebrew have "justify," "account righteous," or "acquit").

not only because his death is incomplete without the resurrection, but also because—as Paul has said in Galatians, 2 Corinthians, and several places in Romans—justification is resurrection to new life. The resurrection of Jesus took place for *our* justification (Rom. 4:24–25)—in other words, *our* resurrection to life, which takes place by dying and being raised with him. That is, in retrospect, from Paul's own position of having died and been resurrected in Christ (and his having witnessed many others do so as well), Abraham's experience is prospectively analogous to what Paul says about all baptized believers: their justification by faith means a participatory experience of resurrection out of death.[58]

There is probably still more: Paul also infers that Abraham has experienced, and indeed has become, a new creation. The gift of his progeny, as an experience of resurrection from the dead, is the work of the God who "gives life to the dead and calls into existence the things that do not exist" (Rom. 4:17). This creation ex nihilo refers in the first place to the creation of progeny from a dead womb, but it also likely means that Abraham and Sarah are re-created; they are now parents, and their nothingness has become something. Their experience hints at the fact that justification involves a new creation (2 Cor. 5:17) that is independent of circumcision (Gal. 6:15) and that entails "newness of life" (Rom. 6:4).[59]

Summary: Abraham the Participant-Prototype

Too often interpreters focus on the "faith" and the "reckoning" ("counting," *logizomai*) language in Romans 4 as if these elements constituted the full sum and substance of justification in chapter 4—and indeed in Romans and even in Paul's writings as a whole. But Paul's reckoning language, and all that goes with it, is inseparable from the language of resurrection; "reckoning" only tells part of the story. And "faith" (Gk. *pistis*) in Romans 4 is related not only to trust for the forgiveness of sins but also to hope in the resurrection of the dead. To be sure, justification is an act of grace and is not earned, for it comes to us who have no right or claim or merit to receive it, but it is

---

58. See also Douglas Campbell's discussion of the participatory nature of Abraham's faith and of Christian faith, inclusive of both trust and fidelity (*Deliverance of God*, 381–95, 750–54). Campbell argues, with a helpful diagram (752), that for Paul Christ's trust in God, who resurrects him, both (1) shapes his portrayal of Abraham as one who trusts in God, who resurrects him, and (2) generates, through participation in Christ's death and resurrection, Christian trust in God for a similar resurrection. For his more general interpretation of faith as participation in the mind of Christ, see Campbell, "Participation and Faith in Paul."

59. For a reading of Abraham and resurrection similar to the one presented here, see Kirk, *Unlocking Romans*, 72–83. Kirk (73n60) draws on an earlier argument by Jon Levenson (similar to the one noted here), but he does not prioritize it or describe Abraham's own participation in resurrection as fully as I do here. He does, however, rightly stress Abraham's deadness (72).

appropriated by trust in God, and specifically in God's promises.[60] "Trust" or "faith" or "faithfulness" or "believing allegiance" (or whatever other term we use to translate *pistis* and its cognate verb *pisteuō*) relates to the promise of life out of death. To be justified is to receive, experience, and embody the promise of life. The latter part of Romans 4 forces us to interpret the earlier part of the chapter, as well as Romans 3:21–26, in a fuller, more robust way. Jonathan Linebaugh, commenting on Romans 3:21–26, rightly says, "'Declare righteous' . . . indicates more than a verdict of an ordinary judge; it is the effective pronouncement of the creator that re-creates sinners as righteous."[61]

Peter Leithart sums this up by saying that justification itself entails death and resurrection and that resurrection is the *form* of justification.[62] Jesus' resurrection does not function merely as proof that God can raise the dead so that we will believe in the resurrecting God. Jesus' resurrection is something in which we may participate, both now and later.[63] We can be raised to life in the form of new (present) and eternal (future) life in Christ as Abraham was raised to life in the form of his son Isaac (present) and all his descendants (future). In this sense, as well as in others, we can share the faith of Abraham (Rom. 4:16). Similarly, Francis Watson states that "Abraham is a model for the *convert*, the one who has passed from ungodliness to righteousness by a transforming event."[64] Resurrection and righteousness, then, go together, for the new life of the justified/baptized is a life of righteousness.

In conclusion, we may affirm that Abraham functions as a prototype of justification in at least five ways:

- Justification is an act of grace and forgiveness for sinners/the ungodly who have a faith like Abraham's, apart from works.
- Justification is for all, the uncircumcised as well as the circumcised.
- Justification is by trust in the God who brings life out of death.
- Justification is a participatory experience of resurrection from the dead.
- Justification commences a new life of righteousness/justice.

60. On the incongruity of divine grace, its unconditional character—but also its conditioned character, requiring an appropriate response—see Barclay, *Paul and the Gift*.

61. Linebaugh, "Righteousness Revealed," 232n39.

62. Leithart, *Delivered from the Elements of the World*, 179–81. As noted in chap. 6, Leithart has wisely coined the term "deliverdict" ("deliver" + "verdict") to show that justification (for Paul, and for theology) is a divine word that liberates (esp. 180–214, 333–54). His contention that resurrection is the "form" of justification does not contradict the substance of my argument in chap. 3 that because participation in Christ is cruciform, it is not resurrectiform but resurrectional. Leithart and I are making the same basic point in different contexts and therefore with different terms.

63. See also Kirk, *Unlocking Resurrection*, esp. 107–23.

64. Watson, *Paul, Judaism, and the Gentiles*, 265.

None of this, however, makes sense, or could take place, apart from the gracious, saving act of God in the Messiah's death and resurrection (Rom. 4:23–25). As in 2 Corinthians 5:21, Isaiah 53 is almost certainly the chief source of the theology in these verses, and Isaiah's servant hymn includes not only representative suffering and death but also the effect of making many righteous (Isa. 53:11) and the reward of life.[65]

Romans 4, then, is about Abraham the justified one and Abraham the resurrected one. He is the paradigm of justification as both forgiveness and transformation/new creation/new life, a life that comes from the death and resurrection of Jesus.[66]

Justification and Reconciliation

We come finally, and much more briefly, to justification and reconciliation. As noted in the previous chapter, one distinctive, explicit contribution to Paul's theology of justification in 2 Corinthians 5:14–21 is the notion of reconciliation, which is expressed in noun or verb form five times in 2 Corinthians 5:18–20. I argued in the previous chapter that reconciliation is, for Paul, not something different from justification, or simply another metaphor in personal rather than forensic terms. It is, instead, at the very core of the meaning of justification for Paul.

We find this to be the case as well in Romans 5, which contains echoes of 2 Corinthians 5. In Romans 5:1–11 the chiastic structure of the passage indicates the overlapping nature of the terms "justification" and "reconciliation":

A Justification by faith means peace with God through Christ (vv. 1–2a)
　　B Hope for glory, guaranteed by the Spirit (vv. 2b–5)
　　　　C Christ's death as the manifestation of God's love (vv. 6–8)
　　B′ Certain hope of future salvation (vv. 9–10)
A′ Reconciliation with God through Christ (v. 11)[67]

---

65. Jipp ("Rereading the Story of Abraham, Isaac, and 'Us,'" 229–31) has a helpful summary of the connections.

66. One might argue, from the fact that Rom. 4 (concerning Abraham's resurrection) follows Rom. 3 (concerning justification), that resurrection is not inherent to justification but is subsequent to justification. This argument would be misguided, however, since the theme of justification is not limited to Rom. 3 but continues into Rom. 4 and actually concludes that chapter (4:25).

67. It might be tempting, especially if 5:1 is taken by itself, to suggest that justification leads to reconciliation rather than justification constitutes reconciliation. The echo of 2 Cor. 5:14–21 and the clear parallel structure (vv. 1–2a being parallel to v. 11) argue for understanding justification as inclusive of reconciliation, not its source.

The center of this passage, both theologically and structurally, is Christ's death as the demonstration of God's love for us when we were weak, ungodly, sinners, and enemies of God (vv. 6–8, 10). What God accomplished in that act is stated in the bookends of the text, verse 1 and verse 11, with justification repeated in verse 9 and reconciliation anticipated in verse 10. This accomplishment, then, is said to be justification and peace with God (v. 1), which means reconciliation (v. 11).

Justification and reconciliation have two major things in common in this text: (1) they are expressed in the passive voice (boldfaced below) and as something received (v. 11), which implies God's gracious activity; and (2) they are accomplished "through our Lord Jesus the Messiah," which means specifically by means of his death/blood (vv. 1, 11; underlined below):

> Therefore, since **we are justified** [*dikaiōthentes*] by faith, we have peace with God <u>through our Lord Jesus the Messiah</u> (v. 1)
>> **we have been justified** [*dikaiōthentes*] <u>by his blood</u> (v. 9)
>> **we were reconciled** [*katēllagēmen*] to God <u>through the death of his Son</u> (v. 10)
>> **having been reconciled** [*katallagentes*] (v. 10)
> we even boast in God <u>through our Lord Jesus the Messiah</u>, through whom **we have now received reconciliation** [*nyn tēn katallagēn elabomen*] (v. 11)

That is, Paul indicates both the source and the means of justification and reconciliation as the same because they refer to the same divine action. Justification is God's act of restoring right relations between himself and sinful human beings.

On the surface, it does not seem that participation per se appears in this important text about justification as reconciliation. Two points can be made to argue against this sort of conclusion, however.

First, as in 2 Corinthians 5, we learn here that reconciliation takes place *through* the death of the Messiah. But this is more than instrumentality, as if God were "using" Jesus. Rather, for Paul God's activity is Christ's activity, and vice versa. As Romans 5:8 implies, God's love is the Son's love, and vice versa; this is made explicit in Romans 8:35–39, where Paul speaks of both "the love of the Messiah" (8:35) and "the love of God in Christ Jesus our Lord" (8:39). In other words, God participates in Christ, as Paul says in 2 Corinthians 5:19 ("God was in the Messiah . . ."). Second, when we read the word "faith" in Romans 5:1, we must carry forward the participatory character of that faith from previous chapters. What kind of faith justifies? The faith that shares the faithfulness of Jesus (3:26), the faith that shares the faithfulness of Abraham (4:16), the faith that results in moving from death to life. In other words, justification is the result of God's righteous, reconciling participation in the

Messiah's ministry of life-giving death, and it means our own participating in and benefiting from that participatory act.

Reconciliation is not, however, merely a "vertical" reality but also a "horizontal" one. As we learn in Romans 1:18–32, humanity's broken relationship with God leads to broken relations with others. When the relationship with God is repaired—by God's own act—the corollary should be, indeed must be, the reparation of relations with other people. This corollary is spelled out in Romans in many ways, but especially in the picture of the multicultural community of hospitality, worship, witness, joy, and justice/righteousness that Paul longs for at Rome, and that he urges the Roman house churches to embody (Rom. 14:1–15:13).

Conclusion

So where have we been, and what have we concluded in this chapter and the previous two? We have been on a journey from Galatians 2 to 2 Corinthians 5 to Romans as a whole. My argument has been that the middle term, so to speak, 2 Corinthians 5:14–21, is a restatement of Galatians 2:15–21 for a new audience and an anticipation of Romans. What holds these together is *a common articulation of justification as a participatory and transformative event of dying and rising with Christ.* That event entails especially becoming *righteous*, or just; being *resurrected* to new life and becoming a new creation; and being *reconciled* to God in a way that also effects, or should effect, our reconciliation with others. That is, justification as a gracious act of divine intervention is an event of transformative participation that entails the following:

1. Righteousness ("righteousness-ification," or "justice-ification")
2. Resurrection
3. Reconciliation[68]

In the next chapter we return to 2 Corinthians in order to see more fully how, in one letter, the "vertical" and "horizontal" aspects of participatory transformation in Christ are brought together.

---

68. By way of a brief addendum to the argument of this chapter, I also suggest that the Letter to the Ephesians (esp. chaps. 2 and 3) understands salvation in this sort of way: resurrection from the dead, good works (righteousness), and reconciliation. That is, Ephesians may well be a continuation of this same trajectory from Galatians to 2 Corinthians to Romans and beyond—which suggests that Ephesians reflects rather well the mind of Paul.

nine

Theosis in 2 Corinthians

In chapter 7 we examined 2 Corinthians 5:14–21 in terms of its continuation of the understanding of justification we find in Galatians 2:15–21, analyzed in chapter 6. I concluded that justification involves participation in Christ, transformation into the justice/righteousness of God, and therefore ethics, including reconciliation. In chapter 8 we found echoes of both Galatians 2 and 2 Corinthians 5 in Romans. That is, in the previous three chapters we followed a justification trajectory.

In this chapter we return to 2 Corinthians in order to follow a related trajectory, this time tracing it within a single Pauline letter that is central to the understanding of life in Christ presented in this book. The analysis of 2 Corinthians 5:14–21 in chapter 7 contributes to a broader (and, for some, controversial) understanding of Paul's spirituality and soteriology—including his understanding of justification—as participatory and transformative. It also raises once again another, even more controversial claim about justification: because justification is transformative participation in the life of the God who is revealed in Christ, justification itself entails what the Christian tradition has called theosis, or deification. It is time, in this chapter, to advocate for the term that I have repeatedly said to be appropriate but not necessary for describing Paul's theology and spirituality.

Elsewhere I have defined "theosis" in the Pauline context as "transformative participation in the kenotic, cruciform character of God through Spirit-enabled conformity to the incarnate, crucified, and resurrected/glorified Christ."[1] In this chapter I wish to highlight four aspects of this Pauline theosis:

1. Gorman, *Inhabiting the Cruciform God*, 7.

1. Because this God is revealed in a Messiah who was *crucified* before being glorified, it is *cruciform* theosis.

2. At the same time (as we emphasized in chap. 3), such cruciform participation in Christ is suffused with the life of the resurrected/glorified Christ, which makes it life-giving; this cruciform theosis is, paradoxically, *resurrectional*. Indeed, otherwise it would not be theosis.

3. We must also stress that for Paul theosis is a communal or corporate reality, not merely an individual experience;[2] in 2 Corinthians 5:21 Paul says that God acted "so that *we* would become" God's righteousness.[3]

4. Finally, realizing this corporate, cruciform, resurrectional theosis constitutes the goal of Paul's mission because he believes it is the mission of God.[4] In sum, theosis in Paul is corporate, cruciform, resurrectional, and missional.

The more specific theses to be further developed here are (1) that 2 Corinthians is a rather comprehensive expression of this Pauline theology of theosis; (2) that Paul's language of "glory" and "justice/righteousness" (*doxa* and *dikaiosynē*) gives succinct expression to this theology; and (3) that 2 Corinthians 5:21, which contains all four aspects of this Pauline soteriology noted above, forms a bridge between the rather general presentation of theosis in 2 Corinthians 3:18 as *doxa* and its concrete expression as the praxis of *dikaiosynē* in 2 Corinthians 8:9.

Thus I will argue that 2 Corinthians as a whole tells us that Paul sees salvation as theosis in the specific sense of humans coming to share in two divine attributes, divine *glory* and divine *justice*; that is, they can and must be both glorified and "justice-ified" (recall the term "justice-ification" at the end of the previous chapter).[5] With respect to 5:21 in particular, I will continue to argue not merely that distinct but closely related Pauline themes (justification/reconciliation, participation, and transformation) appear in that verse and its context, but also that these three aspects of the passage are best understood as expressing three aspects of one reality: corporate, cruciform, resurrectional, missional theosis. Justification takes place in the crucified and exalted Messiah; it is the community's participatory transformation in the life of God

2. See, e.g., Gorman, *Inhabiting the Cruciform God*, 38, 56, 70, 91, 106, 112.

3. My translation; emphasis added.

4. See also my *Becoming the Gospel*.

5. I have made a similar case for Romans, which is indebted to 2 Corinthians, in "Romans: The First Christian Treatise on Theosis," which appears in revised form in *Becoming the Gospel*, 261–96.

such that those who are in the Messiah take on one of the primary divine attributes and activities: justice (*dikaiosynē*). And with respect to 2 Corinthians 8:9 and its context, including its links to the other two main texts, I will argue that theosis finds concrete expression in the collection for Jerusalem as an act of participating in the grace-filled justice of God manifested in Christ. This part of the argument addresses the concerns some have raised about what participation actually means "on the ground"—what practices it generates.[6]

But is "theosis" the right language to describe this transformative, missional participation in Christ?[7] In earlier chapters, and elsewhere, I have suggested that the term is not necessary, although it is accurate and useful. In this chapter I make a more robust case for the language of theosis, furthering arguments made especially in *Inhabiting the Cruciform God*.[8]

Is "Theosis" the Right Language?

"Theosis" (or "deification/divinization"), like the more generic term "participation," is back on the theological table across the Christian traditions and in the study of the New Testament.[9] It is a word with numerous uses and nuances of meaning, but most would agree that it signifies a soteriology of sharing in the divine nature that is grounded in the incarnation and death of God's Son—"He became what we are, so that we could become what he is"[10]—and the transforming work of the Spirit (that is, the indwelling presence of the risen Christ). This transformation is a process of healing and restoration to God's intention for humanity that includes, but is not limited to, sanctification, for its eschatological end is bodily resurrection and transformation. Although theosis is most commonly associated with the Eastern church fathers and with Eastern Orthodoxy, it is not unknown in the West (e.g., Augustine, Aquinas)

6. See esp. Hays, "What Is 'Real Participation in Christ'?," noted in the introduction to this book.

7. Constantine Campbell (*Paul and Union with Christ*) says most recent interpreters say no (63), while he gives a qualified yes (368). See also Finlan, "Can We Speak of *Theosis* in Paul?" (yes).

8. And also in "Romans: The First Christian Treatise on Theosis."

9. On theosis see Christensen and Wittung, *Partakers of the Divine Nature*; Finlan and Kharlamov, *Theōsis*. In addition to the scholars discussed below, Finlan has written significantly on theosis in the New Testament, and numerous other scholars have presented and published conference papers in recent years.

10. This is the spirit of, e.g., Irenaeus, *Against Heresies* 5, preface ("The Lord Jesus Christ ... did, through his transcendent love, become what we are, that he might bring us to be even what he is himself"); cf. Athanasius, *Incarnation of the Word* 54.

and it is, according to some interpreters, at the heart of the soteriology of Calvin, Luther, Wesley, and Torrance.[11]

In an important book, Grant Macaskill argues that the term "theosis" is not helpful for interpreting or describing the New Testament; it is, in fact, "potentially misleading."[12] He rightly insists that the New Testament is replete with language of union, participation, and transformation, and that this language is related to the theology of the new covenant.[13] I agree with the basic thrust of what Macaskill affirms, and I have myself written on the same themes in relation to the new covenant.[14] I take Macaskill's criticisms of my work seriously, but this is not the place to engage them at length.[15] I would contend, however, that neither Macaskill's positive contributions nor his criticisms of my work necessarily negate the claim that various New Testament writers, including Paul, witness to what later theologians call "theosis." Theosis is, however, as Macaskill indicates, a "theologically plastic"—I would say "fluid"—term,[16] and we must allow for ongoing exploration of its meaning or meanings. I would argue, in fact, that a reading of Paul and of the theological tradition can assist in the interpretation of each, and that Paul may actually help us shape an appropriate contemporary understanding of participation, and specifically of theosis.[17]

I would submit, therefore, and will now argue with respect to a particular letter, that we should not abandon the term "theosis" when describing Paul's theology. I suggest, however, that the term's fluidity means that, for the moment, we need to take a fairly minimalist approach to the definition of theosis and its identification in the New Testament. Three exegetical and

11. See, e.g., the chapters in Christensen and Wittung, *Partakers of the Divine Nature.*

12. Macaskill, *Union with Christ*, esp. 42–76; "potentially misleading" is from p. 75. Macaskill does allow, however, that some of the theological elements associated with theosis are significant for New Testament studies.

13. See his summary in Macaskill, *Union with Christ*, 297–99.

14. Gorman, *Death of the Messiah.*

15. See Macaskill, *Union with Christ*, 25–28, 75–76. He is particularly concerned that I have blurred the Creator-creature distinction by speaking of participation in the divine essence. My theological rationale for using the traditional but debated term "essence" was to keep divine act and being together while speaking of believers participating in the narrative identity of God in Christ. Like all orthodox Christian proponents of theosis, I do not intend to blur the Creator-creature distinction. I do wonder, however, whether Macaskill underestimates (though he notes it [26]), both for me and for the New Testament, my fundamental claim that cruciformity is theoformity.

16. Macaskill, *Union with Christ*, 27.

17. Lewis Ayres has said of Gregory of Nyssa, "While I cannot but agree that Gregory actually seems to avoid some of the basic terminology for deification . . . his account of the ways in which Christians become 'like' God actually points to some of the most fruitful ways of giving density to the idea of deification" ("Deification and the Dynamics of Nicene Theology," 377). Similarly, we should not expect Paul to use the same language as subsequent theologians.

theological guidelines present themselves as candidates for the contours of this minimalist position.

First of all, no interpretation of theosis can compromise the Creator-creature distinction. To share in certain divine attributes is not to cease being a creature and to become the Creator.

Second, a text that is theotic will identify, implicitly or explicitly, either one or more divine attributes or else a general divine likeness that is the goal of transformation. This desired likeness can be a present, ethical goal or a future, eschatological one, or both. This proposal means that although certain theological grammars will be especially important for identifying and examining theosis in the New Testament (e.g., exchange or interchange texts such as 2 Cor. 5:21 and 8:9: "Christ became . . . so that we could become . . ."), the presence of theosis is not limited to those particular grammars.

Third, since the New Testament is inherently Christocentric (concerned with the identity and significance of Jesus), there normally needs to be a christological assumption in a potentially theotic text (or its co-text), whether explicit or implicit, that Christ participates in the divine identity. This assumption leads inexorably to the conclusion that, at least in such texts, participation in Christ and/or becoming like Christ means participation in God and/or becoming like God (hence my argument that *cruci*formity is *theo*formity).[18] Further, I would suggest that since the New Testament writers reconfigure theology proper (the doctrine of God) christologically, this assumption undergirds each of the Christologies of the New Testament (though I realize that claim would be debated),[19] which means that theosis, in this christological sense, should be a common rather than a rare New Testament theme. But what about Paul in particular?

Why We Should Expect Theosis in Paul, and Specifically in 2 Corinthians

In a paper delivered at the annual meeting of the Society of Biblical Literature in 2013,[20] Ben Blackwell delineated three current approaches to identifying

18. Gorman, *Inhabiting the Cruciform God*, 4. I do not mean that all christological texts claim that Christ participates in the divine identity, only that such a claim must be at least implicit for a text about participation in Christ to be theotic. There may also, of course, be texts about participation in Christ that are not clearly theotic, as well as texts about participation in God that are not directly linked to participation in Christ (e.g., 2 Pet. 1:4, though even there the context makes christological connections).

19. Though the issues are complex, I think that the work of people like Richard Bauckham, David Capes, and Chris Tilling, noted in chap. 2, is generally persuasive.

20. Blackwell, "Theosis in the New Testament?," presented in a session of the Theological Interpretation of Scripture Seminar.

theosis in the New Testament, especially in Paul: (1) textual logic (with particular attention to the present writer); (2) history of religions, or the comparative approach (especially David Litwa);[21] and (3) history of interpretation, meaning especially patristic interpretations of Paul (especially Blackwell himself).[22] The convergence of these three approaches constitutes an argument that (1) there is an internal logic to Paul's Christology and participationist spirituality that supports understanding Paul's soteriology in terms of theosis; (2) there is historical context and precedent (both Jewish and pagan) for understanding Paul's soteriology in terms of theosis; and (3) there is an early reception history of understanding Paul's soteriology in terms of theosis.

As for 2 Corinthians, three key texts potentially have theotic significance: 3:18, 5:21, and 8:9.[23] Each of these texts has been noted as theotic by virtue of its textual logic, its historical context, or its patristic reception.[24]

Stephen Finlan calls 2 Corinthians 3:18 "the most frankly theotic passage in Paul."[25] It figures in the textual approaches of Litwa, Blackwell, and myself; in Litwa's comparative work; and in some patristic texts noted by Blackwell and others.[26] Gregory of Nyssa, for example, concludes his work *On Perfection* with an argument for the value of change in humans, which is how they will have a share in Christ. The work ends with an interpretation of 2 Corinthians 3:18:

> Therefore let no one be grieved if he sees in his nature a penchant for change. Changing in everything for the better, let him exchange "glory for glory," becoming greater through daily increase, ever perfecting himself and never arriving too quickly at the limit of perfection. For this is truly perfection: never to stop growing toward what is better and never placing any limit on perfection.[27]

The other two texts from 2 Corinthians have a different format and focus, that of the "marvelous exchange" (*admirabile commercium*), or what Morna Hooker has called "interchange" texts, as noted in previous chapters. She explains what she means by "interchange" by appealing to the words of Irenaeus

21. E.g., Litwa, *We Are Being Transformed*; Litwa, "Transformation through a Mirror."
22. Blackwell, *Christosis*.
23. These three do not exhaust the theme. See, e.g., Gordon, "Deification by Ascent."
24. My brief discussion of the fathers here is meant only to be representative of larger themes and additional writers. For convenience, all references are taken from Bray, *1–2 Corinthians*.
25. Finlan, "Can We Speak of *Theosis* in Paul?," 75.
26. Litwa, "2 Corinthians 3:18"; Litwa, *We Are Being Transformed*, esp. 216–25; Litwa, "Transformation"; Blackwell, *Christosis*, esp. 179–93; Gorman, *Inhabiting the Cruciform God*, esp. 91–93, 119–21, 169–70. Blackwell notes, however, that the two fathers he investigates use 3:18 either not at all (Irenaeus) or sparingly (Cyril of Alexandria).
27. Cited in Bray, *1–2 Corinthians*, 224.

("Christ became . . .") and then identifying 2 Corinthians 5:21 and 8:9 as "the clearest examples" of interchange, understood à la Irenaeus, in Paul's letters: *Christ is identified with the human condition in order that we might be identified with his.*[28] Both of these texts figure briefly in the previous textual work I have done, as well as in Litwa's historical work, and 5:21 figures prominently in Blackwell's.[29]

As for the fathers, they also saw theosis in these two passages. The complexity and richness of 2 Corinthians 5:21 are on display in their various treatments of it, including comments on God's benevolence; the incarnation; the means of justification (grace not works—in Chrysostom, for example); Jesus' sinlessness, his assumption of our sins, and his willingness to die; and theosis. Theodoret of Cyrus writes that "Christ was called what we are in order to call us to be what he is."[30] Cyril of Alexandria proclaims, "We do not say that Christ became a sinner. Far from it, but being just, or rather in actuality justice, for he did not know sin, the Father made him a victim for the sins of the world."[31] In addition, some fathers connect this text to the Pauline idea of Christ's becoming a curse for us (Gal. 3:13–14), another instance of the interchange (and thus potentially theosis) texts identified by Morna Hooker.[32]

The fathers also sometimes see 2 Corinthians 8:9 as a text about theosis. Ambrosiaster, for instance, comments as follows: "Paul is saying that Christ was made poor because God deigned to be born as man, humbling the power of his might so that he might obtain for men the riches of divinity and thus share in the divine nature, as Peter says."[33] Augustine echoes Ambrosiaster with a similar sentiment, explaining 2 Corinthians 8:9 in terms of Philippians 2:6–8:

> When he assumed our mortality and overcame death, he manifested himself in poverty, but he promised riches though they might be deferred. . . . To make us worthy of this perfect gift, he [Christ], equal to the Father in the form of God,

28. Hooker, *From Adam to Christ*, 26 (emphasis added). The entire first part of the book is relevant (13–69). See also her article "On Becoming the Righteousness of God." Hooker does not use the terms "theosis" or "deification," probably because she does not think Paul implies "ontological" change (see *From Adam to Christ*, 22).

29. Gorman, *Inhabiting the Cruciform God*, 63n57, 80, 87–90, 91n140, 95; Litwa, *We Are Being Transformed*, 223–24; Blackwell, *Christosis*, esp. 226–32. (Blackwell's treatment of 2 Corinthians includes only chaps. 3–5.)

30. Theodoret of Cyrus, *Commentary on the Second Epistle to the Corinthians* 318, cited in Bray, *1–2 Corinthians*, 249. See also Gregory of Nazianzus, *Theological Oration 5*, in Bray, *1–2 Corinthians*, 250.

31. Cyril of Alexandria, Letter 41, cited in Bray, *1–2 Corinthians*, 250.

32. E.g., Eusebius, *Proof of the Gospel* 4.17, and Gregory of Nazianzus, *Theological Oration 5*, both cited in Bray, *1–2 Corinthians*, 250.

33. Ambrosiaster, *Commentary on Paul's Epistles*, cited in Bray, *1–2 Corinthians*, 269.

became like to us in the form of a servant and refashions us into the likeness of God.[34]

With these brief textual, comparative, and patristic considerations in mind, we are ready to proceed expectantly into our three texts from 2 Corinthians, with the goal of seeing what Paul might have to say about theosis—about sharing in the divine life. (Even those unconvinced by the appropriateness of "theosis" language should appreciate the important connections among these three texts.)

Theosis as Future Resurrection Glory and Present Cruciform Glory: 2 Corinthians 3:18

We begin by setting out the Greek text, in transliteration, and the NRSV translation:

> *hēmeis de pantes anakekalymmenō prosōpō tēn doxan kyriou katoptrizomenoi tēn autēn eikona metamorphoumetha apo doxēs eis doxan kathaper apo kyriou pneumatos.*

And all of us, with unveiled faces, seeing the glory of the Lord as though reflected [*katoptrizomenoi*] in a mirror, are being transformed [*metamorphoumetha*] into the same image from one degree of glory to another; for this comes from the Lord, the Spirit.

David Litwa has been at the forefront of interpreting this passage in terms of deification, and while I do not concur with every aspect of his approach or arguments, I do find his general thesis persuasive, and in what follows I rely in part on his work, as well as Ben Blackwell's. I wish to make five main points.

Transformation

First, this is obviously a text about transformation, whether or not we call that transformation "theosis." The verb that indicates the process, which appears also in Romans 12:1–2, is in the passive voice (*metamorphoumetha*); the agent of the transformation is the Spirit: "This comes from the Lord, the Spirit."[35] The human action that permits this transformation to occur is

---

34. Augustine, *Feast of the Nativity* 194.3, cited in Bray, *1–2 Corinthians*, 269.

35. The famously confusing language about the Spirit and the Lord here need not detain us; the point is that this transformation is the work, not merely of the self or the community, but of "the Spirit of the Lord" (2 Cor. 3:17). This is implied also in Rom. 12:2. The only other

"looking," or better "seeing," specifically "seeing the glory of the Lord [*tēn doxan kyriou*] as though reflected in a mirror," and even more specifically, doing so "with unveiled faces." It was a commonplace of antiquity that gazing on a deity could effect transformation,[36] but Paul makes it clear here that even this ability to gaze at the Lord's glory in an unveiled state (unlike Moses under the old covenant) is the result of grace, indicated by another divine passive: "When one turns to the Lord, the veil is removed" (2 Cor. 3:16).[37] Though it is possible that Paul is here referring to unique visions/revelations of the Lord that he has had (perhaps specifically the one narrated in 2 Cor. 12:1–10), the main point is that this transformation is not unique to Paul, even if his visions are unusual. Indeed, no matter how we translate the tricky participle *katoptrizomenoi* (beholding? reflecting?), the overall sense of the passage in context is that both Paul and the Corinthians are enabled by the Spirit, in Christ, both to *see* and to *be* (i.e., participate in) the glory of God revealed in Christ, and they are doing so *all together* (*pantes*, "all").[38]

From Glory to Glory

Second, Paul specifies the content of this transformation in two closely related phrases: "into the same image" (*tēn autēn eikona*) and "from one degree of glory to another" (*apo doxēs eis doxan*). The latter phrase is better rendered simply "from glory to/toward/into glory." The meaning of these two phrases is warmly debated, but I would suggest that Paul himself provides the most basic interpretation in the context, beginning especially with his description of the content of the gospel as "the glory of Christ, who is the image of God" (2 Cor. 4:4; *euangeliou tēs doxēs tou Christou, hos estin eikōn tou theou*). That is, the transformation is into the likeness of Christ, the image of God (cf. Rom. 8:29, "conformed to the image of his Son," *symmorphous tēs eikonos tou huiou autou*). It is a process of becoming more Christlike and hence more Godlike. Logically (and theologically), then, if we are to speak here of Christification or Christosis (Ben Blackwell's term), we would have to mount a very strong case indeed for not also speaking about deification or theosis.

---

occurrences of the verb *metamorphousthai* are in the transfiguration narrative (Mark 9:2; Matt. 17:2), which may have influenced Paul, perhaps as oral tradition.

36. This phenomenon is documented and assessed with respect to Paul by numerous commentators, including Furnish, *II Corinthians*, 240–42. See esp. Heath, *Paul's Visual Piety*.

37. To be sure, the removal of the veil is predicated on turning to the Lord, which is expressed as an active verb. An interesting dynamic of human and divine activity is at work here, but the emphasis falls on divine action.

38. How this "beholding" or "reflecting" occurs is implicit in the context: in lives of Christlike power-in-weakness. See the discussion below. The word *pantes* ("all") is missing from P[46], but its absence is likely accidental; see Hooker, "On Becoming the Righteousness of God," 365n14.

Yet the content of this Christlikeness still needs to be unpacked (whether here or in the parallel text of Rom. 8:29). Does it refer primarily, or even only, to "moral transformation," or does it also include—or perhaps even refer solely to—something else, even something transcendent or ontological? What does "from glory to/toward/into glory" mean? I would suggest that the primary meaning is the transition from a present, paradoxical, cruciform (yet resurrection-suffused) glory to a future, eschatological, fully anastiform (resurrection-shaped) glory.[39] The process of becoming more Christlike and Godlike is a process of glorification, and it is glorification with both present and future aspects.

Future Glory

Third, then, and to begin with the easier aspect of glorification, the transformation involves *future* glory. In Romans, Paul speaks about the "hope of sharing the glory of God" (5:2; cf. 8:17–21), meaning (at least) conformity to the resurrected and immortal Christ and thereby to share in the glory—the radiant splendor—of God.[40] Paul also speaks of the necessity of cosuffering with Christ as a condition of coglorification with him (8:17). Similarly, in Philippians Paul writes that Christ "will transform the body of our humiliation that it may be conformed to the body of his glory, by the power that also enables him to make all things subject to himself" (3:21).

In 1 Corinthians, Paul says that "we will all be changed" (*pantes de allagēsometha*, another divine passive; 15:51),[41] and he speaks of continuity yet discontinuity with present embodied existence in a "spiritual body" that has been changed from perishability, dishonor, and weakness into imperishability, glory, and power (15:42b–44; cf. 15:51–54). We might refer to this glory as "embodied" or "somatic" immortality. The condition of future glory appears also in 2 Corinthians, summarized in the claim that "we know that the one who raised the Lord Jesus will raise us also with Jesus, and will bring us with you into

39. The term "anastiform" is that of Stephen Finlan ("Can We Speak of *Theosis* in Paul?," 78–79), who claims that the anastiform aspect begins in the present as new life. As argued in chap. 3, "resurrectional" is a better term than "anastiform" or "resurrectiform" (Andy Boakye's term). Future resurrection and glory are, for Paul, somatic, as we will see below. Present glory takes place in the body but does not entail the transformation of the body. Paul's main point is to highlight the move from present, partial glory to future, full glory.

40. The debate about the meaning of glory and glorification in Romans, especially, rages on. I take here a rather minimalist view that could be expanded to include additional dimensions of glory.

41. The similarity of *pantes de allagēsometha* in 1 Cor. 15:51 to *hēmeis de . . . metamorphoumetha* in 2 Cor. 3:18 is worthy of note, the former being a good summary of the future dimension of the latter.

his presence" (4:14), a claim developed in the subsequent verses (4:16–5:11).[42] Yet the previous verses make it equally clear that the *present* situation is one of suffering, of "always carrying in the body the death of Jesus" (4:10b; cf. all of 4:5–12).

Present Glory

But is this present reality also glory? For Paul, it seems to be. Fourth, then, is what Paul says about *present* glory. In each of the texts just mentioned from the various letters, the context makes it clear that the promised future glory is in stark contrast to present existence, which is characterized by suffering, weakness, and death—by cruciform existence. Yet the description of humanity's condition in Romans 3:23—"All . . . fall short of the glory of God"—and the offer of salvation from that condition in Christ *may imply* the possibility of experiencing something of divine glory in the present. But 2 Corinthians 3:18 speaks of a process that *requires* us to acknowledge, for Paul, a present experience of glory. It is almost certainly the theological foundation of the similar (but even more debated) text in Romans 8:30, where Paul claims that those whom God called and justified, God also glorified. The context of 2 Corinthians 3:18 speaks of a paradox—namely, that God's power is manifested in human weakness and that Christ's life is demonstrated in human death, meaning deathlike existence in our mortal bodies (2 Cor. 4:10–11). In other words, there is real participation in divine power and Christic life— the glory of God *and of Christ*—in the present, but that participation is paradoxically marked by what appears to be the opposite of power, life, and glory. Present glory is power in weakness, life in death, glory in suffering, but it is nonetheless glory, nonetheless participation in the life and power of God in Christ. It is *resurrectional* cruciformity. The apostolic practices of being afflicted and persecuted (2 Cor. 4:8–9), of nonretaliation and blessing when cursed (1 Cor. 4:11–13), and so on are fundamentally, then, experiences of glory, the glory of the cross; they are spiritual practices, cruciform practices, theotic practices. And because they are practices of participation in the missional life of God, they are life-giving both for those who practice ministry in this way and for those who benefit from it.

---

42. Contra Litwa (*We Are Being Transformed*, 221), I see no evidence in 2 Cor. 3:18 or its context (or anywhere else) that Paul thinks that physical transformation begins to take place in the present. Blackwell (*Christosis*, 191) rightly calls the transformation "noetic, moral, and somatic embodiment," meaning "inward renewal in the midst of present sufferings and outward renewal in glorified, resurrected bodies in the future"; he designates this "a full christoformity . . . directly in line with the new covenant hope." That is, bodily activity is transformed in the present, but the body itself only in the future.

As we saw in chapter 3, this experience of cruciform glory appears in living, metaphorical color slightly earlier in 2 Corinthians when Paul speaks of God always leading "us" (perhaps primarily a reference to himself and his colleagues) "in triumphal procession"—"in Christ" (2:14). There is both irony and paradox in this claim, for although Paul portrays himself here as the conquered captive, he locates himself in Christ—the living, victorious Christ. In union with Christ, he is both defeated and victorious, dying and living. That Christ was crucified by Rome means that Paul is a conquered victim; that God raised Christ from the dead means that Paul is both alive and a source of life for others (2:16). Although this passage in 2 Corinthians 2 focuses on Paul, who is explaining and defending his ministry, it cannot and does not exclude other believers, for they too are "in Christ," and that is what is determinative of this paradoxical experience and practice of cruciform glory—not apostolicity per se.

The connection of 2 Corinthians 3:18 to Romans 12:1–2, noted above, confirms the universality of the call to transformation in Christ. It also indicates that the transformation Paul has in mind involves both the mind and the body, both ways of perceiving and ways of acting, within the community. In Romans 12 the presentation of the many bodies of believers as one living sacrifice (*parastēsai ta sōmata hymōn thysian zōsan*; cf. Rom. 6:13, 16, 19) is contrasted with being conformed to the present age and equated with (or at least linked to) being transformed. Romans 12 takes up a theme already introduced in Romans 6, where the self-presentation of bodily members that Paul calls for is an offering to God and to "righteousness" (NRSV), or justice, and as weapons and slaves of (God's) righteousness/justice:

> Present yourselves to God as those who have been brought from death to life, and present your members to God as instruments of righteousness.
>
> *parastēsate heautous tō theō hōsei ek nekrōn zōntas kai ta melē hymōn hopla dikaiosynēs tō theō.* (Rom. 6:13b)
>
> Present your members as slaves to righteousness for sanctification.
>
> *parastēsate ta melē hymōn doula tē dikaiosynē eis hagiasmon.* (Rom. 6:19c)

As we observed in the last chapter, these texts echo 2 Corinthians 5:21, which concerns "becoming" the righteousness/justice of God.

In both Romans 6 and Romans 12 there is a clear human role in the process of sanctification (Rom. 6:19) or transformation (Rom. 12:1–2). But Romans 12 identifies the means to this transformation implicitly as God's Spirit (with another divine passive) and explicitly as the renewal of the corporate mind: "Be transformed by the renewing of your minds" (*metamorphousthe tē anakainōsei tou noos*). It is likely, then, that in 2 Corinthians 3:18 Paul has the transformation of both perception and action in mind. Indeed, this is what Paul means when he refers to "the mind of Christ" (1 Cor. 2:16; Phil. 2:5): a Christlike, cruciform mindset and its corollary practices.

Communal Transformation

Fifth and finally, this transformation is more than an individual, and more than an apostolic, experience; it is, as noted earlier, a communal reality ("all of us"),[43] shared by the believers at Corinth with one another, with Paul and his colleagues, and with "all those who in every place call on the name of our Lord Jesus Christ, both their Lord and ours," as Paul describes the church universal in 1 Corinthians 1:2. Furthermore, if theosis means cruciform missional praxis for Paul and his colleagues, then it will mean fundamentally the same thing for the entire church. Theosis is not static but dynamic, and it is not merely about personal transformation in a privatistic sense but about personal transformation into the service of God and others.

David Litwa argues that glorification in 2 Corinthians 3:18 is "moral assimilation to God."[44] The contexts we have examined support that interpretation, but greater clarity and specificity are needed. The God Paul knows has a certain character expressed in particular kinds of acts. And that leads us naturally to 2 Corinthians 5:21.

Theosis as Becoming the Cruciform Justice of God in Christ: 2 Corinthians 5:21

Since we have dealt with 2 Corinthians 5:21 at length in chapter 7, our consideration of it here will be focused specifically on its implications for theosis. It will again be valuable to set out the Greek text, in transliteration, as well as the translation I offered in chapter 7:

> *ton mē gnonta hamartian hyper hēmōn hamartian epoiēsen, hina hēmeis genōmetha dikaiosynē theou en autō.*

For us [or "For our sake"] God made the one who did not know sin [the Messiah Jesus] to be sin so that in him we ourselves would become the justice [or "righteousness"] of God.

43. So also Blackwell, *Christosis*, 183–84.
44. Litwa, *We Are Being Transformed*, 216–23.

I wish to make five critical exegetical points about this "interchange" text, sometimes summarizing points made in chapter 7, but primarily offering new claims or implications of claims made in that chapter. In doing so I assume, for the reasons briefly mentioned in chapter 7, that the first-person-plural pronouns in this verse are inclusive of all who are in Christ, not restricted to Paul and his colleagues.[45]

In the Messiah: The Dynamic Location

The first point should be relatively uncontroversial, though it is not. This is a text about being "in Christ." The preposition "in" (*en*) should be taken locatively, as describing the sphere within which something happens to "us." That is, this something (a "becoming") occurs in the sphere of the crucified and resurrected Messiah.[46] Thus, although the language of the verse is not "transfer" language per se, which is most clearly expressed with the preposition "into" (*eis*),[47] it presumes that such a transfer has occurred—that "we" have moved from being outside Christ to being inside Christ.[48] The language is clearly meant to describe not an impersonal location but rather a deeply

45. So also Grieb, "'So That in Him.'" Wright ("On Becoming the Righteousness of God") and Hooker ("On Becoming the Righteousness of God," 364–75) both read 5:21 as referring to Paul and his ministry team, but Hooker, looking ahead to 2 Cor. 8–9, also thinks others are implicitly included as participants in Paul's, and therefore God's, mission.

46. In addition to debate about the meaning of "in," there is debate about the meaning of "Christ." I generally agree with Novenson (*Christ among the Messiahs*) and Wright (*Paul and the Faithfulness of God*, esp. 817–51) that when Paul says *Christos*, he means "Messiah," so I use the terms interchangeably.

47. See esp. Gal. 2:16 (*eis Christon Iēsoun episteusamen*) and 3:27 (*eis Christon ebaptisthēte*).

48. Constantine Campbell (*Paul and Union with Christ*, 185–87) proposes three strong candidates for the interpretation of "in Christ" here: locative ("the sphere or realm of Christ," 185), instrumental, and unitive (my term)—indicating union with Christ. He rightly rejects the instrumental interpretation but dismisses the locative interpretation because, unlike the nearby text 2 Cor. 5:17, where "realm transfer is in view" (185), in our verse "believers are not described as passing into the realm of God's righteousness but as becoming the righteousness of God" (186). I would note, however, that 5:17 does not speak explicitly of "realm transfer" any more than does 5:21; each verse assumes that such transfer has occurred, with the result being that the transferees are now in Christ. Campbell therefore opts for a rather vague "union with Christ" interpretation that allegedly expresses Paul's understanding of justification as being "made righteous by sharing in his [Christ's] right standing" by virtue of Christ's "sharing in the plight of the sinful" (186–87). Paul, however, here speaks not of union per se but of location. To be sure, this implies participation, and the language of "becoming" in the context of "location" underscores that. However, although Campbell rightly points out that Paul here speaks about believers "becom[ing] righteous" (187), this does not mean "sharing in his right standing" (187), as I argued in chap. 7 and we will see again below. Thus Campbell's decision against a locative interpretation and for a unitive interpretation seems to be controlled by his prior theological understanding of justification as sharing in Christ's right standing. The same seems to be the case in his treatment (114–15) of the somewhat parallel text Gal. 2:17 (discussed briefly below).

personal relationship, even—as suggested in earlier chapters—mysticism. Yet this intimacy, though personal, is not private. "In the Messiah" suggests both a corporate reality and an arena of power, not merely a private love affair or something similar.[49] To be in Christ is to be in a community of people who have come under the influence of this crucified but resurrected (and thus living) Messiah. Thus, the language of location is not static but dynamic; it indicates being in the presence of something—or, better, Someone—possessing the ability to reorient and reshape one's existence in the company of others. It implies, in other words, solidarity and transformation—new creation (2 Cor. 5:17)! For this reason, Paul elsewhere employs the imagery of being clothed with Christ (Rom. 13:14; Gal. 3:27). To be in Christ is to wear him. And since Christ is for believers the *dikaiosynē* (justice/righteousness) *of God* (1 Cor. 1:30), those in him wear (participate in, become), that *dikaiosynē*; they can and will take on that essential divine attribute.

Transfer and Transformation

The second point about 2 Corinthians 5:21, one that we emphasized in chapter 7, is that this is absolutely a text about transformation, about people becoming something they previously were not. The use of the verb *ginomai* ("become") makes this clear; also clear, because of the specific way Paul deploys the verb—in a purpose (*hina*) clause—is that this transformation is both the intended purpose and the desired result of a prior transformation—namely, Christ's having been made sin by the action of God. Transformation begets transformation; that is the essence of the patristic theotic formula.

The process of "becoming" is predicated on the prior (one-time) act of transfer into Christ. That is, we cannot *become* something in Christ until we are actually *in* Christ. This suggests, then, that the purpose of Christ's death was not merely to effect a *status* change in people but to effect an *existential* change among those who have entered the realm of Christ. This suggestion is confirmed by the immediate context of 5:21. Paul has just spoken about "new creation," and whether we take that as a reference to each individual or to the new reality in which all who are in Christ participate, it is hardly the language of status change; it is the idiom of transformation. Furthermore, in an earlier sentence that is semantically parallel to 5:21, Paul has already expressed the purpose of Christ's death in terms of transformation, and also with a purpose (*hina*) clause: "And he died for all so that those who live

---

49. This is how Albert Schweitzer's Pauline "mysticism" is often understood, though Schweitzer himself had sensitivities to the corporate dimensions of Paul's spirituality.

Table 9.1. The Purpose of Jesus' Death in 2 Cor. 5:15, 21

Text	Main clause: the death of Christ narrated	Purpose conjunction	Purpose clause: the goal of Christ's death indicated
5:15	And he died for all	so that (*hina*)	those who live would live [*zōsin*] no longer for themselves, but for him who died for them and was raised.
5:21	For us [or "For our sake"] God made the one who did not know sin to be sin	so that (*hina*)	in him we ourselves would become [*genōmetha*] the justice [or "righteousness"] of God.

would live no longer for themselves, but for the one who died for them and was raised" (5:15 MJG). The parallel with 5:21 is clear (see table 9.1 above). Accordingly, the *aorist* subjunctive verb *genōmetha* ("become") in 5:21 is semantically parallel to the *present* subjunctive verb *zōsin* ("live") in 5:15. To "become the righteousness of God" is materially parallel to "live no longer for themselves, but for him who died for them and was raised."

Morna Hooker has written insightfully about the connection between this transformation claim and the theme of reconciliation found in this section of 2 Corinthians:

> Becoming God's righteousness is not just a matter of being acquitted in God's court or of sharing Christ's status before God. If God's righteousness is a restorative power, bringing life and reconciliation, then those who "become righteousness" will be the means of manifesting that power in the world.[50]

Theosis: Deification and Humanization in Christ

The third point about 2 Corinthians 5:21 is that if it is an interchange text about participation ("location") and transformation, we should at least consider using the term "theosis" to characterize what Paul is describing. Indeed, the term "theosis," or something similar, is arguably the only sort of term that can adequately express what Paul is describing.

Although the christological emphasis in the doctrine of theosis has often been on the incarnation, the doctrine does not exclude the death of Christ, as the patristic evidence indicates.[51] Similarly, the emphasis in Paul's theology of interchange may be on the death of Christ, but it does not exclude his

50. Hooker, "On Becoming the Righteousness of God," 374–75. Cf. Hays, *Moral Vision of the New Testament*, 24.

51. See, e.g., Blackwell (*Christosis*, 111), who notes that patristic exchange formulas even refer to the "whole of Christ's work."

incarnation (cf. esp. 2 Cor. 8:9). The point of theosis is that human beings can share in God's attributes because God has shared in humanity's situation. In the famous image of the seventh-century Byzantine theologian Maximus the Confessor, theosis is like the placing of an iron sword in a fire: it remains an iron sword but also takes on certain properties of the fire—light and heat—by "participating" in it.[52] To put the words of the fathers in slightly more Pauline language:

> In Christ's self-emptying, self-humbling, and self-impoverishment in incarnation and crucifixion, God's fullness, power, wisdom, abundance, holiness, and righteousness (or justice) were revealed in human form so that we might share in that incarnate and cruciform fullness, power, wisdom, abundance, holiness, and justice of God.

To be sure, the doctrine of theosis is about more than moral transformation, or what is often called "sanctification" in the West.[53] It includes both present and eschatological transformation, understood as a single and continuous salvific reality, the former dimension corresponding largely to moral transformation, the latter to the eschatological resurrection and glorification of the body. (We have already seen this in discussing 2 Cor. 3:18.) That is, the primary divine attributes in which humans can participate are holiness (i.e., moral character, which includes righteousness/justice) and immortality.[54]

The paradox of theosis is that when humans become "divine" (in this sense of sharing in these particular divine attributes), they become most fully human. Surely this is a sentiment with which Paul would agree: to become like Christ is to become reshaped into the image of God that God originally intended for humans to embody, as 2 Corinthians 3–4 certainly suggests by using the language of "image." This Christification, in both its moral and its eschatological senses, as I have elsewhere suggested and wish now to re-emphasize, is both deification and humanization.[55]

---

52. Maximus the Confessor, *Ambiguum* 7; cf. *Opuscule* 16.

53. Respondents to those who have been proposing that we return to the language of theosis in describing Pauline soteriology have rightfully been quick to point out that limiting theosis to sanctification is to transform the doctrine almost beyond recognition. This was perhaps Edith Humphrey's main criticism in her response to papers on theosis in the New Testament, and to the scholarly development of using theosis language more generally, in the 2013 session of the Society of Biblical Literature's Theological Interpretation of Scripture Seminar devoted to theosis in the New Testament.

54. Or, in the fathers, "incorruption and sanctification" (Blackwell, *Christosis*, 100). Litwa (*We Are Being Transformed*, 223–24) finds a parallel in Plato's notion of participation in Justice as sharing in the divine nature.

55. See also Gorman, *Inhabiting the Cruciform God*, 37.

Glory and Justice/Righteousness

This topic leads naturally to a discussion of 2 Corinthians 3:18 in connection with 5:21. The fourth point, then, is that 5:21 is materially reminiscent of, and theologically connected to, Paul's earlier theotic text, 3:18, and also to Paul's later presentation of the theotic themes of justification and glorification in Romans.

Elsewhere I contend that Romans tells the story of humanity's restoration to the two divine attributes that it has, in some profound sense, "lost": *doxa* and *dikaiosynē*, "glory" and "justice/righteousness."[56] These two come together in Romans 8:30, where Paul says, "Those whom he [God] justified he also glorified." For Paul, the restoration of justice/righteousness and glory has happened, is happening, and will happen to believers. Paul wants the house churches in Rome to embody the (cruciform) glory and justice/righteousness that they have received in Christ. These same two lost (or, perhaps more theologically precise, diminished) elements of the human condition are also named in 2 Corinthians 3:18 and 5:21: the veil has been lifted by God so that believers can gaze on Christ and become (in a limited, incomplete way) what he is—the *doxa* of God (3:18); and the Messiah has been made sin by God so that people can enter into him and, once in him, become what he is—the *dikaiosynē* of God (5:21; cf. 1 Cor. 1:30). The two verses complement each other and need to be read in tandem, even joined, as they essentially are in Romans 8:30. Glorification means also "justice-ification," which then needs to be worked out in concrete manifestations of justice—as we will see in considering 2 Corinthians 8:9 below.[57]

Theosis and Justification

Fifth and finally, then, 2 Corinthians 5:21 is undoubtedly about justification—by grace. That is one "traditional" reading of this text, and there is support for it going back to the fathers.[58] We have explored this aspect of the verse at length in chapter 7. Although the verb *dikaioō* is not present, most interpreters read the reference to *dikaiosynē* as an indication that the subject is justification. Paul's theological claims here and elsewhere in his corpus support that contention. As we also saw in earlier chapters, the language of reconciliation (2 Cor. 5:18–20), for instance, clearly anticipates Paul's discussion of

56. Gorman, *Becoming the Gospel*, 261–96.
57. On justification as incorporation into the community of the just, see 1 Cor. 6:1–11, discussed in Gorman, *Becoming the Gospel*, 234–40.
58. See, e.g., Chrysostom, *Homilies on the Epistles of Paul to the Corinthians* 11.5, cited in Bray, *1–2 Corinthians*, 249.

justification as reconciliation in Romans 5:1–11. Furthermore, the language of dying and living a new life for Christ (2 Cor. 5:14–15) is reminiscent of Paul's discussion of justification as co-crucifixion and co-resurrection in Galatians 2:15–21, especially 2:19–21. Galatians 2 also makes it clear that justification occurs *in* Christ: *dikaiōthēnai en Christō* ("to be justified in Christ," Gal. 2:17), a phrase parallel to *genōmetha dikaiosynē theou en autō* ("become the justice/righteousness of God in him") in 2 Corinthians 5:21. These constitute some of the main reasons for seeing 2 Corinthians 5:14–21 as both a *restatement* of Galatians 2:15–21 for a new audience and a *foreshadowing* of the central affirmations of Romans on justification (see chap. 7).

If 2 Corinthians 5:21 is about justification, however, it is a text, like Galatians 2:15–21,[59] that demonstrates that for Paul justification is inherently participatory and transformative. Everything we have considered so far in this chapter (not to mention earlier discussions) points to this reality. Justification is in Christ; it is a death and resurrection; it entails reconciliation; it is becoming the righteousness/justice of God. It is—to the unnecessary chagrin of some interpreters—perhaps best characterized as theosis.[60]

Summary: 2 Corinthians 5:21 as Bridge

This second text under consideration in this chapter, then, is about the church becoming the justice of God. It therefore anticipates concrete practices of justice that are, in turn, concrete practices of participation, practices of corporate, cruciform, resurrectional (life-giving), missional theosis. That is, *2 Corinthians 5:21 is a bridge from the heavenly glory of 2 Corinthians 3:18 to its practical, even mundane, embodiment in 2 Corinthians 8:9.*

Theosis on the Ground: Cruciform Economic Justice in 2 Corinthians 8–9

Chapters 8 and 9 of 2 Corinthians contain Paul's appeal to the believers in Corinth for their support of the collection for the Jerusalem church. Specifically, Paul is urging them to fulfill their previous commitment to that effort. The Greek language supplies Paul with a strategic opportunity for a wordplay as he seeks to call the justified/justice-ized community at Corinth (cf. 1 Cor.

---

59. On which, see my *Inhabiting the Cruciform God*, 63–85.

60. E.g., C. Campbell, *Paul and Union with Christ*, 394–95 ("Gorman has gone too far"). Wright, though open to theosis as a post-justification reality (e.g., *Paul and the Faithfulness of God*, 955, 1021–23), finds transformative understandings of justification "dangerous" in their effects (913; cf. 1031).

6:1–11) to practice justice.[61] In 2 Corinthians 8–9 Paul uses the word *charis*, often translated "grace," ten times,[62] with various but interconnected senses: benefaction, generosity, generous act, gratitude. Paul likely draws on both the scriptural sense of God's benefaction (expressed by the Hebrew word *ḥesed* and cognates) and the contemporary Greco-Roman usage of *charis*, which could refer to a generous disposition, a generous gift, or the response of gratitude and subsequent indebtedness to the giver.[63] In addition, Paul uses the cognate *eucharistia*, "thanksgiving," twice, and he quotes Psalm 112:9 (111:9 LXX) in 9:9, which refers to the manifestation of justice (*dikaiosynē*) in generosity to the poor.

Portions of this eloquent piece of rhetoric are worth quoting here. I again cite the NRSV but replace "righteousness" with "justice." Occurrences of "justice," "grace" (variously translated by the NRSV), and "thanksgiving" are in boldface:

> [8:1]We want you to know, brothers and sisters, about the **grace** [*charin*] of God that has been granted to the churches of Macedonia. . . . [3]For, as I can testify, they voluntarily gave according to their means, and even beyond their means, [4]begging us earnestly for the **privilege** [*charin*] of sharing in this ministry to the saints . . . [6]so that we might urge Titus that, as he had already made a beginning, so he should also complete this **generous undertaking** [*charin*] among you. [7]Now as you excel in everything—in faith, in speech, in knowledge, in utmost eagerness, and in our love for you—so we want you to excel also in this **generous undertaking** [*chariti*]. . . .
>
> [9]For you know the **generous act** [*charin*] of our Lord Jesus Christ, that though [or perhaps "because"[64]] he was rich, yet for your sakes he became poor, so that by his poverty you might become rich. . . . [16]But **thanks** [*charis*] be to God who put in the heart of Titus the same eagerness for you that I myself have. . . . [19]He has also been appointed by the churches to travel with us while we are administering this **generous undertaking** [*chariti*] for the glory of the Lord himself and to show our goodwill. . . .
>
> [9:8]And God is able to provide you with every **blessing** [*charin*] in abundance, so that by always having enough of everything, you may share abundantly in every good work. [9]As it is written,

> "He scatters abroad, he gives to the poor;
> his **justice** [*dikaiosynē*] endures forever."

61. Most translations, unfortunately, miss the connections among the various references to justice and injustice in this passage.

62. 2 Cor. 8:1, 4, 6, 7, 9, 16, 19; 9:8, 14, 15.

63. Thus English translations, unfortunately (once again), do not always reveal all the linguistic and theological connections in the text. The cluster of occurrences of *charis* in these two chapters is rivaled only by Rom. 5. Helpful is Barclay, "Manna and the Circulation of Grace"; also Barclay, *Paul and the Gift*.

64. See discussion below.

¹⁰He who supplies seed to the sower and bread for food will supply and multiply your seed for sowing and increase the harvest of your **justice** [*dikaiosynēs*]. ¹¹You will be enriched in every way for your great generosity, which will produce **thanksgiving** [*eucharistian*] to God through us; ¹²for the rendering of this ministry not only supplies the needs of the saints but also overflows with many **thanksgivings** [*eucharistiōn*] to God. ¹³Through the testing of this ministry you glorify God by your obedience to the confession of the gospel of Christ and by the generosity of your sharing with them and with all others [*eis pantas*], ¹⁴while they long for you and pray for you because of the surpassing **grace** [*charin*] of God that he has given you. ¹⁵**Thanks** [*charis*] be to God for his indescribable gift! (2 Cor. 8:1, 3–4, 6–7, 9, 16, 19; 9:8–15)

Laced with the word *charis* and additional rich theological and theocentric language, artfully mixed with the idiom of honor and shame, the appeal for generosity has as its goal something approximating "equality" (so NIV, NAB in 8:13–14 for *isotēs*; NRSV, "fair balance"), or what we would describe as economic justice.⁶⁵ I will make four key exegetical and theological points about 2 Corinthians 8:9 and its immediate context (chaps. 8–9), all of which demonstrate the intermingling of divine justice and human justice that are each "located" in Christ (*en Christō*). *This suggests that 2 Corinthians 8:9 in particular, and all of chapters 8 and 9 in general, constitute a gloss on 2 Corinthians 5:21*—indicating in one situation what becoming the justice of God means and looks like.

God's Generous Justice

First, Paul's appeal to the Corinthians is grounded in what Katherine Grieb has labeled the "generous justice of God,"⁶⁶ which has been manifested concretely in Christ, but also in the Macedonian believers located in Christ. The "generous justice of God in Christ," then, appropriately summarizes what Paul conveys through multiple occurrences of the word *charis* and related terms in conjunction with the two occurrences of *dikaiosynē* (9:9, 10). In 2 Corinthians 8–9 as a unit, Paul speaks of Christ both as the generous, "indescribable gift" of God (*dōrea*, 9:15) and as the gracious self-gift of Christ himself (*charis*, 8:9). The latter text narrates Christ's self-emptying, or kenosis, probably referring to both his incarnation and his death (as in Phil. 2:6–8), in the metaphorical economic language of self-impoverishment for the benefit of others. Paul calls the Corinthians, as beneficiaries of this greatest gift, to participate in it more fully and responsibly—yet freely, cheerfully, and without

---

65. So also Grieb, "'So That in Him,'" esp. 69. Gordon Zerbe (*Citizenship*, 82–87) argues that "economic mutualism" was a consistent part of Paul's teaching in the various assemblies.

66. Grieb, "'So That in Him,'" e.g., 59, 74.

worry—by sharing in the grace of Christ, which is summarized in 8:7–9, and the justice of God, which is summarized in 9:9–10.

"Because He Was Rich"

Second, the translation of 2 Corinthians 8:9 requires some attention. That 2 Corinthians 8:9 is an "exchange" or "interchange" text is quite clear: Christ became poor so that we could become rich. As I and others have argued, the verse echoes the Christ-poem in Philippians 2, and it seems even to have a similar underlying semantic structure: although he was [x], he did not do [y (the natural corollary of x)], but he did do [z (the opposite of x)].[67] As we noted in earlier chapters, the standard translations of both Philippians 2:6 and 2 Corinthians 8:9 render the Greek participles *hyparchōn* and *ōn* (respectively) concessively, with words like "though" or "although": "though he was in the form of God" (Phil. 2:6) and "though he was rich" (2 Cor. 8:9). John Barclay has recently argued, however, that here in 2 Corinthians 8:9 the better interpretation of the participle is as an indicator of cause, not concession, and thus the preferred translation is "because he was rich."[68] Barclay summarizes the two possible readings in the phrases "'wealth' as possession, lost and gained" ("because") versus "'wealth' as generosity, gained in loss" ("although"). His point, then, is that "'wealth' consists not in possession but in generosity," and that "it is precisely in Christ becoming poor that we see in what his 'wealth' consists."[69] Barclay continues: "Paul is less interested here in what Christ gave up than in what he gave out, a momentum of generosity that is not tied solely to one form of giving (giving away) but could be expressed in a variety of forms (including sharing and mutual participation)."[70]

Participating in God's Justice

Third, if Barclay is right, then the hortatory point of 2 Corinthians 8:9 is as follows:

> If Christ's "wealth" consists of his generosity, then the purpose of this momentum is to make "you" rich . . . not in the sense of what you acquire as possessions,

67. To be sure, the [y] element is not explicit in 2 Cor. 8:9, as it is in Phil. 2:6–8, probably because Paul abbreviates the structure of the Philippians poem as he changes the emphasis from kenosis itself to the soteriological purpose (interchange).

68. Barclay, "'Because He Was Rich He Became Poor.'" As Barclay notes (340n19, 343–44), I had earlier made the argument for translating Phil. 2:6 with both the causal and the concessive senses (*Inhabiting the Cruciform God*, 9–39).

69. Barclay, "'Because He Was Rich He Became Poor,'" 340, 341.

70. Barclay, "'Because He Was Rich He Became Poor,'" 341.

but in the sense of becoming *rich in generosity*. . . . The purpose of "enrichment" or "abundance" is not that believers may possess more, but give more.[71]

In my view, this reading (though it may need some nuancing) is correct, and it does not deny but rather enhances a theotic interpretation of 2 Corinthians 8:9. Because Christ is by nature gracious and generous, he has acted generously toward us both to enrich us and to enable us to enrich others. Soteriology is inherently ethical; theosis is missional. This is a fully participatory understanding of salvation, ethics, and mission. Because of the larger context, I would amend Barclay's proposal to include *justice* as inseparably part of the grace/generosity of God, Christ, and believers. The Corinthians are being called to a similar kind of ministry (*diakonia*)[72] to that of Paul and his team, who enrich others (2 Cor. 6:10: "as poor, yet making many rich," *hōs ptōchoi pollous de ploutizontes*).

Throughout the Corinthian correspondence Paul wants the Corinthians' life in Christ and the Spirit to be marked not only by *charismata* (charismatic gifts; 1 Cor. 1:7; 12:4, 9, 28–31) but also by Christlike, cruciform *charis*. In 2 Corinthians 8–9 this desire means that their life in the Spirit given to them in justice-ification (1 Cor. 6:11) needs to be expressed in a "harvest of [their] justice" (2 Cor. 9:10)—which is ultimately the justice of God (2 Cor. 9:9; cf., again, 1 Cor. 6:1–11). "The Corinthians," writes Barclay elsewhere, "are being invited not just to *imitate* God's dynamic of grace [and, we should add, "justice"] toward the world but to *embody* it, to continue and extend it in their own giving to meet the needs of others."[73] Indeed, what is remarkable is that Paul sees such a close relationship between grace and justice, first as the characteristic of God (including Christ and the Spirit) and then as the characteristic of God's people. As an extension of 2 Corinthians 5:21, 2 Corinthians 8:9 could have said, "The grace of God appeared in Christ's self-impoverishing so that you, in turn, might become the grace of God for others." The church participates in God's gracious, justice-creating mission, and Paul indicates this by using the common Greek word for sharing, *koinōnia* (2 Cor. 8:4; 9:13), giving it a profound theological twist.

Missional, Generous Justice

Fourth, in 2 Corinthians 9 Paul uses a common image—the sowing of seed—to further emphasize that God is the ultimate source of generosity and

---

71. Barclay, "'Because He Was Rich He Became Poor,'" 342.
72. See 2 Cor. 5:18; 6:3–4; 8:4, 19, 20; 9:1, 12, 13.
73. Barclay, "Manna and the Circulation of Grace," 420 (emphasis added).

justice for the poor, and that the church participates in that generous justice. Paul invites believers to "sow" bountifully and cheerfully, knowing that God provides abundantly for the doing of good (9:6–11). This point raises the question of the grammatical subject in 9:9, which quotes Psalm 112:9:

> As it is written, "He scatters abroad, he gives to the poor; his righteousness [*dikaiosynē*] endures forever."

Is the one who "scatters abroad" and "gives to the poor," whose "righteousness [justice] endures forever," God, or is it the just and faithful person? In Psalm 112 itself, the subject is the one who fears the Lord, but Paul's use is less clear; the subject may be God. In either case, however, God is the ultimate benefactor who provides and multiplies the seed, blessing the sower to bless others. Thomas Stegman suggests that Paul's thought reflects the flow of Psalms 111 and 112 (110 and 111 LXX): Psalm 111 describes the generous, merciful, and just God who feeds those who fear him, while Psalm 112 describes the one who fears and imitates this God by doing justice and giving to the poor.[74] Both are characterized by justice (*dikaiosynē* in 110:3 LXX; 111:3, 9 LXX). Accordingly, for Paul, "those who give generously to the needy should know that their charitable act is a part of that larger righteousness of God by which they themselves live and in which they shall remain forever."[75] This is a text about *missional* participation.

Participatory Salvation: Interchange, Transformation, Mission

Having made these four main points about 2 Corinthians 8:9, we turn briefly to the text in connection with the letter as a whole. The overall participatory thrust of Paul's gentle but prophetic argument and the presence of *dikaiosynē* language suggest that it is no coincidence that we find another "interchange" text following 5:21. Christ became sin so that we might become just(ice) (5:21), and, similarly, he became poor so that we might become rich (8:9). His generous self-gift to us in our spiritual poverty translates into the generous gift of our material possessions to others in their material poverty.[76] Again, this is not a mere summons to imitation, but rather "the *identification of a divine momentum in which believers are caught up*, and by which they are empowered to be, in turn, richly self-sharing with others."[77]

74. Stegman, *Second Corinthians*, 214.
75. Furnish, *II Corinthians*, 449.
76. "The ultimate goal is not a reversal of fortunes through some kind of class warfare, but 'equality' through the establishment of new economic relationships under the sign of Messiah's economic divestment for the sake of the other" (Zerbe, *Citizenship*, 81–82).
77. Barclay, "Manna and the Circulation of Grace," 421 (emphasis added). Barclay does not use the language of justice, but he describes it in characterizing Paul's vision of equality

Together the two interchange texts in 2 Corinthians suggest that Paul's addressees will be on their way to becoming the justice of God when they are conformed to the cruciform grace of Christ expressed in selfless generosity to the poor. Although Paul's primary concern is the collection for the Jerusalem church, in 2 Corinthians 9, at least, the poor to be cared for are not only believers ("the saints," 9:1, 12) but "all" (9:13, *pantas*; NRSV "all others")—almost certainly meaning outsiders.[78]

It is significant that Paul refers to this generous justice as ministry (*diakonia*, 8:4 [cf. 8:19–20]; 9:1, 12, 13), the same word he uses in 2 Corinthians to describe his own ministry—that is, embodied gospel proclamation (3:8–9; 4:1; 5:18; 6:3; 11:8). Moreover, he refers to his own ministry as a "ministry of righteousness/justice" (*dikaiosynēs*, 3:9), of reconciliation (5:18), and of enriching others (6:10). More precisely, Paul participates in God's ministry, in Christ, of justice, reconciliation, and enrichment—and so do the Corinthians. Morna Hooker writes,

> Paul's appeal to the Corinthians in chapters 8–9 can also be seen as a logical continuation from the conviction that Christians are agents of righteousness. . . . Since God's righteousness abides for ever, he will increase the yield of *their* righteousness (9:8–10): once again, we see the link between God's righteousness and that of Christians—and this righteousness is demonstrated in bringing assistance to those in need. It is certainly no accident that the key appeal in this section is made on the basis of another of Paul's "interchange" statements . . . (8:9). The Corinthians, too, must in their turn bring riches to others. By doing so, they will be sharing in Paul's ministry, and God's saving power will work through them.[79]

In speaking of justice, neither Paul nor we have left either glory or justification behind. As I have noted above and elsewhere, for Paul the inseparability of justification and justice is critical, though few contemporary Pauline scholars have adequately noted or explored this connection.[80] The community of the justified is the community of the just, which is the community of those being transformed and glorified and re-created—all in Christ. *These are not*

---

as the "redistribution of surplus" that is "bilateral" and "reciprocal" because all parties have different sorts of riches to give and needs to be met (423).

78. See Zerbe, *Citizenship*, 80; B. Longenecker, *Remember the Poor*, 291–94. "All," as distinguished from the direct addressees in a letter, is normally Paul's way of referring to, or including, those outside the church. Translations express this interpretation of 9:13 in various ways: CEB, NET, and Wright, *Kingdom New Testament*: "everyone"; NIV: "everyone else"; NKJV: "all men." The NLT has "all believers," which seems unlikely.

79. Hooker, "On Becoming the Righteousness of God," 374.

80. See my *Becoming the Gospel*, 212–60.

different, competing soteriologies or even quasi-independent slices of one soteriological pie. Rather, they are intimately interconnected dimensions of one soteriological reality, such that one aspect cannot be fully or adequately articulated without reference to the others. A comprehensive term or phrase is needed, or at least helpful, to keep these dimensions integrated. "Participatory transformation" or "transformative participation" might work, or simply "union with Christ," "life in the crucified and resurrected Messiah," or "life in the Spirit." But not to be missed are the benefits of using "corporate, cruciform, resurrectional, missional theosis," or "Christosis," or simply, with the ecumenical Christian tradition, "theosis."

Conclusion

So what have we discovered in this chapter? First, we have found that the three main texts we have considered—2 Corinthians 3:18, 5:21, and 8:9—were seen by the church fathers as witnesses to theosis and have been treated as such by several significant recent interpreters of Paul. Second, we have seen that the theosis to which Paul bears witness in 2 Corinthians, at least with respect to its present (as opposed to its eschatological) expression, is corporate, cruciform, resurrectional (though not resurrectiform), and missional. Its corporate (communal) character is clear from the first- and second-person-plural verbs in each verse: "all of us . . . are being transformed" (3:18); "so that in him we might become the righteousness of God" (5:21); and "so that by his poverty you [plural] might become rich" (8:9). Its cruciform and missional character is evident in the texts themselves, and also in the context of each passage and of the letter as a whole. Its resurrectional character is clear from the fact that it involves glory; this glory into which apostles and all believers are being transformed is manifested, paradoxically, in cruciform, life-giving activity; to become the righteousness/justice of God means to share in Christ's gracious self-impoverishment for the benefit of others. These aspects of Paul's understanding of theosis, I would submit, are absolutely fundamental to the apostle's soteriology and ought to be seen as dimensions of theosis that are critical to contemporary appropriation of both Paul's theology and the church's tradition of theosis.

A third finding has been that theosis is not something distinct from justification. Justification is itself the event of initial and ongoing sharing in the justice of God revealed in Christ by the power of the Spirit, and thus of being made just—of being "justice-ified." For believers, the process of justice-ification and glorification has begun already and will be consummated with bodily resurrection and transformation in the future. In the meantime, believers share in the divine attributes of glory and righteousness/justice (*doxa* and *dikaiosynē*) manifested in Christ in a partial but real way such that they become more like Christ, more like God, and more fully human, all by the working of grace and the Spirit of God.[81]

In this regard, 2 Corinthians is much like Romans, which also focuses on Spirit-generated *doxa* and *dikaiosynē*, as well as justification—which, of course, is participatory and transformative. It is, in fact, theotic.

---

81. Indeed, because believers live in the Christ who is the justice of God, and he lives in them, "the church's participation in God is none other than Christ's practicing himself as the embodied practices of the church, in the Spirit, on behalf of the world." Owens, *Shape of Participation*, 183.

Part 2

Paul and Participation Today

The first nine chapters of this book have been primarily studies in Paul's theology and spirituality. While there have been plenty of implications for contemporary Christian theology and practice, and occasional explicit applications, such concerns have not been the primary focus of those chapters. The final two chapters attempt—briefly, and in two very different styles—to bring Paul more directly into conversation with the contemporary Christian church. It would be contrary to the apostle's wishes, I would suggest, not to do so. Much more could, of course, be said; the reflections offered here are not intended to be either the only or the final word.

Being "In Christ" Today

Paul's Letter to the Contemporary Church in North America

From about 1956 to about 1963, the Reverend Martin Luther King Jr. preached various versions of a sermon entitled "Paul's Letter to American Christians," based in part on a similar sermon by Rev. Frederick Meek. It is included in King's collection of sermons entitled *Strength to Love* and elsewhere.[1] King's sermon, an imaginary letter from the apostle Paul to American Christians, extols America's "scientific and technological progress" before questioning America's "moral and spiritual progress." King spends more than half of the sermon addressing divisions in church and society, especially segregation, but also fissures within Christianity. The sermon contains echoes of various Pauline letters and other biblical books, but it most closely resembles 1 Corinthians, with both its emphasis on divisions and its proposed solution: sacrificial love.[2]

Though the 1956 letter is still highly relevant, and I commend it, it might be valuable to continue the Meek-King trajectory with another letter for another time and purpose. This letter is about the mission of God and the

---

1. King, *Strength to Love*, 145–53; see also "Paul's Letter to American Christians." The sermon appears to have been first preached on September 7, 1956, before 10,000 people at the National Baptist Convention in Denver, and then on November 4, 1956, at Dr. King's own church, Dexter Avenue Baptist Church in Montgomery, Alabama. (The earliest reference to the sermon in the King papers is to the Denver sermon: see https://kinginstitute.stanford.edu/encyclopedia /king-delivers-pauls-letter-american-christians-national-baptist-convention-denver.)

2. In fact, the sermon concludes with a remix of 1 Cor. 13, the love chapter.

church in North America in the first half of the twenty-first century. What might Paul say to us today?

Greetings to Those in Christ

Paul, called to be an apostle of Christ Jesus by the will of God, and writing at the request of our mutual friend and brother,[3]

To the church of God that happens to be in North America, to those who are sanctified in Christ Jesus, called to be saints, together with all those from every tribe and race and ethnicity, from minorities and refugees and immigrants around the world and in your own backyard, documented and undocumented, who call on the name of our Lord Jesus Christ, both their Lord and ours:

Grace to you and peace from God our Father and the Lord Jesus Christ. I give thanks to my God always for you because of the grace of God that has been given you in Christ Jesus, for in every way you have been enriched, both spiritually in Christ and materially— though we may need to return to the latter kind of wealth in another letter. God will also strengthen you, so that you may be faithful to the end and blameless on the day of our Lord Jesus Christ. God is faithful; by him you were called to participate in the life of his Son, Jesus Christ our Lord (that which, as I understand it, you generally but rather blandly call "fellowship").

As you know, one of my favorite ways to speak about our life together is with the short phrase "in Christ," or "in the Messiah." You may have noticed that I have already used it a few times. That phrase will be the subject of my letter. It is what you sometimes call "spirituality"; it may surprise you that it also means "mission." It is what our mutual friend calls "cruciformity" (cross-shaped living) or even "cruciform missional theosis."

But before I get too far into my letter, let me go back to those first two words: "grace" and "peace." These are not epistolary niceties, brothers and sisters. They constitute the core of my message, the heart of God's heart.

Grace and Peace

It is evident to me that you are very comfortable with the word "grace." (I would recommend, however, that you take a look at the significant book by my insightful and eloquent interpreter John Barclay, *Paul and the Gift*, to understand the obligations associated with grace more fully. Or you could reread Dietrich Bonhoeffer's classic *Discipleship*,[4] the second half of which is devoted to interpreting my theology and spirituality brilliantly.)

---

3. That is, the author of this volume.
4. Sometimes translated appropriately as *The Cost of Discipleship*.

It is far less apparent to me that you understand the word "peace"—*shalom* in Hebrew. To be sure, this word means inner peace and security. But it signifies much more. It means wholeness and harmony, right relations between us and God, within the human family, and between us and the rest of creation. "Peace" is one of those scriptural words that sums up what God is up to in the world—the mission of God, or *missio Dei*. I use it and many other words and images in my letters to convey the essence of this divine mission: reconciliation, saving justice, new creation, and so on.

But you live in a culture that does not know the way of peace. As I said to the faithful in Rome, quoting Scripture:

> [9]We have already charged that all, both Jews and Greeks, are under the power of sin, [10]as it is written:
>
>> "There is no one who is righteous, not even one;
>>> [11]there is no one who has understanding,
>>> there is no one who seeks God.
>> [12]All have turned aside, together they have become worthless;
>>> there is no one who shows kindness,
>>> there is not even one."
>> [13]"Their throats are opened graves;
>>> they use their tongues to deceive."
>> "The venom of vipers is under their lips."
>>> [14]"Their mouths are full of cursing and bitterness."
>> [15]"Their feet are swift to shed blood;
>>> [16]ruin and misery are in their paths,
>>> [17]and the way of peace they have not known."
>>> [18]"There is no fear of God before their eyes." (Rom. 3:9–18)

Sadly, this is the culture and world in which I lived and in which you live, a world of verbal and physical violence—the culture of death, as one of your great church leaders, John Paul II, called it.[5] Even more sadly, however, this culture has infiltrated much of the church in North America, particularly in the United States. There the Second Amendment trumps the teachings of Jesus, teachings I myself repeated and riffed for several churches, not least for the churches in Rome, the capital of the empire—something like your Washington, DC:

> [14]Bless those who persecute you; bless and do not curse them. [15]Rejoice with those who rejoice, weep with those who weep. [16]Live in harmony with one another; do not be haughty, but associate with the lowly; do not claim to be wiser than you are. [17]Do not repay anyone evil for evil, but take thought for what is noble in the sight of all. [18]If it is possible, so far as it depends on you, live peaceably with all. [19]Beloved, never avenge yourselves, but leave room for the wrath of God; for it is written, "Vengeance is mine, I will repay, says the Lord."

5. See Pope John Paul II, *Evangelium Vitae* (The Gospel of Life), an encyclical issued in 1995.

[20]No, "if your enemies are hungry, feed them; if they are thirsty, give them something to drink; for by doing this you will heap burning coals on their heads." [21]Do not be overcome by evil, but overcome evil with good. (Rom. 12:14–21)

The buzzword in many of your churches today is "missional." If you want to be missional, start with this text. What an amazing witness to Jesus the Lord this would be—a community that practices peace, both internally and externally. This is not merely pragmatic or, worse, idealistic advice. It is what God is up to in the world in Christ, making peace by the blood of his cross in order to reconcile all things to himself, as my letter to the Colossians says (Col. 1:20). (That comment should settle the dispute about authorship!) Or, as I said to the Romans, God reconciled us when we were God's enemies (Rom. 5:10). If that's how God treats enemies, how then shall we live?

Allow me to quote one of my favorite theologians from your era, Miroslav Volf:

> In a world of violence, the cross, that eminently counter-cultural symbol that lies at the heart of the Christian faith, is a scandal. . . .
>
>   There is no genuinely Christian way around the scandal. In the final analysis, the only available options are either to reject the cross and with it the core of the Christian faith or to take up one's cross, follow the Crucified—and be scandalized ever anew by the challenge.[6]

Think of the powerful witness of that Amish community in Christ in Nickel Mines, Pennsylvania, in 2006, when five innocent children were murdered and five others were injured by a gunman in their schoolroom. Their peacefulness and forgiveness touched the world and continue to do so as the shooter's mother bears witness even today. So does the school built to replace the murder site: New Hope School. It was and is amazing, even from my current vantage point.

You are part of a culture gripped by fear. You are afraid of terrorists in other lands, in your cities, in your schools, and even in your churches. But if you learn to practice peace, then you can legitimately quote my letter to the faithful in Philippi:

> [4]Rejoice in the Lord always; again I will say, Rejoice. [5]Let your gentleness be known to everyone. The Lord is near. [6]Do not worry about anything, but in everything by prayer and supplication with thanksgiving let your requests be made known to God. [7]And the peace of God, which surpasses all understanding, will guard your hearts and your minds in Christ Jesus. [8]Finally, beloved, whatever is true, whatever is honorable, whatever is just, whatever is pure, whatever is pleasing, whatever is commendable, if there is any excellence and if there is anything worthy of praise, think about these things. [9]Keep on doing the things that you have learned and received and heard and seen in me, and the God of peace will be with you. (Phil. 4:4–9)

Again: what a witness, what evangelism this kind of peace could be.

6. Volf, *Exclusion and Embrace*, 26.

If you seek peace and pursue it, you will know the truth of another Scripture text I quote to the Roman churches: "The kingdom of God is . . . righteousness and peace and joy in the Holy Spirit" (Rom. 14:17, borrowed from Ps. 85:10 and Isa. 32:16–18).

This does not mean you will escape danger, for God "has graciously granted you [and me] the privilege not only of believing in Christ, but of suffering for him as well" (Phil. 1:29), though I see precious little of that in North America right now, despite claims to the contrary. But it is clearly happening in other parts of the church elsewhere in the world, and you really do need to "weep with those who weep." That is part of *your* mission—to feel the pain of those who are suffering because of their participation in *God's* mission.

Back to Basics

As usual, I have gotten way ahead of myself. (No wonder your commentary writers cannot agree on how to outline one of my letters.) But now I want to get back to basics. What does it mean to be "in Christ"? Let me begin with a few fundamental points based on rereading my letters while observing your particular situation in North America. I hear this is now called "missional hermeneutics." We simply called it "prophecy."

Community

First, to be in Christ is to be *in community*. I think the problem here is the modern version of the English language. When the King James Version was popular, it was better because you had the singular pronouns "thou" and "thee" and "thy" and "thine" in addition to the plural pronoun "ye." Today all you have is "you" and "your." Furthermore, your English verb forms don't distinguish between singular and plural. Is "Go!" directed at one person or a group? So when my letters and other Scripture passages are read, you English-readers don't realize that most of the "you" pronouns are plural and most of the imperative verbs are plural. For example, to the Philippians I wrote:

> [12]Therefore, my beloved, just as you have always obeyed me, not only in my presence, but much more now in my absence, work out your own salvation with fear and trembling; [13]for it is God who is at work in you, enabling you both to will and to work for his good pleasure. (Phil. 2:12–13)

What I meant is this:

> Therefore, my beloved **brothers and sisters**, just as you have always obeyed ~~me~~ [i.e., God; I did not say "me"], not only in my presence, but much more now in my absence, ~~work out~~ **put into practice** your own **corporate** salvation with fear and trembling; for it is God who is at work ~~in~~ **among** you, enabling **all of** you **together** both to will and to work for his good pleasure.

Do you see the difference? Yes, it is important that individuals put their salvation into practice in daily life, but the point of my letters is to form communities into more faithful communities. Together the church is a witness in the world.

This language problem is a serious spiritual matter. It reinforces Western individualism. It suggests that a person can be a "good Christian" without being part of the church. That may be partly true if you're in prison (I speak from experience), but even there you are part of the church. You come from and return to a particular manifestation of the universal church. I did not say it, but it is true: "Outside the church there is no salvation."

By the way, there are some solutions to your English-language problem. You could learn Spanish, which would be very missionally useful anyhow, especially in the United States, because it has plural pronouns and verbs. Or French, which might not be a bad idea in Canada. Or you could learn my language, Greek. Or you could pick up one of the American regional dialects. Here is a rewrite of Philippians 2:1 that demonstrates the possibilities:

> It is God who is at work among **y'all** / **you all** / **you guys** / **youse guys** / **yinz** / **all y'all**, enabling **y'all** / **you all** / **you guys** / **youse guys** / **yinz** / **all y'all** both to will and to work for his good pleasure.

These two verses from Philippians, by the way, are immediately followed by three that stress the importance of communal witness:

> [14]**You guys** must do all things without murmuring and arguing, [15]so that **y'all** may be blameless and innocent, children of God without blemish in the midst of a crooked and perverse generation, in which **you all together** shine like stars in the world. [16]It is by **y'all's** holding fast to [or "holding forth"] the word of life that I can boast on the day of Christ that I did not run in vain or labor in vain. (Phil. 2:14–16 NRSV alt.)

There has been debate about what I meant in 2:16: holding *forth* the word of life, or holding *fast to* the word of life. This may be a legitimate question for a scholarly essay, but theologically and practically it is a false dichotomy. You would not need to hold fast unless you had first held forth! Only the reality of pushback to a public witness—that is, representing Christ outside the believing community, even if in a private setting like a home—and the corollary temptation to capitulate make sense of what I said. That was the situation in Philippi; the believers' faithful witness got them into trouble, just as it had done to me.

My point is this: when we responded to the gospel and were baptized, we entered a family, a body, and it is as a family and a body, not just as individuals, that we are called to bear witness. As Laceye Warner and her colleague Stephen Chapman have said, evangelism is a "group activity" of "living out the reign of God together" that "entails a whole range of practices, habits, dispositions, activities, and choices."[7] I could not agree more; it is what my team and I practiced and taught.

An Alternative Community

This claim by Warner and Chapman leads to my second point. To be in Christ is to be an *alternative* community, even an alternative *political* community. Your Christian communities need to be more political. Those are dangerous words in your cultural environment, so let me explain carefully.

First, let me emphasize what I do *not* mean. I do not—repeat *not*—mean that you should become more involved in local or national politics. (This is not to say that none of you should seek involvement in politics in this normal sense of the word—a question that would take another letter to address fully—but simply that this is not the kind of politics and political involvement I am talking about here.) Specifically, I do not mean that you should be trying to grab political power or looking for ways to restore Christendom's civic muscle and influence. That was and is a really bad idea. Why? Because the central reality of our gospel, the one message I preached everywhere, is Christ *crucified*—and that is the antithesis of worldly political power. Recall what I said to the Corinthian church:

> [23]We proclaim Christ crucified, a stumbling block to Jews and foolishness to Gentiles, [24]but to those who are the called, both Jews and Greeks, Christ the power of God and the wisdom of God. [25]For God's foolishness is wiser than human wisdom, and God's weakness is stronger than human strength. (1 Cor. 1:23–25)

Let me update and expand this a bit for you:

> We proclaim Christ crucified, a stumbling block to those who connect religion with political power, and foolishness to those who actually have secular status and power. But to those who are the called to bear witness to God's way of life, the crucified Christ is the power of God and the wisdom of God. For God's foolishness is wiser than the wisdom of those who seek to foster civil religion for the supposed good of God and country, and God's weakness is stronger than Western military, political, and economic strength.

What I *do* mean by "political" is that the Christian community is an alternative way of being in the world, an alternative way of being human, an alternative way of ordering relationships, an alternative "body." Actually, it is not only *an* alternative. It is *the* alternative—a sign of the new creation that God has inaugurated in the death and resurrection of Jesus.

7. Chapman and Warner, "Jonah and the Imitation of God," 68, 59.

I made this quite clear to the Philippian faithful. Once again, however, English generally fails you, and this time you *really need to learn Greek*. I wrote to the Philippians,

> [27]Live out your citizenship as God's colony [Gk. *politeuesthe*] within the Roman colony of Philippi in a manner worthy of the gospel of Christ, so that, whether I come and see you or am absent and hear about you, I will know that you are standing firm in one Spirit, striving side by side with one mind for the faith of the gospel, and [28]are in no way intimidated by your opponents. (Phil. 1:27–28a MJG)

Notice what I said here:

- The church is a colony within a colony, a city within a city. It is a "contrast society," as some of your interpreters have called it, but it is not an isolated sect, a "holy huddle," to borrow one of your modern idioms.
- Believers' life together must be worthy of the gospel, must reflect the gospel. This is a process of ongoing conversion, as Roman Catholics (especially) aptly say.
- Believers must stand firm and united in their proclamation of the gospel.
- They must not be intimidated by opposition.

It is no accident that I wrote these words in the Philippian letter shortly before the words I quoted earlier about being children of God, shining like stars, a light to the nations (as Isaiah put it), holding forth the word of life in a culture of death, and holding fast to it even in the face of death.

One of my favorite Christian writers, C. S. Lewis, once penned these words:

> Enemy-occupied territory—that is what this world is. Christianity is the story of how the rightful king has landed, you might say landed in disguise, and is calling us all to take part in a great campaign of sabotage.[8]

(By the way, who would have guessed that C. S. Lewis would anticipate the so-called apocalyptic approach to my theology?)

This benevolent sabotage is not aimed at the state or any other institution. It is not a Christian takeover, a religiously based coup d'état. Rather, as Kavin Rowe of Duke said in describing the gist of my colleague's Acts of the Apostles, "New culture, yes—coup, no."[9] The goal is a complete conversion of the human imagination, as Kavin's own distinguished colleague Richard Hays says in multiple places.[10]

The goal of the church, then, is not to take over anything but to be a foretaste of something—the new creation that has come and is coming. One of my finest interpreters,

---

8. Lewis, *Mere Christianity*, 44. This section of the chapter is titled "The Invasion."
9. Rowe, *World Upside Down*, 5.
10. See, e.g., Hays, *Conversion of the Imagination*.

N. T. Wright, puts it this way: the church is a "microcosmos, a little world . . . the proto-type of what [is] to come."[11] It is, he rightly says, a

> place of reconciliation between God and the world; a place where humans might be rec-onciled to one another; a microcosmos in which the world is contained in a nutshell as a sign of what God intends to do for the whole creation; a new sort of polis in which heaven and earth come together.[12]

This reminds me of an extraordinary documentary I recently saw about the people of the French village of Le Chambon during your horrible Second World War. In the midst of brutality, on the one hand, and the spirit of hatred and revenge, on the other, these simple rural people, under the informal leadership of Pastor André Trocmé, became a "conspiracy of goodness," as the narrator said, rescuing and hiding thousands of Jews in their Christian homes. As Pastor Trocmé said in a church newsletter, alluding to my letter to the Ephesians, they would act only with "the weapons of the Spirit."[13]

You North American Christians speak a lot about being "spiritual," but where are the Trocmés in your churches? Where are the churches of Le Chambon? Your current political and cultural climate is one, quite frankly, not only of fear and death but also of idolatry. You are enslaved to your various -isms: consumerism, racism, nationalism, eth-nocentrism, exceptionalism, Americanism, postmodernism, militarism. What a beautiful thing it would be if you could catch God's vision of what the Spirit was up to in my day and is up to in yours: creating an international network of multicultural, socioeconomi-cally diverse communities joyfully acknowledging Jesus as Lord, truly worshiping God, and, by the power of the Spirit, bearing witness in word and deed to God's work of new creation by conformity to his Son.

I rejoice that some of you ("you" plural) are trying to be and do this now, especially in the midst of the world's worst refugee crisis in a long time. It seems that in-Christ communities in Canada are generally doing a better job of cruciform hospitality than many of those in the United States, where some significant conversion of heart and will is needed. As the Macedonians in northern Greece were an example to the Corinthians in southern Greece, perhaps northern assemblies could once again influence southern-ers. We live in hope.

A Living Exegesis of the Gospel

All of this leads to my third point about being in Christ. To be in Christ as an alternative community is *to be a living exegesis, or faithful interpretation, of the gospel*. It is *to be-come like Christ* and therefore, in a profound sense, *to become the gospel* by becoming a

---

11. Wright, *Paul and the Faithfulness of God*, 1492.
12. Wright, *Paul and the Faithfulness of God*, 1492.
13. *Weapons of the Spirit*, produced and directed by Pierre Sauvage (1987).

communal commentary on it. *That*, brothers and sisters, is true fellowship—participation in God's work. Allow me to quote the important missiologist Lesslie Newbigin:

> I have come to feel that the primary reality of which we have to take account in seeking for a Christian impact on public life is the Christian congregation. How is it possible that the gospel should be credible, that people should come to believe that the power which has the last word in human affairs is represented by a man hanging on a cross? I am suggesting that the only answer, the only hermeneutic [means of interpretation] of the gospel, is a congregation of men and women who believe it and live by it.[14]

I have observed the North American church's fascination with the cross of Jesus. I share this commitment to Christ crucified, as I said to the Corinthian church: "I resolved to know nothing among you except Jesus Christ—that is, Jesus Christ *crucified*" (1 Cor. 2:2 MJG). Of course, this does not eliminate the resurrection, as I will stress shortly. But it does remind us, in the words of one of my insightful interpreters from the last century, that the cross is the signature of the one who is risen.[15] But I sense from your hymns and sermons, your books and tapes, that for you the cross is mostly about the cross as the *source* of your salvation. You are fond of arguing about which "model of the atonement" is correct. Well, of course the death of Jesus is the *source* of our salvation, but it is also the *shape* of our salvation. That's what I mean when I said "work out," or put into practice, your salvation.

So people of the resurrection will always be people of the cross. They will learn to wash feet, as my colleague John reported in his Gospel. I actually wrote a poem about that event, with a short introduction (Phil. 2:5–11). I offer the translation of our mutual friend:

> [5]Cultivate this mindset—this way of thinking, acting, and feeling—in your community, which is in fact a community in the Messiah Jesus:
>
>> [6]Although—and because—he was in the form of God,
>>> he did not regard equality with God as something to be exploited for his own advantage,
>> [7]but rather emptied himself
>>> by taking the form of a slave—
>>> that is, by being born as a human being.
>> And being found in human form,
>>> [8]he humbled himself
>>> by becoming obedient to the point of death—
>>> even death on a cross.

14. Newbigin, *Gospel in a Pluralist Society*, 27, in a chapter entitled "The Congregation as Hermeneutic of the Gospel."
15. Käsemann, "Saving Significance of the Death of Jesus," 56.

> ⁹For this reason God superexalted him
>> and bestowed on him the name
>> that is above every name,
> ¹⁰so that at the name of Jesus
>> every knee will bend—
>> in heaven and on earth and under the earth—
> ¹¹and every tongue will acclaim,
>> "Jesus the Messiah is Lord!"
>> to the glory of God the Father.¹⁶

I am quite pleased that some churches still sing this poem in your time and place. Our translator-friend refers to it as my "master story," and I basically approve of that characterization.¹⁷ It is a story of downward mobility, of renouncing power and prestige and status for the benefit of others, like Jesus' foot washing:

> ²And during supper ³Jesus, knowing that the Father had given all things into his hands, and that he had come from God and was going to God, ⁴got up from the table, took off his outer robe, and tied a towel around himself. ⁵Then he poured water into a basin and began to wash the disciples' feet and to wipe them with the towel that was tied around him. (John 13:2b–5)

Jesus interpreted this for his disciples:

> ¹²After he had washed their feet, had put on his robe, and had returned to the table, he said to them, "Do you know what I have done to you? ¹³You call me Teacher and Lord—and you are right, for that is what I am. ¹⁴So if I, your Lord and Teacher, have washed your feet, you also ought to wash one another's feet. ¹⁵For I have set you an example, that you also should do as I have done to you. ¹⁶Very truly, I tell you, servants are not greater than their master, nor are messengers greater than the one who sent them." (John 13:12–16)

Similarly, I interpreted my poem for the churches on several occasions. Here is the interpretation directly connected to the text of the poem in my letter to the Philippians:

> ¹If then there is any encouragement in Christ, any consolation from love, any sharing in the Spirit, any compassion and sympathy, ²make my joy complete: be of the same mind, having the same love, being in full accord and of one mind. ³Do nothing from selfish ambition or conceit, but in humility regard others as better than yourselves. ⁴Let each of you look not to your own interests, but to the interests of others. (Phil. 2:1–4)

In your tradition, this has generally been called *imitatio Christi*, or the imitation of Christ. Others, including our translator of the poem, also call this "resurrectional cruciformity,"

---

16. See Gorman, *Apostle of the Crucified Lord*, 125–28.
17. See esp. Gorman, *Cruciformity*, 88–92.

or cross-shaped living suffused with the power of Christ's resurrection. Some have insisted that this is not merely *imitation*; it is *participation*. I completely agree. It is about Christ being in us and our being in Christ—individually and together.

You may notice that my poem tells a story. As a narrative of downward mobility, the first stanza has three stages. It has sometimes been described as "although [x] not [y] but [z]," where [x] is status, [y] is selfish exploitation, and [z] is self-giving for others.[18]

So let me cut to the chase, brothers and sisters. Is this what your in-Christ community looks like? Is this how you decide your priorities? Your budget? Your mission activity? If you truly believe that Christ crucified is the power of God, and you want the power of God to be at work in and through your Christian community, you will seek to become a community shaped by my master story—which is really God's master story. *Now this may be the most important thing I say in this letter*: You see, the crucified Jesus was a Christophany—revealing what the Messiah is like. But it is also a *theophany*—revealing what *God* is like. And it is also an *ecclesio*phany—revealing what the church is supposed to be like. And ultimately it is also an *anthro*phany—revealing what human beings are meant to be like.

It may appear from Philippians 2 and John 13 that this kind of servanthood is only for life within the community. But that is not what Jesus or John meant, nor I.[19] If you read my letter and John's Gospel carefully, you will see that this self-giving love is meant to be offered to all people. It is what defines you as a Christian community—and what may very well get you in trouble when you take it to the streets. Just read the first chapter of my letter to the Philippians, or the book of Acts, or what happens to the foot-washing Jesus and his disciples. The church's inner and public lives must match, just as the individual believer's private and public lives must match. That is why I told Philemon that the slave Onesimus, newly converted to Christ, was coming back to him "no longer as a slave but more than a slave, a beloved brother . . . both in the flesh and in the Lord" (Philem. 16). In the flesh means "out there in the world" and "in the Lord" means right here in the church.

To participate in the mission of God is to discern, in your particular context, what it means to embody the story of Jesus and thus to "become"—please note the quotation marks—the gospel to and for all. "Become" not in the sense of replacing the gospel, as if you or I were the savior, but in the sense of bearing witness to it in a coherent individual and corporate life of word and deed. And "all" in the sense of the "all" of your world, as you experience it, whether near or far. I made it quite clear on several occasions that we are called to reach out to all, beyond our own churches, but not everyone reads my letters as carefully as they should. I offer just two examples, from one of my earliest

18. See Gorman, *Cruciformity*, 90–91, 164–77, 186–88, 192, 197, 230–38, 243, 252, 261, 330; Gorman, *Apostle of the Crucified Lord*, 80–81, 125–26, 310, 507–9; and elsewhere in his work, including chaps. 1–3 of the present book.

19. For the Gospel of John, see Gorman, *Abide and Go*.

letters (emphasis original): "Increase and abound in love for one another *and for all*" (1 Thess. 3:12); "See that none of you repays evil for evil, but always seek to do good to one another *and to all*" (1 Thess. 5:15).

The paradox in all this is that life comes through death. The life of the world comes through the death of the Messiah, not least because God raised him from the dead. So too, life for the world comes through our cross-shaped existence, which is, paradoxically, being raised to newness of life. I know, it makes no sense at all. But it is true. I experienced it throughout my life, and I wrote about it numerous times, most extensively in my second canonical letter to the Corinthian believers. Of many lines I could quote, here are just a few:

> [8]We are afflicted in every way, but not crushed; perplexed, but not driven to despair; [9]perse-cuted, but not forsaken; struck down, but not destroyed; [10]always carrying in the body the death of Jesus, so that the life of Jesus may also be made visible in our bodies. [11]For while we live, we are always being given up to death for Jesus' sake, so that the life of Jesus may be made visible in our mortal flesh. [12]So death is at work in us, but life in you. (2 Cor. 4:8–12)

Becoming like God

I have just mentioned that the crucified Messiah is an ecclesiophany, revealing what the church is supposed to be like, and an anthrophany, revealing what human beings are meant to be like. *My fourth point is that to be in Christ is to become what God is like, because God in Christ became like us.* I want to explain this a bit more fully by quoting again from my second letter to the Corinthians:

> [14]For the love of Christ urges us on, because we are convinced that one has died for all; therefore all have died. [15]And he died for all, so that those who live might live no longer for themselves, but for him who died and was raised for them.
>
> [16]From now on, therefore, we regard no one from a human point of view; even though we once knew Christ from a human point of view, we know him no longer in that way. [17]So if anyone is in Christ, there is a new creation: everything old has passed away; see, every-thing has become new! [18]All this is from God, who reconciled us to himself through Christ, and has given us the ministry of reconciliation; [19]that is, in Christ God was reconciling the world to himself, not counting their trespasses against them, and entrusting the message of reconciliation to us. [20]So we are ambassadors for Christ, since God is making his appeal through us; we entreat you on behalf of Christ, be reconciled to God. [21]For our sake he made him to be sin who knew no sin, so that in him we might become the righteousness [or justice] of God. (2 Cor. 5:14–21)

This, by the way, is one of my favorite passages. Yes, I was specifically referring to my colleagues and myself as Christ's ambassadors. But I was implying that all believ-ers are ambassadors. Look at the last verse: all of us in Christ are becoming God's righteousness. What a powerful line about transformation! As my early theological successors like Irenaeus and Athanasius said, "He became what we are so that we could become what he is." More recently, one of my very best interpreters, Richard Hays, said this:

> [Paul] does not say "that we might *know about* the righteousness of God," nor "that we might *believe in* the righteousness of God," nor even "that we might *receive* the righteousness of God." Instead, the church is to *become* the righteousness of God: where the church embodies in its life together the world-reconciling love of Jesus Christ, the new creation is manifest. The church incarnates the righteousness of God.[20]

(I am always pleased when an interpreter says something even better than I did.)

What Richard and I are saying is this: God's mission is to "put the world to rights," as Tom Wright likes to say. The prophetic promises of God for a new creation are coming true. That means that God's righteousness—God's saving character and transformative activity that bring about God's kind of justice and *shalom*—is happening now, and we get to be part of it! Yes, it's about individuals being reconciled with God and being transformed into people who no longer live for themselves but for Christ. But it's about much more than that too. It's about those individuals becoming the kind of community that faithfully represents the God who re-creates, rectifies, and renews because God has the whole world in his hand, as you like to sing.

This transformation has sometimes been referred to as "missional theosis."[21] Theosis, or deification, refers to the process of becoming like God by participating in the life of God. This is not a term known to everyone in your time and place, but it's a good one. One of the term's chief proponents even adds more adjectives to the phrase and calls it "communal, cruciform, resurrectional, missional theosis." It means that we become like God when we participate together in the cross-shaped mission and life of God, Father, Son, and Spirit.

Lest you think that either I or some ancient or contemporary Christian theologian invented this idea out of the blue, recall the scriptural mandate, "You shall be holy, for I am holy" (Lev. 11:45; 19:2; 20:26). More specifically, with special relevance for your missional context, recall the words of Deuteronomy, one of my favorite books:

> [14]Although heaven and the heaven of heavens belong to the LORD your God, the earth with all that is in it, [15]yet the LORD set his heart in love on your ancestors alone and chose you, their descendants after them, out of all the peoples, as it is today. [16]Circumcise, then, the foreskin of your heart, and do not be stubborn any longer. [17]For the LORD your God is God of gods and Lord of lords, the great God, mighty and awesome, who is not partial and takes no bribe, [18]who executes justice for the orphan and the widow, and who loves the strangers,

---

20. Hays, *Moral Vision of the New Testament*, 24.
21. See, e.g., Gorman, *Becoming the Gospel*. For a more technical account, see chap. 9 of the present volume.

providing them food and clothing. [19]You shall also love the stranger, for you were strangers in the land of Egypt. (Deut. 10:14–19)

The Lord loves you; the Lord loves the stranger; you too should love the stranger. Then you will be like God. That is missional theosis. (But if you don't care for that word, I would encourage you to find a good substitute.)

A Practical Word before the Conclusion

Before I conclude, I should offer a few practical words about implementing this vision. With the Spirit's help, it is not as difficult as it might appear.

First of all, work at caring for one another and unity in your own congregation. It will spill over to other contexts.

Second, as I told everyone, but especially the Corinthian believers, flee from sexual immorality and idolatry, including especially the false gods of Rights and Power. These are the fundamental sins of every culture I know, but especially yours, and they undermine your integrity as a missional contrast society. Absolute Rights and Absolute Power are absolutely idolatrous. Embrace virtue, and there you will find the joy of the Lord. Embrace weakness, and there you will find the power of God.

Third, as I also told the Corinthians, speak and live the gospel not only in your fellowship but also with your unbelieving family members at home (see 1 Cor. 7:10–16) and with your friends (see 1 Cor. 10:23–11:1).

Finally, for now, as I (once again) also told the Corinthians, make your worship services truly missional. You are fighting about what kind of music, worship style, "messages," and doughnuts or bagels will be most "appealing" to seekers. You are trying to make the gospel palatable. That strategy is demeaning both to our Lord and to those seekers. You have no business trying to make the gospel *palatable*, but you should, as I told the Corinthians (1 Cor. 14), make it *intelligible*.

"You should" means each of you and all of you. It should be clear that my emphasis in this letter on you-plural does not cancel out the importance of you-singular. As our African brothers and sisters say, "I am because we are"—but the "I" has not disappeared.

Conclusion

I lived in the time *before* Christendom in the Roman Empire. You now live in the time *after* Christendom in North America. So our contexts are remarkably similar despite all the differences. I therefore resonate with the words of Bryan Stone, who summarizes his book *Evangelism after Christendom* as follows:

> The most evangelistic thing the church can do today is to be the church—to be formed imaginatively by the Holy Spirit through core practices such as worship, forgiveness, hospitality,

and economic sharing into a distinctive people in the world, a new social option, the body of Christ.[22]

My last words for you would be these, which I consider to be a commissioning prayer. I hope that it will inspire the conversion of your imagination as you—plural and singular— try to discern where and how God is calling you to be the church more fully and thereby to participate in the saving, healing mission of God in your part of the world.

> [14]For this reason I bow my knees before the Father, [15]from whom every family in heaven and on earth takes its name. [16]I pray that, according to the riches of his glory, he may grant that you may be strengthened in your inner being with power through his Spirit, [17]and that Christ may dwell in your hearts through faith, as you are being rooted and grounded in love. [18]I pray that you may have the power to comprehend, with all the saints, what is the breadth and length and height and depth, [19]and to know the love of Christ that surpasses knowledge, so that you may be filled with all the fullness of God.
>
> [20]Now to him who by the power at work within us is able to accomplish abundantly far more than all we can ask or imagine, [21]to him be glory in the church and in Christ Jesus to all generations, forever and ever. Amen. (Eph. 3:14–21)

---

22. Stone, *Evangelism after Christendom*, 15.

eleven

Paul on Practicing and Preaching the Resurrection Today

When Paul resolved to know nothing but Jesus Christ crucified (1 Cor. 2:2), he did not in any way mean to neglect the resurrection.[1] Whether we think of the first century or the twenty-first, the resurrection is both a central and a controversial part of Christian theology and experience. Today, however, we often hear about those who challenge the possibility of resurrection—whether Christ's or ours—both outside and inside the Christian church. Richard Hays, the highly respected New Testament scholar, bluntly describes the situation this way:

> On the issue of resurrection, many preachers and New Testament scholars are unwitting partisans of the Sadducees. Because they deny the truth of Scripture's proclamation that God raised Jesus from the dead—or waffle about it—they leave the church in a state of uncertainty, lacking confidence in its mission, knowing neither the Scriptures nor the power of God.

Hays goes on to say this: "The recent history of theology is replete with attempts to reinterpret the meaning of the New Testament's resurrection in ways that will not conflict with a modern scientific worldview."[2] Hays points out the views of the most influential advocates of this perspective from the last hundred years, including Rudolf Bultmann, Gerd Lüdemann, Bishop John

---

1. Neither do interpreters of Paul who emphasize the cross (including the present writer) mean to minimize the resurrection.
2. Hays, "Reading Scripture in Light of the Resurrection," 216.

Spong, and Robert Funk, as well as the stream of New Atheists who try to debunk the entire Christian faith.

The situation was much the same already in the earliest days of the church. When Paul preached about the resurrection of the dead to the intellectuals of his day, some believed, but others scoffed, according to Luke (Acts 17:32). And much to his chagrin, after Paul preached the resurrection to the Corinthians (1 Cor. 15:1–4), some in the Corinthian church began to say that "there is no resurrection of the dead" (1 Cor. 15:12). Paul then proceeded to write the text on the resurrection that has been foundational and formative for two thousand years of Christian history, 1 Corinthians 15.

We cannot here consider every facet of the biblical witness to the resurrection and how that witness should affect our preaching and living. We will focus, of course, on the apostle Paul, with just a few side glances to the gospel narratives. In our own day of skepticism and misunderstanding about many basic Christian convictions, what can we learn from Paul concerning the theological and spiritual significance of Christ's resurrection and of ours? How might Paul inform our living and preaching? We may approach this topic from four angles, beginning with Christ's resurrection itself.

The Critical Importance of Christ's Resurrection

For the apostle Paul, the resurrection of Christ was not merely one among many Christian convictions; it was the one that guaranteed the significance of all others and provided the rationale for the life of faith, hope, and love expected of those who live in Christ. From Paul's perspective, to deny or misinterpret the resurrection is to undermine the Christian faith.

In his response to the Corinthians who denied the resurrection of the dead, Paul argued logically that if there is no resurrection of the dead, then Christ has not been raised. And if Christ has not been raised, he says, "your faith is futile [CEB, "worthless"] and you are still in your sins" (1 Cor. 15:17). That is, Christ's death on the cross for sins (see 1 Cor. 15:3) has no saving significance without the resurrection. It is merely the Roman crucifixion of a false messiah. Furthermore, the apostle asserts, if Christ is not raised, then

> [18]those also who have died in Christ have perished. [19]If for this life only we have hoped in Christ, we are of all people most to be pitied. . . . [32]If the dead are not raised, "Let us eat and drink, / for tomorrow we die." (1 Cor. 15:18–19, 32b)

In other words, the dead are dead, there is no hope of eternal life, and the idea of living a life of sacrificial devotion to God and others in the present is simply absurd. Instead, let's party! Death is the end, and the only logical thing to do is to enjoy this life to the max: *Carpe diem*. I am reminded of a recent obituary, written by the deceased himself in anticipation of his death, with instructions for the celebration of his life:

> There can be no religion of any kind at my funeral nor any service in a church. And if anyone claims at the end of my life that I accepted the Lord Jesus Christ as my savior, know that they are lying. I've spent my life as an atheist. That's the way I'll die. And hope that hell has been way oversold. . . . Don't say my life was worthwhile because I inspired one person or . . . changed somebody's life. I don't care if my life was worthwhile and have no illusions it should be. . . . [But] I really loved life.[3]

It is unlikely that the naysayers of resurrection in Paul's day or ours recognize the grave consequences of their disbelief. It is one of the tasks of Christian preaching and formation to make these consequences clear.

The Meaning of Christ's Resurrection

Most Christians rightly associate the resurrection of Jesus with the gift of eternal life, and we will return to this topic below. But eternal life does not exhaust the meaning of the resurrection, nor is that topic the best starting point in considering the resurrection. Most Christians also associate the resurrection with the obvious: Jesus is no longer dead but alive: "The Lord is risen indeed" (see Luke 24:34), as we proclaim, or, as many of our hymns put it, "He arose."

Paul, to be sure, does not think Christ is dead. Rather, he exclaims, "But in fact Christ has been raised from the dead" (1 Cor. 15:20a). The wording here is critically important: "Christ has been raised," rather than "Christ arose," implies that someone has raised Christ from the dead. That someone, of course, is God the Father, and Paul almost always uses language about Christ's resurrection that explicitly affirms or implies God's raising of Jesus. By doing so, Paul tells us that the resurrection is God's vindication of Jesus, God's stamp of approval on how Jesus lived and died. Jesus' death, and the life that led to it, are neither misguided nor meaningless. His death was indeed God's provision for the forgiveness of our sins and our liberation from the very power of Sin itself. Moreover, Jesus' life and death reveal the way that

---

3. Out of respect for the family of the deceased, I have not revealed the author of this quotation.

God operates in the world and the way God wants us as the people of God to operate in this world too (1 Cor. 1:18–2:5).

To proclaim *God's* resurrection of Jesus, rather than simply Christ's resurrection, does not diminish Jesus or his significance. Rather, it increases it. God's resurrection of Jesus means that we can, indeed we must, take the way of Jesus seriously. His way is God's way, and therefore our way in and through this world.

Furthermore, in the resurrection of Jesus, God demonstrates that sin, evil, and death do not have the final word in God's world. We know that the twin enemies of the human race, Sin and Death, will be defeated (1 Cor. 15:55–57). In fact, God's resurrection of Jesus initiates a new age characterized by resurrection to new life (power over Sin) in the present and bodily resurrection to eternal life (victory over Death) in the future. We can participate in that new age by sharing in God's resurrection of Jesus through the experience of death and resurrection contained in, and symbolized by, baptism (more on this below).

We must stress here one key point that contemporary Christians often fail to understand or try to avoid: that Christ's resurrection was a *bodily* resurrection. Paul was a Pharisee, not a Platonist, and he did not believe in the immortality of a body-less soul. Bodily resurrection does not mean simply the resuscitation of a corpse, but neither is it merely symbolic language for Christ's ongoing existence in the church as his body, or something similar. *The resurrection is certainly a mystery, but it is not a metaphor.* As N. T. Wright has pointed out in his book *The Resurrection of the Son of God*, in the ancient world early Christian talk of Jesus' bodily resurrection would not have been mistaken as code language for Jesus' living on in the memory of the church, or for a sense of new life within the community. God's resurrection of Jesus means that God takes the created order with the utmost seriousness. Docetism is out for good: flesh matters; bodies matter; creation matters.

Paul's Corinthian audience was apparently confused about the corporeality of resurrection too, so the apostle develops some elaborate analogies to help the Corinthians understand that bodily resurrection means transformation and thus both continuity and discontinuity with respect to our current bodily existence (1 Cor. 15:35–57; see also Luke 24:13–35; John 21:1–14). But resurrection is nonetheless a bodily experience. Paul would have agreed with later Christian writers who repeatedly urged, "What Christ has not assumed [taken on himself], he does not redeem." But Paul might have stated it as follows: "Christ has in fact redeemed that which he assumed [that is, the body]." As we will see below, this has much significance for Christian ethics and mission.

The Present and Future Resurrection of Believers

When contemporary Christians think of their own resurrection, they most often imagine the future reality of eternal life with God, however they conceive of that reality. Paul would certainly not deny the reality—the (transformed) bodily reality—of our future resurrection to eternal life with God (Rom. 5:21; 6:22–23; Gal. 6:8), but he also stresses the present reality of resurrection now. Without neglecting the promise of eternal life, especially in the context of funerals, contemporary Christian preaching needs to pay much more attention to this present reality. Otherwise, the meaning of Christ's resurrection devolves into an occasional celebration of the past (he arose) and the future (eternal life), rather than a past event and future promise with present consequences.

It is true that every Christian funeral is an occasion to offer the hope of eternal life, but it is also the occasion to celebrate a life that, however imperfectly, was lived in the presence and power of the risen Jesus. It is also true that every Sunday is a little Easter, but it is equally true that every *day* for the Christian is a little Easter. Or, to be more Pauline, every day is both a death and resurrection—an embodiment of the Paschal Mystery (a term used especially by Roman Catholics that should be adopted by other Christians too). The life that corresponds to the Paschal Mystery is the participationist spirituality we have designated "resurrectional cruciformity."

In baptism, Paul says, we have shared in Christ's death and resurrection (Rom. 6). Our old self was crucified with Christ (Rom. 6:6), and a new self was raised from the dead so that "just as Christ was raised from the dead by the glory of the Father, we too might live in newness of life" (Rom. 6:4). Paul describes this "newness of life" as dying to sin and living to God (Rom. 6:6, 11). The final outcome of this new life is future eternal life (Rom. 6:5, 22–23), but the main emphasis in Paul's words about baptism is not on future resurrection but on present resurrection—"alive to God in Christ Jesus" (Rom. 6:11). When this present resurrection is properly understood as resurrectional *cruciformity*, the concerns that some have expressed about a present experience of resurrection should disappear.[4]

Preaching about resurrection, whether at Easter, at baptisms and funerals, or throughout the year, should reflect Paul's emphasis far more than it usually does. We misinterpret resurrection and mislead both Christians and others if we convey the idea that resurrection is primarily about "going to heaven when you die." Resurrection is first of all about new life here and now. It is

---

4. The most commonly expressed concern is that speaking of a present experience of resurrection is triumphalistic, especially since it allegedly privileges the "already" and ignores the "not yet" of the kingdom of God/salvation.

about putting on Christ in baptism (Gal. 3:27) and then doing so every day thereafter (Rom. 13:14). This way of looking at resurrection has some critical consequences for Christian living—for spirituality, ethics, and mission.

The Spiritual and Ethical Consequences of Resurrection

The significance for Paul of resurrection to new life could hardly be overestimated. On every page of his letters, he is urging his congregations to embody the new life they have in Christ. We may briefly mention four dimensions of this new life.

First, the new life we live is in fact *the life of Christ within us*. It is a life of *participation*. If Christ has been raised, then he is not dead but alive, and he comes to inhabit his people, both individually and corporately, to infuse them with his very life, which is in fact the life of God: "I myself no longer live, but the Messiah lives in me; and the life I do now live in the flesh, I live by means of the faithfulness of the Son of God, who loved me by giving himself for me" (Gal. 2:19–20 MJG). Too often contemporary Christians underestimate and underutilize the indwelling power of Christ.

Preaching that highlights this aspect of the resurrection will focus on God's transforming and re-creating power. This is not mere metaphor ("Christ's resurrection really means you can have a fresh start") but an affirmation of the nature of God and of God's action in the world. The God of the resurrection is a God of life-giving power. The preacher who believes this will say that the God who brought creation into existence and brought Christ out of the grave is at work in our community, in your life and mine. As the opening prayer in Ephesians says:

> [17]I pray that the God of our Lord Jesus Christ, the Father of glory, may give you a spirit of wisdom and revelation as you come to know him, [18]so that, with the eyes of your heart enlightened, you may know what is the hope to which he has called you, what are the riches of his glorious inheritance among the saints, [19]and *what is the immeasurable greatness of his power for us who believe, according to the working of his great power.* [20]God put this power to work in Christ when he raised him from the dead and seated him at his right hand in the heavenly places. (Eph. 1:17–20, emphasis added)

Second, as the term "resurrectional cruciformity" stresses, the resurrection to new life is—paradoxically—*a life shaped by the cross*. In being raised to new life, we do not leave the cross behind. Not only is our crucifixion with Christ an ongoing experience (again, Gal. 2:19–20), but the very shape of the resurrection life is cross-shaped, or cruciform. That is, the life that Christ lives in us by the power of his Spirit is an extension of the life of obedience to God and love for others that landed him on a Roman cross. Christ's self-giving generosity, service, and hospitality (2 Cor. 8:9; Phil. 2:1–11; Rom. 15:1–3) continue their life in the life of his people. Participating in Christ's resurrection life is a *cruciform* new life.[5]

Preaching that highlights this aspect of the resurrection will also focus on God's transforming and re-creating power. But in doing so, it will recall that Christ crucified is the power of God (1 Cor. 1:18–25). Therefore, God's power is revealed in and through our weakness (2 Cor. 12:9) and through our conformity to Christ's self-giving, life-giving death (2 Cor. 4:8–18). What an odd truth! It leads to the next dimension of resurrection.

Third, the resurrection life is *a countercultural, or alter-cultural, existence* that values the body as God's temple and is dedicated in mind and body to the service of God and others (Rom. 12:1–2). Unlike our culture more broadly, we Christians know (or ought to know) with Paul that our bodies belong to God (1 Cor. 6:19–20) and that God will one day raise them (1 Cor. 6:14). Thus our bodies are to be offered to God (Rom. 6:12–23) in ways that reflect their dignity, purpose, and final end. Good preaching and formation will consistently explore the implications of this kind of bodily resurrection existence for our sexual lives, our vocations, our use of time and money, and much else. The resurrection, in other words, is the foundation of all we are and do.

Preaching that highlights this aspect of the resurrection will help people understand the close connection between misunderstanding of, or disbelief in, the resurrection and daily decisions about lifestyle. Without resurrection, Paul says, the life of faith, hope, and love is an existential mistake that should be replaced with unadulterated hedonism: "If the dead are not raised, 'Let us eat and drink, for tomorrow we die'" (1 Cor. 15:32b). *With* resurrection, every bodily activity becomes a means of worshiping our resurrecting, life-giving, body-valuing God: "The body is meant not for fornication [sexual immorality] but for the Lord, and the Lord for the body. . . . Do you not know that your body is a temple of the Holy Spirit within you, which you have from God, and that you are not your own? For you were bought with a price; therefore glorify God in your body" (1 Cor. 6:13b, 19–20).

Fourth and finally, the resurrection life is *a missional life*. Paul concludes his great chapter on the resurrection with these words: "Therefore, my beloved, be steadfast, immovable, always excelling in the work of the Lord, because you know that in the Lord your labor is not in vain" (1 Cor. 15:58). The

5. For more on resurrectional cruciformity, see esp. chap. 3.

resurrection of Jesus is the divine sign that Jesus is Lord, so we proclaim him to one and all. The resurrection of Jesus is the divine sign that bodies matter, so we feed the hungry and clothe the naked, and we work for (God's kind of) justice on earth. The resurrection of Jesus is the divine sign that God will in fact redeem and restore the creation, so we take care of the earth. And so on.

Preaching that highlights this aspect of the resurrection will help the church make the connection between creation and re-creation. It will remind faithful listeners that the church lives within the grand story of God's mission in the world. The resurrection of Jesus gives us the incentive and the power to join in that mission, as well as the hope that our efforts will not be in vain. At the same time, because we cannot separate the resurrection from the cross, we will avoid any hint of triumphalism or of a "crusader" mentality. The mission inspired by Christ's resurrection, like all of Christian living, still takes the form of the cross.

Final Reflection

No preacher can possibly say everything that needs to be said about Christ's resurrection and ours in one sermon—or even in one lifetime. But the people of God are, I believe, dying for news of the resurrection and its meaning for their *daily* life as well as their eternal life. Preachers, teachers, and others entrusted with the task of Christian formation have the tremendous responsibility—and privilege—of sharing in God's work of transforming the church's imagination and its daily life through the message of Christ's resurrection. Paul's theology and spirituality of participatory resurrectional cruciformity is a rich resource for that transformation.

Bibliography

Adams, Edward. "Abraham's Faith and Gentile Disobedience: Textual Links between Romans 1 and 4." *JSNT* 65 (1997): 47–66.

Aernie, Jeffrey W. "Faith, Judgment, and the Believer: A Reassessment of 2 Corinthians 5:6–10." *CBQ* 79 (2017): 438–54.

———. "Participation in Christ: An Analysis of Pauline Soteriology." *HBT* 37 (2015): 50–68.

Aletti, Jean-Noël. "God Made Christ to Be Sin: Reflections on a Pauline Paradox." In *The Redemption: An Interdisciplinary Symposium on Christ as Redeemer*, edited by S. T. Davis, D. Kendall, and G. O'Collins, 101–20. New York: Oxford University Press, 2004.

Ayres, Lewis. "Deification and the Dynamics of Nicene Theology: The Contribution of Gregory of Nyssa." *SVTQ* 49 (2005): 375–95.

Baker, Mark D., and Joel B. Green. *Recovering the Scandal of the Cross: Atonement in New Testament and Contemporary Context*. 2nd ed. Downers Grove, IL: IVP Academic, 2011.

Baker, Mary Patton. "Participating in the Body and Blood of Christ: Christian κοινωνία [*koinōnia*] and the Lord's Supper." In Thate, Vanhoozer, and Campbell, *"In Christ" in Paul*, 503–28.

Barber, Michael P., and John A. Kincaid. "Cultic Theosis in Paul and Second Temple Judaism." *JSPL* 5 (2015): 237–56.

Barclay, John M. G. "'Because He Was Rich He Became Poor': Translation, Exegesis, and Hermeneutics in the Reading of 2 Cor 8.9." In *Theologizing in the Corinthian Conflict: Studies in the Exegesis and Theology of 2 Corinthians*, edited by Reimund Bieringer, Marilou S. Ibita, Dominika A. Kurek-Chomycz, and Thomas A. Vollmer, 331–44. BTS 16. Leuven: Peeters, 2013.

———. "Manna and the Circulation of Grace: A Study of 2 Corinthians 8:1–15." In *The Word Leaps the Gap: Essays on Theology and Scripture in Honor of Richard B. Hays*, edited by J. Ross Wagner, C. Kavin Rowe, and A. Katherine Grieb, 409–26. Grand Rapids: Eerdmans, 2008.

———. *Paul and the Gift*. Grand Rapids: Eerdmans, 2015.

Barram, Michael. *Missional Economics: Biblical Justice and Christian Formation*. Grand Rapids: Eerdmans, 2018.

Barrett, C. K. *The Second Epistle to the Corinthians*. BNTC. London: A. & C. Black, 1973.

Barth, Markus. "Jews and Gentiles: The Social Character of Justification in Paul." *JES* 5 (1968): 241–67.

Barton, Stephen C. "Spirituality and the Emotions in Early Christianity: The Case of Joy." In *The Bible and Spirituality: Exploratory Essays in Reading Scripture Spiritually*, edited by Andrew T. Lincoln, J. Gordon McConville, and Lloyd K. Pietersen, 171–93. Eugene, OR: Cascade, 2013.

Bates, Matthew W. *Salvation by Allegiance Alone: Rethinking Faith, Works, and the Gospel of Jesus the King*. Grand Rapids: Baker Academic, 2017.

Bauckham, Richard. *Jesus and the God of Israel: God Crucified and Other Studies on the New Testament's Christology of Divine Identity*. Grand Rapids: Eerdmans, 2008.

Betz, Hans Dieter. *Galatians: A Commentary on Paul's Letter to the Churches in Galatia*. Hermeneia. Philadelphia: Fortress, 1979.

Billings, J. Todd. *Union with Christ: Reframing Theology and Ministry for the Church*. Grand Rapids: Baker Academic, 2011.

Bird, Michael F. *An Anomalous Jew: Paul among Jews, Greeks, and Romans*. Grand Rapids: Eerdmans, 2016.

———. *The Saving Righteousness of God: Studies on Paul, Justification, and the New Perspective*. Paternoster Biblical Monographs. Eugene, OR: Wipf and Stock, 2007.

Bird, Michael F., and Preston M. Sprinkle, eds. *The Faith of Jesus Christ: Exegetical, Biblical, and Theological Studies*. Milton Keynes, UK: Paternoster, 2009.

Blackwell, Ben C. *Christosis: Engaging Paul's Soteriology with His Patristic Interpreters*. Grand Rapids: Eerdmans, 2016. Originally published as *Christosis: Pauline Soteriology in Light of Deification in Irenaeus and Cyril of Alexandria*. WUNT 2/314. Tübingen: Mohr Siebeck, 2011.

———. "Immortal Glory and the Problem of Death in Romans 3.23." *JSNT* 32 (2010): 285–308.

———. "Theosis in the New Testament?" Paper presented in a session of the Theological Interpretation of Scripture Seminar, Society of Biblical Literature Annual Meeting, Baltimore, MD, November 23–26, 2013.

Blackwell, Ben C., John K. Goodrich, and Jason Maston, eds. *Paul and the Apocalyptic Imagination*. Minneapolis: Fortress, 2016.

Boakye, Andrew. *Death and Life: Resurrection, Restoration, and Rectification in Paul's Letter to the Galatians*. Eugene, OR: Pickwick, 2017.

———. "Inhabiting the 'Resurrectiform' God: Death and Life as Theological Headline in Paul." *ExpTim* 128, no. 2 (November 2016): 53–62.

Bockmuehl, Markus. *The Epistle to the Philippians*. BNTC. Peabody, MA: Hendrickson, 1998.

Bonhoeffer, Dietrich. *Discipleship*. Translated by Barbara Green and Reinhard Krauss. Dietrich Bonhoeffer Works 4. Minneapolis: Fortress, 2001.

Bowens, Lisa M. "Investigating the Apocalyptic Texture of Paul's Martial Imagery in 2 Corinthians 4–6." *JSNT* 39 (2016): 3–15.

Boyer, James L. "Relative Clauses in the Greek New Testament: A Statistical Study." *Grace Theological Journal* 9 (1988): 233–56.

Bray, Gerald, ed. *1–2 Corinthians*. ACCSNT 7. Downers Grove, IL: InterVarsity, 1999.

Bruce, F. F. *1 and 2 Corinthians*. New Century Bible Commentary. Grand Rapids: Eerdmans, 1971.

Burnett, David. "'So Shall Your Seed Be': Paul's Use of Genesis 15:5 in Romans 4:18 in Light of Early Jewish Deification Traditions." *JSPL* 5 (2015): 211–36.

Cadbury, Henry J. "The Relative Pronouns in Acts and Elsewhere." *JBL* 42 (1923): 150–57.

Caird, G. B. *Paul's Letters from Prison in the Revised Standard Version*. NCB. Oxford: Oxford University Press, 1976.

Calvin, John. *Commentary on Corinthians*, vol. 2. http://www.ccel.org/ccel/calvin/calcom40.xi.iii.html (2 Cor. 5:13–17); http://www.ccel.org/ccel/calvin/calcom40.xi.iv.html (2 Cor. 5:18–21).

Campbell, Constantine R. "Metaphor, Reality, and Union with Christ." In Thate, Vanhoozer, and Campbell, *"In Christ" in Paul*, 61–86.

———. *Paul and Union with Christ: An Exegetical and Theological Study*. Grand Rapids: Zondervan, 2012.

Campbell, Douglas A. *The Deliverance of God: An Apocalyptic Rereading of Justification in Paul*. Grand Rapids: Eerdmans, 2009.

———. "Participation and Faith in Paul." In Thate, Vanhoozer, and Campbell, *"In Christ" in Paul*, 37–60.

———. *Pauline Dogmatics: The Triumph of God's Love*. Grand Rapids: Eerdmans, 2019.

Campbell, William Sanger. "Unity in the Community: Rereading Galatians 2:15–21." In Downs and Skinner, *Unrelenting God*, 226–41.

Canlis, Julie. *Calvin's Ladder: A Spiritual Theology of Ascent and Ascension*. Grand Rapids: Eerdmans, 2010.

Capes, David B. *The Divine Christ: Paul, the Lord Jesus, and the Scriptures of Israel.* Grand Rapids: Baker Academic, 2018.

Chapman, Stephen B., and Laceye Warner. "Jonah and the Imitation of God: Rethinking Evangelism and the Old Testament." *JTI* 2 (2008): 43–69.

Chester, Stephen J. *Reading Paul with the Reformers: Reconciling Old and New Perspectives.* Grand Rapids: Eerdmans, 2017.

Christensen, Michael J. "John Wesley: Christian Perfection as Faith Filled with the Energy of Love." In Christensen and Wittung, *Partakers of the Divine Nature*, 219–31.

Christensen, Michael J., and Jeffery A. Wittung, eds. *Partakers of the Divine Nature: The History and Development of Deification in the Christian Traditions.* Grand Rapids: Baker Academic, 2007.

Claussen, Carsten. "Albert Schweitzer's Understanding of Righteousness by Faith according to Paul's Letter to the Romans." Paper presented at the Annual Meeting of the Society of Biblical Literature, San Diego, 2007. https://www.vanderbilt.edu /AnS/religious_studies/SBL2007/Claussen.pdf.

Collins, Raymond F. *Second Corinthians.* PCNT. Grand Rapids: Baker Academic, 2013.

Cooper, Jordan. *Christification: A Lutheran Approach to Theosis.* Eugene, OR: Wipf and Stock, 2014.

Davey, Wesley Thomas. *Suffering as Participation with Christ in the Pauline Corpus.* Minneapolis: Fortress, 2019.

Davies, Jamie. *Paul among the Apocalypses? An Evaluation of the "Apocalyptic Paul" in the Context of Jewish and Christian Apocalyptic Literature.* LNTS. London: T&T Clark, 2016.

———. "The Two Ages and Salvation History in Paul's Apocalyptic Imagination: A Comparison of *4 Ezra* and Galatians." In Blackwell, Goodrich, and Maston, *Paul and the Apocalyptic Imagination*, 339–59.

de Boer, Martinus C. "Cross and Cosmos in Galatians." In Downs and Skinner, *Unrelenting God*, 208–25.

———. *Galatians: A Commentary.* NTL. Louisville: Westminster John Knox, 2011.

Deissmann, Adolf. *Die neutestamentliche Formel "in Christo Jesu."* Marburg: Elwert, 1892.

———. *Paul: A Study in Social and Religious History.* 2nd ed. London: Hodder and Stoughton, 1926 (German orig., 1925).

———. *The Religion of Jesus and the Faith of Paul: The Selly Oak Lectures, 1923, on the Communion of Jesus with God and the Communion of Paul with Christ.* Translated by William E. Wilson. London: Hodder and Stoughton, 1923. https://ia 802205.us.archive.org/26/items/religionofjesusf00deisuoft/religionofjesusf00deis uoft_bw.pdf.

deSilva, David A. *Galatians: A Handbook on the Greek Text.* Waco: Baylor University Press, 2014.

Despotis, Athanasios. "From Conversion according to Paul and 'John' to Theosis in the Greek Patristic Tradition." *HBT* 38 (2016): 88–109.

———. "ὁ γὰρ ἀποθανὼν δεδικαίωται ἀπὸ τῆς ἁμαρτίας: Rethinking the Application of the Verb δικαιοῦσθαι in Baptismal Contexts from the Perspective of Rom 6:7." In Despotis, *Participation, Justification, and Conversion,* 29–57.

———, ed. *Participation, Justification, and Conversion: Eastern Orthodox Interpretation of Paul and the Debate between Old and New Perspectives on Paul.* WUNT 2/442. Tübingen: Mohr Siebeck, 2017.

Downs, David J., and Matthew L. Skinner, eds. *The Unrelenting God: Essays on God's Action in Scripture in Honor of Beverly Roberts Gaventa.* Grand Rapids: Eerdmans, 2013.

Dunn, James D. G. *A Commentary on the Epistle to the Galatians.* BNTC. London: A. & C. Black, 1993.

———. "The New Perspective on Paul: Whence, What and Whither?" In *The New Perspective on Paul,* 1–98. Rev. ed. Grand Rapids: Eerdmans, 2008.

———. *Romans 1–8.* WBC 38A. Waco: Word, 1988.

———. *The Theology of Paul the Apostle.* Grand Rapids: Eerdmans, 1998.

Dunne, John Anthony. *Persecution and Participation in Galatians.* WUNT 2/454. Tübingen: Mohr Siebeck, 2017.

———. "Suffering and Covenantal Hope in Galatians: A Critique of the 'Apocalyptic Reading' and Its Proponents." *SJT* 68 (2015): 1–15.

———. "Suffering in Vain: A Study of the Interpretation of ΠΑΣΧΩ in Galatians 3.4." *JSNT* 36 (2013): 3–16.

Eastman, Susan Grove. *Paul and the Person: Reframing Paul's Anthropology.* Grand Rapids: Eerdmans, 2017.

———. "Philippians 2:6–11: Incarnation as Mimetic Participation." *JSPL* 1 (2010): 1–22.

Ellington, Dustin W. "So That We Might Become the Righteousness and Justice of God: Re-examining the Gospel in 2 Cor 5:21 for the Church's Contribution to a Better World." *Missionalia* 44 (2016): 175–91.

Finlan, Stephen. "Can We Speak of *Theosis* in Paul?" In Christensen and Wittung, *Partakers of the Divine Nature,* 68–80.

Finlan, Stephen, and Vladimir Kharlamov, eds. *Theōsis: Deification in Christian Theology.* Eugene, OR: Pickwick, 2006.

Fowl, Stephen E. "Christology and Ethics in Philippians 2:5–11." In Martin and Dodd, *Where Christology Began,* 140–53.

———. *Philippians.* THNTC. Grand Rapids: Eerdmans, 2005.

———. *The Story of Christ in the Ethics of Paul: An Analysis of the Function of the Hymnic Material in the Pauline Corpus.* JSNTSup 36. Sheffield, UK: Sheffield Academic Press, 1990.

Fredriksen, Paula. "The Question of Worship: Gods, Pagans, and the Redemption of Israel." In *Paul within Judaism: Restoring the First-Century Context to the Apostle*, edited by Mark D. Nanos and Magnus Zetterholm, 175–201. Minneapolis: Fortress, 2015.

Frick, Peter. "The Means and Mode of Salvation: A Hermeneutical Proposal for Clarifying Pauline Soteriology." *HBT* 29 (2007): 203–22.

Furnish, Victor P. *II Corinthians.* AYB 32A. Garden City, NY: Doubleday, 1984.

Gaventa, Beverly Roberts. "The Singularity of the Gospel Revisited." In *Galatians and Christian Theology: Justification, the Gospel, and Ethics in Paul's Letter*, edited by Mark W. Elliott, Scott J. Hafemann, N. T. Wright, and John Frederick, 187–99. Grand Rapids: Baker Academic, 2014.

Gordon, Joseph. "Deification by Ascent: Paul's Ascent (2 Cor 12:1–10) in Its Historical and Theological Contexts." Paper presented at the Christian Scholars Conference, Nashville, June 6, 2013.

Gorman, Michael J. *Abide and Go: Missional Theosis in the Gospel of John.* Eugene, OR: Cascade, 2018.

———. "'Although/Because He Was in the Form of God': The Theological Significance of Paul's Master Story (Philippians 2:6–11)." *JTI* 1 (2007): 147–69.

———. *Apostle of the Crucified Lord: A Theological Introduction to Paul and His Letters.* 2nd ed. Grand Rapids: Eerdmans, 2017.

———. *Becoming the Gospel: Paul, Participation, and Mission.* Grand Rapids: Eerdmans, 2015.

———. *Cruciformity: Paul's Narrative Spirituality of the Cross.* Grand Rapids: Eerdmans, 2001.

———. *The Death of the Messiah and the Birth of the New Covenant: A (Not So) New Model of the Atonement.* Eugene, OR: Cascade, 2014.

———. "Douglas Campbell's *The Deliverance of God*: A Review Essay by a Friendly Critic." *JSPL* 1 (2011): 103–11.

———. "The Holy Spirit and Cruciformity." In *Holy Spirit: Spokesperson, Scripture, Sermon, Society*, edited by Johnson T. K. Lim, 177–84. Singapore: Armour Publishing & Word N Works, 2018.

———. *Inhabiting the Cruciform God: Kenosis, Justification, and Theosis in Paul's Narrative Soteriology.* Grand Rapids: Eerdmans, 2009.

———. "Justification and Justice in Paul, with Special Reference to the Corinthians." *JSPL* 1 (2011): 23–40.

———. "Participation and Ministerial Integrity in the Letters of Paul." In *Practicing with Paul: Reflections on Paul and the Practices of Ministry in Honor of Susan G. Eastman*, edited by Presian Burroughs, 1–14. Eugene, OR: Cascade, 2017.

———. "Romans 13 and Nonconformity: The Christian Community's Obligation to Oppose Inhumane Laws and Practices." *Cross Talk* (blog), June 17, 2018. http://www .michaeljgorman.net/2018/06/17/romans-13-and-nonconformity-the-christian -communitys-obligation-to-oppose-inhumane-laws-and-practices/.

———. "Romans and the Participationist Perspective." In *Preaching Romans: Four Perspectives*, edited by Scot McKnight and Joseph B. Modica, 59–79. Grand Rapids: Eerdmans, 2019.

———. "Romans: The First Christian Treatise on Theosis." *JTI* 5 (2011): 13–34.

———. "The Self, the Lord, and the Other: The Significance of Reflexive Pronoun Constructions in the Letters of Paul, with a Comparison to the 'Discourses' of Epictetus." PhD diss., Princeton Theological Seminary, 1989.

———. "The This-Worldliness of the New Testament's Other-Worldly Spirituality." In *The Bible and Spirituality: Interpreting Scripture for the Spiritual Life*, edited by Andrew T. Lincoln, J. Gordon McConville, and Lloyd K. Pietersen, 151–70. Eugene, OR: Cascade, 2013.

———. "Wright about Much, but Questions about Justification: A Review of N. T. Wright, *Paul and the Faithfulness of God*." *JSPL* 4 (2014): 27–36.

Grieb, A. Katherine. "'So That in Him We Might Become the Righteousness of God' (2 Cor. 5:21): Some Theological Reflections on the Church Becoming Justice." *ExAud* 22 (2006): 58–80.

Guthrie, George. *2 Corinthians*. BECNT. Grand Rapids: Baker Academic, 2015.

Harrer, G. A. "Saul Who Also Is Called Paul." *HTR* 33 (1940): 19–33.

Harris, Murray J. *The Second Epistle to the Corinthians: A Commentary on the Greek Text*. NIGTC. Grand Rapids: Eerdmans, 2005.

Hays, Richard B. "Apocalyptic *Poiēsis* in Galatians: Paternity, Passion, and Participation." In *Galatians and Christian Theology: Justification, the Gospel, and Ethics in Paul's Letter*, edited by Mark W. Elliott, Scott J. Hafemann, N. T. Wright, and John Frederick, 200–219. Grand Rapids: Baker Academic, 2014.

———. "Christology and Ethics in Galatians: The Law of Christ." *CBQ* 49 (1987): 268–90.

———. *The Conversion of the Imagination: Paul as Interpreter of Israel's Scripture*. Grand Rapids: Eerdmans, 2005.

———. *The Faith of Jesus Christ: The Narrative Substructure of Galatians 3:1–4:11*. 2nd ed. Grand Rapids: Eerdmans, 2002. First published 1983.

———. *The Moral Vision of the New Testament: A Contemporary Introduction to New Testament Ethics*. San Francisco: HarperSanFrancisco, 1996.

———. "Reading Scripture in Light of the Resurrection." In *The Art of Reading Scripture*, edited by Ellen F. Davis and Richard B. Hays, 216–38. Grand Rapids: Eerdmans, 2003.

———. "What Is 'Real Participation in Christ'? A Dialogue with E. P. Sanders on Pauline Soteriology." In *Redefining First-Century Jewish and Christian Identities:*

Essays in Honor of Ed Parish Sanders, edited by Fabian E. Udoh et al., 336–51. Notre Dame, IN: University of Notre Dame Press, 2008.

Heath, J. M. F. *Paul's Visual Piety: The Metamorphosis of the Beholder*. Oxford: Oxford University Press, 2013.

Hellerman, Joseph H. *Reconstructing Honor in Roman Philippi: Carmen Christi as Cursus Pudorum*. SNTSMS 132. Cambridge: Cambridge University Press, 2005.

Hill, Wesley. *Paul and the Trinity: Persons, Relations, and the Pauline Letters*. Grand Rapids: Eerdmans, 2015.

Hogan, Laura Reece. *I Live, No Longer I: Paul's Spirituality of Suffering, Transformation, and Joy*. Eugene, OR: Wipf and Stock, 2017.

Holmes, Stephen R. "Trinitarian Missiology: Towards a Theology of God as Missionary." *IJST* 8 (2006): 72–90.

Hooker, Morna D. *From Adam to Christ: Essays on Paul*. Cambridge: Cambridge University Press, 1990.

———. "On Becoming the Righteousness of God: Another Look at 2 Cor 5:21." *NovT* 50 (2008): 358–75.

Humphrey, Edith. "Becoming the Righteousness of God: The Potency of the New Creation in the World (2 Cor 5:16–21)." In Despotis, *Participation, Justification, and Conversion*, 125–57.

Hurtado, Larry W. "'The Form of God': Philo and Paul." *Larry Hurtado's Blog*, April 19, 2017. https://larryhurtado.wordpress.com/2017/04/19/the-form-of -god-philo-and-paul/.

———. "Jesus as Lordly Example in Philippians 2:5–11." In *From Jesus to Paul: Studies in Honour of Francis Wright Beare*, edited by Peter Richardson and John C. Hurd, 113–26. Waterloo, ON: Wilfred Laurier University Press, 1984.

Jacob, Haley Goranson. *Conformed to the Image of His Son: Reconsidering Paul's Theology of Glory in Romans*. Downers Grove, IL: IVP Academic, 2018.

Jervis, L. Ann. "Time in Romans 5–8." In Downs and Skinner, *Unrelenting God*, 139–49.

Jewett, Robert. *Romans*. Hermeneia. Minneapolis: Fortress, 2007.

Jipp, Joshua W. *Christ Is King: Paul's Royal Ideology*. Minneapolis: Fortress, 2015.

———. "Rereading the Story of Abraham, Isaac, and 'Us' in Romans 4." *JSNT* 32 (2009): 217–42.

John Paul II, Pope. *Evangelium Vitae* (The Gospel of Life). http://w2.vatican.va/con tent/john-paul-ii/en/encyclicals/documents/hf_jp-ii_enc_25031995_evangelium -vitae.html.

Johnson, Andy. "Navigating Justification: Conversing with Paul." Catalyst Resources, November 1, 2010. http://www.catalystresources.org/navigating-justification -conversing-with-paul/.

Johnson, Luke Timothy. *Reading Romans: A Literary and Theological Commentary*. Macon, GA: Smyth & Helwys, 2001.

Kärkkäinen, Veli-Matti. "Deification View." In *Justification: Five Views*, edited by James K. Beilby and Paul Rhodes Eddy, 219–43. Downers Grove, IL: IVP Academic, 2011.

———. "Salvation as Justification and *Theosis*: The Contribution of the New Finnish Luther Interpretation to Our Ecumenical Future." *Dialog* 45 (2006): 74–82.

Käsemann, Ernst. "A Critical Analysis of Philippians 2:5–11." *JTC* 5 (1968): 45–88. Translation of "Kritische Analyse von Phil. 2, 5–11." *ZTK* 47 (1950): 313–60.

———. "The Saving Significance of the Death of Jesus in Paul." In *Perspectives on Paul*, 32–59. Translated by Margaret Kohl. Philadelphia: Fortress, 1971. Reprint, Mifflintown, PA: Sigler, 1996.

Keener, Craig S. *1–2 Corinthians*. New Cambridge Bible Commentary. New York: Cambridge University Press, 2005.

Kimbrough, S. T., Jr. *Partakers of the Divine Life: Participation in the Divine Nature in the Writings of Charles Wesley*. Eugene, OR: Cascade, 2016.

King, Martin Luther, Jr. "Paul's Letter to American Christians." The Martin Luther King, Jr. Research and Education Institute. https://kinginstitute.stanford.edu /king-papers/documents/pauls-letter-american-christians-sermon-delivered-dexter -avenue-baptist-church.

———. *Strength to Love*. Minneapolis: Fortress, 2010.

Kirk, J. R. Daniel. *Unlocking Romans: Resurrection and the Justification of God*. Grand Rapids: Eerdmans, 2009.

Kok, Jacobus (Kobus), and John Anthony Dunne. "Participation in Christ and Missional Dynamics in Galatians." In Despotis, *Participation, Justification, and Conversion*, 59–85.

Kurek-Chomycz, Dominika A. "The Scent of (Mediated) Revelation? Some Remarks on φανερόω with a Particular Focus on 2 Corinthians." In *Theologizing in the Corinthian Conflict: Studies in the Theology and Exegesis of 2 Corinthians*, edited by Reimund Bieringer, Marilou S. Ibita, Dominika A. Kurek-Chomycz, and Thomas A. Vollmer, 69–108. BTS 16. Leuven: Peeters, 2013.

Lambrecht, Jan. *Second Corinthians*. SP. Collegeville, MN: Liturgical Press, 1998.

Leithart, Peter J. *The Baptized Body*. Moscow, ID: Canon, 2007.

———. *Delivered from the Elements of the World: Atonement, Justification, Mission*. Downers Grove, IL: IVP Academic, 2016.

Lewis, C. S. *Mere Christianity*. New York: HarperCollins, 2001. First published 1952.

Linebaugh, Jonathan. "Righteousness Revealed: The Death of Christ as the Definition of the Righteousness of God in Romans 3:21–26." In Blackwell, Goodrich, and Maston, *Paul and the Apocalyptic Imagination*, 219–37.

Litwa, M. David. "2 Corinthians 3:18 and Its Implications for 'Theosis.'" *JTI* 2 (2008): 117–33.

———. "Transformation through a Mirror: Moses in 2 Cor. 3.18." *JSNT* 34 (2012): 286–97.

———. *We Are Being Transformed: Deification in Paul's Soteriology.* BZNW 187. Berlin: de Gruyter, 2012.

Longenecker, Bruce W., ed. *Narrative Dynamics in Paul: A Critical Assessment.* Louisville: Westminster John Knox, 2002.

———. *Remember the Poor: Paul, Poverty, and the Greco-Roman World.* Grand Rapids: Eerdmans, 2010.

Longenecker, Richard N. *The Epistle to the Romans.* NIGTC. Grand Rapids: Eerdmans, 2016.

———. *Galatians.* WBC 41. Waco: Word, 1990.

Macaskill, Grant. "Incarnational Ontology and the Theology of Participation in Paul." In Thate, Vanhoozer, and Campbell, *"In Christ" in Paul,* 87–101.

———. *Living in Union with Christ: Paul's Gospel and Christian Moral Identity.* Grand Rapids: Baker Academic, 2019.

———. *Union with Christ in the New Testament.* Oxford: Oxford University Press, 2013.

Madigan, Kevin J., and Jon D. Levenson. *Resurrection: The Power of God for Christians and Jews.* New Haven: Yale University Press, 2008.

Martin, Ralph P. *A Hymn of Christ: Philippians 2:5–11 in Recent Interpretation and in the Setting of Early Christian Worship.* Downers Grove, IL: InterVarsity, 1997. Originally published as *Carmen Christi: Philippians 2:5–11 in Recent Interpretation and in the Setting of Early Christian Worship* (Cambridge: Cambridge University Press, 1967; 2nd ed., Grand Rapids: Eerdmans, 1983).

Martin, Ralph P., and Brian J. Dodd, eds. *Where Christology Began: Essays on Philippians 2.* Louisville: Westminster John Knox, 1998.

Martyn, J. Louis. "Afterword: The Human Moral Drama." In *Apocalyptic Paul: Cosmos and Anthropos in Romans 5–8,* edited by Beverly Roberts Gaventa, 157–66. Waco: Baylor University Press, 2013.

———. *Galatians: A New Translation with Introduction and Commentary.* AB 33A. New York: Doubleday, 1997.

Maston, Jason. "Plight and Solution in Paul's Apocalyptic Perspective: A Study of 2 Corinthians 5:18–21." In Blackwell, Goodrich, and Maston, *Paul and the Apocalyptic Imagination,* 297–315.

Matera, Frank J. *Galatians.* SP. Collegeville, MN: Liturgical Press, 1992.

———. *2 Corinthians.* NTL. Louisville: Westminster John Knox, 2003.

———. *The Spirituality of Saint Paul: A Call to Imitation.* New York: Paulist Press, 2017.

Meeks, Wayne A. "The Man from Heaven in Paul's Letter to the Philippians." In *The Future of Early Christianity: Essays in Honor of Helmut Koester,* edited by Birger Pearson, 329–36. Minneapolis: Fortress, 1991.

Moo, Douglas J. *Galatians.* BECNT. Grand Rapids: Baker Academic, 2013.

Morales, Isaac Augustine. "Baptism and Union with Christ." In Thate, Vanhoozer, and Campbell, *"In Christ" in Paul*, 151–79.

Morales, Rodrigo Jose. "A Liturgical Conversion of the Imagination: Worship and Ethics in 1 Corinthians." *Letter and Spirit* 5 (2009): 103–24.

———. *The Spirit and the Restoration of Israel*. WUNT 2/282. Tübingen: Mohr Siebeck, 2010.

Moule, C. F. D. "Further Reflexions on Philippians 2:5–11." In *Apostolic History and the Gospel: Biblical and Historical Essays Presented to F. F. Bruce on His 60th Birthday*, edited by W. Ward Gasque and Ralph P. Martin, 264–76. Grand Rapids: Eerdmans, 1970.

Newbigin, Lesslie. *The Gospel in a Pluralist Society*. Grand Rapids: Eerdmans, 1989.

Nikkanen, Pentti Markus. "Participation in Christ: Paul and Pre-Pauline Eucharistic Tradition." PhD diss., University of Aberdeen, 2018.

Novenson, Matthew V. *Christ among the Messiahs: Christ Language in Paul and Messiah Language in Ancient Judaism*. Oxford: Oxford University Press, 2012.

Oakes, Peter. *Galatians*. PCNT. Grand Rapids: Baker Academic, 2015.

O'Brien, Peter T. *The Epistle to the Philippians*. NIGTC. Grand Rapids: Eerdmans, 1991.

Ogereau, Julien M. "The Jerusalem Collection as Κοινωνία: Paul's Global Politics of Socio-Economic Equality and Solidarity." *NTS* 58 (2012): 360–78.

Oropeza, B. J. *Exploring Second Corinthians: Death and Life, Hardship and Rivalry*. Rhetoric of Religious Antiquity 3. Atlanta: SBL Press, 2016.

Owens, L. Roger. *The Shape of Participation: A Theology of Church Practices*. Eugene, OR: Cascade, 2010.

Paul, Pathipati Victor. *Exploring Socio-cultural Aspects of Pauline Ecclesiology: A Study of Paul's Term "in Christ."* Biblical Hermeneutics Rediscovered 13. New Delhi: Christian World Imprints, 2018.

Petroelje, Benj. "What to Do with the Pauline Book?" Centre for the Study of Christian Origins, May 10, 2017. http://www.christianorigins.div.ed.ac.uk/2017/05/10/whattodo/.

Pifer, Jeanette Hagen. *Faith as Participation: An Exegetical Study of Some Key Pauline Texts*. WUNT 2/486. Tübingen: Mohr Siebeck, 2018.

Pitre, Brant, Michael P. Barber, and John A. Kincaid. *Paul, a New Covenant Jew: Rethinking Pauline Theology*. Grand Rapids: Eerdmans, 2019.

Powers, Daniel G. *Salvation through Participation: An Examination of the Notion of the Believers' Corporate Unity with Christ in Early Christian Soteriology*. CBET 29. Leuven: Peeters, 2001.

Rabens, Volker. *The Holy Spirit and Ethics in Paul: Transformation and Empowering for Religious-Ethical Life*. 2nd rev. ed. Minneapolis: Fortress, 2014.

Reumann, John. *Philippians: A New Translation with Introduction and Commentary*. AYB 33B. New Haven: Yale University Press, 2008.

Robertson, A. T. *A Grammar of the Greek New Testament in the Light of Historical Research*. Nashville: Broadman, 1934.

Rowe, C. Kavin. *World Upside Down: Reading Acts in the Graeco-Roman Age*. Oxford: Oxford University Press, 2009.

Rowland, Christopher. "Paul and the Apocalypse of Jesus Christ." In *The Mystery of God: Early Jewish Mysticism and the New Testament*, edited by Christopher Rowland and Christopher R. A. Morray-Jones, 137–65. CRINT 12. Leiden: Brill, 2009.

Sanders, E. P. *Paul and Palestinian Judaism*. 40th anniv. ed. Minneapolis: Fortress, 2017. First published in 1977 by Fortress (Philadelphia).

———. *Paul: The Apostle's Life, Letters, and Thought*. Minneapolis: Fortress, 2015.

Schnelle, Udo. *Apostle Paul: His Life and Theology*. Translated by M. Eugene Boring. Grand Rapids: Baker Academic, 2005.

Schreiner, Thomas R. *Galatians*. ZECNT. Grand Rapids: Zondervan, 2010.

Schweitzer, Albert. *The Mysticism of Paul the Apostle*. Translated by William Montgomery. Baltimore: Johns Hopkins University Press, 1998. First published in German in 1930.

Scougal, Henry. *The Life of God in the Soul of Man*. Christian Classics Ethereal Library. http://www.ccel.org/s/scougal/life/cache/life.pdf.

Seifrid, Mark A. *The Second Letter to the Corinthians*. The Pillar New Testament Commentary. Grand Rapids: Eerdmans 2014.

Shaw, David A. "Apocalyptic and Covenant: Perspectives on Paul or Antinomies at War?" *JSNT* 36 (2013): 155–71.

Silva, Moisés. *Philippians*. BECNT. 2nd ed. Grand Rapids: Baker Academic, 2005.

Stegman, Thomas D. "Paul's Use of *dikaio-* Terminology: Moving beyond N. T. Wright's Forensic Interpretation." *TS* 72 (2011): 496–524.

———. *Second Corinthians*. CCSS. Grand Rapids: Baker Academic, 2009.

Stewart, James S. *A Man in Christ: The Vital Elements of St. Paul's Religion*. London: Hodder and Stoughton, 1935.

Stone, Bryan P. *Evangelism after Christendom: The Theology and Practice of Christian Witness*. Grand Rapids: Brazos, 2006.

Stubbs, David L. "The Shape of Soteriology and the *pistis Christou* Debate." *SJT* 61 (2008): 137–57.

Swartley, Willard M. *Covenant of Peace: The Missing Peace in New Testament Theology and Ethics*. Grand Rapids: Eerdmans, 2006.

Talbert, Charles H. *Romans*. SHBC. Macon, GA: Smyth & Helwys, 2002.

Tan, Rachael. "Conformity to Christ: An Exegetical and Theological Analysis of Paul's Perspective on Humiliation and Exaltation in Philippians 2:5–11." PhD diss., Southern Theological Seminary, 2017. http://digital.library.sbts.edu/handle/10392/5331.

Tannehill, Robert C. *Dying and Rising with Christ: A Study in Pauline Theology*. Berlin: Alfred Töpelmann, 1966.

Tappenden, Frederick S. *Resurrection in Paul: Cognition, Metaphor, and Transformation*. ECL 19. Atlanta: SBL Press, 2016.

Thate, Michael J., Kevin J. Vanhoozer, and Constantine R. Campbell, eds. *"In Christ" in Paul: Explorations in Paul's Theology of Union and Participation*. Grand Rapids: Eerdmans, 2018.

Thrall, Margaret E. *2 Corinthians 1–7*. Vol. 1 of *A Critical and Exegetical Commentary on the Second Epistle to the Corinthians*. ICC. Edinburgh: T&T Clark, 1998.

Tilling, Chris. *Paul's Divine Christology*. Grand Rapids: Eerdmans, 2015.

Tobin, Thomas H. *Paul's Rhetoric in Its Contexts: The Argument of Romans*. Peabody, MA: Hendrickson, 2004.

Vanhoozer, Kevin J. "From 'Blessed in Christ' to 'Being in Christ': The State of Union and the Place of Participation in Paul's Discourse, New Testament Exegesis, and Systematic Theology Today." In Thate, Vanhoozer, and Campbell, *"In Christ" in Paul*, 3–33.

Volf, Miroslav. *Exclusion and Embrace: A Theological Exploration of Identity, Otherness, and Reconciliation*. Nashville: Abingdon, 1996.

Ware, James P. *Paul's Theology in Context: Creation, Incarnation, Covenant, and Kingdom*. Grand Rapids: Eerdmans, 2019.

Watson, Francis. *Paul, Judaism, and the Gentiles: Beyond the New Perspective*. Grand Rapids: Eerdmans, 2007.

Wells, Kyle B. *Grace and Agency in Paul and Second Temple Judaism: Interpreting the Transformation of the Heart*. NovTSup 157. Leiden: Brill, 2014.

Westerholm, Stephen. *Justification Reconsidered: Rethinking a Pauline Theme*. Grand Rapids: Eerdmans, 2013.

Whittle, Sarah. *Covenant Renewal and the Consecration of the Gentiles in Romans*. SNTSMS 161. Cambridge: Cambridge University Press, 2014.

Witherington, Ben, III. *Grace in Galatia*. Grand Rapids: Eerdmans, 1998.

Wolter, Michael. *Paul: An Outline of His Theology*. Translated by Robert L. Brawley. Waco: Baylor University Press, 2015.

Wright, N. T. *The Climax of the Covenant: Christ and the Law in Pauline Theology*. Minneapolis: Fortress, 1993.

———. *Justification: God's Plan and Paul's Vision*. Downers Grove, IL: IVP Academic, 2009.

———. "On Becoming the Righteousness of God: 2 Corinthians 5:21." In *Pauline Theology*, vol. 2, *1 & 2 Corinthians*, edited by David M. Hay, 200–208. Minneapolis: Fortress, 1993.

———. *Paul and the Faithfulness of God*. Vol. 4 of *Christian Origins and the Question of God*. Minneapolis: Fortress, 2013.

————. "Paul, Ethics, and the Church." In *Ecclesia and Ethics: Moral Formation and the Church*, edited by E. Allen Jones III, John Frederick, John Anthony Dunne, Eric Lewellen, and Janghoon Park, 87–96. London: Bloomsbury, 2016.

————. *The Resurrection of the Son of God*. Vol. 3 of *Christian Origins and the Question of God*. Minneapolis: Fortress, 2003.

Wu, Siu Fung, ed. *Suffering in Paul: Perspectives and Implications*. Eugene, OR: Pickwick, 2018.

Yates, John W. *The Spirit and Creation in Paul*. WUNT 2/251. Tübingen: Mohr Siebeck, 2008.

Young, Frances M. "Understanding Romans in the Light of 2 Corinthians." *SJT* 43 (1990): 433–46.

Zerbe, Gordon. *Citizenship: Paul on Peace and Politics*. Winnipeg: CMU Press, 2012.

Scripture Index

Author Index

Subject Index

Note: some subjects are so consistently present in this book (e.g., cruciformity; "in Christ"; justice; justification; participation) that only certain key pages are listed.

Made in the USA
Coppell, TX
01 July 2021

58420100R00177